Almanac of African American History: The Civil Rights Movement

All photos are from the public domain

Published by The Book Shed

All rights reserved.

Cover Design by:

Ty A Shedleski

TyShedleski@gmail.com

ISBN: 978-0-9906061-6-1

Table of Contents

Court Cases

1   Dred Scott v. Sandford – Disallowed citizenship for any African American, free or slave, and invalidated Missouri Compromise of 1820

16   Plessy v. Ferguson – Separate but Equal

71   Brown v. Board of Education – Equal Rights for Education Regardless of Race

330   Heart of Atlanta Motel v. The USA – Challenged Title II of the Civil Rights Act of 1964

418   Loving v. Virginia – Challenged Discrimination of Interracial Marriage

Miscellaneous

453   Emancipation Proclamation

454   13th and 14th Amendment

455   The 15th Amendment

456   Rosa Park's Certificate of Arrest

457   Rosa Park's Fingerprints

458   Map of Rosa Park's Bus

459   Civil Rights Act of 1964

Speeches

485   Henry Highland Garnet – An Address to the Slaves of the USA (1843)

491   Sojourner Truth – Ain't I A Woman? (1851)

492   Frederick Douglass – What to the Slave is the Fourth of July? (1852)

515   Malcolm X – The Ballot or the Bullet (1964)

528   Barack Obama – Knox College Commencement Address (2005)

DRED SCOTT VS. SANDFORD

DRED SCOTT.

SUPREME COURT OF THE UNITED STATES.
No. 137.

DRED SCOTT, Pl'ff in Er.,

vs.

JOHN F. A. SANDFORD.

IN ERROR TO THE CIRCUIT COURT U. S. FOR THE DISTRICT OF MISSOURI.

INDEX.

	Original.	Print.
Declaration	1	3
Marshal's return	3	5
Plea filed	4	5
Plea	4	5
Demurrer to plea filed	5	6
" "	5	6
" " submitted and argued	6	7
" sustained	6	7
Pleas, replications, and statement of facts filed	7	7
Plea No. 1	7	8
" 2	7	8
" 3	8	8
Replication	8	9
Agreed statement of facts	10	9
Judgment	12	11
Motion for new trial filed	12	11
Bill of Exceptions filed	13	12
" "	13	12
Plaintiff's instructions	13	12
Defendant's "	13	12
Motion for new trial	14	12
Writ of error	15	13
Citation and service	17	14
Assignment of errors	18	15

[REC. CXXXVII, D. T. 1854.]—1

assistance of his said wife, and thereby lost great gains and profits, of the value, to wit: of twenty-five hundred dollars; and other wrongs to the plaintiff the defendant then and there did against the peace, and to the plaintiff's damage three thousand dollars. And also for that the defendant heretofore, to wit: on the 1st day of January, A. D. 1853, with force and arms, at St. Louis aforesaid, made an assault on Eliza Scott and Lizzy Scott, then and still infant daughters and servants of the plaintiff, and then and there imprisoned and held as slaves said Eliza and Lizzy for a long space of time, to wit, six hours; and then and there did threaten to beat said Eliza and Lizzy, and to hold them as slaves and restrained of their liberty, so that by means of the premises said Eliza and Lizzy were put in great fear and could not and did not attend to plaintiff's business, as otherwise they might and would have done; and the plaintiff thereby lost the comfort, society, service, and assistance of his said children and servants, of great value, to wit: twenty-five hundred dollars; and other wrongs to the plaintiff the defendant then and there did against the peace, and to the damage of the plaintiff three thousand dollars. And the plaintiff on account of the aforesaid several grievances brings suit, &c., by his attorney,

R. M. FIELD.

(For April Term, 1854.)

Upon the foregoing declaration the following summons issued, viz:—

(*Summons.*)

MISSOURI DISTRICT, SCT:

The President of the United States to the Marshal of the Missouri District, greeting:

You are hereby commanded to summon John F. A. Sandford, a citizen of the State of New York, that he be and appear before the Honorable Circuit Court of the United States for the District of Missouri, at the next term thereof, to be held at the city of St. Louis, in and for said district, on the first Monday of April next, then and there to answer unto Dred Scott, a citizen of the State of Missouri, in a plea of trespass, to the damage of said plaintiff three thousand dollars. Hereof fail not, and have you then there this writ. Witness the Honorable Roger B. Taney, Chief Justice of the Supreme Court of the United States, the second day of November, A. D. 1853.

Issued at office in the city of St. Louis, under the seal of said Court, the day and year last aforesaid.

BEN. F. HICKMAN,
Clerk.

Upon which said summons the Marshal made the following return, viz:—

(Marshal's Return.)

I hereby certify that I executed the within summons on the within named John F. A. Sandford, in the city of St. Louis, Missouri, on this second day of November, 1853, by offering to read the same and the copy of the declaration hereto attached, to and within the hearing of the said Sandford, which he declined hearing, and asked for a copy of said declaration, which I furnished him on this said 2d day of November, 1853.

THOMAS S. BRYANT,
Marshal U. S., Mo. Dist.

By ROBERT K. MOORE,
Dep.

Afterwards, at a Circuit Court continued and held for the District of Missouri, at St. Louis, on Friday, the 7th day of April, 1854, the following order was entered in the foregoing case, viz:—

(Order noting Filing of Plea.)

DRED SCOTT, Plaintiff,
against
JOHN F. A. SANDFORD, Defendant.

This day comes the defendant by his attorney, and files a plea, sworn to, to the jurisdiction of the Court in this case.

Which said plea is as follows, viz:—

(Plea.)

IN THE CIRCUIT COURT OF THE UNITED STATES,
for the District of Missouri:

DRED SCOTT
vs.
JOHN F. A. SANDFORD.
} Plea to the Jurisdiction of the Court.

April Term, 1854.

And the said John F. A. Sandford, in his own proper person, comes and says that this Court ought not to have or take further cognizance of the action aforesaid, because he says that said cause of action, and each and every of them, (if any such have accrued to the said Dred Scott,) accrued to the said Dred Scott out of the jurisdiction of this Court, and exclusively within the jurisdiction of the Courts of the State of Missouri, for that, to wit: the said plaintiff, Dred Scot, is not a citizen of the State of Missouri, as alleged in his declaration, because he is a negro of African descent; his ancestors were of pure African blood, and were brought into this country and sold as negro slaves, and this the said Sanford is ready to verify. Wherefore, he prays judgment whether this Court can or will take further cognizance of the action aforesaid.

JOHN F. A. SANFORD.

John F. A. Sandford, defendant in the above cause, makes oath and says, that the plea hereunto annexed is true in substance and in fact.

J. F. A. SANFORD.

Sworn to and subscribed before me this 16th day of November, 1853.

EDWARD E. ALLEN,
Justice of the Peace.

Afterwards, at a Circuit Court continued and held for the District of Missouri, at St. Louis, on Friday, the 14th day of April, 1854, the following further proceedings were had in said cause, viz:—

(*Demurrer to Plea filed.*)

DRED SCOTT, Plaintiff,
ag'st } Trespass.
JOHN F. A. SANDFORD, Defendant.

This day comes the plaintiff, by his attorney, and files a demurrer to the plea of defendant, heretofore filed to the jurisdiction of this Court in this case.

Which said demurrer is as follows, viz:—

(*Demurrer to Plea.*)

IN THE CIRCUIT COURT OF THE UNITED STATES,
for the District of Missouri:

April Term, 1854.

DRED SCOTT
vs. }
JOHN F. A. SANFORD.

And now comes the plaintiff and demurs in law to the plea of the defendant to the jurisdiction of the Court, and says that the said plea and the matters therein contained are not sufficient in law to preclude the Court of its jurisdiction of this case, and that the plaintiff is not bound by law to reply to said plea; wherefore the plaintiff prays judgment of said plea, and that the defendant answer further to the plaintiff's said action, &c. Field, defendant, joins in the demurrer.

GARLAND,
for Def't.

Afterwards, at a Circuit Court continued and held for the District of Missouri, at St. Louis, on Monday, the 24th day of April, 1854, the following further proceedings were had in said cause, viz:—

(*Demurrer to Plea Submitted and Argued.*)

DRED SCOTT, Plaintiff,
ag'st
JOHN F. A. SANDFORD, Defendant.
} Trespass.

This day came the parties by their attorneys, and the matters of law arising upon the demurrer filed by plaintiff to the plea of defendant filed in this case, were argued and submitted to the Court; but the Court not being sufficiently advised, took time to consider thereof.

Afterwards, at a Circuit continued and held for the District of Missouri, at St. Louis, on Tuesday, the 25th day of April, 1854, the following further proceedings were had in said cause, viz:—

(*Demurrer Sustained.*)

DRED SCOTT, Plaintiff,
ag'st
JOHN F. A. SANDFORD, Defendant.
} In Trespass.

This day come again the parties by their attorneys, and the Court being now sufficiently advised of and concerning the matters of law arising upon the demurrer filed herein by plaintiff to the plea of defendant filed to the declaration of plaintiff, is of opinion that the law is for the plaintiff on said demurrer, and that the plea of said defendant is insufficient, and now orders that the said demurrer be and the same is hereby sustained.

Afterwards, at a Circuit Court continued and held for the District of Missouri, at St. Louis, on Thursday, the 4th day of May, 1854, the following further proceedings were had in said case, viz:—

(*Pleas, Replications, and Statement of Facts filed.*)

DRED SCOTT, Plaintiff,
ag'st
JOHN F. A. SANDFORD, Defendant.
} Trespass.

This day came again the parties by their attorneys, and the said attorneys having agreed at the time that the demurrer filed by plaintiff to the plea in abatement of defendant was sustained by the Court, that other pleas should be filed by the defendant, and that an agreed case should be made up by them, and time being allowed for that purpose, now, in accordance with such agreement, the defendant files pleas Nos. 1, 2, and 3; to all of which pleas the plaintiff files replications; and said attorneys also file an agreement signed by them, agreeing upon the statements of the facts in this case.

Which said pleas are as follows, viz:—

(Plea No. 1.)

IN THE CIRCUIT COURT OF THE UNITED STATES:

DRED SCOTT
vs.
JOHN F. A. SANFORD.
} Plea of Defendant. April Term, 1854.

And the said John F. A. Sanford, by H. A. Garland, his attorney, comes and defends the wrong and injury when, &c., and says that he is not guilty of the said supposed trespass above laid to his charge, or any part thereof, in manner and form as the said Dred Scott hath above thereof complained against him; and of this he, the said Sanford, putteth himself upon the country.

(No. 2.)

And for a further plea in this behalf as to the making the said assault upon the said Dred Scott in the first count of the said declaration mentioned, and imprisoning him, and keeping and detaining him in prison, &c., the said Sanford, by leave of the Court first obtained, says, that the said Dred Scott ought not to have or maintain his aforesaid action thereof against him, because he says that before and at the time when, &c. in the said first count mentioned, the said Dred Scott was a negro slave, the lawful property of the defendant, and as such slave he gently laid his hands upon him, and only restrained him of such liberty as he had a right to do. And this the said Sanford is ready to verify. Wherefore he prays judgment whether the said Scott ought to have or maintain his aforesaid action thereof against him.

(No. 3.)

And for a further plea in this behalf as to the making the said assault upon Harriet, the wife, and Eliza and Lizzie, the daughters of the said Dred Scott, in the second and third counts of the said declaration mentioned, and imprisoning them and keeping and detaining them in prison, &c., the said John F. A. Sanford, by leave of the Court obtained, says, that the said Dred Scott ought not to have or maintain his aforesaid action thereof against him, because he says, that before and at the said time, &c., when, &c., in the said second and third counts mentioned, the said Harriet, wife of said Scott, and Eliza and Lizzie, his daughters, were the lawful slaves of the said Sanford, and as such slaves he gently laid his hands upon them, and restrained them of their liberty, as he had a right to do; and this he is ready to verify. Wherefore he prays judgment, &c.

GARLAND,
for Defendant.

Which said replications are as follows:—

Dred Scott vs. *John F. A. Sandford.*

(*Replications.*)

IN THE CIRCUIT COURT OF THE UNITED STATES,
for the District of Missouri:

DRED SCOTT
vs.
JOHN F. A. SANFORD.

The plaintiff as to the plea of the defendant firstly above pleaded, and whereof he has put himself on the country, doth do like.

FIELD.

And the plaintiff, as to the plea of the defendant secondly above pleaded, as to the said several trespasses in the introductory part of that plea mentioned and therein attempted to be justified, says that the plaintiff, by reason of anything in that plea alleged, ought not to be barred from having and maintaining his aforesaid action against the defendant, because he says, that said defendant at said time when, &c., *of his own wrong, and without the cause by him in his said second plea alleged,* committed the said several trespasses in the introductory part of that plea mentioned, in manner and form as the plaintiff has above in his declaration complained; and this the plaintiff prays may be inquired of by the country, &c.

FIELD.

And the plaintiff, as to the plea of the defendant thirdly above pleaded as to said several trespasses in the introductory part of that plea mentioned, and therein attempted to be justified, says, that the plaintiff, by reason of anything in that plea alleged, ought not to be barred from having and maintaining his aforesaid action against the defendant, because he says that said defendant, at said time when, &c., *of his own wrong, and without the cause by him in his said third plea alleged,* committed the said several trespasses in the introductory part of that plea mentioned in manner and form as the plaintiff has above in his declaration complained. And this the plaintiff prays may be inquired of by the country, &c.

FIELD.

Which said agreed statement of facts is as follows, viz :—

(*Agreed Statement of Facts.*)

IN THE CIRCUIT COURT OF THE UNITED STATES,
for the District of Missouri:

DRED SCOTT
vs.
JOHN F. A. SANFORD.

The parties above named agree on the following statement of facts :—

In the year 1834, the plaintiff was a negro slave belonging to Doctor Emerson, who was a surgeon in the army of the United States. In that year, 1834, said Dr. Emerson took the plaintiff from the State of Missouri to the military post at Rock Island in the State of Illinois, and held him there as a slave until the month of April or May, 1836. At the time last mentioned, said Dr. Emerson removed the plaintiff from said military post at Rock Island to the military post at Fort Snelling, situate on the west bank of the Mississippi river, in the territory known as Upper Louisiana, acquired by the United States of France, and situate north of the latitude of 36 degrees, 30 minutes north, and north of the State of Missouri. Said Dr. Emerson held the plaintiff in slavery at said Fort Snelling, from said last mentioned date until the year 1838.

In the year 1835, Harriet, who is named in the second count of the plaintiff's declaration, was the negro slave of Major Taliaferro, who belonged to the army of the United States. In that year, 1835, said Major Taliaferro took said Harriet to said Fort Snelling, a military post, situated as herein before stated, and kept her there as a slave until the year 1836, and then sold and delivered her as a slave at said Fort Snelling unto the said Dr. Emerson herein before named. Said Dr. Emerson held said Harriet in slavery at said Fort Snelling until the year 1838.

In the year 1836, the plaintiff and said Harriet at said Fort Snelling, with the consent of said Dr. Emerson, who then claimed to be their master and owner, intermarried, and took each other for husband and wife. Eliza and Lizzy, named in the third count of the plaintiff's declaration, are the fruit of that marriage. Eliza is about 14 years old, and was born on board the steamboat Gipsey, north of the north line of the State of Missouri, and upon the river Mississippi. Lizzy is about seven years old, and was born in the State of Missouri at the military post called Jefferson Barracks.

In the year 1838, said Dr. Emerson removed the plaintiff and said Harriet and their said daughter Eliza, from said Fort Snelling to the State of Missouri, where they have ever since resided.

Before the commencement of this suit, said Dr. Emerson sold and conveyed the plaintiff, said Harriet, Eliza and Lizzy, to the defendant as slaves, and the defendant has ever since claimed to hold them and each of them as slaves.

At the times mentioned in the plaintiff's declaration the defendant, claiming to be owner as aforesaid, laid his hands upon said plaintiff, Harriet, Eliza, and Lizzy, and imprisoned them, doing in this respect, however, no more than what he might lawfully do if they were of right his slaves at such times.

Further proof may be given on the trial for either party.

R. M. FIELD,
for Pl'ff.

H. A. GARLAND,
for Def't.

It is agreed that Dred Scott brought suit for his freedom in the Circuit Court of St. Louis county; that there was a verdict and judgment in his favor; that on *on* a writ of error to the Supreme Court the judgment below was reversed and the same remanded to the Circuit Court, where it has been continued to await the decision of this case.

FIELD,
for Pl'ff.
GARLAND,
for Def't.

Afterwards, at a Circuit Court continued and held for the District of Missouri at St. Louis, on Monday, the 15th day of May, 1854, the following further proceedings were had in said case, viz:—

(*Judgment.*)

DRED SCOTT, Plaintiff,
ag'st
JOHN F. A. SANFORD, Defendant. } Case.

This day come again the parties by their attorneys, and, both being ready for trial: It is ordered that a jury come, and thereupon comes said jury, viz: James A. Hardy, Thomas McKenney, John Atkinson, Peter L. Dowling, Samuel Woods, James R. Bridges, R. N. Lock, James A. Scott, John Martin, George Holtzirene, George Berg and Martin Hake, who, after been sworn well and truly to try the issues joined, returned into Court the following verdict, viz: "As to the first issue joined in this case, we of the jury find the defendant not guilty; and as to the issue secondly above joined, we of the jury find that before and at the time when, &c. in the first count mentioned, the said Dred Scott was a negro slave, the lawful property of the defendant; and as to the issue thirdly above joined, we, the jury, find that before and at the time when, &c. in the second and third counts mentioned, the said Harriet, wife of said Dred Scott, and Eliza and Lizzie, the daughters of the said Dred Scott, were negro slaves, the lawful property of the defendant." Whereupon it is now considered by the Court that the plaintiff take nothing by his writ in this case, and that the defendant, John F. A. Sanford, go hence without day, and recover against said plaintiff, Dred Scott, the costs by him expended in the defence of this suit.

Afterwards, on the day and year last aforesaid, the following further proceedings were had in said cause, viz:—

(*Motion for New Trial.*)

DRED SCOTT, Plaintiff,
ag'st
JOHN F. A. SANDFORD, Defendant. } Case.

This day comes again the plaintiff by his attorney and moves the

Court to set aside the verdict and grant him a new trial, upon the grounds and for the reasons set forth in said motion; and the Court being advised of and concerning the same, do order, that said motion be and the same is hereby overruled.

(*Bill of Excep's filed.*)

And thereupon the said plaintiff files his Bill of Exceptions, which is signed, sealed, and ordered to be made part of the record in this case.

Which said Bill of Exceptions is as follows, viz:—

IN THE CIRCUIT COURT OF THE UNITED STATES,
      for the District of Missouri:

(*Bill of Exceptions.*)

DRED SCOTT
 vs.   } April Term, 1854.
JOHN F. A. SANFORD.

On the trial of this cause by the jury, the plaintiff, to maintain the issues on his part, read to the jury the following agreed statement of facts, (inserted on pages 10 and 11 of this transcript.) No further testimony was given to the jury by either party. Thereupon the plaintiff moved the Court to give to the jury the following instruction:—

(*Pl'ff's Instruction.*)

The jury are instructed, that upon the facts agreed to by the parties they ought to find for the plaintiff. The Court refused to give such instruction to the jury, and the plaintiff to such refusal then and there duly excepted. The Court then gave the following instruction to the jury, on motion of the defendant:—

(*Deft's Instruction.*)

The jury are instructed, that upon the facts in this case the law is with the defendant.

To the giving of such instruction the plaintiff then and there duly excepted. The jury found a verdict for the defendant. The plaintiff thereupon immediately filed in Court the following motion for a new trial:—

(*Mo. for New Trial.*)

IN THE CIRCUIT COURT OF THE UNITED STATES,
      for the District of Missouri:

DRED SCOTT
 vs.   } April Term, 1854.
JOHN F. A. SANFORD.

And now, after verdict and before judgment, the plaintiff comes and moves the Court to set aside the verdict and grant a new trial;

because the Court misdirected the jury in matter of law on said trial.
FIELD.

The Court overruled the said motion and gave judgment on the verdict for the defendant, and to such action of the Court the plaintiff then and there duly excepted. The plaintiff writes this Bill of Exceptions and prays that it may be allowed, and signed, and sealed.
FIELD.

Allowed, and signed, and sealed May 15, 1854.
R. W. WELLS. [SEAL.]

MISSOURI DISTRICT:

I, Benjamin F. Hickman, Clerk of the Circuit Court of the United States for the District of Missouri, certify the foregoing fourteen pages, including this, contains a full and complete transcript of the record and proceedings had in said Court in the case of Dred Scott against John F. A. Sanford, as the same remains on file in my office.

In witness whereof I hereunto subscribe my name and affix the seal of said Court at office in the city of St. Louis, this twenty-fifth day of May, eighteen hundred and fifty-four.

[SEAL.] BEN. F. HICKMAN, *Clerk*.

UNITED STATES OF AMERICA,
Missouri District, sct:

The President of the United States of America, to the Judges of the Circuit Court of the United States for the Eighth Circuit and District of Missouri, greeting:

Because in the record and proceedings, as also in the rendition of a judgment in a plea which is in said Circuit Court of the United States for the District of Missouri, before you, between Dred Scott as plaintiff, and John F. A. Sandford as defendant, a manifest error hath happened to the great damage of the said plaintiff Scott, as by his complaint appears, we being willing that error, if any hath been, should be duly corrected, and full and speedy justice done to the parties aforesaid in this behalf, do command you, that if judgment be therein given, that under your seal distinctly and openly you send the record and proceedings aforesaid, with all things concerning the same, to the Supreme Court of the United States, together with this writ, so that you have the same at Washington on the first Monday of December next, in the said Supreme Court, to be then and there held, that the record and proceedings aforesaid being inspected, the said Supreme Court may cause further to be done therein to correct that error, what of right and according to the laws and custom of the United States should be done.

Witness the Honorable Roger B. Taney, Chief Justice of the said

Supreme Court, this 16th day of May, in the year of our Lord one thousand eight hundred and fifty-four.

[SEAL.]   BEN. F. HICKMAN,
Clerk.

Allowed by me,
R. W. WELLS.

MISSOURI DISTRICT, SCT:

I, Benjamin F. Hickman, Clerk of the Circuit Court of the United States for the Missouri District, do hereby certify, that in obedience to the within Writ of Error, I hereby send to the Supreme Court of the United States a certified copy of the record and proceedings had in the case of Dred Scott against John F. A. Sandford, in said Circuit Court.

Given under my hand this 23d day of May, 1854.

BEN. F. HICKMAN,
Clerk C't C't U. S. Mo. Dis.

THE UNITED STATES OF AMERICA,

To JOHN F. A. SANDFORD, greeting:

You are hereby cited and admonished to be and appear at a Supreme Court of the United States, to be holden at Washington on the first Monday of December next, pursuant to a Writ of Error filed in the Clerk's Office of the Circuit Court of the United States for the Missouri District, wherein Dred Scott is plaintiff in error and you are defendant in error, to show cause, if any there be, why the judgment rendered against the said plaintiff in error, as in the said Writ of Error mentioned, should not be corrected, and why speedy justice should not be done to the parties in that behalf. Witness the Honorable Robert W. Wells, District Judge of the United States for the Missouri District, and one of the Judges of the Circuit Court of the United States for said District, this 17th day of May, in the year of our Lord one thousand eight hundred and fifty-four.

R. W. WELLS.

I acknowledge service of the above citation.

H. A. GARLAND,
Counsel for Sandford, Defendant in Error.

June 17, 1854.

IN THE SUPREME COURT OF THE UNITED STATES,
December Term, 1854.

DRED SCOTT, Plaintiff in Error,
vs.
JOHN F. A. SANDFORD, Defendant in Error.

And now comes said plaintiff in error and says that in the record of the proceedings, and in the giving of the judgment below, there is manifest error:

Because the Court below, in the trial of the cause, misdirected the jury in matter of law:

And because the Court below gave judgment for the defendant below, when the judgment should have been for the plaintiff below.

Wherefore, for said errors and others, the plaintiff prays judgment of reversal here, and that he may be restored to all he has lost. By his attorney.

NATH'L HOLMES.

Filed December 30th, 1854.

PLESSY VS. FERGUSON

RECORD, CASE No. 15,248.

233.

SUPREME COURT OF THE UNITED STATES.

OCTOBER TERM, 1893.

Term No., ~~880.~~ No. 210

HOMER ADOLPH PLESSY, PLAINTIFF IN ERROR,

vs.

J. H. FERGUSON, JUDGE OF SECTION "A," CRIMINAL DISTRICT COURT FOR THE PARISH OF ORLEANS.

IN ERROR TO THE SUPREME COURT OF THE STATE OF LOUISIANA.

FILED JANUARY 31, 1893.

RECORD, CASE No. 15,248.

SUPREME COURT OF THE UNITED STATES.

OCTOBER TERM, 1893.

Term No., 880.

HOMER ADOLPH PLESSY, PLAINTIFF IN ERROR,

vs.

J. H. FERGUSON, JUDGE OF SECTION "A," CRIMINAL DISTRICT COURT FOR THE PARISH OF ORLEANS.

IN ERROR TO THE SUPREME COURT OF THE STATE OF LOUISIANA.

INDEX.

	Original.	Print.
Caption	a	1
Petition for writs of prohibition and certiorari	1	1
Exhibit "A"—Affidavit of Chris. C. Cain	5	4
"B"—Information	7	5
"C"—Act No. 111 of 1890	9	6
"D"—Plea to information	14	8
Order on petition	20	10
Writ of prohibition and certiorari	20	10
Sheriff's return	22	12
Answer of respondent	22	12
Certified copy of proceedings in criminal district court	25	14
Information	25	15
Hearing and discharge of defendant on bail	26	15
Hearing and submission	27	15
Order overruling plea, &c.	28	16
Plea	29	16
Demurrer to plea	33	18

JUDD & DETWEILER, PRINTERS, WASHINGTON, D. C., MAY 20, 1893.

INDEX.

	Original.	Print.
Joinder in demurrer	34	19
Opinion	35	19
Clerk's certificate	40	23
Order taking cause under advisement	41	23
Opinion	42	24
Syllabus	53	30
Final judgment	55	31
Petition for rehearing	56	31
Order refusing rehearing	58	32
Petition for writ of error	59	33
Order allowing writ of error	65	36
Bond on writ of error	66	37
Assignment of errors	68	38
Writ of error	73	41
Citation	75	42
Proof of service of citation	76	42
Clerk's certificate	77	43
Chief justice's certificate	77	43
Petition for writ of error	79	44
Order allowing writ of error	88	48
Assignment of errors	90	48

a UNITED STATES OF AMERICA, }
State of Louisiana.

Supreme Court of the State of Louisiana, City of New Orleans.

Ex Parte HOMER ADOLPH PLESSY, Plaintiff in Error. No. 11134.

Albion W. Tourgee and Jas. C. Walker, Esquires, for Homer A. Plessy, plaintiff in error; Lionel Adams, Esq., assistant district attorney for the parish of Orleans, for Jno. H. Ferguson, judge criminal district court, section "A," for the parish of Orleans, respondent, defendant in error.

Writ of error to the supreme court of the State of Louisiana from the Supreme Court of the United States, at the city of Washington, D. C., returnable within 30 days from January 5th, A. D. 1893.

Transcript of Record.

1 Supreme Court of the State of Louisiana.

Ex Parte HOMER A. PLESSY. No. 11134.

Petition for Writs of Prohibition and Certiorari. Filed November 22, 1892.

Ex Parte HOMER A. PLESSY.

To the honl. the supreme court of the State of Louisiana:

The petition of Homer A. Plessy respectfully represents—
That said petitioner is a citizen of the United States and a resident of the State of Louisiana. Moreover, that petitioner is of mixed Caucasian and African descent in the proportion of seven-eighths Caucasian and one-eighth African blood; that the mixture of colored blood is not discernible in petitioner, and he is entitled to every recognition, right, privilege, and immunity secured to citizens of the United States of the white race by the Constitution and laws of the United States, and such right, privilege, recognition, and immunity are of value greatly exceeding the sum of ten thousand dollars, if the same be at all susceptible of being estimated by the standard value of money.

Petitioner further represents that on or about the seventh day of June of the present year, 1892, he engaged and paid for one first-class passage on the East Louisiana railway at and from the city of New Orleans, in the State of Louisiana, to the city of Covington, in St. Tammany parish, also in the State of Louisiana, and thereupon petitioner entered a passenger train of said railway and took possession of a vacant seat in a coach or compartment of said train where passengers of the white race were accommodated.

1—880

2   That said East Louisiana Railway Company is incorporated by the laws of the State of Louisiana as a common carrier, carrying passengers for hire, and is not and cannot be authorized to distinguish between citizens according to race; but, notwithstanding, upon the approach of the conductor of said train petitioner was by him ordered and required, under penalty of ejection from said train and imprisonment, to vacate said coach or compartment and to occupy another seat in another compartment or coach of said train assigned by said company for persons not of the white race, for no other reason announced by said conductor than that petitioner was of the colored race.

That petitioner refused to comply with said unreasonable command and insisted upon occupying and being permitted to occupy and remain in the seat and coach where he then was; whereupon, with the aid of an officer of police, viz., C. C. Cain, as further appears herein, said petitioner was forcibly ejected from said coach and train and hurried off to and imprisoned in the parish jail of New Orleans and there held to answer a charge or affidavit made by said officer to the effect and in substance that petitioner was guilty of having criminally violated an act of the General Assembly of the State of Louisiana approved July 10th, 1890, No. 111 of the sessions acts, in such case made and provided.

That petitioner was subsequently brought before the Honl. A. R. Moulin, recorder of the second recorder's court for the city of New Orleans, for preliminary examination upon the facts set forth in the said affidavit, and petitioner was by the said recorder thereupon committed for trial to the honl. the criminal district court for the parish of Orleans; that said proceedings and affidavit appear by Exhibit "A," hereto annexed and made part of this petition.

3   Petitioner further avers that upon the receipt of the said papers and proceedings by the officers of the said criminal district court for the parish of Orleans the said cause was allotted and assigned to section "A" of the said criminal district court, and, after leave of the honl. the judge of said section "A," the assistant district attorney for the parish of Orleans, prosecuting in behalf of the State of Louisiana, presented and filed an information against petitioner for the subject-matter as herein set forth and as set forth in said above-mentioned affidavit, and said information is hereto annexed, marked Exhibit "B," and made part of this petition, and is predicated only and solely on the facts set forth in said affidavit and on the provisions of said act of the General Assembly of this State approved July 10th, 1890, which petitioner affirms to be in all its parts null and void because in conflict with the Constitution of the United States, as hereinafter appears in detail and specifically set forth in the plea which petitioner interposed against said proceedings.

That petitioner hereto annexes and makes part of this petition, marked Exhibit "C," a verbatim copy of the said act of the General Assembly of this State, No. 111, approved July 10th, 1890.

And petitioner also says that the said criminal district court for the parish of Orleans has no jurisdiction or authority to hear and determine the facts set forth in the said affidavit and information, because the said court is precluded from so doing by reason that the said act of the General Assembly of the State of Louisiana approved July 10th, 1890, is in conflict with the Constitution of the United States in its several parts as aforesaid, and petitioner has thus pleaded and excepted in his defense upon arraignment to answer said information in the said criminal district court, as appears by petitioner's said plea, hereto annexed, marked "D," and made part of this petition. Moreover, that petitioner now repeats and renews in this honl. court all and singular the allegations of the said annexed plea in manner and form as therein recited, the same being too lengthy and numerous to be otherwise referred to.

And petitioner further represents that petitioner's counsel, acting in his behalf, joined issue upon demurrers being filed to the said plea by the said assistant district attorney, and, after hearing argument for the State and for the accused, the said judge of section "A," criminal district court aforesaid, maintained the said demurrer thereto and overruled petitioner's said plea, and has ordered petitioner to answer and plead over to the facts set forth in the said information; that unless said judge of the criminal district court be enjoined by writ of prohibition from further proceeding in said cause the said court will proceed to fine and sentence petitioner to imprisonment, and thus deprive him of his constitutional rights set forth in said plea annexed, notwithstanding that said statute under which petitioner is being prosecuted is in conflict with the Constitution of the United States, and there lies no appeal from such sentence, as the said statute provides, and therefore petitioner is without relief or remedy except to apply to this honl. court for writs of prohibition and certiorari to prohibit the said judge of section "A," criminal district court, from proceeding further with said prosecution against petitioner, and that the record of the same be sent to this honl. court, to the end that the validity of said proceedings be ascertained, and the said proceedings are entitled State of Louisiana vs. Homer A. Plessy, No. 19117 of the docket of the criminal district court for the parish of Orleans.

And petitioner further says that he has duly and formally notified the said honl. judge of section "A," criminal district court, of his intention to apply to this honl. court to issue the said writs, and that he has complied with every other necessary preliminary according to his best knowledge and information.

Wherefore petitioner prays that writs of prohibition and certiorari issue herein, directed to the Honl. J. H. Ferguson, judge of the criminal district court for the parish of Orleans; that he be prohibited from proceeding further with the cause entitled State of Louisiana vs. Homer A. Plessy, No. 19117 of the docket of the said court, until further ordered, and that the record thereof be certified and transmitted to this honl. court, to the end that the validity of said proceedings be ascertained; and petitioner prays that said writ of prohibition be made peremptory in due course, and that he have such other and further relief — the nature of the case requires.

    (Signed)   ALBION W. TOURGÉE,
                          JAS. C. WALKER, *Of Counsel.*

Personally appeared Homer A. Plessy, who, being duly sworn, says that all the facts and allegations set forth in the foregoing petition are true and correct.

    (Signed)   H. A. PLESSY.

Sworn to and subscribed before me this 22d day of November, A. D. 1892.

    [SEAL.]   (Signed)   LOUIS A. MARTINET,
                                                  Not. Pub.

Affidavit Marked Exhibit "A." Filed with Petition Nov'r 22, 1892.

6   Affidavit.

STATE OF LOUISIANA:

    Second Recorder's Court of the City of New Orleans.

              THE STATE
                    vs.
    HOMER ADOLPH PLESSY, 244½ N. Claiborne —.

Personally appeared before me, A. R. Moulin, recorder of the first recorder's court of the city of New Orleans and justice of the peace, duly commissioned and sworn, Detective C. C. Cain, 60 St. Charles —, who, having been duly sworn, doth depose and say—

That Homer Adolph Plessy, late of the parish of Orleans, on the 7th day of June, 1892, within the jurisdiction of this honl. court, on Press St., in the 3rd dist. of this city, then and there being a passenger of the colored race on a train of the East Louisiana Railroad Co., the said East Louisiana Railroad Co. then and there being a railway Co. engaged in carrying passengers for hire in its coaches in the State of Louisiana from the city of New Orleans to the city of Covington and wholly operated within the limits of the said State, unlawfully did insist upon going into and remaining in a compartment of a coach of said passenger train to which by race he, the said Homer Adolph Plessy, did not belong, to wit, a compartment in said coach assigned to passengers of the white race, then being at the time aforesaid afforded by said train equal but separate accommodations thereon for persons of the white and colored races, all against the peace and dignity of the State.

Wherefore deponent charges the accused with violation — sec. 2, act 111 of S. of La., approved July 10, '90, and prays that he be arrested and dealt with according to law.

    (Sig'd)   CHRIS. C. CAIN.

J. H. FERGUSON, JUDGE, ETC.

7 Sworn to and subscribed before me this 8th day of June, 1892.

  (Sig'd)   A. R. MOULIN, *Recorder.*

State witnesses:
 J. L. MOTT,
  19 *Commercial Place.*
 J. J. DOWLING,
  Conductor, 112 *Common.*

Endorsement and certificate: No. 7657. The State *vs.* Homer Adolph Plessy. June 8, '92. Viol. sec. 2, act 111, 1890. Prosecutor, Dect. C. C. Cain. Decision. Examination waived. C. C. D. B., $500. Examination waived. Committed to the hon. the criminal district court for trial as charged. Bond, 500. June 8, 1892. (Signed) A. R. Moulin, judge first recorder's court.

I, J. Malloy, a deputy clerk of the criminal district court for the parish of Orleans, do hereby certify the foregoing copy of affidavit and endorsements thereon to be a true, full, and correct copy of the original as the same appears on file and of record in the aforesaid office.

In testimony whereof I hereunto sign my name and affix the seal of said court, at the city of New Orleans, this 21 day of November, in the year of our Lord one thousand eight hundred and ninety-two, and the one hundred and seventeenth year of the Independence of the United States of America.

 [SEAL.] (Signed)   J. MALLOY, *D'y Cl'k.*

Information, Marked Exhibit "B." Filed with Petition November 22, 1892.

8 THE STATE OF LOUISIANA, ⎱
    Parish of Orleans,   ⎰ *ss:*

  Criminal District Court for the Parish of Orleans.

Lionel Adams, ass't district attorney for the parish of Orleans, who, in the name and by the authority of the said State, prosecutes in this behalf, in proper person comes into the criminal district court for the parish of Orleans, in the parish of Orleans, and gives the said court here to understand and be informed that one Homer Adolph Plessy, late of the parish of Orleans, on the seventh day of June, in the year of our Lord one thousand eight hundred and ninety-two, with force and arms, in the parish of Orleans aforesaid and within the jurisdiction of the criminal district court for the parish of Orleans, being then a passenger, travelling wholly within the limits of the State of Louisiana, on a railroad train — to the East Louisiana Railroad Company, a railway company carrying passengers in their coaches within the State of Louisiana, and on which the officers of the said East Louisiana Railroad Company had power and were required to assign and did then assign the said

Homer Adolph Plessy to the coach used for the race to which he, the said Homer Adolph Plessy, belonged, unlawfully did then and there insist on going into a coach to which by race he did not belong, contrary to the form of the statute of the State of Louisiana in such case made and provided and against the peace and dignity of the same.

(Signed) LIONEL ADAMS,
Ass't District Attorney for the Parish of Orleans.

9   Endorsement and certificate: Section No. 19117. State of Louisiana *versus* Homer Adolph Plessy. Information for violating provisions of act No. 111 of 1890. Filed July 20th, 1892. (S'g'd) F. J. Letten, minute clerk.

I, J. Malloy, a deputy clerk of the criminal district court for the parish of Orleans, do hereby certify the foregoing copy of information and endorsements thereon to be a true, full, and correct copy of the original as the same appears on file and of record in the aforesaid office.

In testimony whereof I hereunto sign my name and affix the seal of said court, at the city of New Orleans, this 21st day of November, in the year of our Lord one thousand eight hundred and ninety-two, and the one hundred and seventeenth year of the Independence of the United States of America.

(Signed) J. MALLOY, *D'y Cl'k.*

Act No. 111 of 1890, Marked " Exhibit C." Filed with Petition November 22, 1892.

10   No. 111.

An act to promote the comfort of passengers on railway trains; requiring all railway companies carrying passengers on their trains, in this State, to provide equal but separate accommodations for the white and colored races, by providing separate coaches or compartments so as to secure separate accommodations; defining the duties of the officers of such railways; directing them to assign passengers to the coaches or compartment set aside for the use of the race to which such passengers belong; authorizing them to refuse to carry on their train such passengers as may refuse to occupy the coaches or compartments to which he or she is assigned; to exonerate such railway companies from any and all blame or damages that might proceed or result from such a refusal; to prescribe penalties for all violations of this act; to put this act into effect ninety days after its promulgation, and to repeal all laws or parts of laws contrary to or inconsistent with the provisions of this act.

11   SECTION I. Be it enacted by the General Assembly of the State of Louisiana, That all railway companies carrying passengers in their coaches in this State, shall provide equal

but separate accommodations for the white, and colored races, by providing two or more passenger coaches for each passenger train, or by dividing the passenger coaches by a partition so as to secure separate accommodations; provided that this section shall not be construed to apply to street railroads. No person or persons shall be permitted to occupy seats in coaches, other than, the ones, assigned, to them on account of the race they belong to.

SECTION II. Be it further enacted, etc., that the officers of such passenger trains shall have power and are hereby required to assign each passenger to the coach or compartment used for the race to which such passenger belongs; any passenger insisting on going into a coach or compartment to which by race he does not belong, shall be liable to a fine of twenty-five dollars or in lieu thereof to imprisonment for a period of not more — twenty days in the parish prison and any officer of any railroad insisting on assigning a passenger to a coach or compartment other than the one set aside for the race to which said passenger belongs shall be liable to a fine of twenty-five dollars or in lieu thereof to imprisonment for a period of not more than twenty days in the parish prison; and should any passenger refuse to occupy the coach or compartment to which he or she is assigned by the officer of such railway, said officer shall have power to refuse to carry such passenger on his train, and for such refusal neither he nor the railway company which he represents shall be liable for damages in any of the courts of this State.

SECTION III. Be it further enacted, etc., That all officers and directors of railway companies that shall refuse or neglect to comply with the provisions and requirements of this act shall be deemed guilty of a misdemeanor and shall upon conviction before any court of competent jurisdiction be fined not less than one hundred dollars nor more than five hundred dollars; and any conductor or other employees of such passenger train, having charge of the same, who shall refuse or neglect to carry out the provisions of this act shall on conviction be fined not less than twenty-five dollars nor more than fifty dollars for each offense; all railroad corporations carrying passengers in this State other than street railroads shall keep this law posted up in a conspicuous place in each passenger coach and ticket office, provided that nothing in this act shall be construed as applying to nurses attending children of the other race.

SECTION IV. Be it further enacted, etc., That all laws or parts of laws contrary to or inconsistent with the provisions of this act be and the same are hereby repealed and that this act shall take effect and be in full force ninety days after its promulgation.

S. P. HENRY,
Speaker of the House of Representatives.
JAMES JEFFRIES,
Lieut. Governor and President of the Senate.

Approved July 10th, 1890.

FRANCIS T. NICHOLS,
Governor of the State of Louisiana.

A true copy from the original.

L. F. MASON,
Secretary of State.

14 *Defendant's Plea to Information, Marked Exhibit "D." Filed with Petition Nov'r 22, 1892.*

Criminal District Court for the Parish of Orleans.

STATE OF LOUISIANA
vs.
HOMER ADOLPH PLESSEY. } No. 19117. Section "A."

Information for occupying railway coach set apart for white passengers.

Defendant's Plea.

And the said Homer Adolph Plessey, in his own proper person, cometh into court here and, having heard the said information read, says that this honorable court ought not to entertain further cognizance of this cause, because, protesting that he is not guilty as in the said information above specified, nevertheless the said defendant says:

1st. That he, the said Homer A. Plessey, is a citizen of the United States and a resident of the State of Louisiana.

2nd. That the East Louisiana Railway Company referred to in the said information is a corporation duly incorporated and organized by the laws of the State of Louisiana as a common carrier, acting by virtue of a public charter and carrying passengers for hire, and cannot be authorized to distinguish between citizens according to race.

3rd. That race is a question of law and fact which an officer of a railroad corporation cannot be authorized to determine.

4th. That said defendant bought and paid for a ticket of said company entitling him to one first-class passage from said city of New Orleans, in the State of Louisiana, to the city of Covington, in the State of Louisiana, and had the same in his possession and unused at the time of the act alleged in the information aforesaid as the basis thereof, and that the coach or car which he went into and occupied was a first-class one, as called for by said ticket, and defendant was being conveyed therein as a passenger of the said railway company from the city of New Orleans to the said city of Covington, and the said ticket is still in said defendant's possession unused up to the present time.

5th. That said defendant was guilty of no breach of the peace, no noisy or obstreperous conduct, and uttered no profane or vulgar language in said car; that he was respectably and cleanly dressed; that he was not intoxicated nor affected by any noxious disease, and that no objection was made to his personal appearance, conduct, or condition by any one in said coach or car, nor could such objection have been truthfully made.

6th. That the information herein is based on an act of the legislature of the State of Louisiana designated as act No. 111 of the sessions acts of the General Assembly of this State, approved July 10th, 1890, and the said act in its several parts is in conflict with the Constitution of the United States.

7th. Defendant further says that section 2 of said act is an essential part of the same; that said section pretends to confer upon the conductor of a railroad train the power to determine the question of race and to assort the passengers upon said train in accordance with his decision of this question; that the refusal of any passenger to abide by the decision of the conductor is attempted to be made a criminal offense by said act and is the gist of the present information; that the legislature has no power to confer judicial functions upon "an officer of a passenger train" nor to make a peaceable refusal to accept his decision as to "the race to which the passenger belongs" a crime or to make said act punishable by fine or imprisonment.

8th. That said section being an essential section of said act it is likewise unconstitutional and void, in that it provides a summary punishment for such pretended criminal act by authorizing the officer to refuse to carry such pretendedly contumacious passenger and exempting both the company and the officer from any claim for damages on the part of said passenger, the same being the imposition of punishment without due process of law and the denial to citizens of the United States of the equal protection of the laws.

9th. That the purpose and object of said act, as appears upon its face, is to assort and classify all passengers upon railroads doing business within the State according to race, and to make the rights and privileges of citizens of the United States dependent on said classification, and is therefore void.

10th. That race is a scientific and legal question of great difficulty; that the State has no power to authorize any person to determine the same without testimony or to make the rights or privileges of any citizen of the United States dependent on the fact of race or its determination by such unauthorized person, to compel the citizen to accept such determination, or to make refusal to comply with the same a penal offence.

11th. That the State has no right to distinguish between the rights and privileges of citizens of the United States on the ground of race as regards place, privilege, or accommodation in public railway trains within said State, a party purchasing a ticket of a particular class being entitled to take any seat in any car of the class for which his passage calls not occupied by another.

12th. The act deprives the citizen of remedy for wrong, and is

2—880

unconstitutional for that reason, and for the further reason that the State neither has nor can have power to distinguish between citizens of the United States as regards any right, privilege, or immunity to be enjoyed or exercised by such citizen on account of race or color.

13th. That a State has no power or authority to grant exclusive rights or privileges to citizens of the United States of one race which are denied to citizens of another race, or to make the refusal to submit to such denial a penal offence.

14th. That the statute in question, to wit, act No. 111, approved July 10th, 1890, establishes an invidious distinction and discriminates between citizens of the United States based on race, which is obnoxious to the fundamental principles of national citizenship, perpetuates involuntary servitude, as regards citizens of the colored race, under the merest pretense of promoting the comfort of passengers on railway trains, and in further respects abridges the privileges and immunities of citizens of the United States and the rights secured by the XIIIth and XIVth amendments of the Federal Constitution; and this the said Homer A. Plessey is ready to verify. Wherefore he prays judgment if this honorable court will or ought to take cognizance of the information aforesaid, and that by the court here he may be dismissed and discharged.

(Original signed)   JAS. C. WALKER,
Of Counsel for Defendant.

Personally appeared Homer A. Plessey, who, being duly sworn, deposes and says that the facts and allegations set forth in the foregoing plea are true and correct, and that the same is not interposed for delay, but that right and justice be done in the premises.

(Original signed)   H. A. PLESSY.

Sworn to and subscribed before me this 13th day of October, A. D. 1892.

(Signed)   F. J. LETTEN,
Minute Clerk.

Endorsement on petition: No. 11134. Supreme court of La. Filed Nov'r 22, 1892. C. W. Buchanan, d'y clerk. *Ex parte* Homer A. Plessy for writs of prohibition and certiorari. Jas. C. Walker, att'y for petitioner.

I accept service of the within petition and exhibits.
New Orleans, La., Nov. 23d, 1892.

           J. H. FERGUSON, *Judge.*

Order on Petition.

It is ordered that the respondent do shew cause, on Saturday, the 26th day of November, A. D. 1892, at 11 o'clock a. m., why the writ of prohibition should not be made perpetual, as prayed for. It is further ordered that the respondent certify and transmit to this court on that date a record of the proceedings had in the said case, entitled and numbered on the docket of the criminal district court for the parish of Orleans "State of Louisiana v. Homer A. Plessy, No. 19117," to the end that the validity of said proceedings be ascertained; and it is further ordered until the further order of this court all proceedings in said case be stayed.

New Orleans, November 22, 1892.

 (Signed)   FRANCIS T. NICHOLLS,
                 Chief Justice of Louisiana.

Writs of Prohibition and Certiorari.   Issued November 22, 1892.

Supreme Court of the State of Louisiana.

CLERK'S OFFICE, NEW ORLEANS, —— —, 189–.

Ex Parte HOMER A. PLESSY.   No. 11134.

21 The judge of the criminal district court for the parish of Orleans, section "A," to Hon. John H. Ferguson, judge of the criminal dist. court for the parish of Orleans, Greeting:

Whereas Homer A. Plessy has this day filed a petition in this honorable court praying for writs of prohibition and certiorari against you in the case entitled State of Louisiana v. Homer A. Plessy, and numbered 19117 on the docket of the criminal district court for the parish of Orleans, and the court, having ordered said writs to issue:

Now, therefore, you are hereby commanded, in the name of the State of Louisiana and of this honorable court, to show cause, on Saturday, twenty-six day of November, A. D. 1892, at 11 o'clock a. m., why the writ of prohibition should not be made perpetual, as prayed for. It is further ordered that you certify and transmit to this court on that date a record of the proceedings had in the said case of State of Louisiana v. Homer A. Plessy, No. 19117 of the docket of the said criminal court for the parish of Orleans, to the end that the validity of said proceedings be ascertained; and it is further ordered until the further order of this court all proceedings in said case be stayed.

 Witness the Honorable Francis T. Nicholls, chief justice of this honorable court, on this the 22nd day of November, in the
[SEAL.] year of our Lord one thousand eight hundred and ninety-two.

 (Signed)   C. W. BUCHANAN, *D'y Clerk.*

Endorsement: No. 11134. Supreme court, State of Louisiana. *Ex parte* Homer A. Plessy. Writs of prohibition and cer-
22 tiorari inside to be served on Hon. John H. Ferguson, judge criminal dist. court. For return.

Sheriff's Return.

Received Wednesday, Nov. 23, 1892, and on the same day, month, and year I served a copy of the within prohibition and accompanying certiorari personally on Hon. John H. Ferguson, judge criminal district court, herein named. Returned same day.

Sheriff's fees, $2.00.
(Signed)
JAMES DUIGNAN,
Deputy Sheriff.

Supreme court of Louisiana. Filed Nov. 28, 1892. (Signed) T. McC. Hyman, clerk.

Answer of Respondent. Filed Nov. 26, 1892.

Supreme Court of La.

Ex Parte HOMER A. PLESSY. No. 11134.

Application for writs of prohibition and certiorari.

To the honorable the supreme court of Louisiana:

Now into court comes John H. Ferguson, presiding judge of section "A" of the criminal district court of the parish of Orleans, State of Louisiana, made respondent in the above entitled and numbered cause, and having suggested that in obedience to the mandate of this honorable court he has herewith transmitted to this honorable court a certified copy of the proceedings in the prosecution entitled "The State of Louisiana *vs.* Homer A. Plessy," being a prosecution by information for violation of the provisions of act No. 111 of 1890, for answer to the writ of prohibition to him directed, with respect says:

That the cognizance of the said cause of the State of Louisiana *vs.* Homer A. Plessy belongs of right to the said section "A" of the criminal district court of the Parish of Orleans, and that your respondent as the presiding judge of the said court is competent to hear and determine the same.

Respondent respectfully represents that so much of the said act No. 111 of 1890 as is charged in the information against the said Homer A. Plessy filed to have been violated is a good and valid statute of the State of Louisiana, and that the said Homer A. Plessy is by the law of the land bound to answer the same; and in support of his said plea respondent annexes hereto and makes part hereof the opinion and decree by him rendered in his official capacity in passing upon the plea to the jurisdiction of the court by the said Homer A. Plessy interposed.

Respondent respectfully avers that nowhere in the information against the said Homer A. Plessy in the said court filed is it alleged either that the said Homer A. Plessy was a white man or a colored man, or that he belonged to the white race or to the colored race; nor is it anywhere in the said hereinbefore-mentioned plea to the jurisdiction of the court by the said Homer A. Plessy interposed either pleaded, averred, or admitted that the said Homer A. Plessy is a colored man or belongs to the colored race, or that he was of mixed Caucasion and African descent, or that belonging to the colored race he was by reason thereof denied and deprived of any right, privilege, or immunity because of his race and color.

Respondent further avers that instead of pleading, averring, or admitting that the said Homer A. Plessy was of and did belong to the colored race, the said Homer A. Plessy, on the contrary, declined and refused, either by pleading or otherwise, to acknowledge and admit that he was in any sense or in any proportion a colored man.

Respondent further respectfully represents that the affidavit of C. C. Cain, made before the recorder of the second recorder's court, against the said Homer A. Plessy, which is annexed to and made part of relator's petition praying for the writ of prohibition herein, forms no part of the proceedings had before your respondent, was at no time produced or offered in any of the proceedings had before your respondent, nor has the same ever been inspected or seen by your respondent, either by copy or in the original, until the service upon him of the writs of prohibition and certiorari issued herein.

Respondent respectfully represents that, so far as the proceedings in his court are concerned, he does not, cannot, and will not know until the trial of the said Homer A. Plessy under the information against him filed whether the said Homer A. Plessy was a white man or a colored man insisting upon going into and remaining in a compartment of a coach to which, by reason of his race or color, he did not belong.

Respondent further avers that, apart from the matters and things set up and alleged in the plea filed by the said Homer A. Plessy in this cause pleaded, there is nothing in the prosecution against him instituted and in the proceedings had thereunder which could or does raise any question under the Constitution and laws of the United States.

Respondent respectfully represents that it was competent for the State of Louisiana, through its legislature, to prohibit the acts of the said Homer A. Plessy which are charged against him as an offence, and that the proceedings had under the penal law of the State forbidding the same have been regular and in pursuance *with* the requirements of the said act.

Wherefore respondent prays that, after due proceedings had, *that* the answer of your respondent be considered as sufficient in law to justify his conduct; that the complaint against him by the said petitioner brought be dismissed, and the said petitioner be sentenced to pay costs.

And your respondent prays for all general and equitable relief.

(Signed)   J. H. FERGUSON,
Respondent.

Certified Copy of Proceedings in Criminal District Court. Filed November 26, 1892.

Criminal District Court.

Certified copy of proceedings *in re—*

The State of La.
vs.
Homer A. Plessy.
} No. 19117. Section "A."

State of Louisiana,
Parish of Orleans,
} ss:

Criminal District Court for the Parish of Orleans.

Lionel Adams, district attorney for the parish of Orleans, who, in the name and by the authority of the said State, prosecutes in this behalf, in proper person comes into the criminal district court for the parish of Orleans, in the parish of Orleans, and gives the court here to understand and be informed that one Homer Adolph Plessy, late of the parish of Orleans, on the seventh day of June, in the year of our Lord one thousand eight hundred and ninety-two, with force and arms, in the parish of Orleans aforesaid and within the jurisdiction of the criminal district court for the parish of Orleans, being then a passenger, travelling wholly within the limits of the State of Louisiana, on a passenger train belonging to the East Louisiana Railroad Company, a railway company carrying passengers in their coaches within the State of Louisiana, and on which the officers of the said East Louisiana Railroad Company had power and were required to assign and did assign the said Homer Adolph Plessy to the coach used for the race to which he, the said Homer Adolph Plessy, belonged, unlawfully did then and there insist on going into a coach to which by race he did not belong, contrary to the form of the statute of the State of Louisiana in such case made and provided and against the peace and dignity of the same.

(Signed) LIONEL ADAMS,
Ass't District Attorney for the Parish of Orleans.

State of Louisiana:

Criminal District Court for the Parish of Orleans.

Thursday, *October 13th*, 1892.

The court met this day, pursuant to adjournment, at 10.30 a. m.
Present: The Honorable John H. Ferguson, judge.
Present: The Honorable C. A. Butler, district attorney.

J. H. FERGUSON, JUDGE, ETC.

STATE OF LOUISIANA
vs. } No. 19117.
HOMER ADOLPH PLESSY.

Information for violating provisions of act 111 of 1890.

The defendant, in person, was placed at the bar of the court, in custody of the sheriff, attended by his counsel, Jas. C. Walker, Esq., to be arraigned on the charge preferred against him in the said information. After the reading of said information by the clerk the defendant was called upon to plead thereto. Now comes said counsel for the defendant and presents to the court a plea in bar to prosecution in the aforesaid information. The court ordered said motion filed. The defendant was discharged on his bond, to await further proceedings.

STATE OF LOUISIANA:

Criminal District Court for the Parish of Orleans.

FRIDAY, *October 28th*, 1892.

The court met this day, pursuant to adjournment, at 10.30 a. m.
Present: The Honorable John H. Ferguson, judge.
    "   "   " C. A. Butler, district attorney.

STATE OF LOUISIANA
vs. } No. 19117.
HOMER A. PLESSY.

Information for violating provisions of act 111 of 1890.

Now comes the assistant district attorney, who prosecutes for the State, and the defendant, in person, was placed at the bar of the court, in custody of the sheriff, attended by J. C. Walker, Esq., of counsel, and the plea in bar filed by counsel for the defense and fixed for hearing to-day came on to be heard. Counsel for the State filed a demurrer to the said plea in bar. Counsel for the defense filed a joinder to said demurrer. After arguments by counsel for the State and defense the court took the matter under advisement.

STATE OF LOUISIANA:

Criminal District Court for the Parish of Orleans.

FRIDAY, *November 18th*, 1892.

The court met this day, pursuant to adjournment, at 10.30 a. m.
Present: The Honorable John H. Ferguson, judge.
    "   "   " C. A. Butler, district attorney.

STATE OF LOUISIANA
vs.
HOMER ADOLPH PLESSY.
} No. 19117.

Information for violating provisions of act 111 of 1890.

The defendant, in person, was placed at the bar of the court in custody of the sheriff, attended by his counsel, Jas. C. Walker, Esq., and the court, for reason on file and of record, overruled the plea in bar herein filed to the aforesaid information. The defendant was discharged on his bond to await further proceedings.

No. 19117. Criminal district court, section A. State of Louisiana vs. Homer A. Plessy. D'f't's plea. (Signed) Jas. C. Walker, att'y. Filed Oct. 13, '92. (Signed) F. J. Letten, minute clerk.

Criminal District Court for the Parish of Orleans.

STATE OF LOUISIANA
vs.
HOMER ADOLPH PLESSY.
} No. 19117. Section A.

29 Information for occupying railway coach set apart for white passengers.

Defendant's Plea.

And the said Homer Adolph Plessy, in his own proper person, cometh into court here and, having heard the said information read, says that this honl. court ought not to entertain further cognizance of this cause, because, protesting that he is not guilty as in the said information above specified, nevertheless the said defendant says:

1st. That he, the said Homer A. Plessy, is a citizen of the United States and a resident of the State of Louisiana.

2d. That the East Louisiana Railway Company referred to in the said information is a corporation duly incorporated and organized by the laws of the State of Louisiana as a common carrier, acting by virtue of a public charter and carrying passengers for hire, and cannot be authorized to distinguish between citizens according to race.

3rd. That race is a question of law and fact which an officer of a railroad corporation cannot be authorized to determine.

4th. That said defendant bought and paid for a ticket of said company entitling him to one first-class passage from said city of New Orleans, in the State of Louisiana, to the city of Covington, in the State of Louisiana, and had the same in his possession and unused at the time of the act alleged in the information aforesaid as the basis thereof, and that the coach or car which he went into and occupied was a first-class one, as called for by said ticket, and defendant was being conveyed therein as a passenger of the said railway company from the city of New Orleans to the said city of

Covington, and the said ticket is still in said defendant's possession unused up to the present time.

30   5th. That said defendant was guilty of no breach of the peace, no noisy or obstreperous conduct, and uttered no profane or vulgar language in said car; that he was respectably and cleanly dressed; that he was not intoxicated nor affected by any noxious disease, and that no objection was made to his personal appearance, conduct, or condition by any one in said coach or car, nor could such objection have been truthfully made.

6th. That the information herein is based on an act of the legislature of the State of Louisiana, designated as act 111 of the sessions acts of the General Assembly of this State, approved July 10th, 1890, and the said act in its several parts is in conflict with the Constitution of the United States.

7th. Defendant further says that section 2 of said act is an essential part of the same; that said section pretends to confer upon the conductor of a railroad train the power to determine the question of race and to arrest the passengers upon said train in accordance with his decision of this question; that the refusal of any passenger to abide by the decision of the conductor is attempted to be made a criminal offence by said act and is the gist of the present information; that the legislature has no power to confer judicial functions upon "an officer of a passenger train," nor to make a peaceable refusal to accept his decision as to "the race to which the passenger belongs" a crime, or to make said act punishable by fine or imprisonment.

8th. That said section being an essential section of said act it is likewise unconstitutional and void, in that it provides a summary punishment for such pretended criminal act by authorizing the officer to refuse to carry such pretendedly contumacious passengers and exempting both the company and the officer from any claim

31   for damages on the part of said passenger, the same being the imposition of punishment without due process of law and the denial to citizens of the United States of the equal protection of the laws.

9th. That the purpose and object of said act, as appears upon its face, is to assort and classify all passengers upon railroads doing business within the State according to race and to make the rights and privileges of citizens of the United States dependent on said classification, and is therefore void.

10th. That race is a scientific and legal question of great difficulty; that the State has no power to authorize any person to determine the same without testimony, or to make the rights or privileges of any citizen of the United States dependent on the fact of race or its determination by such unauthorized person to compel the citizen to accept such determination, or to make refusal to comply with the same a penal offence.

11th. That the State has no right to distinguish between the rights and privileges of citizens of the United States on the ground of race as regards place, privilege, or accommodation in public railway trains within said State, a party purchasing a ticket of a par-

3—880

ticular class being entitled to take any seat in any car of the class for which his passage calls not occupied by another.

12th. The act deprives the citizen of remedies for wrong and is unconstitutional for that reason, and for the further reason that the State neither has nor can have power to distinguish between citizens of the United States as regards any right, privilege, or immunity to be enjoyed or exercised by such citizen on account of race or color.

13th. That a State has no power or authority to grant exclusive rights or privileges to citizens of the United States of one race which are denied to citizens of another race, or to make the refusal to submit to such denial a penal offence.

14th. That the statute in question, to wit, act 111, approved July 10th, 1890, established an insidious destinction and discriminates between citizens of the United States based on race, which is obnoxious to the fundamental principles of national citizenship, perpetuates involuntary servitude as regards citizens of the colored race under the merest pretense of promoting the comfort of passengers on railway trains, and in further respects abridges the privileges and immunities of citizens of the United States and the rights secured by the XIIIth and XIVth amendments of the Federal Constitution.

And this the said Homer A. Plessy is ready to verify. Wherefore he prays judgment of this honl. court will or ought to take cognizance of the information aforesaid, and that by the court here — may be dismissed and discharged.

(Signed) JAS. C. WALKER,
Of Counsel for Defendant.

Personally appeared Homer A. Plessy, who, being duly sworn, deposes and says that the facts and allegations set forth in the foregoing plea are true and correct, and that the same is not interposed for delay, but that right and justice be done in the premises.

(Signed) H. A. PLESSY.

Sworn to and subscribed before me this 13th day of October, A. D. 1892.

(Signed) F. J. LETTEN,
Minute Clerk.

No. 19117. Criminal district court, section A. The State of La. *vs.* H. A. Plessy. Demurrer to def'd's plea. Filed October 28, '92. (Signed) F. J. Letten, minute clerk. (Signed) Lionel Adams, ass't dis't att'y.

Criminal District Court.

THE STATE OF LA.
vs.
H. A. PLESSY.
} No. 19117. Section A.

Now comes Lionel Adams, assistant district attorney for the parish of Orleans, who prosecutes for the State in this behalf, and, as to the said plea of the said H. A. Plessy by him first above pleaded, saith that the same and the matters therein contained, in manner and form as the same are above pleaded and set forth, are not sufficient in law to bar or preclude the said State from prosecuting the said information against him, the said H. A. Plessy, and that the said State is not bound by law to answer to the same; and this he, the said Lionel Adams, who prosecutes as aforesaid, is ready to verify.

Wherefore, for want of a sufficient plea in this behalf, he, the said Lionel Adams, for the State of Louisiana, prays judgment, and that the said H. A. Plessy may be required to plead over the premises in the said information specified.

34

No. 19117. State of Louisiana *vs.* H. A. Plessy. Joinder to demurrer. Filed Oct. 28th, 1892. (Signed) F. J. Letten, minute clerk.

Criminal District Court for the Parish of Orleans.

STATE OF LOUISIANA
vs.
HOMER ADOLPH PLESSY. } No. 19117. Section A.

Joinder by Defendant.

And the said Homer Adolph Plessy saith that his said plea by him heretofore pleaded in this cause and the matters therein contained, in manner and form as the same are therein pleaded and set forth, are sufficient in law to bar and preclude the State of Louisiana aforesaid from prosecuting the said information against him, the said Homer Adolph Plessy, and the said Homer Adolph Plessy is ready to verify and prove the same as the said court shall direct and award. Wherefore, inasmuch as the said district attorney for the said State hath not answered the said plea nor hitherto in any manner denied the same, the said Homer Adolph Plessy prays judgment, and that by the court here he may be dismissed and discharged from the said premises in said information specified.

(Signed)   JAS. C. WALKER,
Of Counsel for Def'd't.

35   Criminal District Court.

STATE OF LA.
vs.
HOMER ADOLPH PLESSY. } No. 19117. Sec. "A."

Information for violating provisions of act 111 of 1890.

The information in this case is based on act No. 111, approved July 10th, 1890. It charges that the defendant unlawfully insisted on going into a coach to which, by race, he did not belong.

There is no averment as to the color of the defendant.

Defendant, before arraignment, filed a plea herein based on fifteen grounds, and prayed therein to be dismissed and discharged.

The title of the act referred to is to promote the comfort of passengers on railway trains; requiring all railway companies carrying passengers on their trains in this State to provide equal but separate accommodations for the white and colored races by providing separate coaches or compartments, so as to secure separate accommodations; defining the duties of the officers of such railways; directing them to assign passengers to the coaches or compartments set aside for the use of the race to which such passengers belong; authorizing them to refuse to carry on their train such passengers as may refuse to occupy the coaches or compartments to which he or she is assigned; to exonerate such railway companies from any and all blame or damages that might proceed or result from such a refusal; to prescribe penalties for all violations of this act, &c.

It is urged by defendant'- attorney that the title of the act to promote the comfort of railway passengers *it* is evidently not the design of the act; that its purpose is to legalize a discrimination between classes of citizens based on race and color.

This law is clear and free from all ambiguity, and the letter of it is not to be disregarded under the pretext of pursuing its spirit.

Judges have nothing to do with the policy of particular acts passed by the legislature.

The will of the law given being understood, nothing remains but to carry it into effect. 3 R., 465.

It is claimed also and, in fact, it is conceded by the State's attorney that such part of the statute as exempts from liability the railway companies *at its* officers is unconstitutional.

It is a rule of interpretation that a law may be unconstitutional in part and valid in all other parts. H. D., vol. 1, pp. 779, '80, No. 10 & 31; p. 782, Nos. 3 & 6. Eliminate the clause which is objected to — remains a perfectly valid and constitutional enactment.

It is further urged in support of the plea herein that judicial functions are delegated to the conductor of the train by the legislature, and that it has exceeded its authority by so doing.

In an analogous case reported in the Federal Reporter, vol. XXIII, page 319, it was held that the conductor was the proper officer to decide upon her (a colored woman) right to ride in the ladies' car.

The act in question authorizes the officers of the train to assign passengers to the coach or compartment used for the race to which such passenger belongs; to decide upon the right of defendant to ride in a certain car.

The officer, it is true, determines for the time being the question of color.

He does so at his peril. His decision is subject to subsequent judicial investigation and determination. Clearly railway companies have the right to adopt reasonable rules and regulations for their protection and for the proper conduct of their business and to designate who shall execute said regulations. It is in the nature of a police regulation.

If, therefore, said companies have such right, it follows that the legislature, the law-maker, has the undoubted right to so declare in an expression of legislature will.

Counsel for defendant contends that the accused is deprived by the said power delegated to the conductor of liberty and property without due process of law, in violation of the Constitution of the United States.

It would be impracticable—in fact, almost impossible—to organize and utilize a circuit court or any tribunal with special jurisdiction to *instanter* the train by and determine the color of a passenger when the question was special- put at issue.

The defendant herein was not in a proper sense deprived of his liberty by the act of the officer of the company.

There is no pretense that he was not provided with equal accommodations with the passengers of that class to which he did not belong. He was simply deprived of the liberty of doing as he pleased and of violating a penal statute with impunity.

It is urged that defendant was deprived of his property because he purchased a first-class ticket and never used it by reason of the act of the conductor. The railway company was blameless in the matter. The ticket purchased by the defendant was not used simply because the defendant refused to ride in the car or compartment to which he was assigned by the conductor, without a valid reason for said refusal, and insisted on going into a coach — which by race he did not belong, according to the information.

Another ground is that said act does not afford an equal protection, in violation of art. XIV of the Constitution. The act expressly provides that all railway companies carrying passengers in their coaches in this State shall provide equal accommodations for the white and colored races; also that any passenger insisting on going into a coach or compartment to which by race he *does not belong* shall be liable to — according to its provisions. Should a white passenger insist on going into a coach or compartment to which by race he does not belong, he would thereby render himself liable to punishment according to this law. There is, therefore, no distinction or unjust discrimination in this respect on account of color. The important question for consideration in this case — *that* the legislature — the right to authorize and empower railway companies within the State to provide equal but separate cars or compartments for the different races.

In the case entitled Logqood and Wife *vs.* Memphis & C. R. R. Co.—

Judge Hammond, of the circuit court, charged the jury that common carriers are required by law not to make any unjust discrimination and must treat all passengers paying the same price alike. Equal accommodations do not mean identical accommodations. Races and nationalities under some circumstances, to be determined on the facts of each case, may be separated, but in all cases the carrier must furnish substantially the same accommodation to all by providing equal comforts, privileges, and pleasures to every class. Colored people and white people may be so separated, if carriers proceed according to this rule.

If a railroad company furnishes for white ladies a car with special privileges of seclusion and other comforts, the same must be substantially furnished for colored women.

All travelers have to submit to some discomforts and inconveniences and should not be too exacting.

The break-man on the train having referred Mrs. Logwood to the conductor, who was the proper officer to decide upon her right to ride in the ladies' car, and she having gone to him, the question in this case must be determined by what occurred between them, and if you believe from the proof that the conductor ratified the act of the break-man by telling her she must ride in the front car and would not be permitted to go into the ladies' car, the company is undoubtedly liable for damages, unless you conclude from the evidence that the front car was, under the rule already announced, equal to the ladies' car.

But if you believe that the conductor told her that at his convenience he would admit her to the ladies' car, and there was no unreasonable delay or discomfort in so doing, the plaintiff cannot recover in this case.

In the case entitled Murphy vs. Western & A. R. R. and Others the circuit court of Tennessee held that a railroad company may set apart certain cars to be occupied by white people and certain cars to be occupied by colored people, but if it charges the same fare to each race it must furnish substantially like and equal accommodations.

It was held in Maryland in an admiralty proceeding that on a night steamboat plying on the Chesapeake bay colored female passengers may be assigned a different sleeping cabin from white female passengers.

The right to make such separation can only be upheld when the carrier in good faith furnishes accommodations equal in quality and convenience to both alike. Federal Reporter, vol. XXII, p. 843.

In the year 1888 the legislature of the State of Mississippi passed an act of which the act under consideration is identical.

In a case reported in the 133 United States Reports, at page 591, the Supreme Court, in interpreting the Mississippi statute, use the following language:

"So far as the first section is concerned (and it is with that alone we have to do), its provisions are fully complied with when to trains within the State is attached a separate car for colored passengers. This may cause an extra expense to the railroad company, but not more so than State statutes requiring certain accommodations at depots, compelling trains to stop at crossings of other railroads, and a multitude *by* other matters confessedly within the power of the State."

The argument herein by the counsel for the defendant displayed great research, learning, and ability. The court, however, is of the opinion, after mature deliberation and careful consideration — questions involved and of the authorities cited in support of the grounds presented — the able argument of the dist. att'y, for the reasons stated,

J. H. FERGUSON, JUDGE, ETC.

that the plea herein filed by defendant should be dismissed, and it is further ordered that defendant plead over.

Clerk's Certificate.

STATE OF LOUISIANA:

Criminal District Court for the Parish of Orleans.

I, W. J. McGheehan, clerk of the criminal district court for the parish of Orleans, do hereby certify that the within and foregoing 24 pages contain a full, true, and correct transcript of the record, proceedings, and judgment in the cause No. 19117 of the docket of this court, and entitled the State of Louisiana *vs.* Homer Adolph Plessy, as the same appears of record and on file in the clerk's office of the criminal district court for the parish of Orleans.

Given under my hand and seal this 26th day of November, in the year of our Lord one thousand eight hundred and ninety-two, and the one hundred and seventeenth year of the Independence of the United States.

[SEAL.]   (Signed)   W. J. McGHEEHAN,
Clerk of the Criminal District Court for the —

Cause Heard and Submitted.

Extract from the Minutes.

NEW ORLEANS, SATURDAY, *November 26, 1892.*

The court was duly opened pursuant to adjournment.

Present: Their honors Francis T. Nicholls, chief justice; Charles E. Fenner, Lynn B. Watkins, Samuel D. McEnery, Joseph A. Breaux, associate justices.

Ex Parte HOMER A. PLESSY.   No. 11134.

This cause came on this day to be heard on the application of the relator for writs of prohibition and certiorari.

Whereupon the return of the respondent to the rule *nisi* was presented and filed, and, the counsel for the respective parties having submitted the cause, the court took time to consider.

Opinion of the Court. Filed Dec'r 19, 1892.

UNITED STATES OF AMERICA, }
    State of Louisiana.

Supreme Court of the State of Louisiana.

NEW ORLEANS, MONDAY, *December 19th, 1892.*

The court was duly opened pursuant to adjournment.

Present: Their honors Francis T. Nicholls, chief justice; Charles E. Fenner, Lynn B. Watkins, Samuel D. McEnery, Joseph A. Breaux, associate justices.

His honor Mr. Justice Fenner pronounced the opinion and judgment of the court in the following case:

Ex Parte HOMER A. PLESSY. No. 11134.

Application for certiorari and prohibition.

We have held that when a party is prosecuted for crime under a law alleged to be unconstitutional, in a case which is unappealable and where a proper plea setting up the unconstitutionality has been overruled by the judge, a proper case arises for the exercise of our supervisory jurisdiction in determining whether the judge is exceeding the bounds of judicial power by entertaining a prosecution for a crime not created by law.

State *ex rel.* Walker *v.* Judge, 39 Annual, 132.
State *ex rel.* Abbott *v.* Judge, 44 Annual, 583.

Relator's application conforms to all the requirements of this rule. He alleges that he is being prosecuted for a violation of act No. 111 of 1890; that said act is unconstitutional; that his plea of its unconstitutionality has been presented to and overruled by the respondent judge, and that the case is unappealable.

He therefore applies for writs of certiorari and prohibition in order that we may determine the validity of the proceedings, and, in case we find him entitled to such relief, may restrain further proceedings against him in the cause.

The judge, in his answer, maintains the constitutionality of the law and the validity of his proceeding.

The legislative act in question is entitled:

"An act to promote the comfort of passengers on railway trains; requiring all railway companies carrying passengers on their trains in this State to provide equal but separate accommodations for the white and colored races by providing separate coaches or compartments, so as to secure separate accommodations; defining the duties of the officers of such railways; directing them to assign passengers to the coaches or compartments set aside for the use of the race to which such passengers belong; authorizing them to refuse to carry on their trains such passengers as may refuse to occupy the coaches or compartments to which he or she is assigned; to exonerate such railway companies from any and all blame or damages that might proceed from such refusal; to prescribe penalties for all violations of this act," etc.

The 1st section of the act requires that "all railway companies carrying passengers in their coaches in this State shall provide equal but separate accommodations for the white and colored races by providing two or more passenger coaches for each passenger train or by dividing the passenger coaches by a partition, so as to secure separate accommodations," and that "no person or persons shall be permitted to occupy seats in coaches other than the ones assigned to them on account of the race they belong to."

The 2nd section provides "that the officers of such passenger trains shall have power and are hereby required to assign each passenger to the coach or compartment used for the race to which such passenger belongs; any passenger insisting on going into a coach or compartment to which by race he does not belong shall be liable to a fine of $25, or in lieu thereof to imprisonment for a period of not more than twenty days in the parish prison," and a like penalty is imposed on "any officer of any railroad insisting on assigning a passenger to a coach or compartment other than the one set aside for the race to which said passenger belongs;" and it is further provided that "should any passenger refuse to occupy the coach or compartment to which he or she is assigned by the officer of such railway said officer shall have power to refuse to carry such passenger on his train, and for such refusal neither he nor the railway company shall be liable for damages in any of the courts of this State."

The 3rd section provides penalties upon officers, directors, conductors, and employees of railway companies who shall refuse or neglect to comply with the provisions of the act.

We have had occasion very recently to consider the constitutionality of this act as applicable to interstate passengers, and held that if so applied it would be unconstitutional, because in violation of the exclusive right vested in Congress to regulate commerce between the States.

State *ex rel.* Abbott v. Judge, 44 Annual, 583.

The instant case presents no such application of the statute; but it appears on the face of the information that relator was proceeded against as "a passenger travelling wholly within the limits of the State of Louisiana on a passenger train belonging to the East Louisiana Railroad Company, carrying passengers in their coaches within the State of Louisiana." It thus appears that the interstate-commerce clause of the Constitution of the United States is not involved.

The relator's plea of the unconstitutionality of the statute contains no less than fourteen enumerated paragraphs, which do not require reproduction, because most of them are argumentative, and no provisions of the State or Federal constitutions are referred to as violated by the statute except the thirteenth and fourteenth amendments to the Constitution of the United States. The whole gravamen of relator's plea is contained in the 14th ground, which is as follows:

"That the statute in question establishes an invidious distinction and discrimination between citizens of the United States based on race which is obnoxious to the fundamental principles of national citizenship, perpetuates involuntary servitude as regards citizens of the colored race under the merest pretense of promoting the comforts of passengers on railway trains, and in further respects abridges the privileges and immunities of the citizens of the United States and the rights secured by the 13th and 14th amendments of the Federal Constitution."

So far as the thirteenth amendment is concerned, its application to this statute may be at once eliminated, because the Supreme

4—880

Court of the United States has clearly decided that it does not refer to rights of the character here involved. We will, for the sake of brevity, quote only the syllabus of the decision, as follows:

"The XIII amendment relates only to slavery and involuntary servitude (which it abolishes), and although by its reflex action it establishes universal freedom in the United States, and Congress may probably pass laws directly enforcing its provisions, yet such legislative power extends only to the subject of slavery and its incidents, and the denial of equal accommodations in inns, public conveyances, and places of public amusements imposes no badge of slavery or involuntary servitude upon the party, but at most infringes rights which are protected from State aggression by the XIVth amendment."

Civil Rights cases, 109th United States, 3.

We may therefore confine ourselves to the question whether or not the statute violates the XIVth amendment, which provides that "no State shall make or enforce any law which shall abridge the privileges or immunities of citizens of the United States; nor shall any State deprive any person of life, liberty, or property without due process of law, nor deny to any person within its jurisdiction the equal protection of the laws."

A further elimination may be made of the question whether a statute requiring separate accommodations for the races, without requiring the accommodations to be equal, would contravene the amendment, because the statute here explicitly requires that the accommodations shall be equal.

We thus reach the sole question involved in this case, which is whether a statute requiring railroads to furnish separate but equal accommodations for the two races and requiring domestic passengers to confine themselves to the accommodations provided for the race to which they belong violates the XIV amendment.

The first branch of the above question, as to the binding effect of the statute on railways, has been definitely decided by the Supreme Court of the United States on a statute almost identical, holding that the provision requiring railroads to furnish separate but equal accommodations was valid.

Louisville & C. Railway Company *v.* Mississippi, 133 United States, 587.

But the court said: "Whether such *such* accommodations shall be a matter of choice or compulsion" (on the part of passengers) "does not enter into this case."

The validity of such statutes, in so far as they require passengers, under penalties, to confine themselves to the separate and equal accommodations provided for the race to which they belong has not as yet been directly presented to or decided by the Supreme Court of the United States.

But the validity of such statutes and of similar regulations made by common carriers in absence of statute and the validity of similar regulations or statutes, as applied to public schools, have arisen in very many cases before the highest courts of the several States and before inferior Federal courts, resulting in an almost uniform course of decision to the effect that statutes or regulations enforcing the separation of the races in public conveyances or in public schools, so long at least as the facilities or accommodations provided are substantially equal, do not abridge any privilege or immunity of citizens or otherwise contravene the XIV amendment.

We refer to the following, amongst other, numerous decisions:

West Chester R. R. Co. *v.* Miles, 55 Pa. State, 209.
State *v.* McCann, 21 Ohio, 210.
People *v.* Gallagher, 93 New York, 438.
Cory *v.* Carter, 48 Ind., 337.
State *v.* Duffy, 7 Nev., 342.
People *v.* Gaston, 13 Abb., N. Y., 160.
Louisville & C. R'way *v.* State, 66 Mississippi, 662.
Lehew *v.* Brummell (Mo.), 15 S. W. Rep., 765.
Dawson *v.* Lee, 83 Ky., 49.
48 Ward *v.* Flood, 48 Cal., 36.
Chesapeake R. Co. *v.* Wells, 85 Tenn., 613.
Bertouneau *v.* Directors, 3 Woods (C. C. R.), 177.
The Sue, 22 Federal Reporter, 843.
Logwood *v.* Memphis, 23 *ib.*, 318.
Murphy *v.* Weston R. Co., 23 *ib.*, 637.

It would little boot for us to make extensive quotations from these decisions. They all accord in the general principle that in such matters equality and not identity or community of accommodations is the extr-me test of conformity to the requirements of the XIV amendment.

The cogency of the reasons on which this principle is founded perhaps accounts for the singular fact that notwithstanding the general prevalence throughout the country of such statutes and regulations and the frequency of decisions maintaining them no one has yet undertaken to submit the question to the final arbitrament of the Supreme Court of the United States.

In a case which arose as far back as 1849 the supreme court of Massachusetts, through its great Chief Justice Shaw, considered this subject, saying: "Conceding, therefore, in the fullest manner, that colored persons, the descendants of Africans, are entitled by law to equal rights, constitutional and political, civil and social, the question then arises whether the regulation in question, which provide separate schools for colored children, is a violation of any of these rights," and the court held that it was not, saying, in conclusion:

"It is urged that this maintenance of separate scools tends to deepen and perpetuate the odious distinction of caste, founded
49   in a deep-rooted prejudice in public opinion. This prejudice, if it exists, is not created by law and cannot be changed by law. Whether this distinction and prejudice, existing in the opinions and feeling of the community, would not be as effectually fostered by compelling colored and white children to associate together may well be doubted."

Roberts *v.* Boston, 5 Cush., 198.

The general rule applied to carriers is well stated by Mr. Hutchinson: "If the conveyance employed be adapted to the carriage of passengers separated into different classes, according to the fare which may be charged, the character of the accommodations afforded, or of the persons to be carried, the carrier may so divide them, and any regulation confining those of one class to one part of the conveyance will not be regarded as unreasonable if made in good faith for the better accommodation and convenience of the passengers."

Hutchinson on Carriers, paragraph 542.

In applying this rule the supreme court of Pennsylvania said: "The right to separate passengers being clear in proper cases and it being the subject of sound regulation, the question remaining to be considered is whether there is such a difference between the white and the black races in this State, resulting from nature, law, and custom, as makes it a reasonable ground of separation." The court then proceeds to discuss these differences, taking care to say: "To assert separateness is not to declare inferiority in either. It is simply to say that, following the order of divine Providence, human authority ought not to compel these widely separated races to intermix." Concluding, the court said: "Law and custom having sanctioned a separation of races, it is not the province of the judiciary to legislate it away. * * * Following these guides, we are compelled to declare that, at the time of the alleged injury, there was that natural, legal, and customary difference between the white and black races in this State which made their separation as passengers in a public conveyance the subject of a sound regulation to secure order, promote comfort, preserve the peace, and maintain the rights both of the carriers and passengers."

West Chester R. R. Co. v. Miles, 55 Penn. St., 209.

Both the decisions from which we have quoted were rendered before the adoption of the XIV amendment, but in States where the civil rights of the colored race were fully recognized. We have referred to them as indicating the germinal principles which have been followed in the numerous decisions cited above applying to the XIV amendment. That amendment, it is well settled, created no new rights whatever, but only extended the operation of existing rights and furnished additional protection for such rights.

Barbier v. Connelly, 113 United States, 27.
United States v. Cruikshanks, 92 United States, 542.
Slaughter-house cases, 16 Wallace, 36.

The statute here in question is an exercise of the police power and expresses the conviction of the legislative department of the State that the separation of the races in public conveyances, with proper sanctions enforcing the substantial equality of the accommodations supplied to each, is in the interest of public order, peace, and comfort. It undoubtedly imposes a severe burden upon railways, but the Supreme Court of the United States has held that they are bound to bear it. It impairs no right of passengers of either race, who are secured that equality of accommodations which satisfies every reasonable claim.

The regulation of domestic commerce is as exclusively a State function as the regulation of interstate commerce is a Federal function. It is as much within the control of State legislation as the public-school system or the law of marriage. To hold that the requirement of separate though equal accommodations in public conveyances violated the XIVth amendment would on the same principles necessarily entail the nullity of statutes establishing separate schools and of others, existing in many States, prohibiting intermarriage between the races. All are regulations based upon difference of race, and if such difference cannot furnish a basis for such legislation in one of these cases it cannot in any.

The statute applies to the two races with such perfect fairness and equality that the record brought up for our inspection does not disclose whether the person prosecuted is a white or a colored man. The charge is simply that he "did then and there unlawfully insist on going into a coach to which by race he did not belong." Obviously, if the fact charged be proved the penalty would be the same whether the accused were white or colored.

We have been at pains to expound this statute because the dissatisfaction felt with it by a portion of the people seems to us so unreasonable that we can account for it only on the ground of some misconception. Even were it true that the statute is prompted by a prejudice on the part of one race to be thrown in such contact with the other, one would suppose that to be a sufficient reason why the pride and self-respect of the other race should equally prompt it to avoid such contact if it could be done without the sacrifice of equal accommodations. It is very certain that such unreasonable insistence upon thrusting the company of one race upon the other, with no adequate motive, is calculated, as suggested by Chief Justice Shaw, to foster and intensify repulsion between them rather than to extinguish it.

We will conclude by noticing some charges made against the statute by relator, based, as we think, on an utterly unwarranted construction.

He claims that the statute vests the officers of the company with a judicial power to determine the race to which the passenger belongs; that they may assign the passenger to a coach to which by race he does not belong, and that such assignment is binding on the passenger, and that, though wrongfully made, the officer and the railway companies are exempted from any legal responsibility.

The reading of the statute utterly repels these charges.

Not only does not the statute authorize the conductor or other officer to assign a passenger to a coach to which by race he does not belong, but it affirmatively requires him "to assign each passenger to the coach used for the race to which such passenger belongs," and it punishes for failure to make such assignment.

When the statute authorizes the conductor to refuse to carry any passenger who shall "refuse to occupy the coach to which he or she is assigned by the officer of such railway," it obviously means an assignment according the the requirements of the act—*i. e.*, to the coach to which the passenger by race belongs; and the exemption from damages is subject to the same construction.

It is too clear for discussion that a refusal to carry a passenger because he had refused to obey an assignment to a coach to which his race did not belong would not be exempted from redress in action for damages.

The discretion vested in the officer to decide primarily the coach to which each passenger by race belongs is only that necessary discretion attending every imposition of a duty to determine whether the occasion exists which calls for its exercise. It is a discretion to be exercised at his peril and at the peril of his employer.

It is very certain that if relator shall prove in this prosecution that he did not, as charged, "insist on going into a coach to which by race he did not belong," an erroneous assignment by the conductor would not stand in the way of his acquittal or exempt the officer and the railway from an action for damages, whatever defenses might lie open to them based on good faith and probable cause.

It is therefore ordered that the provisional writ of prohibition herein issued be now dissolved and set aside, and that the relief sought be denied, at relator's cost.

(*Syllabus.*)

1. Act 111 of the legislature of 1890, regulating accommodations of the races on railways, does not violate the XIII amendment of the United States Constitution, because such accommodations involve no badge of slavery or involuntary servitude, which is the sole subject of that amendment. Civil Rights cases, 109 United States, 3.
2. A long line of decisions, State and Federal, maintain that statutes or regulations enforcing the separation of the white and colored races in public conveyances and in public schools, so long at least as the facilities or accommodations provided are substantially equal, do not abridge any privilege or immunity of citizens or otherwise contravene the XIVth amendment of the United States Constitution.
3. In such matters equality and not identity or community of accommodations is the extreme test of conformity to the requirements of the amendment.
4. The regulation of domestic commerce is as exclusively a State function as the regulation of interstate commerce is a Federal function. This statute is a exercise of the police power and expresses the legislative conviction that the separation of the races in railway conveyances, with proper sanctions for substantial equality of accommodations, is in the interest of public order, peace, and comfort. It is a matter of legislative power and discretion with which courts cannot interfere.

5. A proper construction of the statute does not (as contended by relator) authorize a conductor to assign a passenger to a coach to which his race does not belong, nor does it bind the passenger to accept such wrongful assignment, nor exempt the officers from action for damages in case of such wrongful assignment and refusal to carry when disobeyed. The discretion vested in the conductor to decide primarily the coach to which each passenger belongs is only the necessary discretion, attending every imposition of any duty, to determine whether the circumstances under which the duty arises exists. He exercises such discretion at his peril and that of his employer.

Final Judgment.

Extract from the Minutes.

NEW ORLEANS, MONDAY, *December* 19, 1892.

The court was duly opened pursuant to adjournment.

Present: Their honors Francis T. Nicholls, chief justice; Charles E. Fenner, Lynn B. Watkins, Samuel D. McEnery, Joseph A. Breaux, chief justices.

Ex Parte HOMER A. PLESSY. No. 11134.

It is ordered that the provisional writ of prohibition herein issued be now dissolved and set aside, and that the relief sought be denied at the relator's costs.

56   *Petition for Rehearing. Entered and Filed Dec.* 26, 1892.

Ex Parte HOMER A. PLESSY. No. 11134.

To the honorable the supreme court of Louisiana:

The petition of Homer A. Plessy respectfully represents—

That he begs leave to direct attention to the following points, to which reference has not been made in the opinion and decree pronounced by this honl. court in this cause, viz:

1. Act No. 111 of the legislature of this State, approved July 10, 1890, is subversive of petitioner's rights under the XIII amendment of the U. S. Constitution, because the said statute authorizes the officers of railway trains to class petitioner as a colored man, notwithstanding petitioner's lawful status is that of a white man from the fact, as heretofore represented, that petitioner is of mixed Caucasian and African descent in the proportion of seven-eighths Caucasian and one-eighth African blood, and the admixture of colored blood is not discernible in petitioner's complexion; that the distinction under which this classification is made is arbitrary and unfounded, save as an observance and badge of servitude imposed by ancient custom in this State heretofore compulsorily exacted by citizens of the pure white race and now sought to be perpetuated by the said act of the legislature. Civil Rights cases, 109 U. S., p. 3.

2. That the said statute has not defined the term "colored race," which is not merely a question of fact, but is a question of law to be determined by legislative enactment or judicial interpretation.

3. The act, it is true, requires that the railway companies shall provide "equal, but separate, accommodations for the white and colored races," and that "the officers of such passenger trains shall have power and are required to assign each passenger to the coach used for the race to which such passenger belongs," under penalty, &c., &c.; but further on in the text of the statute, section 11 is imperative and less guarded in point of expression, enacting that "should any passenger refuse to occupy the coach or compartment to which he or she is assigned by the officer of such railway, said officer shall have power to refuse to carry such passenger on his train, and for such refusal neither he nor the railway company which he represents shall be liable for damages in any of the courts of this State, thus leaving it to implication that the coach to which the passenger is assigned is equal to the others in the way of accommodation, notwithstanding penal statutes are construed *stricti juris* and not by implication. Besides this, the special exemption of the officers and company from liability for damages in any of the courts of this State, petitioner humbly submits, violates that provision of the XIVth constitutional amendment which secures to all the equal protection of the laws.

4. Act 111 of 1890 is amenable to the charge of class legislation, whether contemplated as a regulation of domestic commerce or as an exercise of the police powers, because the statute, while purporting to separate the races on railway trains operated within the State, discriminates in favor of servants employed as nurses and against persons lawfully married to others of a different race and their children, and the law does not apply to all white persons and all colored persons indiscriminately.

5. The statute is invalid because directed against the colored race, a class of citizens of the United States entitled to equal rights, privileges, and immunities in common with all citizens under the law, and therefore in contravention of the XIVth amendment of the United States Constitution.

Wherefore petitioner prays that a rehearing be allowed in this cause, and for general relief.

Respectfully, &c., &c.

(Signed)   ALBION W. TOURGÉE,
JAS. C. WALKER,
Att'ys for Pet'r.

New Orleans, Dec'b'r 26th, 1892.

Rehearing Refused.

Extract from the Minutes.

NEW ORLEANS, MONDAY, *January* 2, 1893.

The court was duly opened, pursuant to adjournment.
Present: Their honors Francis T. Nicholls, chief justice; Charles

E. Fenner, Lynn B. Watkins, Samuel D. McEnery, Joseph A. Breaux, associate justices.

Ex Parte HOMER A. PLESSY.   No. 11134.

It is ordered that the rehearing applied for in this case be refused.

59   *Petition for Writ of Error and Order. Filed Jan'y 5, 1893.*

Ex Parte HOMER A. PLESSY.   No. 11134.

To the honl. the chief justice of the supreme court of the State of Louisiana:

The petition of Homer A. Plessy, a citizen of the United States, respectfully represents—

That he is aggrieved by the final judgment rendered by this honl. court in the proceedings entitled *Ex parte* Homer A. Plessy, No. 11134 of the docket of this court, wherein petitioner prayed to this honl. court for writs of prohibition and certiorari, to be directed to the Honl. J. H. Ferguson, judge of section "A" of the criminal district court for the parish of Orleans, and petitioner is advised the judgment and decree of this hon. court therein is erroneous and to his prejudice, and he desires to prosecute a writ of error to reverse said judgment to the Supreme Court of the United States.

Petitioner shows that these proceedings were brought by him to enjoin and prohibit the said judge of the criminal district court for the parish of Orleans from entertaining further cognizance and jurisdiction and from proceeding further in the cause entitled the State of Louisiana *vs.* Homer A. Plessy, No. 19117 of the docket of the said criminal district court for the parish of Orleans, wherein it was charged and alleged, upon information filed against petitioner by the Hon. Lionel Adams, assistant district attorney for the parish of Orleans, prosecuting in said cause in behalf of the State of Louisiana, that your petitioner " did, on the seventh day
60   of June of the present year, 1892, with force of arms, in the parish of Orleans and within the jurisdiction of the criminal district court for the parish of Orleans, being there a passenger travelling wholly within the limits of the State of Louisiana on a passenger train of the East Louisiana Railroad Company, a railway company carrying passengers in their coaches within the State of Louisiana, and on which the officers of the said East Louisiana Railroad Company had power and were required to assign and did then assign the said Homer Adolph Plessy to the coach used for the race to which he, the said Homer Adolph Plessy, belonged, unlawfully did then and there insist upon going into a coach to which by race he did not belong, contrary to the form of the statute of the State of Louisiana in such case made and provided and against the peace and dignity of the same."

And there was also drawn in question in this cause and in the said proceedings in the criminal district court for the parish of Orleans aforesaid the validity and constitutionality under the XIIIth

5—850

and XIVth amendments of the Constitution of the United States of an act of the General Assembly of the State of Louisiana, approved July 10th, 1890, No. 111 of the sessions acts of the legislature of the said State, entitled "An act to promote the comfort of passengers on railway trains; requiring all railway companies carrying passengers on their trains in this State to provide equal but separate accommodations for the white and colored races by providing separate coaches or compartments, so as to secure separate accommodations; defining the duties of the officers of such railways; directing them to assign passengers to the coaches or compartment set aside for the use of the race to which such passengers belong; authorizing them to refuse to carry on their train such passengers as may refuse to occupy the coaches or compartments to which he or she is assigned; to exonerate such railway companies from any and all blame or damages that might proceed or result from such a refusal; to prescribe penalties for all violations of this act; to put this act into effect ninety days after its promulgation, and to repeal all laws or parts of laws contrary to or inconsistent with the provisions of this act," for the reasons, viz:

That the East Louisiana Railway Company is incorporated by the laws of this State as a common carrier of passengers for hire, and cannot be authorized to distinguish between citizens according to race; that race is a question of law and fact which an officer of a railroad corporation cannot be authorized to determine.

That said act No. 111, approved July 10th, 1890, is in its several parts in conflict with the Constitution of the United States.

That section 2 of said act pretends to confer on a railroad conductor the power to determine the question of race and to assort the passengers in accordance with his decision, and the refusal of any passenger to abide by the decision of the conductor is attempted to be made a criminal offence by said act.

That the legislature has no power to confer judicial functions upon an officer of a passenger train, nor to make a peaceable refusal to accept his decision as to the race to which the passenger belongs a crime, or to make said act punishable by fine and imprisonment; that the statute provides a summary punishment for such pretended criminal act by authorizing the officer to refuse to carry such passenger for said cause, and exempts both the company and the officer from any claim for damages, thus imposing punishment without due process of law and the denial to citizens of the United States of the equal protection of the laws.

That said statute is void because the purpose of said act on its face is to classify according to race all passengers upon railroads operated within the State and to make the rights and privileges of citizens of the United States dependent on said classification.

That the State has no power to authorize any person to determine the question of race without testimony or to make the rights or privileges of any citizen of the United States dependent on the fact of race or its determination by such unauthorized person; to compel the citizen to accept such determination or to make refusal to comply with the same a penal offence.

That the State has no right to distinguish between the rights and privileges of citizens of the United States on the ground of race as regards place, privilege, or accommodation in public railroad trains within this State.

The act deprives the citizen of remedy for wrong, and is unconstitutional for that reason, and for the further reason that the State neither has nor can have power to distinguish between citizens of the United States as regards any right, privilege, or immunity to be enjoyed or exercised by such citizen on account of race or color.

That the State has no power or authority to grant exclusive rights or privileges to citizens of the United States of one race which are denied to citizens of another race, or to make the refusal to — such denial a penal offence.

That the statute in question, to wit, act No. 111, approved July 10th, 1890, establishes an invidious distinction and discrimination between citizens of the United States based on race, which is obnoxious to the fundamental principles of national citizenship, perpetuates involuntary servitude as regards citizens of the colored race under the merest pretense of promoting the comfort of passengers on railway trains, and in further respects abridges the privileges and immunities of citizens of the United States and the rights secured by the XIIIth and XIVth amendments of the Federal Constitution.

And there was also drawn in question in said proceedings the right, privilege, and immunity of petitioner under said constitutional amendments as a citizen of the United States to the enjoyment of equal rights and privileges with citizens of the white race travelling as passengers on the said East Louisiana railway and on all other railway trains operated within the limits of the State of Louisiana.

All of which said reasons petitioner relied on and set up in this cause as conferring upon petitioner the right to invoke and have perpetuated by this honl. court the said writs of prohibition and certiorari against the said honl. judge of section "A," criminal district court for the parish of Orleans.

That the judgment of this honl. court was adverse to said rights claimed under the aforesaid XIIIth and XIVth amendments to the Constitution of the United States and maintained the validity of the said statute of the State of Louisiana for the reasons following:

The said statute is not a violation of any right under the XIIIth and XIVth amendments. The statute is an exercise of the police power of the State, enforces substantial equality of the accommodations supplied to each, and is in the interest of public order, peace, and comfort and impairs no right of passengers of either race, who are secured the equality of accommodations which satisfies every reasonable claim.

That the subject-matter of the said statute is a regulation of domestic commerce, and therefore exclusively a State function.

That the sole question involved in this case is whether a statute requiring railroads to furnish separate but equal accommodations for the two races and requiring domestic passengers to confine themselves to the accommodations provided for the race to which they belong violates the XIVth amendment.

That the said statute explicitly requires that the accommodations shall be equal, and does not authorize the officers of the railway train to assign passengers according to their own judgment and without reference as to whether the accommodations are equal or not; that the said statute infringes no rights which are protected from State aggression by the XIIIth and XIVth amendments.

That the statute does not authorize the conductor or other officer to assign a passenger to a coach to which by race he does not belong; that it obviously means that the coach to which the passenger is assigned shall be according to the requirements of the act—to the coach to which the passenger by race belongs.

That the said statute does not exempt the officer or conductor from damages for refusing to carry a passenger who refuses to obey an assignment to a coach to which his race did not belong. It is very certain * * * an erroneous assignment by the conductor would not exempt the officer and the railway from an action for damages.

The discretion vested in the officer to decide primarily the coach to which each passenger by race belongs is only that necessary discretion attending any imposition of duty, to be exercised at his peril and at the peril of his employer.

The XIII amendment does not apply or refer to rights of the character here involved.

The statute utterly repels the charge that it vests the officers of the company with a judicial power to determine the race to which the passenger belongs.

All of which appears by the pleadings and judgment in this cause, specially referred to for fuller explanation and greater certainty, by reason of all which the said judgment of this court against petitioner setting aside and revoking the provisional writ of prohibition herein granted by this honl. court against said judge of section "A," criminal district court for the parish of Orleans, and rejecting petitioner's prayer to perpetuate and make the said writ of prohibition peremptory, is within the jurisdiction of the Supreme Court of the United States to review the cause involving the Federal questions aforesaid, passed upon and decided by this court adverse to the right claimed by petitioner, and maintaining the validity of the said statute of the State of Louisiana under said Constitution of the United States and the said XIIIth and XIVth amendments thereto, and petitioner desires a writ of error from the Supreme Court of the United States to review said decision of this honl. court.

Wherefore petitioner prays that said writ of error be allowed him in this case, returnable to the honl. Supreme Court of the United States in thirty days, the said writ to operate as a supersedeas upon petitioner's furnishing bond, with good and sufficient surety, in the sum of — dollars, conditioned as the law directs, and that said respondent, Honl. J. H. Ferguson, judge of section "A," criminal district court for the parish of Orleans, be cited to answer the said writ, and for general relief.

(Signed)   ALBION W. TOURGÉE,
JAS. C. WALKER,
Att'ys for Pet'r.

Writ allowed on bond of three hundred dollars, conditioned as the law provides, being furnished.

New Orleans, January 5th, 1893.

(Signed)   FRANCIS T. NICHOLLS,
Chief Justice.

Bond for Writ of Error. Filed January 5th, 1893.

Know all men by these presents that we, Homer Adolph Plessy, who resides in the city of New Orleans, in the State of Louisiana, as principal, and Paul Bonseigneur, as surety, are held and firmly bound unto the Honorable J. H. Ferguson, judge of the section "A" of the criminal district court for the parish of Orleans, in the full and just sum of three hundred dollars, to be paid to the said Honorable J. H. Ferguson, judge of the section "A" of the criminal district court for the parish of Orleans, his certain attorney, executors, administrators, or assigns; to which payment, well and truly to be made, we bind ourselves, our heirs, executors, administrators, jointly and severally, by these presents.

Sealed with our seals and dated this fifth day of January, in the year of our Lord one thousand eight hundred and ninety-three.

Whereas lately, in the supreme court of the State of Louisiana, in a suit depending in said supreme court of the State of Louisiana, wherein the said Homer A. Plessy was relator and said Honl. J. H. Ferguson, judge of the section "A," criminal district court for the parish of Orleans, was defendant, judgment was rendered against the said Homer A. Plessy dissolving and setting aside the provisional writ of prohibition therein issued and refusing the relief prayed for by relator, at relator's costs; and the said Homer Adolph Plessy having obtained a writ of error and filed a copy thereof in the clerk's office of the said supreme court of the State of Louisiana to reverse the judgment in the aforesaid suit, and a citation directed to the said Honorable J. H. Ferguson, judge of the section "A," criminal district court for the parish of Orleans, citing and admonishing him to be and appear at the Supreme Court of the United States to be holden at Washington within thirty days from the date thereof:

Now, the condition of the above obligation is such that if the said Homer Adolph Plessy shall prosecute said writ to effect and answer

all damages and cost- if he fail to make his plea good, then the above obligation to be void; else to remain in full force and virtue.
(Signed)   H. A. PLESSY. [L. S.]
P. BONSEIGNEUR. [L. S.]

Approved January 5th, 1893.
(Signed)   FRANCIS T. NICHOLLS,
Chief Justice.

UNITED STATES OF AMERICA,
State of Louisiana, City of New Orleans, } ss:

Personally appeared Paul Bonseigneur, who, being duly sworn, deposes and says that he is the surety on the within bond; that he resides at No. 179 N. Claiborne St., in the city of New Orleans, and is worth the full sum of three hundred dollars over and above all his debts and liabilities and property exempt from execution.
(Signed)   P. BONSEIGNEUR.

Subscribed and sworn before me this fifth day of January, 1893.
[SEAL.]   (Signed)   T. McC. HYMAN,
Clerk Supreme Court of Louisiana.

68   *Assignment of Errors. Filed January 5th, 1893.*

October Term, 1892.

Ex Parte HOMER A. PLESSY.

Assignment of errors.

To the honl. the Supreme Court of the United States:

Now comes the relator, Homer A. Plessy, plaintiff in error, through his attorneys, Albion W. Tourgée and Jas. C. Walker, and assigns for error and says that in the record and proceedings aforesaid there is manifest error, in this, to wit:

First. The court erred in its opinion and decree maintaining the constitutional validity of the act of the General Assembly of the State of Louisiana, No. 111, approved July 10th, 1890, entitled An act to promote the comfort of passengers on railroad trains, &c., &c., and that the same is not in conflict with nor a violation of any right under the XIIIth and XIVth amendments of the Constitution of the United States; that the same is the lawful exercise of the police power of the State; that the subject-matter thereof is a regulation of domestic commerce, and therefore exclusively a State function; enforces substantial equality of accommodations supplied to passengers of both races on railroad trains operated within the limits of the State of Louisiana; that the same is in the interest of public order, peace, and comfort, and impairs no right of passengers of either race.

This was error (1) for the reason that the statute imports a badge of servitude imposed by State law; perpetuates the distinction of race and caste among citizens of the United States of both races, and observances of a servile character coincident with the institution of slavery, heretofore exacted by the white race and compulsorily submitted to by the colored race. The said statute discriminates between citizens of the white race and those of the colored race, and does not apply to all white persons and all colored persons alike, and the same abridges the rights, privileges, and immunities of citizens on account of race and color.

(2.) The said statute does not enforce substantial equality of accommodations to be furnished to passengers of both races on railroad trains, but authorizes the officers thereof to assign passengers to separate coaches without reference thereto.

(3.) The statute impairs the right of passengers of the class to which relator belongs, to wit, octoroons, to be classed among white persons, although color be not discernible in their complexion, and makes penal their refusal to abide by the decision of a railroad conductor in this respect.

(4.) The said statute does not extend to all citizens alike the equal protection of the laws, and provides for the punishment of passengers on railroad trains without due process of law by authorizing the officers of railroad trains to refuse to carry such persons as refuse to abide by their decision as to the race to which said passengers belong, and by making said refusal a penal offence.

(5.) The statute is not in the interest of public order, peace, and comfort, but is manifestly directed against citizens of the colored race.

(6.) The statute exempts individuals of a certain class, to wit, nurses attending children of the other race, from the operation of the law, and is therefore amenable to the charge of class legislation.

(7.) The said statute is an invasion and deprivation of the natural and absolute rights of citizens of the United States to the society and protection of their wives and children travelling in railroad trains, when said citizens are married to persons of the other race under the law and the sacrament of the church — marital unions between persons of both races, which are not forbidden by the laws of Louisiana.

(8.) The statute deprives the citizen of remedy for wrong, and is unconstitutional for that reason.

(9.) Neither the said statute, nor the laws of the State of Louisiana, nor the decisions of its courts have defined the terms "colored race" and "persons of color," and the law in question has delegated to conductors of railway trains the right to make such classification and made penal a refusal to submit to their decision.

(10.) The East Louisiana railroad and other railroads to which said statute applies are organized by the laws of the State of Louisiana as common carriers, acting by virtue of public charters and carrying passengers for hire, and cannot be authorized to distinguish between citizens according to race.

(11.) Race is a question of law and fact which an officer of a railroad corporation cannot be authorized to determine.

(12.) The State has no power to authorize the officers of railway trains to determine the question of race without testimony, to make the rights and privileges of citizens to depend on such decision, or to compel the citizen to accept and submit to such decision.

Second. The court erred in the opinion and decree that the statute in question explicitly requires that the accommodations shall be equal, and does not authorize the officers of the railway trains to assign passengers according to their own judgment and without reference as to whether the accommodations are equal or not.

This was error, because criminal statutes are construed *stricti juris* and not by implication, and the literal text of the law terminating the second secton of the statute is as follows:

* * * "And should any passenger refuse to occupy the coach or compartment to which he or she is assigned by the officer of such railway, said officer shall have power to refuse to carry such passenger on his train, and for such refusal neither he nor the railway company which he represents shall be liable for damages in any of the courts of this State."

Third. The court erred in its opinion and decree that the statute does not authorize the conductor or other officer to assign a passenger to a coach to which by race he does not belong; that it obviously means that the coach to which the passenger is assigned shall be, according to the requirements of the act, to the coach to which the passenger by race belongs.

This was error, for the same reason. The aid of implication is required to help out the construction of a criminal statute—that the coach to which the passenger is assigned must be the coach to which by race he belongs—when the text of the law subjects the passenger to fine and imprisonment if he "should refuse to occupy the coach or compartment to which he or she is assigned."

Fourth. The court erred in its opinion and decree that the said statute does not exempt the officer or conductor from damages for refusing to carry a passenger who refuses to obey an assignment to a coach to which his race did not belong.

This was error, because the text of the statute is plain: "Said officer shall have power to refuse to carry such passenger on his train, and for such refusal neither he nor the railway company which he represents shall be liable for damages in any of the courts of this State."

Fifth. The court erred in its opinion and decree that the discretion vested in the officer to decide primarily the coach to which by race each passenger belongs is only that necessary discretion attending any imposition of a duty to be exercised at his peril and at the peril of his employer. The statute utterly repels the charge that it vests the officers of the company with a judicial power to determine the race to which the passenger belongs.

This was error, because the 2nd section of the act expressly provides "that the officers of such passenger trains shall have power and are hereby required to assign each passenger to the coach or compartment used for the race to which such passenger belongs," and terminates with the provision that in case of refusal on the part of the passenger to occupy the coach to which he is assigned "said officer shall have power to refuse to carry such passenger on his train, and for such refusal neither he nor the railway company which he represents shall be liable for damages in any of the courts of this State."

Wherefore, for these and other errors apparent on the record, the said Homer A. Plessy prays that the said judgment of the honl. the supreme court of the State of Louisiana be reversed, and that the said writ of prohibition prayed for and provisionally issued in these proceedings be made peremptory.

(Signed) ALBION W. TOURGÉE,
JAS. C. WALKER,
Att'ys for Pl'ff in Error.

73 UNITED STATES OF AMERICA, *ss:*

The President of the United States of America to the honorable the judges of the supreme court of the State of Louisiana, Greeting:

Because in the record and proceedings, as also in the rendition of the judgment of a plea which is in the said supreme court of the State of Louisiana, before you or some of you, being the highest court of law or equity of the said State in which a decision could be had in the said suit between Homer Adolph Plessy, as relator, and Honorable J. H. Ferguson, judge of section "A," criminal district court for the parish of Orleans, as defendant, wherein was drawn in question the validity of a treaty or statute of or an authority exercised under the United States and the decision was against their validity, or wherein was drawn in question the validity of a statute of or an authority exercised under said State, on the ground of their being repugnant to the Constitution, treaties, or laws of the United States, and the decision was in favor of such their validity, or wherein was drawn in question the construction of a
74 clause of the Constitution or of a treaty or statute of or commission held under the United States and the decision was against the title, right, privilege, or exemption specially set up or claimed under such clause of the said Constitution, treaty, statute, or commission, a manifest error hath happened, to the great damage of the said Homer A. Plessy, relator, plaintiff in error, as by his complaint appears, we, being willing that error, if any hath been, should be duly corrected and full and speedy justice done to the parties aforesaid in this behalf, do command you, if judgment be therein given, that then, under your seal, distinctly and openly, you send the record and proceedings aforesaid, with all things concerning the same, to the Supreme Court of the United States, together with this writ, so that you have the same at Washington within thirty days from the date hereof, in the said Supreme Court, to be then and there held, that, the record and proceedings aforesaid being inspected, the said Supreme Court may cause further to be done therein to correct that error what of right and according to the laws and customs of the United States should be done.

Witness the Honorable Melville W. Fuller, Chief Justice of the said Supreme Court, the fifth day of January, in the year of our Lord one thousand eight hundred and ninety-three.

[Seal U. S. Circuit Court for the 5th Circuit & Eastern District of La.]

E. R. HUNT,
Clerk of the Circuit Court of the United States for the Eastern District of Louisiana.

Allowed by—
FRANCIS T. NICHOLLS,
Chief Justice Supreme Court of Louisiana.

[Endorsed:] Filed 5 Jan'y, 1893. T. McC. Hyman, clerk.

75   THE UNITED STATES OF AMERICA:

Supreme Court of the State of Louisiana.

The President of the United States to the Honorable J. H. Ferguson, judge of section "A," criminal district court for the parish of Orleans, Greeting:

You are hereby cited and admonished to be and appear at a Supreme Court of the United States, to be holden at the city of Washington within thirty days from the date hereof, pursuant to a writ of error filed in the clerk's office of the supreme court of the State Louisiana, at New Orleans, wherein Homer Adolph Plessy is plaintiff in error and you are defendant in error, to show cause, if any there be, why the judgment rendered against the said Homer A. Plessy, plaintiff in error, as in said writ of error mentioned, should not be corrected and why speedy justice should not be done to the parties in that behalf.

Witness the Honorable Melville W. Fuller, Chief Justice of the Supreme Court of the United States, this fifth day of January, in the year of our Lord one thousand eight hundred and ninety-three.

[Seal Supreme Court of the State of Louisiana.]

FRANCIS T. NICHOLLS,
Chief Justice of the Supreme Court of the State of Louisiana.

76   [Endorsed:] Supreme court of the State of Louisiana. No. 11134. *Ex parte* Homer A. Plessy. Citation. Filed Jan'y 6, 1893. T. McC. Hyman, clerk.

Sheriff's Return.

Received Friday, Jan. 6, 1893, and on the 6th day of January, 1893, I served a copy of the within citation personally on the Honorable J. H. Ferguson, judge of section "A," criminal district court for the parish of Orleans.

Returned same day.

JAMES DUIGNAN,
Deputy Civil Sheriff, Parish of Orleans, La.

James Duignan, deputy sheriff of the parish of Orleans, being duly sworn, deposes and says that the facts set forth in the foregoing return are true and correct.

JAMES DUIGNAN.

Sworn to & subscribed before me, at the city of New Orleans, this 6th day of January, A. D. 1893.

[Seal Supreme Court of the State of Louisiana.]

T. McC. HYMAN,
Clerk Supreme Court of Louisiana.

77 *Clerk's Certificate.*

UNITED STATES OF AMERICA:

Supreme Court of the State of Louisiana.

I, Thomas McCabe Hyman, clerk of the supreme court of the State — Louisiana, at the city of New Orleans, do hereby certify the foregoing seventy-four pages contain a full, true, and complete copy and transcript of the record of all the proceedings had and documents and exhibits filed and evidence adduced in the supreme court of the State of Louisiana in the suit entitled *Ex parte* Homer A. Plessy, on application for writs of certiorari and prohibition, No. 11134 of the docket of the said court, wherein the said Homer A. Plessy is relator and J. H. Ferguson, judge of section "A," criminal district court for the parish of Orleans, is respondent.

Seal Supreme Court of the State of Louisiana.

In testimony whereof I have hereunto set my hand and affixed the seal of said court, at the city of New Orleans, this 13th day of January, anno Domini 1893, and in the 117th year of the Independence of the United States of America.

T. McC. HYMAN, *Clerk.*

Certificate of Chief Justice.

I, Francis Tillou Nicholls, chief justice of the supreme court of the State of Louisiana, do hereby certify that Thomas McCabe Hyman is clerk of the supreme court of the State of Louisiana, at New Orleans; that the signature of Thomas McCabe Hyman to the foregoing certificate is in the proper handwriting of him, the *the* said clerk, and that said certificate is in due form of law,

78 and that full faith and credit are due to all of his official acts as such.

Seal Supreme Court of the State of Louisiana.

In testimony whereof I have hereunto set my hand and seal, at the city of New Orleans, this 13th day of January, anno Domini eighteen hundred and ninety-three, and in the one hundred and seventeenth year of the Independence of the United States of America.

FRANCIS T. NICHOLLS,
Chief Justice.

79 *Ex Parte* HOMER A. PLESSY. No. 11134.

To the honl. the chief justice of the supreme court of the State of Louisiana:

The petition of Homer A. Plessy, a citizen of the United States, respectfully represents—

That he is aggrieved by the final judgment rendered by this honl. court in the proceedings entitled *Ex parte* Homer A. Plessy, No. 11134 of the docket of this court, wherein petitioner prayed to this honl. court for writs of prohibition and certiorari, to be directed to the Honl. J. H. Ferguson, judge of section "A" of the criminal district court for the parish of Orleans, and petitioner is advised the judgment and decree of this hon. court therein is erroneous and to his prejudice, and he desires to prosecute a writ of error, to reverse said judgment to the Supreme Court of the United States.

Petitioner shows that these proceedings were brought by him to enjoin and prohibit the said judge of the criminal district court for the parish of Orleans from entertaining further cognizance and jurisdiction and from proceeding further in the cause entitled The State of Louisiana *vs.* Homer A. Plessy, No. 19117 of the docket of the said criminal district court for the parish of Orleans, wherein it was charged and alleged, upon information filed against

80 pet'r by the Hon. Lionel Adams, assistant district attorney for the parish of Orleans, prosecuting in said cause in behalf of the State of Louisiana, that your petitioner "did, on the seventh day of June of the present year, 1892, with force of arms, in the parish of Orleans and within the jurisdiction of the criminal district court for the parish of Orleans, being then a passenger, travelling wholly within the limits of the State of Louisiana, on a passenger train of the East Louisiana Railroad Company, a railway company carrying passengers in their coaches within the State of Louisiana, and on which the officers of the said East Louisiana Railroad Company had power and were required to assign and did then assign the said Homer Adolph Plessy to the coach used for the race to which he, the said Homer Adolph Plessy, belonged, unlawfully did then and there insist upon going into a coach to which by race he did not belong, contrary to the form of the statute of the State of Louisiana in such case made and provided and against the peace and dignity of the same."

And there was also drawn in question in this cause and in the said proceedings in the criminal district court for the parish of Orleans aforesaid the validity and constitutionality, under the

81 XIIIth and XIVth amendments of the Constitution of the United States, of an act of the General Assembly of the State of Louisiana, approved July 10th, 1890, No. 111 of the sessions acts of the Legislature of the said State, entitled "An act to promote the comfort of passengers on railway trains; requiring all railway companies carrying passengers on their trains in this State to provide equal but separate accommodations for the white and colored races by providing separate coaches or compartments, so as to secure separate accommodations; defining the duties of the

officers of such railways; directing them to assign passengers to the coaches or compartment set aside for the use of the race to which such passengers belong; authorizing them to refuse to carry on their train such passengers as may refuse to occupy the coaches or compartments. to which he or she is assigned; to exonerate such railway companies from any and all blame or damages that might proceed or result from such a refusal; to prescribe penalties for all violations of this act; to put this act into effect ninety days after its promulgation, and to repeal all laws or parts of laws contrary to or inconsistent with the provisions of this act," for the reasons, viz:

That the East Louisiana Railway Company is incorporated by the laws of this State as a common carrier of passengers for hire and cannot be authorized to distinguish between citizens according to race.

82   That race is a question of law and fact which an officer of a railroad corporation cannot be authorized to determine.

That said act No. 111, approved July 10th 1890, is in its several parts in conflict with the Constitution of the United States.

That section 2 of said act pretends to confer on a railroad conductor the power to determine the question of race and to assort the passengers in accordance with his decision, and the refusal of any passenger to abide by the decision of the conductor is attempted to be made a criminal offence by said act.

That the legislature has no power to confer judicial functions upon an officer of a passenger train, nor to make a peaceable refusal to accept his decision as to the race to which the passenger belongs a crime, or to make said act punishable by fine and imprisonment.

That the statute provides a summary punishment for such pretended criminal act by authorizing the officer to refuse to carry such passenger for said cause, and exempts both the company and the officer from any claim for damages, thus imposing punishment without due process of law, and the denial to citizens of the United States of the equal protection of the laws.

83   That said statute is void because the purpose of said act on its face is to classify according to race all passengers upon railroads operated within the State, and to make the rights and privileges of citizens of the United States dependent on said classification.

That the State has no power to authorize any person to determine the question of race without testimony or to make the rights or privileges of any citizen of the United States dependent on the fact of race or its determination by such unauthorized person, to compel the citizen to accept such determination, or to make refusal to comply with the same a penal offence.

That the State has no right to distinguish between the rights and privileges of citizens of the United States on the ground of race, as regards place, privilege, or accom-odation in public railroad trains within this State.

The act deprives the citizen of remedy for wrong and is unconstitutional for that reason, and for the further reason that the State neither has nor can have power to distinguish between citizens of the United States as regards any right, privilege, or immunity to be enjoyed or exercised by such citizen on account of race or color.

That the State has no power or authority to grant exclusive rights or privileges to citizens of the United States of one race which are denied to citizens of another race, or to make the refusal to such denial a penal offence.

That the statute in question, to wit, act No. 111, approved July 10th, 1890, establishes an invidious distinction and discrimination between citizens of the United States, based on race, which is obnoxious to the fundamental principles of national citizenship; perpetuates involuntary servitude, as regards citizens of the colored race, under the merest pretense of promoting the comfort of passengers on railway trains, and in further respects abridges the privileges and immunities of citizens of the United States and the rights secured by the XIIIth and XIVth amendments of the Federal Constitution.

And there was also drawn in question in said proceedings the right, privilege, and immunity of petitioner, under said constitutional amendments, as a citizen of the United States, to the enjoyment of equal rights and privileges with citizens of the white race travelling as passengers on the said East Louisiana railway and on all other railway trains operated within the limits of the State of Louisiana.

All of which said reasons petitioner relied on and set up in this cause as conferring upon petitioner the right to invoke and have perpetuated by this hon. court the said writs of prohibition and certiorari against the said honl. judge of section "A," criminal district court for the parish of Orleans.

That the judgment of this honl. court was adverse to said rights claimed under the aforesaid XIIIth and XIVth amendments to the Constitution of the United States, and maintained the validity of the said statute of the State of Louisiana for the reasons following:

The said statute is not a violation of any right under the XIIIth and XIVth amendments.

The statute is an exercise of the police power of the State, enforces substantial equality of the accommodations supplied to each, and is in the *the* interest of public order, peace, and comfort, and impairs no right of passengers of either race, who are secured the equality of accommodations which satisfies every reasonable claim.

That the subject-matter of the said statute is a regulation of domestic commerce, and therefore exclusively a State function.

That the sole question involved in this case is whether a statute requiring railroads to furnish separate but equal accommodations for the two races and requiring domestic passengers to confine themselves to the accommodations provided for the race to which they belong violates the XIVth amendment.

That the said statute explicitly requires that the accommodations shall be equal and does not authorize the officers of the railway train to assign passengers according to their own judgment and without reference as to whether the accommodations are equal or not.

That the said statute infringes no rights which are protected from State aggression by the XIIIth and XIVth amendments.

That the statute does not authorize the conductor or other officer to assign a passenger to a coach to which by race he does not belong; that it obviously means that the coach to which the passenger is assigned shall be, according to the requirements of the act, to the coach to which the passenger by race belongs.

That the said statute does not exempt the officer or conductor from damages for refusing to carry a passenger who refuses to obey an assignment to a coach to which his race did not belong. It is very certain * * * an erroneous assignment by the conductor would not exempt the officer and the railway from an action for damages.

The discretion vested in the officer to decide primarily the coach to which each passenger by race belongs is only that necessary discretion attending any imposition of a duty to be exercised at his peril and at the peril of his employer.

87 The XIIIth amendment does not apply or refer to rights of the character here involved.

The statute utterly repels the charge that it *it* vests the officers of the company with a judicial power to determine the race to which the passenger belongs.

All of which appears by the pleadings and judgment in this cause, specially referred to for fuller explanation and greater certainty; by reason of all which the said judgment of this court against petitioner, setting aside and revoking the provisional writ of prohibition herein granted by this honl. court against said judge of section "A," criminal district court for the parish of Orleans, and rejecting petitioner's prayer to perpetuate and make the said writ of prohibition peremptory, is within the jurisdiction of the Supreme Court of the United States to review the cause involving the Federal questions aforesaid, passed upon and decided by this court adverse to the right claimed by petitioner and maintaining the validity of the said statute of the State of Louisiana under said Constitution of the United States and the said XIIIth and XIVth amendments thereto, and petitioner desires a writ of error from the Supreme Court of the United States to review said decision of this honl. court.

88 Wherefore petitioner prays that said writ of error be allowed him in this case, returnable to the honl. Supreme Court of the United States in thirty days, the said writ to operate as a supersedeas upon petitioner's furnishing bond, with good and sufficient surety, in the sum of — dollars, conditioned as the law directs, and that said respondent, Honl. J. H. Ferguson, judge of section "A," criminal district court for the parish of Orleans, be cited to answer the said writ, and for gen'l relief.

ALBION W. TOURGÉE,
JAS. C. WALKER,
Att'ys for Pet'r.

Writ allowed on bond of three hundred dollars, conditioned as the law provides, being furnished.

New Orleans, January 5th, 1893.

FRANCIS T. NICHOLLS,
Chief Justice.

89 [Endorsed:] No. 11134. Supreme Court of Louisiana. *Ex parte* Homer A. Plessy. Petition for writ of error and order. Filed Jan'y 5, 1893. T. McC. Hyman, clerk.

90 *Assignment of Errors.*

October Term, 1892.

Ex Parte HOMER A. PLESSY.

To the honl. the Supreme Court of the United States:

Now comes the relator, Homer A. Plessy, plaintiff in error, through his attorneys, Albion W. Tourgée and Jas. C. Walker, and assigns for error and says that in the record and proceedings aforesaid there is manifest error, in this, to wit:

First. The court erred in its opinion and decree maintaining the constitutional validity of the act of the General Assembly of the State of Louisiana, No. 111, approved July 10th, 1890, entitled An act to promote the comfort of passengers on railroad trains, &c., &c., and that the same is not in conflict with nor a violation of any right under the XIIIth and XIVth amendments of the Constitution of the United States; that the same is the lawful exercise of the police power of the State; that the subject-matter thereof is a regulation of domestic commerce, and therefore exclusively a State function; enforces substantial equality of accommodations supplied to passengers of both races on railroad trains operated within
91 the limits of the State of Louisiana; that the same is in the interest of public order, peace, and comfort, and impairs no right of passengers of either race.

This was error (1) for the reason that the statute imports a badge of servitude imposed by State law; perpetuates the distinction of race and caste among citizens of the United States of both races, and observances of a servile character coincident with the institution of slavery, heretofore exacted by the white race and compulsorily submitted to by the colored race. The said statute discriminates between citizens of the white race and those of the colored race, and does not apply to all white persons and all colored persons alike, and the same abridges the rights, privileges, and immunities of citizens on account of race and color.

(2.) The said statute does not enforce substantial equality of accommodations to be furnished to passengers of both races on railroad trains, but authorizes the officers thereof to assign passengers to separate coaches without reference thereto.

(3.) The statute impairs the right of passengers of the class to which relator belongs, to wit, octoroons, to be classed among white persons, although color be not discernible in their complexion, and makes penal their refusal to abide by the decision of a railroad conductor in this respect.

(4.) The said statute does not extend to all citizens alike the equal protection of the laws, and provides for the punishment of passengers on railroad trains without due process of law by authorizing the officers of railroad trains to refuse to carry such persons as refuse to abide by their decision as to the race to which said passengers belong, and by making said refusal a penal offence.

(5.) The statute is not in the interest of public order, peace, and comfort, but is manifestly directed against citizens of the colored race.

(6.) The statute exempts individuals of a certain class, to wit, nurses attending children of the other race, from the operation of the law, and is therefore amenable to the charge of class legislation.

(7.) The said statute is an invasion and deprivation of the natural and absolute rights of citizens of the United States to the society and protection of their wives and children travelling in railroad trains, when said citizens are married to persons of the other race under the law and the sacrament of the church — marital unions between persons of both races, which are not forbidden by the laws of Louisiana.

(8.) The statute deprives the citizen of remedy for wrong, and is unconstitutional for that reason.

(9.) Neither the said statute, nor the laws of the State of Louisiana, nor the decisions of its courts have defined the terms "colored race" and "persons of color," and the law in question has delegated to conductors of railway trains the right to make such classification and made penal a refusal to submit to their decision.

(10.) The East Louisiana railroad and other railroads to which said statute applies are organized by the laws of the State of Louisiana as common carriers, acting by virtue of public charters and carrying passengers for hire, and cannot be authorized to distinguish between citizens according to race.

(11.) Race is a question of law and fact which an officer of a railroad corporation cannot be authorized to determine.

(12.) The State has no power to authorize the officers of railway trains to determine the question of race without testimony, to make the rights and privileges of citizens to depend on such decision, or to compel the citizen to accept and submit to such decision.

Second. The court erred in its opinion and decree that the statute in question explicitly requires that the accommodations shall be equal, and does not authorize the officers of the railway trains to assign passengers according to their own judgment and without reference as to whether the accommodations are equal or not.

This was error, because criminal statutes are construed *stricti juris* and not by implication, and the literal text of the law terminating the second section of the statute is as follows:

* * * "And should any passenger refuse to occupy the coach or compartment to which he or she is assigned by the officer of such railway, said officer shall have power to refuse to carry such passenger on his train, and for such refusal neither he nor the railway company which he represents shall be liable for damages in any of the courts of this State."

Third. The court erred in its opinion and decree that the statute does not authorize the conductor or other officer to assign a passenger to a coach to which by race he does not belong; that it obviously means that the coach to which the passenger is assigned shall be, according to the requirements of the act, to the coach to which the passenger by race belongs.

This was error, for the same reason. The aid of implication is required to help out the construction of a criminal statute—that the coach to which the passenger is assigned must be the coach to which by race he belongs—when the text of the law subjects the passenger to fine and imprisonment if he " should refuse to occupy the coach or compartment to which he or she is assigned."

Fourth. The court erred in its opinion and decree that the said statute does not exempt the officer or conductor from damages for refusing to carry a passenger who refuses to obey an assignment to a coach to which his race did not belong.

This was error, because the text of the statute is plain: "Said officer shall have power to refuse to carry such passenger on his train, and for such refusal neither he nor the railway company which he represents shall be liable for damages in any of the courts of this State."

Fifth. The court erred in its opinion and decree that the discretion vested in the officer to decide primarily the coach to which by race each passenger belongs is only that necessary discretion attending any imposition of a duty to be exercised at his peril and at the peril of his employer. The statute utterly repels the charge that it vests the officers of the company with a judicial power to determine the race to which the passenger belongs.

This was error, because the 2nd section of the act expressly provides " that the officers of such passenger trains shall have power and are hereby required to assign each passenger to the coach or compartment used for the race to which such passenger belongs," and terminates with the provision that in case of refusal on the part of the passenger to occupy the coach to which he is assigned " said officer shall have power to refuse to carry such passenger on his train, and for such refusal neither he nor the railway company which he represents shall be liable for damages in any of the courts of this State."

Wherefore, for these and other errors apparent on the record, the said Homer A. Plessy prays that the said judgment of the honl. the supreme court of the State of Louisiana be reversed, and that the said writ of prohibition prayed for and provisionally issued in these proceedings be made peremptory.

ALBION W. TOURGÉE,
JAS. C. WALKER,
Att'ys for Pl'ff in Error.

97 [Endorsed:] No. 11134. Supreme court of Louisiana. *Ex parte* Homer A. Plessy. Assignment of errors. Filed Jan'y 5, 1893. T. McC. Hyman, clerk.

Endorsed on cover: Case No. 15,248. Louisiana supreme court. Term No., 880. Homer Adolph Plessy, plaintiff in error, *vs.* J. H. Ferguson, judge of section "A," criminal district court for the parish of Orleans. Filed January 31st, 1893.

BROWN VS. BOARD OF EDUCATION

TRANSCRIPT OF RECORD

Supreme Court of the United States

OCTOBER TERM, 1953

No. 1

OLIVER BROWN, MRS. RICHARD LAWTON, MRS. SADIE EMMANUEL, ET AL., APPELLANTS,

vs.

BOARD OF EDUCATION OF TOPEKA, SHAWNEE COUNTY, KANSAS, ET AL.

APPEAL FROM THE UNITED STATES DISTRICT COURT FOR THE DISTRICT OF KANSAS

FILED NOVEMBER 19, 1951
Probable jurisdiction noted June 9, 1952

SUPREME COURT OF THE UNITED STATES

OCTOBER TERM, 1952

No. 8

OLIVER BROWN, MRS. RICHARD LAWTON, MRS. SADIE EMMANUEL, ET AL., APPELLANTS,

vs.

BOARD OF EDUCATION OF TOPEKA, SHAWNEE COUNTY, KANSAS, ET AL.

APPEAL FROM THE UNITED STATES DISTRICT COURT FOR THE DISTRICT OF KANSAS

INDEX

	Original	Print
Record from U.S.D.C. for the District of Kansas	1	1
Caption (omitted in printing)	a	
Amended complaint	1	1
Motion for a more definite statement and to strike	8	8
Docket entry—Motion denied, except as to paragraph 8, which is to be amended	11	10
Amendment to paragraph 8 of amended complaint	12	10
Answer to amended complaint as amended in paragraph 8 thereof	13	11
Separate answer of the State of Kansas	17	14
Transcript of proceedings of pre-trial conference	19	15
Appearances	19	15
Colloquy between court and counsel	21	16
Reporter's certificate (omitted in printing)	98	

JUDD & DETWEILER (INC.), PRINTERS, WASHINGTON, D. C., JULY 8, 1952.

—2734

INDEX

	Original	Print
Record from U.S.D.C. for the District of Kansas—Continued		
Order correcting transcript of record	99	62
Transcript of proceedings, June 25, 1951	105	63
Caption	106	63
Colloquy between Court and counsel	107	63
Offers in evidence	108	64
Testimony of Arthur H. Saville	115	68
Kenneth McFarland	121	72
Lena Mae Carper	136	81
Katherine Carper	141	85
Oliver L. Brown	145	88
Darlene Watson	155	94
Alma Jean Galloway	158	96
Sadie Emanuel	160	97
Shirley Mae Hodison	164	100
James V. Richardson	167	102
Lucinda Todd	169	103
Marguerite Emmerson	171	104
Zelma Henderson	173	105
Silas Hardwick Fleming	176	107
Hugh W. Speer	182	111
James H. Buchanan	233	143
R. S. B. English	248	153
Wilbur B. Brookover	263	162
Louisa Holt	272	168
John J. Kane	283	175
Bettie Belk	291	180
Dorothy Crawford	303	187
Clarence G. Grimes	309	191
Thelma Mifflin	317	196
Kenneth McFarland (Recalled)	331	205
Ernest Manheim	342	213
Colloquy between court on counsel	347	216
Opening argument on behalf of plaintiff	349	217
Argument on behalf of defendants	363	225
Closing argument on behalf of plaintiff	372	231
Colloquy between Court and counsel	377	233
Reporter's certificate (omitted in printing)	384	
Clerk's certificate (omitted in printing)	385	
Opinion, Huxman, J.	386	238
Findings of fact and conclusions of law	393	244
Decree	397	247
Petition for appeal	398	248
Assignment of errors and prayer for reversal	400	249
Order allowing appeal	403	251
Citation on appeal (omitted in printing)	405	
Note re cost bond	406	252
Statement required by paragraph 2 rule 12 of the rules of the Supreme Court (omitted in printing)	407	

INDEX

Record from U.S.D.C. for the District of Kansas—Continued	Original	Print
Praecipe for transcript (omitted in printing)	412	
Order extending time to file and docket record on appeal	414	253
Clerk's certificate (omitted in printing)	415	
Statement of points to be relied upon and designation of parts of record to be printed	416	
Order noting probable jurisdiction	418	254

[fol. a]

IN UNITED STATES DISTRICT COURT FOR THE DISTRICT OF KANSAS

[Caption omitted]

OLIVER BROWN, Mrs. RICHARD LAWTON, Mrs. SADIE EMMANUEL, Mrs. Lucinda Todd, Mrs. Iona Richardson, Mrs. Lena Carper, Mrs. Shirley Hodison, Mrs. Alma Lewis, Mrs. Darlene Brown, Mrs. Shirla Fleming, Mrs. Andrew Henderson, Mrs. Vivian Scales, Mrs. Marguerite Emmerson, and

LINDA CAROL BROWN, an infant, by Oliver Brown, her father and next friend,

VICTORIA JEAN LAWTON and CAROL KAY LAWTON, infants, by Mrs. Richard Lawton, their mother and next friend,

JAMES MELDON EMMANUEL, an infant, by Mrs. Sadie Emmanuel, his mother and next friend,

NANCY JANE TODD, an infant, by Mrs. Lucinda Todd, her mother and next friend,

RONALD DOUGLAS RICHARDSON, an infant, by Mrs. Iona Richardson, his mother and next friend,

KATHERINE LOUISE CARPER, an infant, by Mrs. Lena Carper, her mother and next friend,

CHARLES HODISON, an infant, by Mrs. Shirley Hodison, his mother and next friend,

[fol. b] THERON LEWIS, MARTHA JEAN LEWIS, ARTHUR LEWIS and Frances Lewis, infants, by Mrs. Alma Lewis, their mother and next friend,

SAUNDRIA DORSTELLA BROWN, an infant, by Mrs. Darlene Brown, her mother and next friend,

DUANE DEAN FLEMING and SILAS HARDRICK FLEMING, infants, by Mrs. Shirla Fleming, their mother and next friend,

DONALD ANDREW HENDERSON and VICKI ANN HENDERSON, infants, by Mrs. Andrew Henderson, their mother and next friend,

1—8

RUTH ANN SCALES, an infant, by Mrs. Vivian Scales, her mother and next friend,

CLAUDE ARTHUR EMMERSON and GEORGE ROBERT EMMERSON, infants, by Mrs. Marguerite Emmerson, their mother and next friend, Plaintiffs,

vs.

BOARD OF EDUCATION OF TOPEKA, SHAWNEE COUNTY, KANSAS; Kenneth McFarland, Superintendent of Schools of Topeka, Kansas; and Frank Wilson, Principal of Sumner Elementary School, Defendants,

and

THE STATE OF KANSAS, Intervening Defendant

No. T-316 Civil

[fol. 1] AMENDED COMPLAINT—Filed March 22, 1951

1. (a) The jurisdiction of this Court is invoked under Title 28, United States Code, section 1331. This action arises under the Fourteenth Amendment of the Constitution of the United States, section 1, and the Act of May 31, 1870, Chapter 114, section 16, 16 Stat. 144 (Title 8, United States Code, section 41), as hereinafter more fully appears. The matter in controversy exceeds, exclusive of interest and costs, the sum or value of Three Thousand Dollars ($3000.00).

(b) The jurisdiction of this Court is also invoked under Title 28, United States Code, section 1343. This action is authorized by the Act of April 20, 1871, Chapter 22, section 1, 17 Stat. 13 (Title 8, United States Code, section 43), to be commenced by any citizen of the United States or other persons within the jurisdiction thereof to redress the deprivation, under color of a state law, statute, ordinance, regulation, custom or usage, or rights, privileges and immunities secured by the Fourteenth Amendment to the Constitution of the United States, section 1, and by the Act of May 31, 1870, Chapter 114, section 16, 16 Stat. 144 (Title 8, United States Code, section 41), providing for the equal rights of citizens and of all other persons within the jurisdiction of the United States, as hereinafter more fully appears.

3

(c) The jurisdiction of this Court is also invoked under Title 28, United States Code, section 2281. This is an action for an interlocutory injunction and a permanent injunction restraining the enforcement, operation and execution of statutes of the State of Kansas by restraining the action of defendants, officers of such state, in the enforcement and execution of such statutes.

2. This is a proceeding for a declaratory judgment and injunction under Title 28, United States Code, section 2201, for the purpose of determining questions in actual contro-
[fol. 2] versy between the parties to wit:

(a) The question of whether the state statute, ch. 72-1724 of the General Statutes of Kansas 1935, is unconstitutional in that it gives to defendants the power to organize and maintain separate schools for the education of white and colored children in the City of Topeka, Kansas.

(b) The question of whether the customs and practices of the defendants operating under Ch. 72-1724 of the General Statutes of Kansas, 1935, are unconstitutional in that they deny infant plaintiffs the rights and privileges of enrolling in, attending and receiving instruction in public schools of the district within which they live while such rights and privileges are granted to white children similarly situated; where the basis of this refusal and grant is the race and color of the children, and that alone.

(c) The question of whether the denial to infant plaintiffs, solely because of race, of educational opportunities equal to those afforded white children is in contravention of the Fourteenth Amendment to the United States Constitution as being a denial of the equal protection of the laws.

3. (a) Infant plaintiffs are citizens of the United States, the State of Kansas, and Shawnee County, the City of Topeka, Kansas. They are among those classified as Negroes. They reside within various school districts in the City of Topeka, satisfy all requirements for admission to schools within the districts within which they live, have presented themselves for enrollment and registration at the proper times and places, and were denied the right to enroll therein, on account of their race and color. Instead, they

are required, solely because of race, to attend schools where they do not and cannot receive educational advantages, opportunities and facilities equal to those furnished white [fol. 3] children.

(b) Adult plaintiffs are citizens of the United States and the State of Kansas, are residents of and domiciled in Topeka, Shawnee County, Kansas, are taxpayers of said county, of the State of Kansas, and of the United States. They are the parents and natural guardians of infant plaintiffs named herein. By being compelled to send their children to schools outside the districts wherein they live rather than to schools within said districts, they must bear certain burdens and forego certain advantages, neither of which is suffered by parents of white children situated similarly to children of plaintiffs.

(c) Plaintiffs bring this action on their own behalf and also on behalf of all citizens similarly situated and affected, pursuant to Rule 23A of the Federal Rules of Civil Procedure, there being common questions of law and fact affecting the rights of all Negro citizens of the United States similarly situated who reside in cities in the State of Kansas in which separate public schools are maintained for white and Negro children of public school age, and who are so numerous as to make it impracticable to bring them all before the Court.

4. The State of Kansas has declared public education a state function in the Constitution of the State of Kansas, Article 6, Sections 1 and 2. Pursuant to this mandate, the Legislature of Kansas has established a system of free public schools in the State of Kansas, according to a plan set out in Chapter 72 of the General Statutes of Kansas, 1935, and supplements thereto. The establishment, maintenance, and administration of the public school system of Kansas is vested in a Superintendent of Public Instruction, County Superintendent of Schools, and City School Boards. (Constitution of Kansas, Article 6, section 1.)

[fol. 4] 5. The public schools of Topeka, Shawnee County, Kansas are under the control and supervision of the defendants.

(a) Defendant, Board of Education, is under a duty to enforce the school laws of the State of Kansas (General Statutes of Kansas, 1935, [and supplements thereto,] * section 72-1809); to maintain an efficient system of public schools in Topeka, Shawnee County, Kansas; to determine the studies pursued, the methods of teaching, and to establish such schools as may be necessary to the completeness and efficiency of the school system. It is an administrative department of the State of Kansas, which discharges governmental functions pursuant to the Constitution and the laws of the State of Kansas. (Constitution of Kansas, Article 6, sections 1 and 2, General Statutes, 1935, and supplements thereto of Kansas, section 72-1601). It is declared by law to be a body corporate and is sued in its governmental capacity.

6/22/51 amended at Pre-Trial A.J.M.

1949
72-1724

(b) Defendant Kenneth McFarland is Superintendent of Schools, and holds office pursuant to the Constitution and the laws of the State of Kansas, as an administrative officer of the free public school system of the State of Kansas. He has immediate control of the operation of public schools in Topeka, Shawnee County, Kansas. He is sued in his official capacity.

6. Defendant, Board of Education of Topeka, Shawnee County, Kansas, has established and at the present time maintains in the City of Topeka, State of Kansas, elementary schools for the education of the school children of the City of Topeka. They are located within different districts of the City of Topeka, whose boundaries are designated by the defendant, Board of Education.

7. White Children of elementary school age go to the school within the designated boundaries of the district in which they live.

[fol. 5] Infant plaintiffs live within the boundaries of these districts, but they are required to leave the districts within which they live and travel from one and one-half miles to

---

* Struck out in copy.

two miles to separate all-Negro schools, solely because of their race and color and in violation of their rights under the Fourteenth Amendment to the Constitution of the United States.

8. The educational opportunities provided by defendants for infant plaintiffs in the separate all-Negro schools are inferior to those provided for white school children similarly situated in violation of the equal protection clause of the Fourteenth Amendment to the Constitution of the United States.

9. Adult plaintiffs are required to send their children outside the school districts in which they reside to separate all-Negro schools, whereas parents of white children are permitted to send their children to schools close at hand within the district in which they live, solely because of race and color. Thus adult plaintiffs are being denied the equal protection of the laws in violation of the Fourteenth Amendment to the Constitution of the United States.

10. Infant plaintiffs and adult plaintiffs are thereby being wilfully and unlawfully discriminated against by the defendants on account of their race and color, in that infant plaintiffs are compelled to attend schools outside the school districts in which they live, while white children similarly situated are not so compelled; infant plaintiffs and adult plaintiffs are being deprived of their rights guaranteed by the Constitution and laws of the United States.

11. Plaintiffs are suffering irreparable injury and face irreparable injury in the future by reason of the acts herein complained of. They have no plain, adequate or complete remedy to redress the wrongs and illegal acts herein complained of, other than this suit for a declaration of rights [fol. 6] and an injunction. Any other remedy to which plaintiffs might be remitted would be attended by such uncertainties and delays as to deny substantial relief; would involve a multiplicity of suits; and would cause further irreparable injury not only to plaintiffs, but to defendants as governmental agencies.

Wherefore, plaintiffs respectfully pray that:

1. The Honorable Court, upon filing of this complaint, notify the Chief Judge of this Circuit as required by 28 U. S. C. A., section 2284, so that the Chief Judge may desig-

nate two other judges to serve as members of a three-judge court as required by Title 28, U. S. C. A., section 2281, to hear and determine this action.

2. The Honorable Court enter a judgment or decree declaring that the General Statutes of Kansas, 1935, 72-1724, is unconstitutional insofar as it empowers defendants to set up separate schools for Negro and white school children.

3. The Honorable Court enter a judgment or decree declaring that the policy, custom, usage and practice of defendants in operating under Ch. 72-1724, General Statutes of Kansas, 1935, in denying plaintiffs and other Negro children residing in Topeka, Shawnee County, Kansas, solely because of race or color, the right and privilege of enrolling in, attending and receiving instruction in schools within the district within which they reside as is provided for white children of like qualifications, are denials of the equal protection clause of the United States Constitution and are therefore unconstitutional and void.

4. The Honorable Court issue a permanent injunction forever restraining and enjoining the defendants from executing so much of Ch. 72-1724, General Statutes of Kansas, 1935, as empowers them to set up separate schools for Negro and white school children.

[fol. 7] 5. The Honorable Court issue a permanent injunction forever restraining defendants from denying the Negro school children of Topeka, Shawnee County, Kansas, on account of their race or color, the right and privilege of attending public schools within the district wherein they live, and from making any distinction based upon race or color in the opportunities which the defendants provide for public education.

6. The Honorable Court will allow plaintiffs their costs herein, reasonable fees for attorneys, and such other and further relief as may appear to the Court to be equitable and just.

7. The Honorable Court retain jurisdiction of this cause after judgment to render such relief as may become necessary in the future.

   Bledsoe, Scott, Scott & Scott, by Chas. E. Bledsoe,
  Charles S. Scott, John J. Scott, Attorneys for
  Plaintiffs.

Duly sworn to by Charles E. Bledsoe. Jurat omitted in printing.

[fol. 8] IN UNITED STATES DISTRICT COURT

DEFENDANTS' MOTION FOR A MORE DEFINITE STATEMENT AND TO STRIKE—Filed May 15, 1951

Defendants move the court for an order, as follows:

1. Requiring plaintiffs to amend their amended complaint, paragraph 3 (a), last sentence thereof, which reads as follows: "Instead, they are required, solely because of race, to attend schools where they do not and cannot receive educational advantages, opportunities and facilities equal to those furnished white children." by making a more definite statement therein setting forth the facts upon which plaintiffs base their conclusion as to unequal advantages, opportunities and facilities, for the reason that the present statement is so vague or ambiguous that defendants cannot reasonably be required to frame a responsive pleading thereto.

2. Requiring plaintiffs to amend their amended complaint, paragraph 3 (b), last sentence thereof, which reads as follows:

> "By being compelled to send their children to schools outside the districts wherein they live rather than to schools within said districts, they must bear certain burdens and forego certain advantages, neither of which is suffered by parents of white children situated similarly to children of plaintiffs."

by making a more definite statement therein setting forth the facts upon which plaintiffs base their conclusion that adult plaintiffs must bear certain burdens and forego certain benefits; for the reason that the present statement is so vague and ambiguous that defendants cannot reasonably be required to frame a responsive pleading thereto.

3. Requiring plaintiffs to strike from their amended complaint the following language in paragraph 7 thereof:

> "and in violation of their rights under the Fourteenth Amendment to the Constitution of the United States."

[fol. 9] for the reason that the same is a conclusion and is redundant.

4. Requiring plaintiffs to amend the eighth paragraph of their amended complaint, which reads as follows:

> "The educational opportunities provided by defendants for infant plaintiffs in the separate all-Negro schools are inferior to those provided for white school children similarly situated in violation of the equal protection clause of the Fourteenth Amendment to the Constitution of the United States."

by making a more definite statement therein setting forth the facts upon which plaintiffs base their conclusion that educational opportunities claimed therein are inferior to those provided for white children; for the reason that the present statement is so vague and ambiguous that defendants cannot reasonably be required to frame a responsive pleading thereto, and further requiring plaintiffs to strike from said paragraph 8, the following language:

> "in violation of the equal protection clause of the Fourteenth Amendment to the Constitution of the United States."

for the reason that the same is a conclusion and is redundant.

5. Requiring plaintiffs to strike from paragraph 9 of the amended complaint the last sentence thereof which reads as follows:

> "Thus adult plaintiffs are being denied the equal protection of the laws in violation of the Fourteenth Amendment to the Constitution of the United States."

for the reason that the same is a conclusion and is redundant.

6. By requiring plaintiffs to amend their amended complaint by striking all of paragraph 10 thereof, which reads as follows:

> "Infant plaintiffs and adult plaintiffs are thereby being wilfully and unlawfully discriminated against by the defendants on account of their race and color, in

that infant plaintiffs are compelled to attend schools outside the school districts in which they live, while white children similarly situated are not so compelled; infant plaintiffs and adult plaintiffs are being deprived [fol. 10] of their rights guaranteed by the Constitution and laws of the United States."

for the reason that the same is a conclusion and is redundant.

 Lester M. Goodell, George M. Brewster, 401 Columbian Building, Topeka, Kansas, Attorneys for Defendants.

[fol. 11]   In United States District Court

Docket Entry

"May 25, 1951. At Topeka, before Huxman, Mellott, and Hill, JJ.: Defendants' Motion for more definite statement and to Strike denied except as to paragraph 8 which is to be amended; plaintiffs given five days to amend paragraph 8 and defendants to have five days to plead or ten days to answer."

[fol. 12]   In United States District Court

Amendment to Paragraph Eight of the Amended Complaint—Filed May 29, 1951

8. The educational opportunities provided by defendants for infant plaintiffs in the separate all-Negro schools are inferior to those provided for white school children similarly situated in violation of the equal protection clause of the Fourteenth Amendment to the Constitution of the United States. The respects in which these opportunities are inferior include the physical facilities, curricula, teaching, resources, student personnel services, access and all other educational factors, tangible and intangible, offered to school children in Topeka. Apart from all other factors, the racial segregation herein practiced in and of itself constitutes an inferiority in educational opportunity offered

to Negroes, when compared to educational opportunity offered to whites.

   Bledsoe, Scott, Scott & Scott, by Chas. E. Bledsoe.

Duly sworn to by Charles E. Bledsoe. Jurat omitted in printing.

[fol. 13]   In United States District Court

Answer of Defendants to Amended Complaint as Amended in Paragraph 8 Thereof—Filed June 7, 1951

1. Defendants admit the allegations stated in paragraphs 4 and 6 of the Amended Complaint, except that defendants allege that the City of Topeka is one school district, as hereinafter set forth. Defendants deny all the allegations stated in Amendments to paragraph 8 of the Amended Complaint, and further deny all the allegations stated in paragraphs 9, 10 and 11 of the Amended Complaint.

2. Defendants admit the allegations stated in paragraph 1 (a) of the Amended Complaint, except defendants deny that the amount in controversy, exclusive of interest and costs, exceeds $3,000.00.

3. Defendants admit the allegations stated in paragraph 2, except defendants deny that infant plaintiffs are denied rights and privileges of enrolling in, attending and receiving instruction in public schools within the district in which they live; and deny that they have denied infant plaintiffs educational opportunities equal to those afforded white children.

4. Defendants allege that the City of Topeka, Kansas, is in and of itself one school district; that acting pursuant to authority vested in it, defendants have designated and defined 22 separate territories within the City of Topeka and in each of said territories have established and maintain a public elementary school, and white children are required to attend the elementary school located in the territory in which they live; that defendants have also established and maintain four separate elementary schools for colored children within said district, and only colored children in the City of Topeka may attend said four schools. [fol. 14] Defendants further allege that the colored school

children, including infant plaintiffs, may attend any one of these four schools.

5. Defendants allege that said separate schools are established and maintained pursuant to the laws of the State of Kansas, G. S. 1949, 72-1724, and separate schools are provided only for elementary school children, to-wit, the first six grades.

6. Defendants allege that they have established and maintain junior high schools throughout the City of Topeka and have designated and defined territories for each of said schools; that both colored and white children may attend these schools and are required to attend the junior high school located within the territory in which they live.

7. Defendants allege that transportation facilities are provided for colored school children attending the four colored schools mentioned in paragraph 4 hereof, and said transportation facilities are furnished any colored school child attending elementary schools, upon request; that no transportation is furnished white children by the defendants.

8. Defendants admit the allegations stated in paragraph 3 (b) that adult plaintiffs are citizens of the United States, the State of Kansas, Shawnee County and the City of Topeka, Kansas, and deny the remainder of said paragraph. Defendants further deny that adult plaintiffs are compelled to send their children to schools outside the district wherein they live.

9. Defendants admit the allegations stated in paragraph 3 (a) that infant plaintiffs are citizens of the United States, State of Kansas, Shawnee County and the City of Topeka, Kansas, and that they are among those classified as negroes. [fol. 15] Defendants allege that infant plaintiffs have presented themselves for enrollment and registration in elementary schools for white children but were denied the right to enroll therein. Defendants allege that infant plaintiffs, because of race and color, do not satisfy the requirements for admission to schools for white children and by reason thereof they were denied admission. Defendants deny the remainder of paragraph 3 (a).

10. Defendants allege that they are without knowledge or information sufficient to form a belief as to the truth of the allegations stated in paragraph 3 (c) of the Amended

Complaint, or that adult plaintiffs are taxpayers of Shawnee County, the State of Kansas, and the United States, as stated in paragraph 3 (b).

11. Defendants admit the allegations stated in paragraph 5 of the Amended Complaint, but deny that they are governed by General Statutes 1935, and supplements thereto, section 72-1809, for the reason that said statute applies to public schools in cities of the second class and not to public schools in cities of the first class to which class the City of Topeka belongs.

12. Defendants deny the allegations stated in paragraph 7 of the Amended Complaint, and allege that white school children of elementary school age in the City of Topeka are required to go to the elementary schools within the designated boundaries of the territory in which they live, and that these schools are within the school district of the City of Topeka; that infant plaintiffs go to elementary schools within the district in which they live, namely, the school district of the City of Topeka, Kansas, and they may attend any of the colored elementary schools within the City of Topeka, as set forth in paragraph 4 hereof. Defendants further allege that the distance traveled by colored children [fol. 16] in reaching the schools they attend is not on the average greater than the distance white children are required to travel.

Wherefore, Defendants pray that plaintiffs take naught; and that defendants have judgment and costs.

  Lester M. Goodell, George M. Brewster, Topeka, Kansas, Attorneys for Defendants.

Duly sworn to by Lester M. Goodell. Jurat omitted in printing.

14

[fol. 17] [File endorsement omitted]

In United States District Court

[Title omitted]

Separate Answer of the State of Kansas—Filed June 15, 1951

Comes now the State of Kansas, an intervening defendant, by Edward F. Arn, Governor of said State, and Harold R. Fatzer, the Attorney General thereof, and for its answer to the amended complaint herein alleges as follows:

I

That the amended complaint in said cause fails to state a claim or cause of action against this intervening defendant upon which relief may be granted to the plaintiffs.

II

This intervening defendant admits the allegations contained in paragraph 1 of the amended complaint except that it denies the amount in controversy exceeds, exclusive of interest and costs, the sum or value of $3,000.00.

III

This intervening defendant admits the allegations contained in paragraph 2 (a) of the amended complaint except that it expressly denies Chapter 72-1724 of the General Statutes of Kansas, 1935 (1949), is unconstitutional. This defendant is without knowledge or information to either admit or deny the truth or the allegations contained in paragraph 2 (b), (c), and paragraph 3 (a), (b) of the amended complaint.

[fol. 18] IV

This defendant admits the allegations contained in paragraphs 4 and 5 of the amended complaint, but denies that the defendant, Board of Education of Topeka, Shawnee County, Kansas, is governed by the General Statutes of Kansas, 1935, and supplements thereto, Section 72-1809, for the reason that said statute has no application to public schools in cities of the first class to which class the city of Topeka belongs.

V

For further answer herein this intervening defendant states it is without knowledge or information to either admit or deny the truth of the allegations contained in paragraphs 6, 7, 8 as amended, 9 or 10 of the amended complaint. All other allegations contained in the amended complaint which are not hereinbefore admitted or explained are hereby expressly denied.

Wherefore this intervening defendant prays that plaintiffs take naught by this action and that defendants have judgment for all costs herein expended.

    Harold R. Fatzer, Attorney General for the State of Kansas; Willis H. McQueary, Assistant Attorney General for the State of Kansas; C. Harold Hughes, Assistant Attorney General of the State of Kansas.

[Verified by Willis H. McQueary.]

[fol. 19]   In United States District Court

[Title omitted]

Transcript of Proceedings of Pre-Trial Conference—Filed October 30, 1951

Appearances:

Hon. Walter A. Huxman, Judge, United States Court of Appeals, Tenth Circuit.

Hon. Arthur J. Mellott, Judge, United States District Court, District of Kansas.

Charles S. Scott, Topeka, Kansas; John Scott, Topeka, Kansas; Charles Bledsoe, Topeka, Kansas; Robert L. Carter, New York, New York, and Jack Greenberg, New York, New York. Appeared on behalf of Plaintiffs.

Lester M. Goodell, Topeka, Kansas, and George M. Brewster, Topeka, Kansas. Appeared on behalf of Defendants, Board of Education, Topeka, Shawnee County, Kansas, et al.

Harold R. Fatzer, Attorney General, State of Kansas, by Willis H. McQueary and Charles H. Hobart, Assistant Attorneys General, State of Kansas, Topeka, Kansas. Appeared on behalf of State of Kansas.

Harold Pittell, Official Reporter.

[fol. 20] Be it remembered, on this 22nd day of June, A.D. 1951, the above matter coming on for hearing before Honorable Walter A. Huxman, Judge, United States Court of Appeals, Tenth Circuit and Honorable Arthur J. Mellott, Judge, United States District Court, District of Kansas, and the parties appearing in person and/or by counsel, as hereinabove set forth, the following proceedings were had:

* * * * * * *

[fol. 21] COLLOQUY BETWEEN COURT AND COUNSEL

Judge Mellott: Do you have the appearances, Mr. Reporter?

The Reporter: Yes, Your Honor.

Judge Huxman: Gentlemen, the purpose of this session this morning is to hold a pre-trial conference to see whether we can simplify the matters and what can be agreed to before we go to trial next Monday.

Judge Mellott has called my attention to Rule 16. It provides for conference to simplify the issues, whether there is any necessity for amendments to the pleadings and to inquire into the possibility of obtaining admissions of fact concerning which there can be no dispute, limitation of the number of expert witnesses, the advisability of a preliminary reference of the issues to a master for findings and any such other matters as may simplify the issues at the time of the trial.

All the parties have entered—are in court and have filed pleadings; that is true of the State of Kansas, is it not?

Mr. McQueary: It is, Your Honor.

Judge Huxman: Is there a desire on the part of anybody to amend the pleadings in any manner; any necessity for amendment of pleadings?

Mr. Charles Scott: Yes, if the Court please. We have one amendment we desire to make.

[fol. 22] Judge Mellott: To what paragraph?

Mr. Charles Scott: Paragraph 5, sub-paragraph (a) of the plaintiffs' amended complaint.

Mr. Goodell: What was that again?

Mr. Charles Scott: Paragraph 5, sub-paragraph (a).

Judge Huxman: Paragraph 5 what?

Mr. Charles Scott: Paragraph 5(a).

Judge Mellott: Let me orient myself and Judge Huxman. Did you file a complete amended complaint?

Mr. Charles Scott: No, sir.

Judge Mellott: You filed an original complaint.

Mr. Charles Scott: And an amended complaint and——

Judge Mellott: And then in the amended complaint—there was an amendment to the amended complaint.

Mr. Goodell: I interpret that they did file——

Judge Mellott: You did file an amended complaint on March 22nd, didn't you?

Mr. Charles Scott: Yes.

Judge Mellott: The motion to make more definite was addressed to that amended complaint.

[fol. 23] Mr. Charles Scott: That is correct.

Judge Mellott: And then you filed an amendment to the amended complaint, under date of May 29th, did you not?

Mr. Charles Scott: That is correct, sir.

Judge Huxman: What do you desire presently?

Mr. Charles Scott: We desire to correct the statute of 72-1809 of the General Statutes of 1935 and the supplements thereto.

Judge Mellott: Let me get this in the pleading here. You are now talking about your original amended complaint, aren't you?

Mr. Charles Scott: The original amended complaint.

Judge Mellott: And you say you want to refer to paragraph 5 of that.

Mr. Charles Scott: 5(a).

Judge Mellott: 5(a). Your amendment is what; you want to make reference to the General Statutes of '49 instead of 1935, is that what you are saying?

2—8

Mr. Charles Scott: We also want to make reference to the General Statutes of 1949 and also strike therefrom Section 72-1809 and insert therein 72-1724.

Judge Mellott: 72-1724.

Mr. Charles Scott: That is correct.

[fol. 24] Judge Mellott: And does that read, then, that that is the General Statutes of Kansas for 1949?

Mr. Charles Scott: That is correct.

Judge Mellott: You wish to leave out the words, "and supplements thereto."

Mr. Charles Scott: Yes, we can take that out, that's true.

Judge Mellott: Let me see if I understand what you are doing. Paragraph 5(a), as amended, now reads: "Defendant, Board of Education, is under a duty to enforce the school laws of the State of Kansas (General Statutes of Kansas, 1949, Section 72-1724)", is that the amendment you are making?

Mr. Charles Scott: That is correct, sir.

Judge Mellott: Any other amendments?

Mr. Charles Scott: That is all we have.

Judge Huxman: Any objections to that? No objections; the amendment will be——

Mr. Goodell: If I understand his point, he cited in his amended complaint, which he now desires to correct, a statute which applies to cities of second class, erroneously when he intended to use—so we have no objection.

Judge Huxman: All right; the amendment will be ordered.

Judge Mellott: The Court will make the amendment by [fol. 25] interlineation.

Judge Huxman: Any other amendment to the pleadings?

Mr. Goodell: We have none, Your Honor.

Judge Huxman: No further amendments to any of the pleadings.

Mr. Bledsoe: If the Court please, at this time I would like to inform the Court we have two attorneys who are interested in this case with the plaintiffs, and they are here now, and I would like to present them to the Court at this time.

Judge Huxman: I will ask Judge Mellott to handle that because he knows how that matter is handled.

Judge Mellott: Very well. You may introduce them, if you will, and tell me who they are.

Mr. Bledsoe: They would like to be admitted for the purpose of this case only.

Judge Mellott: Present them.

Mr. Bledsoe: If the Court please, this gentleman here is Robert Carter, from New York. This, gentlemen, is Judge Huxman of the Tenth Circuit Court of Appeals; the gentleman over here is Jack Greenberg, of New York, and this is Judge Mellott of the District of Kansas Federal Court.

Judge Mellott: Are these gentlemen members of the bar?
[fol. 26] Mr. Bledsoe: They are.

Judge Mellott: In what state?

Mr. Bledsoe: New York.

Judge Mellott: In good standing?

Mr. Bledsoe: They are.

Judge Mellott: And are they admitted to practice in federal courts and courts such as this in their home jurisdiction?

Mr. Bledsoe: They are.

Judge Mellott: Never been disbarred. You vouch for them.

Mr. Bledsoe: I do.

Judge Mellott: Without further formality, then, they will be permitted to appear as counsel, along with the other gentlemen who presently appear as counsel in this case. Thank you, gentlemen; you may be seated.

Judge Huxman: Unless there is something else preliminary, we might——

Mr. Carter: Your Honor, if I may, I would like to raise one point. I don't think an amendment would be necessary to our pleadings, but we erroneously refer to school districts in Topeka, where it should be "territories", and we were going to make a stipulation with the defendants that they are territories rather than districts—and there is one school district.

[fol. 27] Judge Huxman: I think that is covered.

Mr. Carter: I just want to be sure.

Judge Mellott: I suppose, if necessary, for all proper purposes in this case, the Court can consider that where you use the word "district" in your pleading, that really what you are referring to is "territories." I believe I suggested that at an earlier proceeding here. It was my understanding Topeka was one school district, so you were referring to territories.

Judge Huxman: There is one other matter that might come up during the trial—at least I think the Court might want to make inquiry—will either or any of the parties to this litigation want to use expert witnesses?

Mr. Carter: Well, Your Honor——

Judge Huxman: For what purpose?

Mr. Carter: We want to use expert witnesses for the general purpose of showing that the segregation, which is the issue in the case, the segregation of the plaintiffs and of the class they represent in the negro schools is in fact a denial to them of their right to equal educational opportunities, that they are not getting equal educational opportunities by virtue of that. That is the purpose of our expert testimony.

Judge Huxman: Will there be any opposition to expert witnesses?

[fol. 28] Mr. Goodell: The——

Judge Huxman: —the use of expert witnesses by the plaintiffs?

Mr. Goodell: The way the question was stated, we will certainly object to that. We think that is a question of law. I, of course, don't know what turn it will take.

Judge Huxman: Well, the question of whether such testimony is competent, does not need to be decided at this time. The purpose of this inquiry is to ascertain how many such witnesses you will request and whether there shall be a limit. How many witnesses do you gentlemen desire on that question, assuming that the Court rules it is competent.

Mr. Carter: Well, Your Honor, I think that we were not certain of the exact number but approximately nine. We have approximately nine or ten people who we want to call who have made studies of this.

Judge Huxman: Well, the Court feels that nine witnesses on that one issue is too many witnesses. In other words, the issue is whether segregation itself, I presume, is not a denial of due process, irrespective of whether everything else is equal, to that furnished in the white schools, is that not your general contention?

Mr. Carter: Yes, sir.

Judge Huxman: Because of the effect it has upon the

[fol. 29] mind, upon the student, upon his outlook; I presume that would be your position.

Mr. Carter: That is absolutely correct, Your Honor.

Judge Huxman: Could nine witnesses give different testimony, or would their testimony be largely the same?

Mr. Carter: I doubt that, Your Honor. Our testimony will not be cumulative. Our purpose of getting these people was in order to give a rounded picture with respect to the subject that we have just raised. Now, we will have some witnesses who will testify as to tangible and physical inequalities also among those people, so that I think that it would be a great hardship to us if we were limited. We have no intention of merely bringing on witnesses to be cumulative.

Judge Mellott: That is the thing the Court thinks it should avoid. We shouldn't hear nine witnesses testify cumulatively even as experts, it seems to me, on the same thing.

Mr. Carter: I agree, but, Your Honor, we have no—we are not going to have duplication. Each of the people that we are asking to come here to testify will handle a different phase of this.

Judge Mellott: Then we should not limit you if that is what you expect to do.

[fol. 30] Judge Huxman: The Court feels this way, that it's difficult for it at this time to see where nine witnesses could testify on this one subject, to nine different sets of facts, unrelated facts, but you may be right; we do not intend to deny you the right to fully present your case. The Court, however, feels that after it has heard five witnesses, expert witnesses, if the Court then feels that the witnesses that you are offering thereafter are merely duplicating what has been said, an objection to their testimony on that ground will be sustained. If, on the other hand, the testimony is clearly different from what has been given, why you then should have the right to present your nine witnesses. But at the end of five, the Court will certainly scrutinize the testimony of the other four quite carefully to see whether it is duplication or additional testimony.

Mr. Carter: All right, sir.

Judge Huxman: Do you gentlemen then stipulate that, in any event, the expert witnesses which you request will be limited in number to nine.

Mr. Carter: Your Honor, frankly, our difficulty in making any stipulation like that is that Mr. Greenberg and I have just gotten here from New York this morning about——

Judge Huxman: This isn't the first case of this kind you were in. You were in the South Carolina case, weren't [fol. 31] you?

Mr. Carter: Yes, sir; but the thing is we haven't really had an opportunity to go over this. I would not want to make that stipulation. What I will say and what Your Honor has ruled is that after five, you will scrutinize whatever testimony we present for duplication, and we will certainly attempt to avoid that, but I wouldn't want to say that we would only have nine.

Judge Huxman: That was your statement in response.

Mr. Carter: I said approximately; I didn't want to be tied down to that number at all.

Judge Mellott: How much leeway do you want?

Mr. Carter: Well, I frankly think that we won't have more than nine, but I just would prefer not to be tied down. I am not going to, believe me, Your Honor, we are not going to parade a lot of witnesses here merely to keep you tied down.

Mr. Goodell: It would be under ninety, wouldn't it?

Mr. Carter: It will be under fifteen.

Mr. Goodell: Nine to ninety.

Judge Huxman: It would be the order of the Court that expert witnesses on behalf of the plaintiff, in the first [fol. 32] instance, will be limited to five, but if at that point the plaintiffs have additional witnesses which they feel have testimony to offer which has not been covered by these five, they will not be denied the right to present that testimony, is that correct, judge?

Judge Mellott: Yes, at this time, I think.

Judge Huxman: But that after five have been heard, the Court will reserve the right to reject any further evidence if it should feel that the evidence that is being offered is cumulative and not additional to what the first five have testified, is that fair to you boys?

In view of the fact that there has been a statement that plaintiffs will offer expert witnesses on this subject, assuming that the testimony will be received, will the defendants, or any of them, want to on their part offer expert testimony along this same line?

Mr. Goodell: Well, I am a little at a handicap of knowing exactly what their line is. They mention there is to be testimony from experts, as I understood it, on some physical facts which, of course, I don't know what they are referring to except I take it to mean that inferiority to—as to some—something relating to the school system and, of course, if that comes up, we will probably want to rebut that, not with experts, I don't think.

[fol. 33] Judge Huxman: Judge Mellott——

Mr. Goodell: As to the other phase which I understand is the psychological aspect and sociological, until I have heard their testimony, I am at a loss to know whether we will want to rebut it or attempt to rebut it.

Judge Mellott: Well, would it not be proper if the Court thought in terms of the same basic premise that in the event you do decide to offer experts rebutting the testimony of the plaintiffs' experts, that a limitation somewhat along the line suggested by Judge Huxman to the plaintiff should, likewise, apply to you.

Mr. Goodell: I certainly think so.

Judge Huxman: All right; that will be the order of the Court at this time.

Now, is there anything else, gentlemen, as to preliminary matters that we want to discuss before we go into these requests for admissions. Anything else that might be helpful in shaping the issues, shortening this trial.

I may state for myself, as a member of this court, that it would certainly be my purpose to afford the parties a full and complete hearing and an opportunity to present the issues fully and completely but, on the other hand, I would be very loathe to just permit the introduction of a great mass of testimony for any purpose whatever that has no bearing upon the issues; it merely prolongs and drags out [fol. 34] this trial.

Anything else preliminary? Do you care to say anything more?

Judge Mellott: I am quite sure Judge Hill and I concur entirely as to what you have just said, though my authority, of course, to speak is only to speak for myself.

Judge Huxman: In a preliminary conference, Judge

Mellott, to bring you up to date, purely informal, with attorneys for the plaintiffs and the defendants, I suggested that, as a preliminary to this pre-trial conference, each side prepare requested admissions of fact and serve them on the other side.

Judge Mellott: I am sure that was quite helpful.

Judge Huxman: We have that here this morning and, if there is nothing further, suppose, gentlemen, we proceed to see how many of these requests we can agree upon.

We will take up the defendants' requests for stipulations first.

No. 1 is a request for an agreement that the City of Topeka, Kansas, constitutes one school district.

Mr. Carter: We agree.

Judge Huxman: That is agreed to.

Judge Mellott: Thank you, gentlemen.

[fol. 35] Judge Huxman: Request No. 2:

"That defendants have designated within the City of Topeka, Kansas, eighteen territories and in each of these territories have established and maintain a public elementary school for white children only; in addition thereto defendants have established and maintain in the City of Topeka, Kansas, four separate elementary schools for colored children and attendance at these four schools is restricted to colored children. Exhibit A, which is made a part hereof by reference, is a map of the City of Topeka and adjacent territories attached to Topeka School District for school purposes only. Said Exhibit A correctly designates the school territory for white schools for the City of Topeka, Kansas. Said map also designates the four colored schools, which are Buchanan, McKinley, Monroe and Washington. Colored school children in the City of Topeka, Kansas, may attend any one of these four colored schools, and the choice of schools is made by the colored school children or their parents. The territory colored blue on Exhibit A represents areas not within the City of Topeka except for school purposes, and children residing in said areas attend schools in the City of Topeka, Kansas."

Now, before you make any request, Judge Mellott has not seen Exhibit "A". As a preliminary question, may I ask, Mr. Goodell, who prepared that exhibit?

[fol. 36]   Mr. Goodell: The clerk of the Topeka Board of Education.

Judge Huxman: Do you vouch for its territorial correctness and integrity?

Mr. Goodell: Absolutely.

Judge Huxman: All right. With that preliminary statement, is there any objection to the admission requested in request No. 2?

Mr. Carter: Well, Your Honor, this is the first—I think we have no objection on Exhibit "A", but going over on to page 2—about the fifth line from the top——

Judge Huxman: Fifth line from the top on page 2.

Mr. Carter: "and the choice of schools is made by the colored school children or their parents." I should think we have to get more information on that before we could agree. With that exception, we will agree.

Mr. Goodell: For clarity, what is meant there, of course, is choice of which of the four colored schools. It doesn't mean to say——

Mr. Carter: It is a question in our minds as to whether that is true.

Judge Huxman: Do you have testimony to the effect that that is not true?

Mr. Carter: We may.

[fol. 37]   Judge Huxman: You may.

Mr. Carter: Yes, sir.

Judge Huxman: Well, do you have reasons to believe that it is not true?

Mr. Carter: Well, the only thing I can say at this time, Your Honor, is that up to—as far as this is concerned, we have to know—we would have to make a little further investigation on this ourselves. We might stipulate, agree, that this is true by Monday, but I don't think we can do it today.

Judge Huxman: All right. I just feel this way, that there ought to be a perfect willingness on the part of both parties to freely and frankly agree to facts concerning which there just can't be any dispute. Now, if there is a question about a fact, that should not be agreed to, of course, but you have local colored counsel here who no doubt went to schools here, these segregated schools.

Mr. Carter: That is——

Judge Huxman: Do you agree to the request with the exception of that portion starting—with this exception: "Colored school children in the City of Topeka, Kansas, may attend any one of these four colored schools, and the choice of schools is made by the colored school children or their parents."

Mr. Carter: All we reject is of the choice.

[fol. 38] Judge Huxman: Do you agree to everything but that?

Mr. Carter: We agree with the first part of the statement. All we don't know about is the choice.

Judge Huxman: I am just taking the one sentence. I don't like to divide a sentence. You want to reserve the agreement to that until Monday.

Mr. Carter: Yes, sir.

Judge Huxman: And, in the meantime, you will make an investigation and if you find that that is a fact——

Mr. Carter: We will agree to it.

Judge Huxman: Mr. Scott, you have been a resident of Topeka all your life.

Mr. Charles Scott: Yes, sir.

Judge Huxman: Are you able to say whether that is or is not a fact as the schools are administered.

Mr. Charles Scott: Qualified, Your Honor. We are allowed to go to the schools that are closest to our home. Now, whether or not the school board has any control over that or not, I don't know, but, as a practical matter, naturally, the colored students go to the school closest to their home.

Judge Huxman: I tell you what I wish you would do with your New York counsel. I wish you would have a confer-[fol. 39] ence with the members of the school board between now and Monday and ask them if a colored student wants to attend any one of these four schools whether there is any restriction upon his right to do so.

Mr. Charles Scott: I will do that, Your Honor.

Judge Huxman: And then come in Monday morning——

Mr. Goodell: Of course, my information came from the board and the administrative officers on all these matters.

Judge Huxman: They should have the right to get that information themselves.

It is agreed, then, that request for admission No. 2 is argeed to with the exception of that portion which has just been read by the Court and, as to that portion, inquiry will be made by Monday and a statement by counsel for plaintiffs will be made then as to whether they agree to that portion which is presently eliminated.

We will take up No. 3:

"That the same curriculum is used in the elementary colored schools in the City of Topeka, Kansas, as is used in the elementary white schools in said city."

Mr. Carter: After conference, Your Honor, we cannot stipulate to that.

[fol. 40] Judge Huxman: Do you claim that that is not so?

Mr. Carter: We would change in the first sentence where it reads, "That the same curricula is used", we would change that to "prescribed" as long as curricula is understood to mean courses of study.

Judge Huxman: That is what the curricula means, isn't it, courses of study.

Mr. Goodell: That is what I intended by it.

Mr. Carter: I am not sure.

Judge Huxman: Do you have a different meaning of curricula?

Mr. Carter: Yes, sir.

Judge Huxman: Is there any objection to the elimination of the word "curricula" and the substitution of the "studies are used"?

Mr. Carter: "Prescribed" is what we want to use.

Judge Huxman: That wouldn't be any admission. The question is, is it actually used, that is the test.

Mr. Carter: We are advised that that is not true, Your Honor.

Judge Huxman: How?

[fol. 41] Mr. Carter: We at this table don't feel that we can stipulate to that at this time.

Judge Huxman: Well, do you intend to offer evidence to show that that is not so?

Mr. Carter: Yes, sir.

Judge Huxman: In what respect do you contend that there is a difference?

Mr. Carter: Well, there are several things that I have

right now at my fingertips that I can indicate. One is that there is a difference in terms of the special teachers and the special—there are special teachers that are used at the White schools. No special teachers or special courses for certain classes of the student body are at the Negro School.

Judge Huxman: The teachers have nothing to do with the courses of study?

Mr. Carter: Yes, sir. They have set up, as we understand it, Your Honor, set up at the White school a special course of study for children who are somewhat retarded who are not able to come up to the part of their class. Now, no such course is available at the Negro school. We also have a question right now as to whether even though the same courses of study are prescribed, and we think that we have evidence to show that it is not used, that this is not followed out at the Negro school generally.

[fol. 42] Judge Huxman: Mr. Goodell, what do you say with regard to the statement that special courses prescribed in white schools for sub-normal children are not in colored schools?

Mr. Goodell: I don't think that is curricula that is special —that comes under a heading later in our brief about special services which they cover in paragraph 8, which I don't think is embraced in the question of curricula.

Judge Mellott: I am wondering if you gentlemen perhaps are in dispute primarily about the definition of the word "curricula." I wonder if that is your difficulty.

Mr. Goodell: I think—my interpretation of it and the use I intended is the—as meaning the subjects taught, programs used in the school and the subjects taught, courses of study.

Judge Mellott: Well, do you wish to rephrase it so that it does limit it to those particular terms? Maybe your adversary will agree if you rephrase it.

Mr. Goodell: I am willing to change it, Your Honor, by striking out the word "curricula" and substituting therefor "that the same course of study"—"courses of study".

Judge Mellott: I suggest that counsel for the plaintiff give attention to what is being said.

[fol. 43] Mr. Carter: Yes, sir.

Judge Huxman: He is suggesting that perhaps a change in the word "curricula" might make this understandable so you do agree upon its meaning and perhaps get closer to a stipulation.

Mr. Goodell: "That the same course of study is used in the elementary colored schools in the City of Topeka as is used in the elementary white schools." It will read, Your Honor, my suggested amendment.

Judge Huxman: Also keep in mind, gentlemen, that under Mr. Goodell's explanation this special matter which you mentioned for abnormal children is not meant to be included in here, and the agreement to this stipulation would not bar you from showing that some special services are rendered to white children that are not rendered to colored children. With that statement, are you willing to agree with this?

Mr. Charles Scott: At this time, Your Honor, I don't think we are inclined to accept it.

Judge Mellott: Your associates think they are. They say if you limit it to simply saying that the same course of study is used, that they don't have any objection.

Mr. Charles Scott: Well, this is the reason, Your Honor: We have examined a greater portion of the curricula, as prescribed by the school board, and we have found that [fol. 44] there are some differences, certain course of studies are offered in some schools and are not offered in some of the colored schools, and so I don't think we are inclined to accept it on those basis.

Judge Huxman: Can you name a specific instance?

Mr. Charles Scott: Yes, sir.

Judge Huxman: All right, let's have it.

Mr. Charles Scott: They have a course entitled "Literature Appreciation" that is offered in the fifth and sixth grades in several of the white schools, and it is not offered in one or two of the colored schools. Then you have——

Judge Huxman: Is that shown by the exhibits?

Mr. Charles Scott: Yes, sir.

Judge Huxman: All right. What would you say to this: Would you agree that the courses of study as outlined in these exhibits—what are the exhibits?

Mr. Charles Scott: If the Court please, now they label——

Judge Huxman: Are the courses of studies that are used.

30

Mr. Charles Scott: They call it the school program, but it appears to be the course of study.

[fol. 45] Judge Huxman: That is quibbling about words, isn't it?

Mr. Charles Scott: Well——

Mr. Goodell: I am willing to limit that again. I am not familiar with that matter he points out—to have it read. "That the same course of study required by the Kansas"—by law—"by the Kansas statute is given." I think what he is talking about is some extra-curricular subject that some teachers of their own volition give, like outside reading, reference texts, and so forth, rather than a prescribed course of study.

Mr. Charles Scott: No, I beg to differ with counsel. This is prescribed by the school board and sent down.

Mr. Goodell: I am talking about what the state law requires to be taught in our Kansas elementary public school system.

(Colloquy was here had between counsel off the record.)

Mr. Goodell: If we are going to have a lawsuit here and pursue factual inquiry as to—as to school by school, of which there are twenty-two, we will be chasing down each textbook for outside reading that Miss Jones may prescribe at Randolph which Miss Baker at another school doesn't like, and she prescribes another text for outside [fol. 46] reading. Suppose they are taking history; one likes this for outside reading and another teacher likes another. That will frequently occur.

Judge Mellott: Do you have a printed course of study?

Mr. Goodell: Absolutely.

Judge Mellott: Do you have one?

Mr. Goodell: I have it attached as an exhibit here. And what I meant to convey and what I mean by this stipulation and will reframe it——

Judge Mellott: Where is it attached?

Mr. Brewster: Exhibit "F".

Mr. Goodell: That the course of study required by our Kansas statute is followed in all of the schools without any distinction between the white and colored elementary schools.

(Colloquy was here had between counsel off the record.)

Judge Huxman: Shall we then eliminate request No. 3?
Mr. Goodell: Let's pass that, Your Honor.
Judge Huxman: We will pass request No. 3 and take up No. 4:

"That the same school books are used in the elementary colored schools in the City of Topeka, Kansas, as are used in [fol. 47] the elementary white schools in said city."

Is that not related to 3 and also covered by your exhibits?
Mr. Goodell: Yes.
Judge Huxman: Shall we pass it?
Mr. Goodell: Yes, that is satisfactory.
Mr. Carter: Your Honor, we are having one of our expert witnesses, that is going to be a librarian, who is at the present time checking the holdings of all the schools.
Judge Huxman: Is what?
Mr. Carter: The holdings, the library holdings of all of the schools, and we therefore are not—we can't——
Judge Huxman: We passed 4.
Mr. Goodell: I would like to amend, in view of his remarks, I would like to amend that to read, "The same textbooks"—"school textbooks" so that it doesn't——
Judge Huxman: All right, that will be permitted.
Judge Mellott: Do you agree that the same textbooks are used?
Mr. Carter: I think we will agree.
Judge Mellott: Very well.
Judge Huxman: Did you, Mr. Reporter, get request No. [fol. 48] 4, as amended?
The Reporter: Yes, Your Honor.
Judge Huxman: We will take No. 5:

"That each of the four colored elementary schools in the City of Topeka, Kansas, is situated in neighborhoods where the population is predominantly colored."

Mr. John Scott: That is agreeable, Your Honor.
Judge Huxman: That is agreed to.
Judge Huxman: No. 6:

"That transportation to and from school is furnished colored children in the elementary schools of the City of

Topeka, Kansas, without cost to said children or their parents. No such transportation is furnished white children in the elementary schools of the City of Topeka."

It would seem to me that is either a fact or isn't a fact.
Mr. Charles Scott: We will agree to that.
Judge Huxman: All right. No. 6 is agreed to.
No. 7:

"That the same services are offered to colored and white elementary schools by the school authorities of the City of Topeka, Kansas, except in the case of transportation, as [fol. 49] set out in the preceding paragraph hereof."

Now, before you speak on that, I would like to ask a preliminary question: I am not sure that I understand, Mr. Goodell, what you mean by the "same services."

Mr. Goddell: I mean services like supervised play of the children at recess and noon period; I mean services of public health, nursing, which is furnished the elementary schools, both white and colored alike; I mean services that are entailed in departmental heads calling on the elementary school system, such as music department, and giving supervision and advice to the teachers. That is what I mean.

Judge Huxman: Is there anything else that you include in services?

Mr. Goodell: No, that is what I mean.

Judge Huxman: All right. And your request, requested admission, that these services which you have mentioned are furnished both in the colored schools and in the white schools.

Mr. Goodell: That is correct.

Mr. John Scott: We don't accept that, if Your Honor please. I think that is a little too indefinite; we need a little more definite and certain——

Judge Huxman: That is the reason I asked you to state [fol. 50] specifically the kind of services he had in mind.

Mr. John Scott: Yes, Your Honor, I understand that, but as it stands in the stipulation at the present time, we wouldn't have a way of knowing.

Judge Huxman: The stipulation as it reads in the printed record isn't going to be the record. The record that is made is as modified by the statements of Mr. Goodell. They are the ones that go into the record.

All right; is that agreed to, then?

Mr. Carter: That is agreeable, Your Honor.

Judge Huxman: That is agreeable.

Judge Mellott: Well, are there any other services that either side thinks should be incorporated. Now, I have in my mind some three or four services. Now, in order to make that complete, do you wish to give us a more detailed or do you wish to add anything to the services which Mr. Goodell has referred to?

Mr. Carter: No, sir. We have one item that I think I spoke of before. I think that Mr. Goodell indicated that it was a service, but he doesn't include that in his special statements. The statement is satisfactory to us.

Judge Mellott: The word "services" is rather big and broad and all-inclusive.

Judge Huxman: Of course, it—all right, that is agreed [fol. 51] to, then, as modified by the explanation; the furnishing of services as stated is agreed to.

We will take up No. 8:

"That the distance traveled by colored children in reaching the schools they attend is not on the average greater than the distance white children are required to travel to reach the schools they attend."

Mr. Carter: Well, Your Honor, I don't think we want to stipulate on this. I don't think it has anything to do with the case. I think it's irrelevant.

Mr. Goodell: If the Court please, on that point, it is merely a mathematical proposition. That map, Exhibit "A", shows the whole City of Topeka and territory outside of the city is in blue, which is in Topeka for school purposes. We have marked on the map, Exhibit "A", each school territory. It shows, of course, the physical facts of distances which appear on this city map and can be computed. Children, in other words, living, for example—taking Exhibit "A"—in the blue territory over here in the corner (indicating) their school that they would have to go to, white children, would be Randolph, and all of that. Of course the matter of various school distances are written in

3—8

on the map—are identified. Of course to get at it any more accurately, which would be almost an intolerable job, would be to get each child that went to the city schools and get the [fol. 52] actual distance travelled divided by the number of children, and then you would get the average, and then get each colored child and get the actual distance divided by number of children, and then you would have the average.

Judge Huxman: Mr. Goodell, I doubt whether the Court would want that kind of a stipulation agreed to. That might be mathematically correct when you take an outlying territory. Now, to reach that result, you take territory that is not in the city limits and that——

Mr. Goodell: I have done some computing with a ruler, and I have taken the school population of the various schools, and I have taken distances in various different territories, and I know that as a matter of fact, it's a conservative statement, it's on the conservative side.

Judge Huxman: Well, now you may be right, but I wouldn't want this, as far as I am concerned; I wouldn't be content to have it established by stipulation that you can have four schools in the City of Topeka for one group of people and eighteen for another in that same territorial limit and yet those in the four schools would not be required to travel greater distances than the children that have eighteen schools. Now maybe it's a fact, I don't know.

Mr. Goodell: Keep in mind, Your Honor, that the colored schools have been, and that is covered by prior stipulation which is admitted, are located in neighborhoods in each case [fol. 53] which are predominantly colored neighborhoods; consequently, you don't have a situation in the case of where four colored schools have children living blocks—thirty some blocks—away from the nearest school which we—which does obtain in the case of many of our white schools—several of them—because of the population trends in the southwest part of our city in the last few years, particularly since the war. We have had great population trends out toward the west and southwest which has caused the territory to be taken in for school purposes and, in some cases, annexed territory, and has brought about that situation.

Furthermore, I—except for paragraphs 8, when they make that as one of their grounds for inequality, is the matter of distance travelled or inaccessibility of their schools. I can't see where that is too important because we do transport them in every case where they ask to be transported.

Judge Huxman: Now that is a conclusion which flows from what is done, and you might be right on that, but the fact is a different thing, and Judge Mellott and I are in agreement that the Court does not want the stipulation as an admitted fact in this case.

Mr. Goodell: Would it add anything to it for me to have some witness get on the stand and testify as to just what the map shows and testify that the children do come from [fol. 54] the territories as shown by the map, to the various schools. Now, to make anything——

Judge Huxman: Speaking for myself alone, Mr. Goodell, as I get—if I understand the effect of what you are trying to say, is that the average distances travelled by the white children are as great as the average distance travelled by the colored children.

Mr. Goodell: That's right.

Judge Huxman: I wouldn't be impressed with that in the case at all. If the fact remained that a colored child over here had to travel two miles and a number of colored children had to travel two miles by virtue of the fact that there weren't so many of them and you had an outlying district of white children which brought their average travelled distance to as great as the colored children had to travel. I still think it might be an imposition upon a colored child if it had to travel two miles whereas a white child did not have to travel two miles.

Mr. Goodell: We will have an isolated case. When I talk about travel, I say again, in the stipulations, have already been admitted on that; that they are furnished transportation so that travel doesn't seem to me as a very significant issue.

Judge Huxman: That is a different matter.

Mr. Goodell: But, be that as it may, you still have iso- [fol. 55] lated cases where a colored child may go twenty-four blocks by bus.

Judge Huxman: The Court is of the view that the request for stipulation No. 8 might be eliminated, so we might as well pass it for the time being.

Mr. Goodell: As I understand the Court, I have to prove

the distance all the white children go to school and the distance the colored children go to school, is that my understanding, is that correct? We would be here for days and days on that.

Judge Mellott: You have your map here, and I think you can demonstrate—you already have indicated what you think your demonstration would consist of. What Judge Huxman, as I understand, is suggesting, and I am in accord with his views, is a mere mathematical calculation out of which flows an average allocated in one instance to the colored pupils and in another instance to the white pupils, wouldn't be particularly helpful.

Mr. Goodell: Of course there is inequality within the white structure. You have some white kids living next door and half a block away from the schoolhouse and others living thirty-six blocks away. To cure that we would have to have a schoolhouse on every corner. There always has to be that disparity.

Judge Huxman: But, as Judge Mellott has just stated, [fol. 56] an average distance travelled arrived upon the composite of a great number, has very little weight with me.

Mr. Goodell: I admit that fallacies in it, of course. I have to prove that because they have injected that as an issue.

Judge Huxman: They might be willing to concede that you having arrived at this by average, that the total distance travelled by all the white children and the total distance travelled by the colored children would produce this result; that is a different matter. But, anyhow, it wouldn't take you very long to prove that, how this computation was arrived at.

Mr. Goodell: Your Honor, I am not trying to say that I proved that on a school attendance record. I took—arbitrarily—distances and assume there would be children going to school in some of their territory. Now, that was an assumption. To get at that on a factual basis, I would have to get the school attendance from each and every one of these schools, look up the records where each kid lives, put those altogether, those children and distances, divided by the number of children to get at the average distance, and I would be all summer doing that.

Judge Mellott: I don't think we would ever ask you to do that or permit you to do it.

Judge Huxman: Request No. 8 is omitted.

[fol. 57] Mr. Brewster: One statement, judge. Plaintiffs' objection to this stipulation was the fact that distance travelled was immaterial. If that is what he meant, are you willing to stipulate, then, that the distance the students are required to travel is not an issue in the lawsuit.

Mr. Carter: No; I didn't say that. I said that the stipulation was immaterial.

Judge Huxman: No use or purpose would be served by pursuing the inquiry further because the Court itself has eliminated request No. 8.

Mr. Brewster: The point was——

Judge Huxman: We will come to No. 9:

"That Exhibits B-1 to B-22, inclusive, attached hereto and made a part hereof, are correct compilations for each of the elementary public schools in the City of Topeka, Kansas, and correctly state for the 1950-1951 school period the following as to each school designated:

"1. Name of elementary school.
"2. Name of principal.
"3. Class-room units.
"4. Enrollment.
"5. Kindergarten units.
"6. Kindergarten enrollment.
"7. Names of teachers, grades taught, enrollment for each grade, and average daily attendance."

[fol. 58] Now, before we go to that, I think I would like to clear up in my mind a matter that is somewhat cloudy. I want to be sure that I understand these designations. "SP" means what?

Mr. Goodell: Special.

Judge Huxman: Special teacher. What does "K" mean?

Mr. Goodell: Kindergarten.

Judge Huxman: And the figures appearing after "K" is the number of kindergarten students, or what is that? For instance, in Buchanan, you have this: "Teacher, SP K 1 1-2 2 2-3".

Judge Mellott: I suppose those are first grades.

(Colloquy was here had between Court and Counsel off the record.)

Judge Mellott: Do you stipulate, gentlemen, that these exhibits are correct and reflect those various matters?

Mr. Charles Scott: If the Court please, we agree to everything. I think there is a typographical error in the name of Mildred Starnes, as appears on Exhibit "B-1." The name should be changed to Myrtle. It isn't material.

Judge Mellott: Any correction such as that is not very material, but if you want them corrected——

[fol. 59] Judge Huxman: Do plaintiffs agree to request for admissions as contained in No. 9, then.

Mr. Carter: Yes, sir.

Judge Huxman: No. 9 is agreed to.

No. 10:

"That Exhibits C-1 to C-22 inclusive, attached hereto and made a part hereof, are correct compilations for each of the elementary public schools in the City of Topeka, Kansas, and correctly state for the 1950-1951 school period the following as to each school designated:

"1. Name of teacher or principal.
"2. Total service.
"3. Degree or hours credit.
"4. 1950-1951 salary.
"5. 1951-1952 salary."

Is there any objection to agreeing to that?

Mr. Charles Scott: No, sir.

Judge Huxman: All right. Request No. 10 is agreed to in toto.

No. 11:

"That in arriving at the salary to be paid teachers in the elementary public schools of Topeka, Kansas, the determining factors are the same for colored teachers as for white teachers, and the application of these factors is the [fol. 60] same."

Mr. Carter: Well, Your Honor, we can't say that this is a fact. We don't think it's important.

Judge Huxman: That's rather a conclusion, isn't it?

Mr. Goodell: Maybe it is, except what is meant by it, the

clear implication of it, what I meant to say, if it can be made plainer, I will amend it to say it. No distinction is made in the matter of payment of salaries between white and colored teachers.

Judge Huxman: Well, Mr. Goodell——

Mr. Goodell: ——because of color.

Judge Huxman: The Court is of the view that No. 11 perhaps would serve no useful purpose if agreed to, and it is of such a nature that the plaintiff's perhaps shouldn't be required to agree to it. I doubt if they make an issue of that.

Mr. Goodell: If the Court please——

Judge Mellott: They have covered it in the preceding paragraph admitting what the salaries are, haven't they?

Mr. Goodell: That admits salaries, yes. That shows the physical facts of what the salaries being paid are, yes.

(Colloquy was here had off the record.)

[fol. 61] Judge Huxman: What is it you state?

Mr. Goodell: The amendment to the amended complaint which is amending paragraph 8 of the amended complaint filed in this case makes blanket allegations. They don't go into particularity, but they make blanket allegations of disparities that exist between the white and the colored elementary schools. Now one of the disparities covered by that pleading in amendment to paragraph 8 of the original —of the amended complaint, is teaching. Now I take it that under that allegation it would be fair—it would be a fair line of proof for them to admit—to introduce evidence that we are treating the teacher differently with respect to their contracts and their salary and so forth. So of course you don't get as good work and their children are suffering because they are not getting the benefit of a well-paid teacher.

Judge Huxman: Speaking for myself, Mr. Goodell, I am still of the opinion that even if that is so, if that is their position, it's a matter that you can't very well reduce to an absolute agreement. They may not——

Mr. Goodell: I see the Court's point about that.

Judge Huxman: ——they may not contend that. If they do, it's their burden to establish. If they fail to establish it, it's out of the case. If they make the contention it's a very simple matter for you to prove that it isn't so.

[fol. 62] Mr. Goodell: Of course they know that whether it's a fact or not. I say that it's a fact, but I agree with you that they may not care to admit it and perhaps shouldn't be required to.

Judge Huxman: No. 11 is out. All right. No. 12:

"That Exhibit D, attached hereto and made a part hereof, is a correct compilation of statistics of the transportation costs for the colored elementary schools in the City of Topeka for the 1950-1951 school period."

Mr. Goodell: That is shown by our records, the treasurer's office.

Judge Mellott: Do you contend that that is not an accurate compilation, gentlemen?

Mr. Charles Scott: We agree to it.

Mr. John Scott: That is admitted.

Judge Huxman: No. 13:

"That Exhibits E-1 to E-5 inclusive, attached hereto and made a part hereof, are correct compilations of statistics relating to public school nurses in the City of Topeka, Kansas, and correctly set forth statistics relating to public health nurses in the City of Topeka for the 1950-1951 school period."

Mr. Goodell: Now all that exhibit is is to show the num-
[fol. 63] ber of persons or children served by the various public school nurses over the city as reflecting on the question of whether there are enough nurses to give adequate service to the colored schools. In other words, it shows the load per pupil for the nurses.

Mr. Carter: Your Honor, there again is one of the things that we don't know. We are not going to controvert it.

Mr. Goodell: Our records show it.

Judge Huxman: If the records show it, could you not agree to the exhibit without agreeing to the matter which they intend to establish by it. You don't have to agree to that. You could agree that this is a fact or the facts shown by this exhibit are correct. You don't have to agree to the conclusion that flows from that.

Mr. Carter: All right.

Judge Huxman: All right. It is then agreed that Exhibits "E-1" to "E-5", as attached to the request for stipulations, are correct.

Mr. Carter: Yes, sir.

Mr. Goodell: The record is correct.

Judge Huxman: And the facts therein reflected are the facts.

Mr. Carter: All right.

Judge Huxman: All right.

[fol. 64] No, No. 14:

"That Exhibits F-1 to F-22 inclusive, attached hereto and made a part hereof, are correct compilations of the elementary public school program for each of the designated elementary schools in the City of Topeka, Kansas, for the 1950-1951 school period."

Any objections to that?

Mr. Carter: No, sir. We agree to that.

Judge Huxman: You agree.

Mr. Carter: Yes, sir.

Judge Huxman: All right. Request for admission No. 14, as read, is agreed.

Judge Mellott: Let me be on the record for just a moment.

I believe that if I have understood correctly what Judge Huxman has accomplished so far in the pre-trial, it has resulted in the receipt in evidence of all of these exhibits here, is not that correct, gentlemen?

Mr. Charles Scott: That is correct.

Judge Mellott: I am wondering if we shouldn't just turn these exhibits over to the clerk and let him mark them as exhibits admitted in evidence for all purposes, and then they constitute a part of the formal record.

Mr. Brewster: We have additional ones, supplemental requests.

[fol. 65] Judge Huxman: I think that is a good suggestion, Judge Mellott, and the parties have agreed to it.

Mr. Goodell: If Your Honor please, we were going back to the preceding paragraphs which were passed for the moment in the light of this last exhibit.

42

I am willing to amend paragraph 3 by substituting for "curricula" the words, "course of study."

Judge Huxman: Mr. Goodell, let me ask you, for my information, these exhibits, I forget what the numbers of them are, set out the courses of study.

Mr. Goodell: "F-1."

Judge Huxman: The "F" series of exhibits sets out the actual courses of study that are taught in all of these schools.

Mr. Goodell: That's right.

Judge Huxman: What does your request for admission No. 3 add to what those exhibits actually show?

Mr. Brewster: How would it be if on 14 we just added, "And said program includes all courses of study prescribed by the law of the State of Kansas." Is that what you are getting at?

Mr. Goodell: I wanted to make that plan that we were following the prescribed course of study.

Judge Huxman: You have actually set out the courses of study that you say are taught.

[fol. 66] Mr. Goodell: All it takes to pick it up and make it complete——

Judge Huxman: There is no contention made that they don't conform to the state requirements. If they want to claim it, let them prove it. You say those are the courses of study.

Mr. Goodell: I don't care to belabor the point.

Judge Huxman: What would 3 add?

Mr. Goodell: Three supplements 14 only in respect, that it ties up and shows that it's a legal course of study being followed or taught.

Judge Mellott: May I suggest that the reporter read what Mr. Brewster interpolated and see if, perhaps, his interpolation may not be added as a part of your admission with reference to Exhibit "F".

(Portion referred to by Judge Mellott read aloud by the reporter.)

Judge Mellott: Is there any reason why you couldn't supplement No.——

Mr. Carter: I think, if I may, Your Honor——

Judge Mellott: Any reason why you couldn't supplement No. XI which you have agreed to, by the addition of what Mr. Brewster just said.

[fol. 67] Mr. Carter: I frankly am unable to see where it adds anything. We have admitted the facts.

Judge Mellott: I don't think it adds much. You are not contending that Topeka in the operation of its school system is refusing to abide by the statutes of Kansas and the orders of the state superintendent of public instruction with reference to courses of study, are you; you are not making that contention.

Mr. Carter: I would prefer, however, Your Honor, if the exhibit which sets out the courses and they are admitted in the record, I think they speak for themselves.

Judge Mellott: You haven't answered my question. I think you should answer it. Do you contend that the board of education of the City of Topeka, Kansas, is not complying with the state law and the regulations and the orders of the state superintendent of public instruction?

Mr. Carter: That is not our contention, no.

Judge Mellott: All right.

Judge Huxman: Then why do you object to this addition? The only reason you could object to it is that you claim they aren't complying.

Mr. Carter: Well, Your Honor, the point is that we have admitted the courses of study. These are facts which [fol. 68] they have set forth in the record; these are the courses of study which are taught.

Judge Mellott: Well, I think we would take his statement as an admission that of course he is not contending that the Board of Education of Topeka is doing other than complying with the Kansas statutes so far as course of study is concerned. I would certainly spell that out of counsel's statement.

Judge Huxman: With that statement by counsel perhaps the addition isn't necessary.

Judge Mellott: I don't think so.

Judge Huxman: Let's take up the supplemental requests for stipulations which have been filed by the defendants.

No. 15:

"That Exhibit G, attached hereto and made a part hereof, is a correct statement taken from the records of the Board of Education of the City of Topeka, Kansas, pertaining to bus schedules for colored elementary school children for transportation furnished said children by the said Board of Education for the 1950-1951 school year."

Is there any objection to agreeing to that stipulation?

Mr. Carter: We agree to that, Your Honor, with the exception of line 9.

[fol. 69] Judge Huxman: Line 9?

Mr. Carter: Line 2 under "Monroe"; that is on the exhibit itself.

Judge Mellott: That is on the exhibit.

Mr. Carter: Line 2 under "Monroe."

Judge Huxman: Which says, "8:10—First and Kansas." You don't agree to that.

Mr. Goodell: You mean that is erroneous? What should it be?

Mr. Charles Scott: Should be First and Quincy.

Mr. Goodell: Is that correct, First and Quincy?

Judge Mellott: Let's change it to First and Quincy, then.

Mr. Goodell: I am writing that in as an amendment then.

Judge Huxman: And, as amended, plaintiffs agree to request 15 for admissions.

Mr. Carter: Your Honor, Mr. Scott brought something to our attention. This addendum down here, "Bus picks up students also anywhere along route."

Judge Mellott: You haven't gotten to that yet, have you?

Mr. Carter: That is on the same exhibit—on the exhibit.

[fol. 70] Judge Huxman: "Bus picks up students also anywhere along route." You don't agree to that?

Mr. Carter: I understand that they picked them up at these various stops.

Mr. Goodell: They do and, in addition, along the way at not designated stops they will pick them up. That is what they tell me; I don't know. That is what the clerk's office tells me has been the practice for years.

Judge Mellott: Well, do you Topeka lawyers especially, do you know whether that is a fact or not?

Mr. Charles Scott: No, sir.

Judge Mellott: Suppose we admit the exhibit, then, eliminating from it the parenthetical clause and let that remain as an item requiring proof, if that is required.

Judge Huxman: If requested. As so modified, do you agree to the admission?

Mr. Charles Scott: Yes, sir.

Judge Huxman: All right.

No. 16:

"That Exhibit H attached hereto and made a part hereof, is a correct statement of facts from the records of the Board of Education of the City of Topeka pertaining to teacher load in the kindergartens of the Topeka public schools for [fol. 71] the 1950-1951 school year."

Any objection to agreeing to that?

Mr. Carter: Our witness informs us that this is not correct.

Judge Mellott: Who is your witness?

Mr. Carter: Dr. Speer.

Judge Mellott: What does he know about it; has he checked the records?

Mr. Carter: Yes, sir.

Judge Mellott: Is he here now?

Mr. Carter: No, he isn't.

Judge Mellott: How much of that is covered here in exhibits which are already in evidence.

Mr. Carter: I don't know.

Judge Mellott: You have stipulated with refere, I believe it was "E" or "F", has already been covered. Let me refer back here.

Mr. Brewster: Series "B", I imagine.

Judge Mellott: You have shown here what the number of kindergarten children were in each of the schools, and you have shown what the average daily attendance of the kindergarten was. I don't know what is shown by "H".

Mr. Carter: Isn't this the teacher load? These are facts taken from that other report, isn't it, Mr. Goodell?

[fol. 72] Mr. Goodell: Sure. It's a breakdown of each school in the City of Topeka showing the teaching load per teacher. In other words, children each teacher has under her for particular grades starting with kindergarten.

Judge Mellott: What I am asking is simply this: Isn't Exhibit "H" a mere assembling of the data which is already in Exhibit "B"?

Mr. Goodell: It's calculations drawn therefrom from that other data; it's a mathematical, in other words, reduction of what the other exhibits show. I can prove that; I don't care to argue it.

Judge Huxman: Now, gentlemen, the Court is of this view, that this exhibit is just a compilation of the other exhibits already in there.

Mr. Carter: But, Your Honor, Mr. Goodell himself says it's a calculation based upon it which is entirely different.

Judge Huxman: That is what I mean, a compilation made from data already in. It's a simple calculation, and it's either right or it's wrong.

Mr. Goodell: Calculation—it's a reduction of the figures used down to teaching load.

Judge Huxman: The Court is of this view, that we will not ask for an admission at this time, and we will give both parties an opportunity to check this exhibit again, against [fol. 73] the basic data which is contained in these other exhibits, and then, before we start into the trial Monday morning, we will again ask Mr. Goodell whether he is satisfied with the correctness, and we will also ask plaintiff- then if they still contend that this computation is not correct, to have for the benefit of the Court your computation in which you point out the manner and respect in which this is not correct. Now if it is not correct, it shouldn't go in. If it is correct, I know both parties want to agree to it.

Now, that is 16, isn't it?

Mr. Goodell: Yes.

Judge Huxman: That will be passed until Monday morning.

Both parties here have shown a spirit of fairness and cooperation and I see no reason in the world why you shouldn't get together on the question of whether this exhibit is or is not correct.

No. 17:

"That Exhibit I attached hereto and made a part hereof is a correct statement of facts from the records of the Board of Education of the City of Topeka pertaining to teacher load in the first six grades of the elementary schools of the Topeka public school system for the 1950-1951 school year."

[fol. 74] Mr. Carter: We could shorten this, Your Honor, if we might have the same ruling as you made on the last one apply to this one.

Judge Huxman: All right. We pass No. 17 to Monday.

Mr. Brewster: As I understand it, their claim is, using the first series of exhibits, we haven't computed correctly, is that what they mean?

Mr. Goodell: No, they are challenging the reductions we made there.

Judge Huxman: No. 18:

"That Exhibit J attached hereto and made a part hereof is a correct statement of facts from the records of the Board of Education of the City of Topeka pertaining to auditoriums and gymnasiums in the elementary schools of the City of Topeka, Kansas."

Mr. Goodell: I think there is a typographical error in that which I would like to correct.

Judge Huxman: All right. Where is that.

Mr. Goodell: Exhibit "J". On the Monroe School where I have in my exhibit "combination", meaning that they have combination auditorium and gymnasium, that is erroneous, according to my later information, that they do not have a gymnasium, only an auditorium.

Judge Huxman: Only an auditorium.

[fol. 75] Judge Mellott: What do you want to do, strike out the word "combination" and put in the word "yes" under "Auditorium."

Mr. Goodell: That's right and "no" under "Gymnasium."

Judge Huxman: And "no" under "Gymnasium", all right. That correction will be made.

Mr. Carter: Your Honor, we don't feel that we can accept this at this time. We are today, as of today, our experts are now checking these items, and we cannot say whether they are true or not, so we are not willing to accept them as of now.

48

Judge Huxman: We will pass that as we have some of these others until Monday morning.

Judge Mellott: May I inquire if counsel understand that we are expecting you to tell us Monday morning whether these are correct and, if they are not, you will give us what you say the correct data is.

Mr. Carter: I understand that completely.

Judge Huxman: No. 19:

"That no distinction is shown by the Board of Education of the City of Topeka in school plant facilities and equipment, because of race or color. Instead, the same factors are considered and applied by said Board of Education as to plant facilities and equipment in both white and colored [fol. 76] elementary schools."

Mr. Carter: We can't agree to that.

Judge Huxman: All right, plaintiffs will not be required to agree to No. 19.

No. 20:

"That Exhibit K attached hereto and made a part hereof, is a correct statement of facts from the records of the Board of Education of the City of Topeka pertaining to original cost of school buildings in the City of Topeka, Kansas, and correctly states the following:

"1. Name of building or school.
"2. Year of construction.
"3. Structural cost.
"4. Land cost.
"5. Equipment cost."

Mr. Carter: We agree.

Judge Huxman: 20 is agreed to.

No. 21:

"That Exhibit L attached hereto and made a part hereof, is a correct statement from the records of the Board of Education of the City of Topeka pertaining to the present appraised value of the school buildings and equipment, for both white and colored elementary schools; that said appraised value is the appraised value furnished by the appraisers for the insurance underwriters for the purpose of [fol. 77] fixing values of said buildings and equipment for issuing insurance thereon."

Mr. Carter: We agree to that.

Judge Huxman: No. 21 is agreed to.

Now, that completes the defendants' request for agreement.

Judge Mellott: In the light of what has just been gone through, the Exhibits "G" and "K" and "L" seem now to be ready for admission formally, is not that correct, gentlemen?

Mr. Charles Scott: That is correct.

Judge Mellott: The clerk, then, will mark them as admitted in evidence. The others just covered, namely, the others, "H", "I" and "J" may be handed to the clerk and marked for identification only.

How has the map been marked, if at all.

Mr. Goodell: Exhibit "A", Your Honor.

Judge Mellott: Exhibit "A". It may be marked and admitted in evidence, subject to any corrections that counsel may desire to call to the Court's attention based upon the draftsmanship of the map.

Mr. Goodell: I do think this, Your Honor, I want to re-check it. I think since this map was prepared, the copy prepared which came from the map that the Board of Education clerk's office keeps, that there is a segment of that southwest territory that may have been annexed so it wouldn't be correctly outside of the city now.

[fol. 78] Judge Huxman: Yes.

Judge Mellott: Well, I believe we all know and can take judicial notice of the fact that under the statutes of Kansas pertaining to cities of the first class, schools within and adjoining cities of the first class, that the statutes contemplate, and most of the cities of Kansas do, attach to the cities for school purposes territory which is outside of the city, and that is what you refer to as property attached to the city for school purposes.

Mr. Goodell: Yes.

Judge Mellott: Now since your map indicates that certain of that territory has been attached for school purposes but that there may be some inaccuracies in that, you have not

4—8

checked to see if subsequently some of the territory has actually been annexed to and brought into the city for all purposes.

Mr. Goodell: I will reconcile that with all the later annexations.

Judge Huxman: Let me ask you this, Mr. Goodell, is it your understanding that this map is accurate and correct as to the close of the school year?

Mr. Goodell: Yes.

Judge Huxman: Then it would seem to me, that is, on the questions which we have, that what has taken place in the last three or four months or as to the annexation of [fol. 79] additional territory, would not be any factor in determining the constitutionality — the questions before us in this case, do you gentlemen agree with that?

Mr. Charles Scott: Yes.

Judge Huxman: And if this map is correct as drawn, any changes since would not need to be shown.

(A brief recess was here had at the conclusion of which the following further proceedings were had:)

Judge Huxman: Let me address this remark to attorneys for plaintiffs: Has your request for admission No. 1 not already been met by defendants' request for admission 1. There is no difference in them, is there?

Mr. John Scott: Except for the latter part, Your Honor, "That Negro children of elementary school age are compelled to attend one of the four Negro schools aforementioned because of their race and color, pursuant to the custom and usage provided in General Statutes 1949, 72-1724."

Judge Huxman: That is a fact, isn't it?

Mr. John Scott: Yes, sir.

Judge Huxman: I am asking Mr. Goodell now. That latter part is a fact now, isn't it?

Mr. Goodell: I think it's embraced in our stipulation.

Judge Huxman: You do not have that—you do not have [fol. 80] in your request the statement, "Negro children of elementary school age are compelled to attend one of the four negro schools because of their race and color pursuant to the custom and usage provided in G. S. 1949, 72-1724." You do not have that in your——

Mr. Goodell: We don't use the statute; we say they are required to attend instead of compelled.

Judge Huxman: That is a fact that it is because of their——

Mr. Goodell: That's right.

Judge Huxman: All right, then—is it then agreed, gentlemen, that it is a fact and so stipulated for the purpose of this trial that negro children of elementary school age are compelled to attend one of the four negro schools provided for in Topeka because of their race and color pursuant to the custom and usage provided in G. S. 1949, 72-1724.

Mr. Goodell: Well, that is a fact. I don't think the "custom and usage" is provided by the statute. It's simply an authorization, but we won't quibble about that.

Judge Huxman: Suppose we eliminate "custom and usage" as authorized.

Mr. Goodell: That is all right.

Judge Mellott: I understand there isn't any dispute.
[fol. 81] Mr. Goodell: We will admit it.

Judge Mellott: —that they are, you say, required—the word "required" connotes about the same thing as compelled.

Judge Huxman: He objected to the words "custom and usage" provided by the statute. The statute doesn't perhaps provide a custom.

Mr. Goodell: I would say pursuant to the statute.

Judge Huxman: All right. We will put in the word "pursuant", is that agreed to?

Mr. Goodell: Yes.

Judge Huxman: All right.
Now, we will take up No. 2:

"2. That the distance be computed based on city blocks from given points of residence of infant plaintiffs and other Negro children similarly situated, to the designated Negro schools where they must attend as outlined on the official map of the City of Topeka."

Judge Mellott: Since we did not require you to go into that average one, it seems to me that you wouldn't want to insist upon this, would you, Mr. Scott?

Mr. John Scott: Well, if Your Honor please——

Judge Huxman: In other words, do you want to go back [fol. 82] now to the defendants' request No. 8 and add to it what you now have, is that what you want to do?

Mr. John Scott: No, sir. We will withdraw that.

Judge Huxman: You will withdraw request No. 2.

Mr. Carter: No, sir. We are talking about an entirely different point there, Your Honor.

Judge Mellott: I don't understand what you are talking about.

Mr. Carter: I will try to explain it for a moment. When the defendants are talking about averages, insofar as we are concerned, we feel that that is irrelevant because it has nothing to do with the individual disadvantage. When we speak here of a distance which is travelled by individual plaintiffs we are attempting to show an individual disadvantage which these plaintiffs have in making the trip. We are not talking about general averages; we are talking about what affects the individual plaintiff, and I think that is entirely a different point.

Judge Huxman: Mr. Counsel, we didn't permit the defendants to commit you to a yardstick of measuring distances and why should we——

Mr. Carter: We will put on proof to that effect.

[fol. 83] Judge Huxman: Let me just finish my sentence for the record so it doesn't stand up there in the air. Why should we permit you to commit them to a yardstick of measurement?

Request for admission No. 2 is withdrawn.

Request No. 3:

"Infant plaintiffs and other Negro children similarly situated are transported by buses to the Negro schools where they attend and are picked up by said buses at designated points along prescribed routes in accordance with schedules and designated pick-up points outlined by the School Board or its agents. A copy of the schedule of routes is hereto attached marked Exhibit 'A' and made a part hereof."

That schedule has already been agreed to, hasn't it, and request No. 3 will therefore, I presume, be withdrawn.

Judge Mellott: That is Exhibit "G" which has been admitted in evidence with the parenthetical clause, "Bus picks up students also anywhere along the route." eliminated.

Now you gentlemen did tell us, did you not, that you would make inquiry and find out, if you can, by Monday morning whether the parenthetical clause is or is not applicable, can you not do that?

[fol. 84] Mr. John Scott: Yes, sir.

Judge Huxman: That's right.

Judge Mellott: Then that probably covers everything that you have. Now you have a copy of the schedule of routes.

Mr. John Scott: Yes, sir.

Judge Huxman: Is it any different from Exhibit "G"?

Mr. Charles Scott: No.

Mr. John Scott: No, it's exactly the same.

Judge Mellott: Do you propose to offer it in evidence as an additional exhibit?

Mr. John Scott: No, sir. The one that the defendants offered——

Judge Huxman: The entire request No. 3 is withdrawn in view of the admissions already made.

Mr. John Scott: That's right, sir.

Judge Huxman: Request for admission No. 4:

"That no provision made for shelter or protection against inclement weather conditions or safety regulations at designated pick-up points for infant plaintiffs and other Negro children similarly situated while waiting for the arrival of their respective buses."

[fol. 85] What do the attorneys for the defendant say as to that request?

Mr. Goodell: We don't have shelter-houses, so I would say we do admit that. "Safety regulations" is pretty broad. I don't know what they mean by that.

Judge Huxman: Well, what would you say to this: Safety regulations other than those provided for traffic generally.

Mr. Brewster: The board of education doesn't provide the lights anyway.

Mr. Goodell: In Topeka the Police Department and the

54

traffic control division have jurisdiction over those matters.

Judge Huxman: Don't you gentlemen feel that the question of safety regulations could be deleted? What value is there to——

Mr. John Scott: Well, if Your Honor please——

Judge Huxman: Now you can show, if you want to, that there are no added regulations or precautions. Of course the Court will take knowledge, in the absence of anything else, that the usual conditions with respect to traffic and travel in the city obtains, and no other, unless it's shown.

Mr. John Scott: Yes, I think that is sufficient, don't [fol. 86] you?

Mr. Carter: Yes.

Mr. John Scott: I think that is sufficient.

Judge Huxman: Then is it agreed that request for admission No. 4, as follows, is agreed to:

"That no provision made for shelter or protection against inclement weather"—"That no provision is made for shelter or protection against inclement weather conditions."

Do the defendants agree to that?

Mr. Goodell: That is correct.

Judge Huxman: And we will omit from your request the reference to any additional safety regulations.

Mr. John Scott: Yes, sir.

Judge Huxman: I didn't go quite far enough, Mr. Reporter. The admission should read as follows:

"That no provision is made for shelter or protection against inclement weather conditions at designated pick-up points for infant plaintiffs and other Negro children similarly situated while waiting for the arrival of their respective buses."

That is the admission as it is agreed to.

Judge Mellott: The affirmative answer was made by counsel for the School Board.

Mr. Goodell: Yes.

[fol. 87] Judge Huxman: No. 5:

"That said buses make only two trips a day to and fro to the respective all Negro schools in the morning as prescribed"——

Judge Mellott: We don't have the exhibit, so I suppose——

Judge Huxman: Would you object if we substituted for your Exhibit "A" the number of their exhibit to which——

Judge Mellott: Exhibit "G".

Mr. John Scott: That will be perfectly all right.

Judge Huxman: "in the morning as prescribed in Defendants' Exhibit 'G' admitted in the record and in the evening at the close of school."

Judge Mellott: I understand that is admitted.

Mr. John Scott: Yes, sir.

Judge Mellott: Correct, Mr. Goodell?

Mr. Goodell: Yes.

Judge Huxman: I wanted to stop there purposely; so far you admit that much of the request of No. 5.

Mr. Goodell: The schedule shows that they are taken to the school in the morning and returned at night.

[fol. 88] Judge Huxman: Now, we will take up the rest of the request because we might run into trouble there. The further request is made for an admission, "As a result, infant plaintiffs and other Negro children similarly situated are required to spend the entire day at their respective school without the opportunity and benefit of seeing their parents during the noon hour and are required to eat cold lunches which are prepared by their parents before leaving home in the morning."

Mr. Goodell: We are not prepared to admit. It's a conclusion.

Judge Huxman: That is a conclusion, isn't it, that flows from the admission.

Mr. John Scott: We can prove that, Your Honor.

Judge Huxman: That portion of the request will be denied.

Mr. Goodell: I don't think it's a proper issue in the case because they are treated no differently than white children. If they want to go home for lunch, they go, and if they don't, they stay and eat lunch.

Judge Huxman: That is argumentative, in any event.

Request No. 6:

"That the respective buses are without any supervisor other than the driver to exercise disciplinary measures [fol. 89] and control of said children."

Is that agreed to?

Mr. Goodell: I don't think we send a guard along; I believe that is accurate; we just have a driver.

Judge Huxman: You agree to that, then.

Mr. Goodell: I would like to check it. I think it's correct.

Judge Huxman: Let's put it this way, you agree to that, subject to your right to check and withdraw your agreement if your further investigation shows otherwise.

Mr. Goodell: Yes.

Judge Huxman: No. 7:

"That Buchanan School does not have an auditorium or gymnasium; such facilities are available at Sumner,"— before we go further, gentlemen, we have already covered the question of auditoriums and gymnasiums in the series of exhibits designated "J".

Mr. John Scott: Yes, sir.

Judge Mellott: We have not yet admitted "J", but you were to——

Mr. John Scott: —check it.

Judge Mellott: —check it and give us any corrections on Monday morning.

Mr. John Scott: That's right.

Judge Huxman: Then we should not agree to request [fol. 90] No. 7 here and that can be ironed out on your investigation as to Exhibit "J", as proffered by the defendant.

Mr. John Scott: Yes. We will withdraw that.

Judge Huxman: Request for admission No. 7 is withdrawn because of these other matters in the record.

No. 8:

"That Monroe School's playground or a portion thereof is separated by a public thoroughfare adjacent to the building and located on the easterly side of said playground is the A. T. S. F. Railroad right-of-way and track."

Is that a fact, Mr. Goodell?

Mr. Goodell: I believe that is accurate, yes.

Judge Huxman: Then you admit request No. 8 as read.

Mr. Goodell: Yes.

Judge Huxman: All right.

No. 9:

"That no provisions are made for electrically operated school stop signs and safety signals at any of the Negro schools and no safety measures are provided for Infant Plaintiffs and other Negro children similarly situated who are required to cross the intersection of First and Kansas [fol. 91] Avenue at a time when the vehicular traffic is dense, while they are enroute to the designated bus pick-up points and at other busy intersections throughout the City of Topeka where Infant Plaintiffs and other Negro children similarly situated are required to cross enroute to designated bus pick-up points."

Mr. Goodell: We can't admit that because it isn't an accurate statement. Furthermore, we have no control over traffic lights, electric devices. The City of Topeka Police Department takes traffic counts at various points in town and, from their determination, decide that a designated point should have school blinker signs, and we have several cases, the evidence will show if we get in that point,—in several cases requested signs which they on the traffic count didn't think it was justified and wouldn't put them in. We don't have any control over it.

Mr. John Scott: If Your Honor please——

Judge Huxman: Didn't we, when we had up defendants' request for agreement, agree that there were no extra safety or traffic regulations provided at these places.

Mr. Goodell: I don't think so. There are some——

Judge Mellott: Let me ask this question: You agree, do you not, Mr. Scott and counsel for the plaintiffs, that Mr. [fol. 91a] Goodell is correct in his statement that the Board of Education has nothing whatever to do with putting in blinker lights and safety devices for school children and others to cross the public streets, but at best, can only request that the traffic department of the state and the city police department take care of those matters; do you not agree that that is a fact?

Mr. John Scott: We agree that that is a fact and also, to extend that, Your Honor, I think the first part of that request is a fact, that there are no——

Judge Mellott: Well, I suppose that if you divide the

request, there may be some merit, "That no provisions are made for electrically operated school stop signs and safety signals at any of the Negro schools." Now, I suppose——

Mr. Goodell: If the Court please, that is not accurate.

Judge Mellott: Then you should not agree upon it.

Mr. John Scott: It is accurate.

Mr. Goodell: No, it isn't accurate.

Mr. John Scott: We can prove it, Your Honor.

Judge Huxman: The Court feels that that is a very minor matter, whatever the electrical arrangements are or aren't, and, if you can't agree on it, it will take only fif-
[fol. 92] teen minutes of evidence to establish what the fact is.

Mr. Goodell: They make a broad statement, as I understand it, no safety devices in any of the areas traversed by the colored children to go to their schools——

Judge Huxman: They don't say that at all.

(Colloquy was here had off the record.)

Mr. Goodell: For example, on 10th Street, you have Parkdale School and Washington School in very close proximity. The negro children who have to cross 10th Street to get to Washington School that walk and don't ride, they use that traffic sign—I mean there is a designated crossing for school children where they cross over 10th there for Parkdale. Now it's splitting hairs to say that is solely for Parkdale and no benefit to Washington.

Judge Huxman: Well, the Court feels that is a minor matter.

Mr. Goodell: We have got that situation in other parts of town.

Judge Huxman: It's a simple matter, and we will not require the parties to agree on that—request No. 9.

Mr. John Scott: We can prove it very easily, Your Honor.

[fol. 93] Judge Huxman: I believe the attorneys for the plaintiffs will agree that this case, the outcome, doesn't hinge upon that one little factor; I doubt whether it's going to be determinative too much.

Now, does that conclude plaintiffs' requests for admissions?

Mr. John Scott: Yes, sir.

Judge Huxman: We want to ask at this point counsel for the State of Kansas whether they have at this time any requests for admissions of fact in addition to what has been agreed to and, if not, whether they go along with, and agree to, these admissions which have been made by the respective parties to this litigation.

Mr. McQueary: If Your Honor please, the position of the State of Kansas, insofar as this lawsuit or this controversy is concerned, is going to be to endeavor to uphold the constitutionality of the statute in question, and our participation will be limited to that field, and so far as equal facilities or the conditions provided by the Board of Education of the City of Topeka or the facilities enjoyed by the negro, by the plaintiffs, we are not going to make that a matter of issue insofar as we are concerned. We have no knowledge as to that; we haven't investigated it. That will be left solely to the other parties in this matter.

Judge Huxman: Then I understand your position is that you have no request for admissions of fact.

[fol. 94] Mr. McQueary: We have none, Your Honor.

Judge Huxman: And that the state has no interest in these admissions which have been made by the parties, the plaintiff and defendant, other than the state, because you do not think that they touch the state's phase of this case.

Mr. McQueary: That is a correct statement.

Judge Huxman: All right.

Mr. Goodell: I have one more matter. I would like to request a stipulation that the—as an exhibit, that seventeen cites, first and second class cities of the State of Kansas, operate separate colored and white schools in the elementary grades, and I have an exhibit.

Judge Huxman: I am not sure that I understand that, Mr. Goodell.

Mr. Goodell: I have an exhibit with the names of the cities showing that seventeen cities in the State of Kansas are operating their elementary school systems similar to Topeka—strike that—operating separate white and colored schools in the elementary grades pursuant to the same statute.

Judge Huxman: Is there any objection to that admission?

60

Mr. Greenberg: Yes, Your Honor. We object on the [fol. 95] ground that what may happen in any other city in the State of Kansas is not relevant to the rights of our particular plaintiffs who operate in this school system here and now.

Judge Huxman: Since there is one member of the Court not here, in any event we will—and since this is the trial court, we will receive it. You have no objection to the correctness of the statement.

Mr. Greenberg: We don't know, as a matter fact; we haven't——

Judge Huxman: You have no reason to doubt the correctness of the statement.

Mr. Greenberg: We have had no occasion to investigate it because we haven't thought it pertinent.

Judge Huxman: The exhibit will be received subject to its materiality.

Judge Mellott: It will be marked as Exhibit "M", Defendants' Exhibit "M".

Judge Huxman: Also subject to the right of counsel before trial, if he so desires, to attack it as to its correctness.

Mr. Greenberg: That is agreeable.

Judge Huxman: Is there anything else?

Judge Mellott: That may be taken up Monday also.

[fol. 96] Judge Huxman: Is there anything else now, gentlemen?

Judge Mellott has a matter that he would like to inquire about. Go ahead, judge.

Judge Mellott: I was only going to suggest to my associates on the bench that we may not have covered categorically sub-division (6) of Rule 16 which says that it's proper for us at a pre-trial to give consideration to such other matters as may aid in the disposition of the action. That is, of course, only a general statement. Does either side care to suggest, in line with that sub-section, any other matters which you think might be taken up with the Court at this time which would aid in the disposition of the action.

Mr. Goodell: I think of none, Your Honor.

Judge Mellott: Very well. The concluding sentences of the rule under which we are now functioning provides that, "The court shall make an order which recites the action taken at the conference, the amendments allowed to the pleadings, and the agreements made by the parties as to any of the matters considered, and which limits the issues for trial to those not disposed of by admissions or agreements of counsel;".

Now, where a pre-trial is handled as intelligently and as expeditiously as this has been handled by reason of the [fol. 97] preliminary requests for admissions having been made and secured to some extent, it seems to me that perhaps it is wholly unnecessary for this tribunal to make any order because your record itself shows just what disposition has been made.

Counsel may desire to secure from the reporter copies of what has been accomplished, but I believe that the way in which this has been handled that everybody has it pretty well in mind, and I am suggesting that perhaps it would be mere supererogation and wholly unnecessary for the Court in this particular instance to dictate into the record a lengthy order inasmuch as Judge Huxman has pretty well covered that as we have proceeded.

Do you think this Court should make a separate order or not?

Mr. Goodell: No, I think not.

Judge Huxman: All right. Anything else that anyone has to suggest which might tend to expedite this hearing before we recess. If not, the pre-trial conference will be recessed until 10:00 o'clock Monday morning when we will take up for final disposition the matters that we have left here in abeyance and which you gentlemen on your respective parts will investigate and see if you can satisfy yourselves, and we will then make final disposition of that and immediately go into the trial of this case at the conclusion —final conclusion of the pre-trial conference.

* * * * * * *

[fol. 98] (Reporter's Note:) The further proceedings in the pre-trial conference had on June 25, 1951, are contained in the transcript of proceedings of the hearing proper.

* * * * * * *

Reporter's Certificate (omitted in printing).

[fol. 99] [File endorsement omitted]

In United States District Court

[Title omitted]

Order Correcting Transcript of Record—Filed August 27, 1951

It has been called to the attention of the Court that certain minor typographical errors exist in the certified record filed in the Court in the above entitled cause. The Court Reporter has checked the record and confirms the existence of these minor typographical errors.

So that the record may speak the truth, it is considered, ordered and adjudged that it be corrected in the following respects:

That on Page 10, Line 4, the name "Dr. Spee" be corrected to read "Dr. Speer"; that on Page 56, Line 2, the phrase "Hold are they" be corrected to read "How old are they?"; that on Page 115 in the last two lines the word "depredations" be changed to read "deprevations"; that on Page 119, Line 2, the sentence there should be made [fols. 100-103] to read ". . . United States *there* are . . ."; that the index record be corrected to correctly reflect the name of Horace B. English as it appears on Page 145 of the record; that at Page 162, Line 4, the phrase "minor groups" be changed to read "minority groups"; that on Page 164 in Line 7 from the bottom the word "roll" be changed to "role"; that at Page 169 the record be corrected to show "direct examination was by Mr. Carter"; that at Page 173 in the third line of the paragraph marked "Q" the last word "them" be deleted; that at Page 212 in Line 9 from the bottom the word "minitors" be changed to "monitors"; that at Page 219, 11 Lines from the top, the sentence should read "of the entire school system?"; that at Page 248, 6 Lines from the bottom, the semi-colon after the word "individual" be changed to a comma; that at Page 249, 12 Lines from the top the word "disadvantages" be changed to "disadvantaged"; that at Page 251 and 255 where the case name McLawrin appears the record be changed to show the name of the case to be "McLaurin".

It is by the Court further considered, ordered and adjudged that a filing of this order constitute the correction of the record and that copies of this order be furnished to the parties requesting or now having a copy of the record.

(S.) Walter A. Huxman, United States Circuit Judge.

[fol. 104]   In United States District Court

[Title omitted]

[fol. 105]   Transcript of Proceedings—Filed October 16, 1951

[fol. 106]   Be it remembered, on this 25th day of June, A.D. 1951, the above matter coming on for hearing before Honorable Walter A. Huxman, Judge, United States Court of Appeals, Tenth Circuit; Honorable Arthur J. Mellott, Judge, United States District Court, District of Kansas, and Honorable Delmas C. Hill, Judge, United States District Court, District of Kansas, duly constituted as a Three-Judge Court under Chap. 155, Title 28, U.S.C., and the parties appearing in person and/or by counsel, as hereinabove set forth, the following proceedings were had:

[fol. 107] Colloquy Between Court and Counsel

Judge Huxman: I take it there are no additional parties to be entered of record. All of that was done the other day, was it? Anyone else to be entered as an attorney of record?

Mr. Goodell: If the Court please, this is Mr. Bannon, attorney for the Board of Education of Leavenworth, Kansas.

Judge Huxman: Do you desire to have your name entered as——

Mr. Bannon: As appearing, Your Honor, but I do not know whether or not the Board might ask for authority to file a brief at some later stage of the proceeding.

Judge Huxman: All right.

Mr. Goodell: The attorney for the Board of Education at Coffeyville.

Judge Mellott: I suppose he should be admitted only as amicus curiae at this time since he filed no pleading.

Mr. Goodell: I suppose so.

Mr. Dallas Knapp, attorney for the Board of Education at Coffeyville called me and asked to have his name entered and wanted to be allowed to participate for filing a brief.

Judge Huxman: Well, we will have his name entered at this time, and we will determine——

[fol. 108] Mr. Goodell: The same is true of Mr. Hal Harlan, of Manhattan, Kansas, who is attorney for the Board of Education there.

Judge Huxman: What do they desire?

Mr. Goodell: To have his name entered and be permitted to file a brief.

Judge Huxman: His name will be entered, and the question of filing of briefs amicus curiae will be determined at the conclusion of the hearing.

Mr. Goodell: Surely.

Judge Huxman: Now, at the conclusion of our pre-trial conference Friday there were certain matters that were passed for final determination this morning. The first one I have noted is Stipulation 16, which reads as follows: "That Exhibit "H", attached hereto and made a part hereof, is a correct statement of facts from the records of the Board of Education of the City of Topeka, pertaining to teacher load in the kindergarten of the Topeka public schools for the 1950 and 1951 school years." Attorneys for plaintiff wanted opportunity to check into that. What do you say this morning?

Mr. Carter: We are willing to accept that.

Offers in Evidence

Judge Mellott: Let the record show Exhibit "H" is formally admitted then in evidence.

Defendants' Exhibit "H", having been offered and [fol. 109] *received in evidence*, is contained in the case file.

Judge Huxman: All right. Request 17; "That Exhibit 'I', attached hereto and made a part hereof, is a correct statement of facts from the Board of Education of the City of Topeka, pertaining to teacher load in the first six grades of the elementary schools of the Topeka public school system for the school years 1950 and 1951."

Mr. Carter: We will accept that, too.

Judge Huxman: The record may show that their request No. 17 is agreed to, stipulated, and that Exhibit "I" is admitted.

Defendants' Exhibit "I", having been offered and received in evidence, is contained in the case file.

Judge Huxman: Request No. 18, "That Exhibit 'J', attached hereto and made a part hereof, is a correct statement of facts from the records of the Board of Education of the City of Topeka pertaining to auditoriums and gymnasiums in the elementary schools of the City of Topeka, Kansas."

Mr. Carter: On that we have a question, Your Honor; definition, I suppose. Our investigation reveals——

Judge Huxman: I didn't understand.

Mr. Carter: We have a question. I suppose it's one of definition and——

Judge Huxman: Let's look at Exhibit "J". Is that in [fol. 110] the original exhibits?

Mr. Carter: That is in the supplement attached to the supplement that you were reading; pertains to auditoriums and gymnasiums.

Mr. Goodell: Which one are you talking about now?

Mr. Carter: Exhibit "J".

Mr. Goodell: Any particular part of Exhibit "J"?

Judge Huxman: All right. Now what is it?

Mr. Carter: We are unable to accept the definition under "Buchanan" "Yes", as having an auditorium because our investigation shows that there are two rooms, makeshift rooms, that have been thrown together in which there are chairs. Now we think that is totally different from the feeling of an auditorium which has been built in the school. With that reservation, we will accept that part.

Judge Huxman: If we eliminated "Buchanan" do you accept the statements in Exhibit "J" as to the auditorium and gymnasium in Central Park, Clay—what are the three colored schools?

Mr. Goodell: Monroe.

Judge Huxman: Do you accept the rest of the exhibit with the exception of that pertaining to Buchanan?

Mr. Carter: Well, just three items, Your Honor. If you [fol. 111] read down there to Lafayette——

Judge Huxman: Is that a colored school?

Mr. Carter: No, sir; that is not. It is shown here "yes" an auditorium, "no" gymnasium. We have found that there is a playroom in the school building which is ample, and we think that that should be entered on the record.

Mr. Goodell: We say "yes" it has an auditorium.

Judge Huxman: Suppose we change the "no" to "playroom", what do you say, Mr. Goodell?

Mr. Goodell: I don't think it's accurate; neither is his statement accurate about Buchanan. We will offer evidence on it.

Judge Huxman: All right. If you can't agree, we will eliminate Lafayette from the exhibit.

Mr. Carter: And we have the same——

Judge Huxman: Just a minute. How about Buchanan? You won't agree to Buchanan as stated in the exhibit?

Mr. Carter: No, sir.

Judge Huxman: We will eliminate Buchanan.

Mr. Carter: We agree with everything else on the exhibit with the exception of Polk and Potwin and in both of those schools there are playrooms, even though there is no gymnasiums.

Judge Huxman: Polk and Potwin. All right. We will [fol. 112] eliminate Polk and Potwin. With Buchanan, Lafayette, Polk and Potwin eliminated, do you agree to Exhibit "J" as it now remains?

Mr. Carter: Yes, sir.

Judge Huxman: The record will then shown that it is agreed that Exhibit "J", with Buchanan, Lafayette, Polk and Potwin eliminated therefrom, will be admitted and received in the record as evidence.

Defendants' Exhibit "J", as agreed to above, having been offered and received in evidence, is contained in the case file.

Judge Huxman: Now, that is all that I have marked that was left for consideration today. Have I omitted anything?

Mr. Carter: No, sir, not that I know of.

Judge Huxman: Any other stipulations that the parties wish or can agree to as to evidence?

Mr. John Scott: If the Court please, we have prepared a map of the City of Topeka for the purpose of showing valuations of the buildings that are located within the City of Topeka school district.

Judge Huxman: That is a- evaluation of the school buildings?

Mr. John Scott: The school buildings; that is correct, sir, and we would like to enter this as a stipulation in this [fol. 113] particular case.

Mr. Goodell: I couldn't agree to that without knowing something about it. Who appraised it?

Mr. John Scott: Dr. Speer.

Mr. Goodell: I wouldn't agree to such a thing as that. It's some school teacher that gave an expert opinion about——

Mr. John Scott: It's no such a thing.

Judge Huxman: Now, gentlemen, don't get to quarreling with each other before the real trial starts.

Mr. John Scott: This was taken from your exhibits.

Judge Huxman: Now, just a minute; you address your remarks to the Court, please. If you can't agree to it, why you can offer it in the due course of time, and we will then rule on it at that time.

Judge Mellott makes this suggestion, and I agree with him: This case to the Court is just another burden that we have in a trial to be decided by us and approached by us just as any other case that comes before the Court. It will be the endeavor of the Court to decide this case according to the law and the evidence. We realize that, of course, there is considerable sentiment in this case that you can't get away from. We trust that, first, there will be no quarreling or bickering among counsel; it's not [fol. 114] called for; it isn't necessary; doesn't add anying to the value of the case. We trust that counsel will keep that in mind. Also, there will be no demonstration on the part of the audience or spectators in any way. This, of course, is a public trial. We want all those who are interested to be here; but the decorum that is maintained in federal courts must be maintained throughout the trial.

Is there anything else before we proceed to the trial of the case? If not, the Court is ready to proceed with the trial of case No. T-316, Orville Brown and others vs. Board of Education of Topeka, Shawnee County, Kansas.

Mr. Carter: If Your Honor please, plaintiffs would like to invoke Rule 43(b) of the Federal Rules of Civil Procedure and call as the first witness the president of the Board of Education, Mr. Kelsey Petry.

Judge Mellott: That is what, calling your adversary as a hostile witness?

Mr. Carter: Yes, sir.

Judge Mellott: "A party may interrogate any unwilling or hostile witness by leading questions. A party may call an adverse party or an officer, director, or managing agent" and so forth. Proceed.

Judge Huxman: You may proceed.

Judge Mellott: The witness that was called come forward; Mr. Speer, was that his name?

[fol. 115] Mr. Goodell: It is my understanding that this witness was out of the city.

Judge Huxman: Who is the witness?

Mr. Goodell: Mr. Petry, who is president of the board.

Judge Huxman: Is he here? Is Mr. Petry here?

Mr. Goodell: He was out of the city, I think, when the subpoena was issued, in Colorado.

Mr. Carter: Then we will call Mr. Saville.

Judge Huxman: Mr. Saville present? Come forward and be sworn.

ARTHUR H. SAVILLE, having been first duly sworn, assumed the stand and testified as follows:

Direct examination.

By Mr. Carter:

Q. Mr. Saville, how long have you been a member of the Board of Education of Topeka?

A. About twelve years.

Judge Mellott: May I have the witness' name?
The Witness: Arthur H. Saville.

By Mr. Carter:

Q. What are your duties and responsibilities as a member of the Board of Education?
[fol. 116]   A. To adopt policies that are carried out by the school administration, build a budget and various things of that sort.

Q. Does the Board of Education promulgate rules and regulations governing the entire school system of Topeka?
A. Yes, sir.

Q. You maintain, do you not, eighteen schools, elementary schools, in Topeka that are located in eighteen territories, is that correct?
A. Elementary schools? I think there are twenty-two.

Judge Huxman: Isn't that all stipulated to, the number of schools that are maintained.
Mr. Carter: Yes, sir; it's stipulated to, but I am leading up to a question.
Judge Huxman: All right.

By Mr. Carter:

Q. Well, you maintain a total of twenty-two.
A. I believe so, yes, that is correct.

Q. Eighteen are for white children and four for negro children.
A. That's right.

Q. Now, why is it that the Board of Education requires negro children to attend the four separate schools in Topeka?

Mr. Goodell: Object to that as incompetent, irrelevant and immaterial and invading the province of the Court. The pleadings show the issues are joined, that they are doing it, [fol. 117] and they are doing it under a permissive statute, 72-1724. The personal feelings of a board member has nothing to do——
Judge Huxman: I think the objection will be sustained.
Mr. Carter: I think, if I may——

Judge Huxman: It's agreed they are doing it under statute and the ordinance of the City of Topeka.

Mr. Carter: I know that, Your Honor, but I think that I would be entitled to inquire as to whether there are any rules and regulations that the board adopted.

Judge Huxman: You did inquire that and you ask him now why they maintain them. The objection is sustained.

By Mr. Carter:

Q. In your opinion, as a member of the Board of Education, would the board—wouldn't the board have a much simpler problem, since it must maintain the high schools on an unsegregated basis, to integrate negro and white children at the elementary school level?

Mr. Goodell: Object to that as incompetent, irrelevant and immaterial, not having any probative force on the issues in this case.

Judge Huxman: The objection will be sustained.

By Mr. Carter:

Q. Mr. Saville, are you familiar with the document known [fol. 118] as the comprehensive plan of the City of Topeka and Shawnee County, Kansas. I might add that this was—this document was sponsored jointly by the Board of City Commissioners, the Board of County Commissioners and the Board of Education of Topeka and, at the time of the sponsorship, your name, A. H. Saville, is listed as being on the board.

A. Yes.

Q. You are familiar with this.

A. Is that the Bartholomew plan?

Q. Yes, sir.

A. I believe I remember it.

Q. Can you tell me whether or not this plan has been adopted, is being followed at the present time by the Board of Education.

Mr. Goodell: Object to that as incompetent, irrelevant and immaterial; has to do with a long-range view building plan; outside the issues of the case.

Judge Huxman: The objection will be overruled. He may answer.

71

The Witness: Frankly, I don't remember. What was the date of that?

By Mr. Carter:

Q. The document was published May, 1945.

A. I couldn't tell you; I couldn't answer that yes or no.

Q. You can't say whether before this document was [fol. 119] published you looked at it as a member of the Board of Education and approved it.

A. Yes, I looked at it—I am familiar to some extent with the contents of the document, but I have no recollection at this time what's contained in it.

Q. Well, if I may, I would like to address your attention to several extracts from the document and find whether this is the policy of the board or whether you approved of it. The document reads as follows, under Schools, Chapter 7. "Schools and Recreational Facilities. No city affords satisfactory living facilities unless adequate parks and schools are available to all persons living therein. Just as the economic welfare of the community is largely dependent upon the extent and diversity of its commerce and industry, the mental and physical wellbeing of the population are largely dependent upon the educational and recreational facilities available. The vital role which public education plays in democracy has long been recognized." Would you subscribe to that statement?

Mr. Goodell: We object to that as pursuit here of an academic matter of a report prepared by Bartholomew which this witness didn't prepare.

Judge Huxman: What's the purpose of this line of questioning?

Mr. Carter: This is a document, Your Honor, which was [fol. 120] sponsored by the Board of Education. It is true that it sets up a long-range plan. The document was prepared by Harlan Bartholomew, but it is indicated in the document that changes were made in it, and so forth, at the suggestion of the various people here listed, the members of the Board of Education. I think that I am entitled to attempt to find out whether or not this witness, as a member of the Board of Education, either had anything to do with the preparation of the document, whether he agrees with the

72

statements, some of the statements which are listed here and whether they are being followed. Now, Mr. Saville indicates he does not know whether this plan is now being followed by the Board of Education.

Judge Huxman: Mr. Counsel, the question before the Court in this case is not what the viewpoint of anyone is or might be as to the future, the present or the past; but it seems to me the question in this case turns upon what the City of Topeka has and is doing, and what they may think about it is immaterial, if they are furnishing adequate facilities. If they are doing that, then what they are thinking about is immaterial. The objection to this line of questioning is sustained.

Mr. Carter: Your Honor, I don't want to press this point too much, but I think the Court is being unduly severe. [fol. 121] There are statements in here which have to do with a question of the adequacy of facilities.

Judge Huxman: That is a long-range program laid down by a man, Bartholomew, who is not even a member of the Board of Education. It has nothing to do with what the City of Topeka is doing or is not doing with regard to its school system. No, the objection will be sustained. That line of questioning will not be pursued.

Mr. Carter: All right, Your Honor. I think that is all.

Judge Huxman: Any questions?

Mr. Goodell: No questions.

Judge Huxman: Any need for this witness remaining longer or may he be excused from attendance?

Mr. Carter: We have no further need for him.

Judge Huxman: You are not required to attend further upon the Court.

(Witness excused.)

KENNETH MCFARLAND, having been first duly sworn, assumed the stand and testified as follows:

Direct examination.

By Mr. Carter:

Q. Mr. McFarland, you are at present the superintendent [fol. 122] of schools of Topeka, Kansas?

A. Correct.

Q. How long have you been superintendent?

A. Nine years.

Q. Are there any rules and regulations that you know of that are in force with regard to the choice of schools by negro pupils in the school system, among the four that are set aside for them?

A. Well, we have administered the schools as they were organized at the time this administration took over in 1942. The four negro districts were established at that time.

Q. What I am driving at is what determines, in terms of the place in the city where a negro child lives, what determines what school that child will attend?

A. Those districts were drawn prior to 1942 and adopted by the Board of Education, and we have administered them in essentially the same form.

Q. Well, may I have what they are?

A. Well, you have a map.

Judge Huxman: Doctor, what he asks is what determines the location, if you know. Is that what you want?

Mr. Carter: I am trying to ask—there are four negro schools—the white schools—the school system is divided into territories. That apparently is not true of the negro [fol. 123] schools. Now a negro who lives—out let's say—let's say the Randolph area, what determines what school, what colored school, he or she will attend? That is what I am trying to find out. Are there any rules about that? ered by the admitted state of facts.

Mr. Goodell: Object to this as already having been covered by the admitted state of facts.

Judge Huxman: I am sorry; repeat that question.

(The last preceding question was here read by the reporter.)

Mr. Goodell: The objection is that this is in conflict with the admitted statement of facts.

Judge Mellott: Was it admitted? I have overlooked it, and that is what I was asking Judge Huxman, is the reason he didn't hear you. In paragraph 2, I believe, of your original stipulation——

Mr. Goodell: On Page 2, Your Honor, there was that—that portion was not agreed to.

Judge Mellott: That is what I thought.

Mr. Goodell: I withdraw my objection.

Mr. Carter: That is what I am trying to find out.

Mr. Goodell: Our pleadings allege that a colored child may attend any one of the four colored schools based upon [fol. 124] the selection of his parents.

Judge Mellott: As I recollect it, counsel did not agree upon that Friday, so I think he should pursue it.

Judge Huxman: The witness may answer.

The Witness: Theoretically, the plan would be to give the best coverage possible with four buildings in relationship to where children live and with relationship to bus routes, and so forth.

By Mr. Carter:

Q. Now, Mr. McFarland, the defendants have introduced a series of exhibits relating to school program, teacher salaries, bus schedules and transportation costs. Are you familiar with those exhibits?

A. Not in detail. I am familiar with the fact that the exhibits were prepared and delivered to the counsel.

Q. They were prepared in your office.

A. By my office, yes.

Mr. Carter: If I may get the exhibit "F"(1) to "F"(22).

Mr. Goodell: You have copies of that.

Mr. Carter: All right.

By Mr. Carter:

Q. I want to direct your attention—these are the exhibits. Now, those exhibits "F"(1) to (22) relate to the school schedule program for the school year in each of the schools. [fol. 125] Judge Mellott: You said "F"(22).

Mr. Carter: "F"(1) to (22) covering the twenty-two schools.

By Mr. Carter:

Q. That is the school program for each of the schools. What I want to know, we do not have any information as to the hours that school is in session. Would you have that at your fingertips?

A. Well, 9:00 o'clock until 4:00 o'clock is the general hour for elementary schools.

Q. Is there any difference with respect to—does that apply from the first grade through the sixth grade?

A. No, first grades convene a little later, adjourn a little earlier, so do kindergartens. They also have different schedules for the first few weeks of school than they do later.

Q. Without regard for the first few weeks of school, I would like to get the accurate figures on that, if available. When does kindergarten convene and when does it let out?

A. Well, we have let the kindergartens out at 11:30.

Q. They convene at 9:00?

A. And convene at 9:00.

Q. Do you have any in the afternoons?

A. 1:30 and 3:30.

Q. 1:30 and 3:30.

A. I think most of those——

[fol. 126] Q. What about the first year, the first grade?

A. We usually, during warm weather, when the schools first start, we are more lenient on those; we will start about fifteen minutes later.

Q. That would be 9:15.

A. 9:15. We will let them out at 11:30 and sometimes 11:45.

Q. 11:30, 11:45. They reconvene at what time?

A. 1:30, 1:15.

Q. Until 4:00. What about the second through sixth?

A. 1:15 to 4:00.

Q. What about the morning schedule?

A. 9:00 to 12:00.

Q. 9:00 to 12:00. An hour for lunch.

A. Right; an hour or a half or an hour and fifteen minutes, depending.

Q. In order that I may be absolutely correct on this, you have half session of kindergarten, half day of kindergarten from 9:00 to 11:30 or from 1:30 to 3:30.

Judge Huxman: Answer, doctor.
The Witness: Yes.

By Mr. Carter:

Q. You have in the first grade, you convene at approximately 9:00 or 9:15; you let out at approximately 11:30, 11:45.

A. Right.

Q. And reconvene at 1:15 to 4:00.

[fol. 127] A. That's right; those are approximately right. There are some variations in that. We have a schedule here, if you want it, admitted in evidence.

Q. If you have the schedule.

A. We have a complete schedule of that and will be glad to get it.

Q. Well, I think it would be—if it's here I would like to see it because I am going to ask some questions.

Mr. Goodell: If the Court please, we introduced, and it's admitted, the program. I don't understand—do you claim they don't get as many hours of instruction?

Mr. Carter: What I am trying to find out is the hours of the classes. You have introduced the program but not the hours of the school.

Mr. Goodell: If the Court please, we submit it would be immaterial unless he claims there is disparity between the two schools as to hours of instruction.

Judge Huxman: I don't see much probative value to that unless there is discrimination, if you will not pursue it too far——

Mr. Carter: I am going to ask some questions on it, Your Honor, and I think the questions will be germane. I wanted [fol. 128] to be certain that Mr. McFarland is certain of his hours. I don't want to have an approximation, and I am not trying to lead you or trap you. I merely want to get the facts. I think it's important for us to know the school schedule.

The Witness: We should prepare a schedule and hand it to you for every school, in that case.

By Mr. Carter:

Q. You mean there are differences?
A. And differences in season, difference in time.

Judge Huxman: Does counsel contend there is a discrimination in those hours between colored schools and white schools?

Mr. Carter: We are trying to find out something which we think is—affects the school program with regard to a particular school in terms of—that would—it would be important for us to know what hours the classes are in session, and it is for that reason I am particularly anxious to find that out.

Judge Huxman: Do you contend there is any discrimination between the hours in the colored schools and in the white schools?

Mr. Carter: That is not what we are directing it to, Your Honor. We would contend there is discrimination if certain facts occur with regard to the hours that the school operates. For example, I would be interested chiefly in [fol. 129] Washington School. I am chiefly interested in what the schedule is in Washington School, particularly the first grade, kindergarten and the second to sixth grade.

Judge Huxman: Mr. Counsel, the Court feels that this is purely a fishing expedition at this time. You don't make an allegation that there is discrimination in the hours of school in colored schools as against the white schools. You are just, by your frank admission, you are stating that you are trying to see whether there is or not. The Court is going to sustain this objection; going to sustain an objection to this line of questioning at this time. You have an opportunity at recess to get this schedule and go over it. If you can find anything material in it, why you may then pursue this line of examination and Dr. McFarland will be available. But just to go into a fishing expedition in all of this line of testimony, the Court doesn't think it's proper. The objection will be sustained at this time.

Doctor, you will make available to counsel those schedules for their examination, if you have them.

The Witness: We have them.

Judge Huxman: Then if you want to renew your request for this examination later on, you may pursue it, but at this time the objection is sustained.

[fol. 130] Mr. Carter: The thing I want to find out, I think I can find out.

By Mr. Carter:

Q. Now, I would like to direct your attention to Exhibit "G", which is the morning schedule, bus schedule, to take the negro children to school, is that correct?

A. Yes.

Judge Mellott: What is your——
Mr. Carter: Exhibit "G".
Judge Mellott: Exhibit "G".

By Mr. Carter:

Q. I understand that from—from Mr. Goodell that there was not submitted a schedule for taking the children home, but he has advised me that that would be available. Now, I would also like to address your attention to Exhibit "D" and then we can take "D" and "G" together.

Mr. Goodell: Exhibit what?
Mr. Carter: "D".
Judge Huxman: "D" like in dog.
Mr. Carter: "D" like in dog.

By Mr. Carter:

Q. Now, I am directing your attention to both of those schedules, both of those exhibits. I note that you—the Board of Education paid a Miss Washington for transportation of negro pupils in 1950-1951. Can you tell me what part of the schedule on Exhibit "G" Miss Washington [fol. 131] handled?

Judge Huxman: What is the materiality of that?

Mr. Carter: I want to find out, Your Honor—I want to find out the bus schedule for each—who is handling each of the bus schedules because we think it's material.

Mr. Goodell: We object to this as being outside——

Judge Huxman: Will you state in what respect it's material.

Mr. Carter: Well, for example, I want to find out whether Mr. Grimes handles both the schedule which is listed at the top to Washington and the one listed at Monroe; whether Mr. Grimes handles the 8:00 o'clock pick-up to

8:29 and then—I think I want to find out how that operates. I want to find out what bus—which of these people handles the taking of the children to McKinley and which handles the taking of the children to Buchanan.

Mr. Goodell: I object to this as incompetent, irrelevant and immaterial, and outside the scope of the issues made up by the pleadings and the admitted stipulation of facts. The two exhibits that he's asked to compare with, one of them is [fol. 132] a regularly maintained bus; the other he has called attention to are some teachers, an isolated case of a teacher or two in the kindergarten who has taken her private car and taken children home, which ordinarily would be done by taxi cabs or by the bus, but to let the teacher make a little extra money, at their request voluntarily, she has taken them home and has been paid by the Board of Education.

Judge Huxman: Mr. Counsel, the Court fails to see any materiality in the question as to who drove the bus. The Court can't see how it makes any difference.

Mr. Carter: Let me pursue it for a moment; I won't take up your time, Your Honor.

By Mr. Carter:

Q. The bus schedule, as listed here, indicates that with regard to Monroe School, children are taken to Monroe; they begin at 8:00 o'clock; they are let off at Monroe School at 8:29. Now, it's my understanding—I would like to have it cleared up—that this same bus driver and this same bus then has a pick-up at 6th and Brannan at 8:30. Now I— the only way I can find that out——

Judge Huxman: Ask the witness if he knows whether that is a fact or not.

Mr. Carter: That is what I asked, Your Honor, whether Mr. Grimes handled both of these schedules. Mr. Grimes is the one who is involved in this.

[fol. 133] Mr. Goodell: Do I understand it that you challenge the accurateness of that exhibit now? You want to inquire into its accuracy, is that what you are getting at?

Mr. Carter: I would like to find out whether Mr. Grimes handles both of these and, therefore, I have a right to, of course, inquire into that.

Mr. Goodell: If the Court please, we renew our objection. They have admitted the bus schedule as being accurate excepting only that they stop at additional places other than the scheduled bus stops.

Judge Huxman: The doctor may answer, if he knows. I fail to see the materiality of it.

The Witness: I don't know.

Mr. Carter: All right, that's okay.

By Mr. Carter:

Q. Now, Mr. McFarland, in your schools are there anything that you call special rooms that you have set aside for white children in your public school system?

A. Yes.

Q. Are there any such special rooms for negro children in the public schools?

A. We have no special rooms for negro children. We have health rooms for both, but not special rooms.

Q. What is the nature of these special rooms?

A. Special rooms are for groups that are, for one reason [fol. 134] or another, unable to fit into regular classroom, do regular work and still we would consider as public school people.

Q. If you know, can you tell us why there are no special rooms for negro children?

A. We haven't had the need. We haven't had, we felt, sufficient numbers of them who were far enough out of line from the regular group to warrant special rooms.

Q. Are any provisions made in the school system for hot lunches, aside from the health rooms? I understand the health rooms are for undernourished children.

A. That's right.

Q. Aside from that, are any provisions made for hot lunches?

A. Not in elementary schools.

Q. I see. Now that would apply to the negro children regardless of the fact that whether they were too far to go home to lunch, you make no provisions for hot lunches for them, is that right?

A. Outside the health rooms, no provision. You understand we have two health rooms for four colored schools, where we have only two health rooms for eighteen white schools.

Q. I understand. Can you tell me, in terms of the transportation of pupils to school, if you know, can you tell me what is the number of children that are transported, negro children that are transported to school, total number.

[fol. 135] A. I couldn't give you that figure. I don't have it at hand.

Q. Is that figure available?

A. We can get that for you.

Q. Would I be able to get that from you?

A. Yes.

Mr. Carter: That's all.

Judge Huxman: Any questions by defendants?

Mr. Goodell: We have no questions.

Judge Huxman: Anyone request the presence of Dr. McFarland any further, or may he be excused?

Mr. Carter: Well, I would like for Dr. McFarland to be able to get from him the school schedule and the number of pupils transported, and I think——

Dr. McFarland: You mean class schedule or hours? You want hours?

Mr. Carter: Hours that the school is in session, that is, including the afternoon recess.

Judge Huxman: Can you furnish that, doctor?

Dr. McFarland: Yes.

Judge Huxman: Will you furnish that to counsel on each side and also copies for the Court?

Dr. McFarland: Yes, sir.

(Witness excused.)

[fol. 136] LENA MAE CARPER, having been first duly sworn, assumed the stand and testified as follows:

Direct examination.

By Mr. John Scott:

Q. State your name to the Court please.

A. Lena Mae Carper.

Q. Are you one of the plaintiffs in this action?

6—8

82

A. Yes.
Q. Where do you live, Mrs. Carper?
A. 1217 Hillsdale.
Q. 1217.
A. Yes.

Mr. Goodell: Twelve what?
The Witness: 1217 Hillsdale.

By Mr. John Scott:

Q. Is that in the City of Topeka?
A. Yes.
Q. Are you married, Mrs. Carper?
A. Yes.
Q. And do you have children or a child of school age?
A. I have one.
Q. What is her name?
A. Katherine Louise Carper.
Q. How old is she?
A. She's ten years old.
[fol. 137]   Q. Will you state to the Court what school she attends?
A. She attends the Buchanan School.
Q. The Buchanan School. What grade is she in?
A. Fifth grade.
Q. Fifth grade.

Mr. John Scott: For the purpose of the record, the residence the plaintiff, Mrs. Carper, has testified to appears to be in the district Gage and Randolph indicated on the official map of Topeka, the same being Exhibit—Defendants' Exhibit "A".

Mr. Goodell: No, that is our exhibit "A". Oh, pardon me. Did you say was in both of those school districts?

Mr. John Scott: Yes, and it's also indicated on the map in the color of red and blue.

Mr. Goodell: Do you mean it's in Gage and Randolph?
Mr. John Scott: Gage-Randolph.
Mr. Goodell: There are two different territories.
Mr. John Scott: She lives in the same district.

By Mr. John Scott:

Q. Now, Mrs. Carper, how does your child go to school?

A. She has to walk about four blocks on Huntoon and then [fol. 138] has to cross the highway at Huntoon and Gage and catch a school bus.

Q. What time does she catch the school bus?

A. The school bus is supposed to be there at 8:40. However, I go to work, and I go with her each morning she goes to school, and sometimes it has been as high as five minutes to nine before the bus showed up.

Q. Can you state to the Court the approximate distance from the school—strike that—the approximate distance of the pick-up point to the Buchanan School.

A. Oh, in the neighborhood of about—oh, I say about twenty-four blocks, anyhow.

Q. And can you state to the Court what schools that you live near?

A. She—we live near the Gage Park or the Randolph School.

Q. Randolph School. And is there also a school now under construction located at 17th and Stone?

A. Yes.

Q. Do you know the name of that school now under construction?

A. No, I don't.

Q. Are you also located near that particular site?

A. Yes.

Q. Now, Mrs. Carper, do you prepare a lunch for your child?

A. Yes.

[fol. 139] Q. Every day that she attends school?

A. Yes.

Q. Does she come home for dinner?

A. No.

Q. What time does she return home?

A. She usually gets home around 4:30.

Q. Around 4:30. Have you ever had an occasion to observe the number of people riding the bus that your child rides?

A. When the bus comes for my child it's nearly loaded.

Q. When you say "nearly loaded" be more explicit about that, Mrs. Carper.

A. Sometimes it is really overloaded.

84

Mr. Goodell: Move to strike that answer as a conclusion of the witness.

Judge Huxman: Overruled.

By Mr. John Scott:

Q. And I believe you stated, Mrs. Carper, that there have been times that the bus has been late, is that correct?

A. Many times.

Q. Would that be during the cold winter months?

A. Yes.

Q. And what would your child and other children be doing at that time?

A. They would usually stand in the cold waiting for the bus until they couldn't stand it any longer, and then we would take them to a small grocery store on Gage and [fol. 140] take them in there and try to get them warm until the bus come. When the bus come, I would get out and hail the bus in front of the store to pick them up.

Q. Are there any shelters or any means of protection against weather conditions there on the corner where the bus stops?

A. None.

Q. Is there a stop signal there at Huntoon and Gage?

A. Absolutely none.

Q. Can you tell the Court what the traffic conditions are where your little girl catches the bus?

Mr. Goodell: Object to this as outside the scope of the issues and the pleadings. There is no evidence that the Board of Education has any control over safety devices, the installation or operation of them.

Mr. John Scott: If the Court please——

Judge Huxman: Just a minute. The objection will be overruled.

By Mr. John Scott:

Q. Did you understand the question?

(The last preceding question was here read by the reporter.)

A. At that time of the morning the cars are really congested going along that highway. It's really congested traffic along there at that time. In the morning most people are going to work at that time.

[fol. 141] Mr. John Scott: I believe that is all. You may cross examine.

Mr. Goodell: No questions.

Judge Huxman: You may step down; call your next witness.

(Witness excused.)

KATHERINE CARPER, having been first duly sworn, assumed the stand and testified as follows:

Direct examination.

By Mr. John Scott:

Q. Katherine, don't be nervous; these gentlemen up here are your friends. Now, what is your name?
A. Katherine Carper.
Q. Katherine, how old are you?
A. Ten.
Q. When is your birthday?
A. February 24th.
Q. February 24th.
A. Yes.
Q. Where do you live, Katherine?
A. 1217 Hillsdale.
Q. What—was that your mother that was just on the stand?
A. Yes, sir.
Q. Do you know the difference between right and wrong, [fol. 142] Katherine?
A. Yes, sir.
Q. And you know what it means to tell the truth, don't you?
A. Yes, sir.
Q. Now, Katherine, you attend Buchanan School, is that correct?
A. Yes, sir.
Q. And you also ride the bus.
A. Yes, sir.

86

Q. I want you to tell these three gentlemen up here—strike that. Just tell the Court how many people, the conditions of the bus that you ride when you catch it in the morning,

A. It is loaded, and there is no place hardly to sit.

Q. There is no place hardly to sit, is that right?

A. No, sir.

Q. People are standing up.

A. Yes, sir.

Q. And you have stood on the corner when it was cold, is that right?

A. Yes, sir.

Q. And did your hands get cold?

A. Yes, sir.

Q. Now what grade are you in, Katherine?

A. Fifth.

[fol. 143]   Q. Fifth grade.

A. Yes, sir.

Q. Do you know what time you arrive at school in the morning?

A. Quarter to nine.

Q. And what time does school—what time does school start?

A. Nine o'clock.

Q. Nine o'clock. And what time do you get out at noon?

A. Quarter to twelve.

Q. Quarter to twelve.

A. Yes, sir.

Q. Do you know what time the first grade gets out?

A. Eleven thirty.

Q. And do you know Mrs. Crawford?

A. Yes, sir.

Q. What grade does she teach?

A. The first and half the second.

Q. Is that at Buchanan School?

A. Yes, sir.

Q. And does she do anything else other than teach school?

A. Takes the kindergarten home.

Q. The kindergarten children home.

A. Yes, sir.

Q. What time does she take the kindergarten children home?

A. Eleven thirty.

Q. Eleven thirty. And what does she do with her class?
[fol. 144] A. Let's them go into Miss McBrier's room.

Q. Mrs. McBrier?

A. Yes, sir.

Q. What grade does she teach?

A. The third and half the second.

Q. The third and half the second. Is her class out at the time that Mrs. Crawford's children go in there?

A. Yes, sir.

Q. They are out. Katherine, I want you to tell these three gentlemen what the conditions of the bus in the evening are when you go home.

A. Sometimes when I get on the bus it is loaded, and there is no place to sit.

Q. And are the children sitting on top of each other?

A. Yes, sir.

Mr. Goodell: We object to this whole line of leading questions of counsel testifying rather than the child.

Judge Huxman: They are slightly leading, but try not to lead the witness. The objection is overruled.

By Mr. John Scott:

Q. In your neighborhood, Katherine, do you live in a neighborhood with white children?

A. Yes, sir.

Q. Do you play with them?
[fol. 145] A. Yes, sir.

Q. What schools do they go to?

A. Randolph.

Mr. Goodell: I object to that as incompetent, irrelevant and immaterial, outside the issue.

Judge Huxman: Objection to this line of questioning will be sustained.

Mr. John Scott: I believe that is all.

Judge Huxman: Any questions? You may be excused.

(Witness excused.)

Mr. Goodell: If the Court please, if they will tell me where these children live, what the distance is to the pick-up point, we will agree to all of this and shorten this up.

Judge Huxman: They are entitled to make their case. We will proceed this way, at least presently.

OLIVER L. BROWN, having been first duly sworn, assumed the stand and testified as follows:

Direct examination.

By Mr. Bledsoe:

Q. You may state your name to the Court, please.
A. Oliver Leon Brown.
Q. And where do you live, Mr. Brown?
[fol. 146]   A. 511 West First Street.
Q. Are you a citizen of the United States?
A. I am.
Q. And you are a plaintiff in this lawsuit?
A. I am.

Judge Huxman: Talk a little louder, Mr. Brown.
Judge Mellott: He didn't answer yet.
The Witness: Yes.

By Mr. Bledsoe:

Q. What is your business or occupation?
A. Carman welder.

Mr. Bledsoe: Speak a little louder.
The Witness: A carman welder.
Judge Huxman: Mr. Brown, it's difficult to hear you. I wish you would make an effort to speak so we can hear you distinctly; we want to hear what you say.

By Mr. Bledsoe:

Q. Are you married?
A. Yes.
Q. And, if so, who constitutes the members of your family
A. I do.
Q. What I mean by that, who constitute the members of your family?
A. I have a wife and three children.

Q. What are the ages of your children?

[fol. 147] A. My oldest daughter is eight years old; I have one four and another one five months.

Q. What is the name of your daughter, oldest daughter?

A. Linda Carol Brown.

Q. In what school district or territory do you live, Mr. Brown?

A. I live in the Sumner District.

Q. Sumner School District.

A. Yes.

Mr. Bledsoe: For the purpose of the record, if the Court please, let it be shown that the witness resides in Sumner School District. I think it's this district here marked (indicating on exhibit)—that is colored red.

Judge Mellott: Well, I am afraid your testimony standing alone isn't too intelligent; it isn't to me. Now, as I understand it, Topeka is one school district, you agreed at the pre-trial, but you said that there were certain territories.

Mr. Bledsoe: Well, I may sushstitute territory for— if I may—territory for district.

Judge Huxman: Wouldn't it be more helpful to the Court if you just had these witnesses locate their residence with reference to the colored school that they attend, rather than having it defined by the various territories. [fol. 148] That is the important factor, how far they are from school.

By Mr. Bledsoe:

Q. Now, Mr. Brown, where do you live with reference to Monroe School?

A. Well, — stated that I live at 511 West First Street which is fifteen blocks, approximately, from Monroe School.

Mr. Goodell: I didn't get that.

Judge Mellott: Fifteen blocks from Monroe School.

The Witness: Twenty-one blocks, pardon me; approximately twenty-one blocks.

By Mr. Bledsoe:

Q. You are talking about now the way your daughter has to travel to go to Monroe School, is that correct?

A. That is true.

Q. Does your daughter ride the school bus?

A. Yes.

Q. All right. Now, Mr. Brown, what time does your daughter leave home in the morning to walk to First and Quincy, the bus pick-up point, to go to school; what time does she leave home?

A. She leaves at twenty minutes 'till eight o'clock.

Q. Twenty minutes of eight.

A. Every school morning.

Q. What time, or thereabouts, does she board the bus [fol. 149] at First and Quincy?

A. Well, she is supposed to be there at eight o'clock and which she has been, in many instances, but many times she has had to wait through the cold, the rain and the snow until the bus got there, not knowing definitely what time it gets there all the time.

Q. All right. Now, Mr. Brown, she boards that bus about eight o'clock. What time does she arrive at the school?

A. She's supposed to arrive at the school around 8:30.

Q. Eight thirty. And, as I understand it, what time does the classes begin at school?

A. Nine o'clock.

Q. What does your daughter do between the time the bus arrives at the school at 8:30 and 9:00 o'clock?

A. Well, there is sometimes she has had to wait outside the school until someone came to let them in, through the winter season and likewise, many times.

Q. What else does she do, if anything?

A. Well, there is nothing she can do except stand out and clap her hands to keep them warm or jump up and down. They have no provisions at all to shelter them.

Q. And what you want the Court to understand is that your daughter is conveyed to the school, she gets there by 8:30 in the morning, and that she has nothing to do until school starts at 9:00 o'clock, is that right?

[fol. 150] A. That is correct.

Q. Now, Mr. Brown, you don't—withdraw that, please. What provisions are made by the school board for your daughter to have warm lunch, if any.

A. There are no provisions made at all.

Judge Huxman: Mr. Bledsoe, hasn't it been agreed and testified to by Dr. McFarland that no provision is made for warm lunches?

Mr. Bledsoe: I beg your pardon; I believe you are correct, if the Court please.

Judge Huxman: That stands admitted, doesn't it?

Mr. Bledsoe: That's right; that is all right. Let me withdraw that, please.

By Mr. Bledsoe:

Q. Now, then, your child—you don't get to see your child during the daytime until she returns home in the evening, is that right?

A. That is correct, sir.

Q. Would you, Mr. Brown, would you like to have your daughter home, have the same opportunity of giving her parental guidance as the white fathers and mothers might do their child.

A. Yes, sir.

Mr. Goodell: We object to the form of that question as assuming a state of facts not in evidence and, in fact, con-
[fol. 151] trary to some of the admitted stipulation of facts.

Judge Huxman: The objection will be sustained.

By Mr. Bledsoe:

Q. But you do not see your daughter from the time she leaves in the morning until she returns in the evening, is that correct?

A. I do not.

Q. What time is that?

A. She gets home around fifteen minutes to five.

Q. Fifteen minutes to five. Do you know whether or not there is any provisions made to shelter or protect your daughter while she is standing on the street or the designated bus pick-up——

Judge Huxman: Mr. Bledsoe, that has been testified to, and I think it's conceded no shelter is provided in any of these points where colored children are picked up, is that not so, Mr. Goodell?

Mr. Goodell: That's right.

By Mr. Bledsoe:

Q. Now, Mr. Brown, what is the condition of the area there between your residence and First and Quincy where your daughter boards the bus?

A. Well, there are a considerable amount of railroad tracks there; they do a vast amount of switching from the Rock Island yards and from the time that she leaves [fol. 152] home until she gets to Quincy, First and Quincy, to board the bus, she has to pass all of these switch tracks and she—also including the main thoroughfare, Kansas Avenue and First; there is a vast amount of traffic there morning and evening when she goes and returns. There is no provisions at all made for safety precautions to protect those children passing these thoroughfares at all.

Q. Now, Mr. Brown, if your daughter were permitted to attend Sumner School would there be any such obstructions or any such conditions as she will meet on her way to First and Quincy?

A. Not hardly as I know of.

Q. How far is it from your residence to Sumner School?
A. Seven blocks.

Q. Seven blocks. Mr. Brown, are you assessed a tax for the support and maintenance of the public schools of the City of Topeka?
A. I am.

Mr. Goodell: We object to that, if the Court please; it's wholly outside the scope——
Judge Huxman: He may answer.
The Witness: I am, sir.

By Mr. Bledsoe:

Q. Mr. Brown, do you consider it an advantage to have a school in the neighborhood in which you live near your home? Do you consider that an advantage?
[fol. 153] Mr. Goodell: We object to that as incompetent, irrelevant and immaterial what he considers.
Judge Huxman: Objection sustained.
Mr. Bledsoe: If the Court please, I believe that is really a part of our case.

Mr. Goodell: If the Court please, every parent would like to have a school next door, but that is impossible.

Judge Huxman: I think it flows naturally it's an advantage to live closer to a school than to have one far away. I don't think we need to spend much time to establish that fact. I think the Court will take judicial knowledge of the fact that if it had children of school age it would rather have them go to a close school than one far away.

By Mr. Bledsoe:

Q. Mr. Brown, is there a more direct route from your residence, 511 West First Street, to the bus pick-up point at First and Quincy; is there any more direct route than there?

A. Than just my family do you mean?

Q. No, for your daughter going down to the bus pick-up point, is there a more direct route for her to travel?

A. No, there isn't.

Q. There is not.

Judge Huxman: Any questions?

[fol. 154] Cross-examination.

By Mr. Goodell:

Q. Mr. Brown, you see that map there, Defendants' Exhibit "A"?

A. I do.

Q. You understand that the portions colored there form the school territory for the whole city of Topeka.

A. I do.

Q. And, directing your attention to the corner here or all the area in blue, you understand that that is territory outside of the city limits of Topeka, but in Topeka for school purposes alone.

A. I understand.

Q. What?

A. I understand that.

Q. You say your child goes four blocks to the bus pick-up point.

A. She goes six blocks to the pick-up point.

Q. Six blocks, pardon me. Don't you know as a matter of fact that in many, many instances there are children that go to the white schools in this town that go thirty and thirty-five blocks and walk to get there.

Mr. Carter: I object to that.
The Witness: Where at?
Mr. Carter: I see no materiality to this question.
[fol. 155] Judge Huxman: Objection will be sustained. That is not proper cross-examination of this witness.
Mr. Goodell: No further questions.
Judge Huxman: The Court will take a short recess of approximately ten minutes.

(The Court then, at 11:15 o'clock a.m., stood at recess until 11:25 o'clock a.m., at which time the following further proceedings were had:)

Judge Huxman: You may proceed:

DARLENE WATSON, having been first duly sworn, assumed the stand and testified as follows:

Direct examination.

By Mr. Bledsoe:

Q. State your name to the Court, please.
A. Darlene Watson.
Q. Where do you live?
A. I live at 508 West First.
Q. Do you have children of school age?
A. Yes, I do.
Q. And what school do your children attend?
A. They go to Sumner.
Q. Sumner School. Are you acquainted with Oliver Brown and his family, the Oliver Brown who just left the stand.
A. Yes; we are neighbors.
[fol. 156] Q. You are neighbors. Now, Mrs. Watson, are you able to tell the Court what time Linda Brown leaves in the morning to go to school?

95

Mr. Goodell: We object to this as repetition; simply cumulative; already been testified to.

Judge Huxman: Yes, this evidence is cumulative but plaintiff is entitled to reasonable latitude.

Mr. Goodell: We will admit the time you say is right; we will admit that.

Judge Huxman: You may answer.

The Witness: I have watched her leave at 7:40.

by Mr. Bledsoe:

Q. Now, do you have a son who attends Sumner School?
A. Yes.
Q. What time does you son leave; you live directly across the street from Mr. Brown.
A. That's right.
Q. Now, what time does your son leave to go to Sumner School?

Mr. Goodell: We object to this as incompetent, irrelevant and immaterial, and not tending to prove any burden within the scope of the 14th Amendment which is what this lawsuit involves, for the reason that if this is a proper inquiry, then we have got to subpoena all of the parents of the white children and show in some cases they live [fol. 157] thirty-six blocks away, and they have to leave maybe at 7:15. It's pure accident where families may live close to schoolhouses. We can't have schoolhouses next door to everybody.

Judge Huxman: The objection will be overruled.

The Witness: My boy leaves at 8:40, twenty minutes of nine.

Q. Twenty minutes of nine.
A. Yes.
Q. How far is it from your home to the Sumner School?
A. It's seven blocks.
Q. Seven blocks. And you just testified that Linda leaves home at 7:40 in the morning.
A. That's right.

Mr. Goodell: We object to this as repetition.

Mr. Bledsoe: That is all.

Judge Huxman: Mr. Bledsoe, speaking for myself alone, for your future guidance, I will take judicial knowledge of the fact that where there are only four colored schools in a town of this size, against eighteen white schools, that there are innumerable instances of this kind where colored children will go by a white school and go much farther to [fol. 158] a colored school than they would be required to go if they had the privilege of attending the white school. That is what you are trying to establish, isn't it?

Mr. Bledsoe: That is, if the Court please.

Judge Huxman: I think we can take judicial knowledge of the fact that that is inevitable where you have only four colored schools as against eighteen white schools.

Mr. Bledsoe: That is. You may take the witness.

Mr. Goodell: No questions.

ALMA JEAN GALLOWAY, having been first duly sworn, assumed the stand and testified as follows:

Direct examination.

By Mr. John Scott:

Q. State your name to the Court, please.
A. Alma Jean Galloway.
Q. Mrs. Galloway, please speak right out enough so the Court and the reporter may hear you, please. Where do you live, Mrs. Galloway?
A. 428 North Lake.
Q. 428 North Lake.
A. Yes.
Q. Do you have a child or children of school age?
[fol. 159] A. Yes; I have two.
Q. Have two. How old are they?
A. One is six and one is five.
Q. And do they attend any of the public schools in the City of Topeka?
A. Washington School.
Q. Washington School. Do you know the approximate distance Washington School is from your residence?
A. I think it's sixteen blocks.
Q. How do they go to school?
A. Well, they take the school bus.

Q. Where does the school bus pick them up?
A. On the corner of Chandler and Greeley.
Q. How far is the bus pick-up point from your residence?
A. Well, it's two and a half blocks.
Q. Two and a half blocks. Are you located near any school that might be within close proximity of your home?
A. Yes, State Street School.
Q. State Street School. Have you ever had an opportunity to observe the conditions of the buses that take your children to school?
A. Well, no, I haven't.
Q. Are you required to fix a lunch in the morning?
A. Yes.
Q. And your children do not come home at noon, is that [fol. 160] correct?
A. No.
Q. What time do they arrive home in the evening?
A. Well, about five or ten minutes past four.
Q. I see. And what time do they leave in the morning?
A. About between 8:20 and 8:25.

Mr. John Scott: That will be all. You may cross-examine.
Judge Huxman: Any cross-examination?
Mr. Goodell: No.
Judge Huxman: You may step down.

(Witness excused.)

SADIE EMANUEL, having been first duly sworn, assumed the stand and testified as follows:

Direct examination.

By Mr. John Scott:
Q. State your name to the Court, please.
A. Mrs. Sadie Emanuel.
Q. Are you one of the plaintiffs in this actions, Mrs. Emanuel?
A. I am.
Q. Where do you live?
A. I live at 1606 East Third.
Q. 1606 East Third Street.

7—8

98

[fol. 161] A. Yes.

Q. Are you a parent of children of school age?

A. I have one boy in school.

Q. How old is he?

A. He is nine years old.

Q. And what school does he attend?

A. He attends Washington School.

Q. Washington School.

A. Yes.

Q. Do you know the approximate distance Washington is from your home?

A. Well, I don't know just exactly, but I imagine it would be from our place to Washington around about fifteen or sixteen blocks, I just imagine; I don't know.

Q. How does your child travel to school?

A. I send him to school on the city bus.

Q. State to the Court why you send your child to school on the city bus.

A. Well, when he was in kindergarten, the kindergarten teacher she picked him up at our home, and then he would return on the school bus in the evenings, and I would meet the school bus which he had about five blocks to come from the bus line when he was in kindergarten, and the reason why that I stopped him—after he got out of kindergarten and started in the first grade when I would [fol. 162] meet the school bus the children would be hanging out of the bus and when they would get so far the other larger children would push the smaller children on the ground, and I bought him a cap and when he came home he said some of the children pulled his cap off and threw it out of the bus, so we were only just one block from the city bus, and he has been riding on the city bus ever since, and I just didn't like it because it seemed that there wasn't any order on the school bus, and I just didn't like the condition; it was so crowded and congested until I just didn't like the idea so I send him to school on the city bus.

Q. And you pay his fare each and every day.

A. I sure do.

Q. Approximately how long have you been doing that, Mrs. Emanuel?

A. Ever since he has been in the first grade.

Q. What grade is he in now?

A. He is going into the fourth.
Q. Do you prepare a lunch for him in the morning?
A. Yes, I do.
Q. Therefore he stays at school and eats his lunch, is that right?
A. Yes.

Judge Huxman: Mr. Counsel, can't we stipulate and [fol. 163] agree that in all instances lunches are prepared, and the colored students stay from the time they come there in the morning until they go home at night.

Mr. Goodell: That would be true as to the children transported, but it is not an accurate statement as to——

Judge Huxman: That is what I mean, as to those who are transported. Can we stipulate that into the record that all colored school children who are transported stay at the school from the morning; they take their lunch with them and leave the school building only when school is completed in the afternoon.

Mr. John Scott: Yes, sir.

Mr. Goodell: The stipulation ought to be that they are not required to stay.

Judge Huxman: They are not required but, of necessity, they do that.

Mr. John Scott: Convenience.

Judge Huxman: They have no place else to go.

Mr. Goodell: Which is precisely like it is in the white schools where children live far away.

Judge Huxman: We will not add that on to it.

Mr. John Scott: That is your case.

[fol. 164] Judge Huxman: Nothing gained by asking each witness whether they prepare the lunch and whether their children stay there and don't come home until evening because that seems to be the pattern.

By Mr. John Scott:

Q. Is there a school located near your home?
A. Two blocks.
Q. Two blocks. What's the name of that school?
A. Lafayette School.
Q. Lafayette School.

Mr. John Scott: I believe that is all.

100

Judge Huxman: Any questions; cross-examination?
Mr. Goodell: No.

SHIRLEY MAE HODISON, having been first duly sworn, assumed the stand and testified as follows:

Direct Examination.

By Mr. John Scott:

Q. State your name to the Court, please.
A. Shirley Mae Hodison.
Q. Are you one of the plaintiffs in this action?
A. Yes.
Q. Where do you live?
A. 734 Garfield.
[fol. 165] Q. Do you have a child or children of school age?
A. I have one of school age.
Q. What is his name?
A. Charles Hodison, Jr.
Q. How old is he?
A. He is nine.
Q. Do you know what grade he is in?
A. He is in the fifth.
Q. What school does he attend.
A. Buchanan.

Judge Mellott: What school?
The Witness: Buchanan.

By Mr. John Scott:

Q. Does he ride the school bus?
A. Yes, he does.
Q. What time does he—do you prepare him to catch the school bus in the morning?
A. Well, I have him to leave about ten after eight.

Mr. Goodell: If the Court please, we don't want to be obstreperous. We object to this whole line of questioning on the basis that it could not furnish the basis of recovery, distance travelled, and a long line of decisions by the federal courts have held that that is not such a situation that would invoke the 14th Amendment. I have a long line of decisions on that.

Mr. John Scott: We have——

[fol. 166] Mr. Goodell: That is, those are disparities that are bound up here in any school system, and it occurs within the white districts and that that is not a ground for invoking the equal protection of the laws.

Judge Huxman: The objection will be overruled and, if a study of the authorities should convince the Court that this testimony is incompetent, of course, it would be disregarded in reaching our conclusion. We can't stop to analyze all the cases at this stage.

By Mr. John Scott:

Q. What time did you say he left for school?
A. Ten after eight.
Q. Is that the time the bus arrives?
A. It's supposed to be there about a quarter after.
Q. And where do you catch the bus?
A. On 7th and Garfield.
Q. On 7th and Garfield. That is a block from your home.
A. Just about; I live the second house from the corner of 8th and Garfield.
Q. Do you know the approximate distance Buchanan School is from your home?
A. I am not sure; I believe it's about eight blocks, I imagine.
Q. Would you say twelve?
A. I am not sure.
Q. Do you know what time your child arrives at school?
[fol. 167] A. No, I don't.
Q. Is there a school located near your home?
A. Yes.
Q. What's the name of that school?
A. Clay.
Q. Clay School.

Mr. John Scott: It has already been stipulated about the lunches so we don't have to go into that.

Judge Huxman: Any questions?

Mr. Goodell: No questions.

102

JAMES V. RICHARDSON, having been first duly sworn, assumed the stand and testified as follows:

Direct examination.

By Mr. Bledsoe:

Q. State your name to the Court, please.
A. James V. Richardson.
Q. Where do you live, Mr. Richardson?
A. 1035 Jewell.
Q. 1035 Jewell. Do you have a—children of school age?
A. One boy.
Q. What is his name?
A. Ronald.
Q. Did you tell me how old he was?
A. Seven years old.
[fol. 168] Q. Seven years old. What school does he now attend?
A. Holy Name School.
Q. The Holy Name. That is a parochial school?
A. That's right, sir.
Q. Why do you send your child to a parochial school, Mr. ——
A. Simply because I do not believe in segregation.

Mr. Goodell: Move to strike out that testimony as incompetent, irrelevant and immaterial.
Judge Huxman: The objection will be overruled.

By Mr. Bledsoe:

Q. Now, did your child ever attend Buchanan School?
A. Yes, sir.
Q. How far is Buchanan School from you?
A. Oh, approximately ten or eleven blocks.
Q. How far is Lowman School from——
A. Two or three blocks.
Q. Two or three blocks.

Mr. Bledsoe: I believe that's all.
Judge Huxman: Any questions?
Mr. Goodell: No questions. You may step down.

(Witness excused.)

[fol. 169] LUCINDA TODD, having been first duly sworn, assumed the stand and testified as follows:

Direct examination.

By Mr. Bledsoe:

Q. State your name to the Court, please.
A. Lucinda Todd.
Q. Where do you live, Mrs. Todd?
A. At 1007 Jewell.
Q. Do you have a daughter of school age?
A. Yes, I do.
Q. Now what school does your daughter attend?
A. Buchanan.
Q. Buchanan School. How far is Buchanan School from your residence?
A. About ten blocks.
Q. About ten blocks. Is there a school nearer your home than——
A. Yes, there is.
Q. What school is that?
A. Lowman Hill.
Q. How far is that school from your residence?
A. About three blocks.
Q. Does your child ride the bus?
A. Yes, she does.
Q. What time does she leave in the morning?
[fol. 170] A. About twenty minutes of nine.
Q. About twenty minutes of nine. And of course she doesn't return for the noontime.
A. No.
Q. She does not. What time does your daughter get home in the evening?
A. About four fifteen, four twenty.
Q. And she rides—comes home on the bus, does she?
A. Yes, she does.
Q. Have you noticed the condition of that bus as to how many rides it?
A. Yes, I have; it's very crowded.
Q. Mrs. Todd, do you know of any instances where your daughter suffered from waiting for the school bus?

A. Oh, many instances; she has been stranded on the corner waiting for the bus from a half-hour to forty-five minutes many times.

Mr. Bledsoe: I believe that is all.
Judge Huxman: Any questions?
Mr. Goodell: No questions.
Judge Huxman: You may step down, please.

(Witness excused.)

[fol. 171] MARGUERITE EMMERSON, having been first duly sworn, assumed the stand and testified as follows:

Direct examination.

By Mr. John Scott:

Q. State your name to the Court, please.
A. Marguerite Emmerson.
Q. Are you one of the plaintiffs in this action?
A. Yes, I am.
Q. Where do you live?
A. 1029 Grand.
Q. Are you a parent of a child or children of school age?
A. Yes, I have two.
Q. What are their names?
A. Claude Arthur and George Robert.
Q. How old are they?
A. They are nine and eight—nine and seven.
Q. Do you know what grades they are in?
A. They are in the second and fourth grades.
Q. What school do they attend?
A. Buchanan.
Q. How do they get to school?
A. On the school bus.
Q. What time does the school bus pick up your children?
A. Around a quarter to nine and ten minutes to nine.
[fol. 172] Q. Where do they catch the bus?
A. On 11th and Woodward.
Q. Has there ever been any instances that your children have missed the bus?
A. Yes, there has been.

Q. You can state to the Court what you did, if anything.
A. Well, they have missed the bus, and I have called the school, and they have sent the bus back after them.
Q. They sent the bus back after them.
A. Yes.
Q. Have there been any instances that they missed the bus and your child didn't go to school at all?
A. No, because when he has missed the bus before that I have sent him on the city bus.
Q. On the city bus, I see. Is there a school located near your residence?
A. Yes, there is.
Q. What's the name of that school?
A. Lowman Hill.
Q. How far is it from your residence?
A. About five blocks.
Q. About five blocks.

Mr. John Scott: That is all. You may cross examine.
Mr. Goodell: No questions.

[fol. 173] Judge Huxman: Step down, please.

(Witness excused.)

ZELMA HENDERSON, having been first duly sworn, assumed the stand and testified as follows:

Direct examination.

By Mr. Bledsoe:

Q. State your name to the Court, please.
A. Zelma Henderson.
Q. Where do you live, Mrs. Henderson?
A. 1307 North Jefferson.
Q. Now, Mrs. Henderson, do you have children of school age?
A. Yes, I do; I have two.
Q. What school does your children attend?
A. McKinley.
Q. How old are your children?

106

A. Seven and five.

Q. Seven and five. Do you have a child in the kindergarten now?

A. Yes, she just completed the kindergarten.

Q. In what grade—the other?

A. In the first grade.

Q. Is there a school nearer your residence than McKinley School?

A. Yes, there is.

[fol. 174] Q. How far is that school from——

A. I would say approximately five blocks.

Q. What is the name of that school?

A. Quincy.

Q. What time does your children leave home in the morning?

A. All the way from 8:15 to 8:30.

Q. Do they ride the bus?

A. Yes, they do.

Q. And, of course, they don't come back for lunch.

A. No; the little girl did at noon, of course, but the little boy stayed all day.

Q. What time would they return home in the evening?

A. About 4:15.

Q. Now, tell the Court whether or not you prepare lunches for your son.

A. Yes, I prepare lunch but——

Mr. Goodell: Object to this as having already been stipulated to.

Mr. Bledsoe: If the Court please, I have something else I want to——

Judge Huxman: All right, you may ask.

By Mr. Bledsoe:

Q. Do you prepare lunch for your son?

A. Yes, I do.

Q. Tell the Court whether or not your son is able to eat his lunches.

[fol. 175] A. My son——

Mr. Goodell: We object to that; that might depend on a lot of things rather than that the school board——

Judge Huxman: I think the objection will be sustained.

By Mr. Bledsoe:

Q. Have you noticed any physical difference in your son due to his eating the lunch?
A. Yes.
Mr. Goodell: Wait a minute. We object to this as this witness is not qualified to give an opinion of that character.
Judge Huxman: Objection sustained.

By Mr. Bledsoe:

Q. Have you observed your son; what was his condition?
A. One month after starting to first grade he was ill.

Mr. Goodell: Just a minute, we object to that unless—we are not trying the physical elements of these children unless it's connected up with discrimination and violation of the 14th Amendment.
Judge Huxman: I think the answer would be immaterial. Furthermore, the question is so vague; you couldn't tell what condition was referred to. What effect the eating of a lunch would have upon one individual wouldn't throw any light on the constitutional question involved. The objection [fol. 176] is sustained.
Mr. Bledsoe: That will be all. Thank you.
Mr. Goodell: No questions.

(Witness excused.)

SILAS HARDRICK FLEMING, having been first duly sworn, assumed the stand and testified as follows:

Direct examination.

By Mr. John Scott:

Q. State your name to the Court, please.
A. Silas Hardrick Fleming.
Q. Where do you live, Mr. Fleming?
A. 522 Liberty.
Q. Are you a parent of a child or children of school age?
A. Yes, sir.
Q. What are there—how many?
A. Two.

108

Q. What are their names?
A. Silas Hardrick Fleming, Jr., and Duane Dean Fleming.
Q. And state to the Court their ages?
A. Well, ten and seven.

Mr. Goodell: What was that again, please?
The Witness: Ten and seven.

By Mr. John Scott:

Q. What school do they attend?
A. Washington School.
[fol. 177] Q. Do you know the approximate distance Washington is from your school—I mean from your home.
A. Oh, between ten, twelve blocks, I would say; I don't know the exact distance.
Q. How do they get to school?
A. They ride the East Tenth Street bus.
Q. They don't ride the school bus.
A. No.
Q. You state to the Court why they don't ride the school bus.
A. Well, the school bus is about six or eight blocks away. It comes across Brannan Street; that is about six or seven blocks away from Sixth and Liberty.
Q. You mean that is the pick-up point?
A. That's right.
Q. I see. Go ahead. Well, how far do you have—the children have to walk to catch the regular city bus?
A. Half a block going to school and about a block starting home.
Q. Do you pay their fare?
A. Yes, sir.
Q. Each and every day?
A. That's right.
Q. Is there a school located near your home?
A. Yes, there is one two blocks away from me, and there [fol. 178] is one about four or five blocks. They pass two schools going to their school.
Q. They pass two schools.
A. Two white schools, yes.
Q. What's the name of those schools, if you know?
A. Lafayette is one and Parkdale the other.

Q. Which of the two schools is closer to your home?
A. How's that?
Q. Which of the two schools that you just mention are closer to your home?
A. I guess it's Parkdale; it's two blocks away, Parkdale.
Q. You are mistaken——
A. It's Lafayette.
Q. That's right. Is there any other reason you don't permit your children to ride the school bus?
A. How's that?
Q. Is there any other reason that you don't permit your children to ride the regular school bus?
A. No; my only reason is that it's just about as far away from the bus as they would be from the school. They are only a few blocks away from the school to pick up the bus. I will ask the Court, Your Honor——

Judge Mellott: I can't hear the witness.
The Witness: I would ask this for a few minutes to explain why I got into the suit whole soul and body.
[fol. 179] Mr. Goodell: We object to the voluntary statement.
Judge Huxman: I can't hear what you say.
Mr. Goodell: He wants to explain why he got in with the other plaintiffs to bring this lawsuit.
Mr. John Scott: He has a right to do that.
Judge Huxman: Didn't you consent to be a plaintiff in this case?
The Witness: That's right.
Judge Huxman: You did not?
Judge Mellott: He said he did, but he wants to tell the reason why.
The Witness: I want to tell the cause.
Judge Huxman: You want to tell the Court why you joined this lawsuit?
The Witness: That's right.
Judge Huxman: All right, go ahead and tell it.
The Witness: Well, it wasn't for the sake of hot dogs; it wasn't to cast any insinuations that our teachers are not capable of teaching our children because they are supreme, extremely intelligent and are capable of teaching my kids or white or black kids. But my point was that not only I and

my children are craving light, the entire colored race is [fol. 180] craving light, and the only way to reach the light is to start our children together in their infancy and they come up together.

Judge Huxman: All right, now you have answered and given us your reason.

The Witness: That was my reason.

Mr. John Scott: Thank you.

By Mr. John Scott:

Q. Just one more question, Mr. Fleming. What time do your children leave in the morning to go to school?

A. About 8:20.

Q. What time do they get home in the evening?

A. Oh, about 4:10 or 4:15; sometimes the bus is a little early and sometimes late.

Judge Huxman: The Court is going to adjourn presently at 12:00 o'clock. Before we adjourn, we would like to request that counsel on both sides meet with the Court in the district courtroom chambers.

We will adjourn to 1:30. We would like to have counsel meet us at 1:15 in the district courtroom chambers.

You may announce a recess of the court until 1:30.

(The court then, at 12:00 o'clock noon, stood at recess until 1:30 o'clock p.m., at which time court was reconvened [fol. 181] and the following further proceedings were had:)

Judge Huxman: You may proceed.

Mr. Goodell: If the Court please, we do have one of the records that was asked for on the schedule, the hourly schedule, of the elementary schools. I have that record.

Judge Huxman: Is that what they promised to furnish?

Mr. Goodell: Yes.

Judge Huxman: I don't think we have that in the record here. One of those should be marked.

Mr. Goodell: Dr. McFarland said he would furnish it. It was what the witness, McFarland, Dr. McFarland said he would furnish.

Judge Huxman: And that has been prepared.

Mr. Goodell: This is it.

Judge Huxman: Is this offered as an exhibit in the case?

111

Mr. Goodell: Yes.

Judge Mellott: What is the next exhibit number, Mr. Clerk?

The Clerk: "N".

Judge Mellott: "N". Let it be admitted as Defendants' Exhibit "N".

[fol. 182] Defendants' Exhibit "N", having been offered and received in evidence, is contained in the case file.

Hugh W. Speer, having been first duly sworn, assumed the stand and testified as follows:

Direct examination.

By Mr. Greenberg:

Q. Will you please tell the Court your name.
A. Hugh W. Speer.
Q. And what is your occupation?
A. I am chairman of the Department of Education at the University of Kansas City.
Q. Have you ever been in public school work, Mr. Speer?
A. Yes, I was in public school work in Kansas for about twelve years.
Q. You mentioned the Department of Education, University of Kansas City, what is the function of the Department of Education?
A. Our chief function at the present time is the training of elementary school teachers.
Q. Do you train teachers eligible to teach in Kansas?
A. Yes, and a number of them do.
Q. How many members are on the teaching staff of your Education Department under your supervision?
[fol. 183] A. At the present about twenty.
Q. Do you have any other responsibilities at your university?
A. Well, I am a member of the President's Advisory Committee; I am chairman of the Curriculum Committee of the university.
Q. Do you regularly come into contact with elementary schools?

112

A. Yes, we conduct an elementary school of our own. We call it the demonstration school in the summer. We do practice teaching in the public schools in our locality, which means we are in and out of the schools constantly.

Q. Would you tell us something of your educational background, Dr. Speer; where did you attend public school?

A. Attended public schools at Olathe, Kansas.

Q. And what universities did you attend and what degrees do you hold?

A. I hold a Bachelor's Degree from American University in Washington, D. C., a Master's Degree from George Washington University, and a PhD. Degree from the University of Chicago.

Q. What was your major field in your doctorate?

A. Evaluation.

Q. Would you please explain to the Court what evaluation means.

A. Evaluation is a rather general term. We sometimes evaluate educational programs or buildings or the behavior changes that are produced in children as a result of educa-
[fol. 184] tional programs.

Q. Do you belong to any professional organizations, Dr. Speer?

A. I am a key member of the National Education Association, a member of the Missouri State Teachers Association, a member of the National Vocational Guidance Association; that is about it.

Q. Do you hold any honors or scholarships?

A. I have recently been granted a Fullbright scholarship by the United States Department of State to lecture on education in Iran.

Q. What will be the purpose of your visit in Iran?

A. I will work through the University of Tehran to help improve the school system of Iran.

Q. Dr. Speer, have you ever made an examination of the elementary schools of Topeka?

A. Yes.

Q. When?

A. During the last month.

Q. Why did you make this examination, Dr. Speer?

A. At the request of counsel for plaintiffs.

Q. What aspects of the schools did you examine during your examination?

A. We examined the more important aspects that we thought had a bearing on the major issues in this case. We [fol. 185] have examined the buildings, the curriculum, the equipment, the library, the preparation and experience of the teaching staff and the salaries, the class loads, the size of classes and a few other minor points.

Q. Now, I am going to ask you some questions about your findings. What did you find concerning the comparison of teachers in the colored schools with those of the white schools?

A. I found only minor differences between the two groups, and these differences tend to balance each other. For example, in preparation, all the colored teachers have Bachelor's degree and all but 15% of the white teachers have Bachelor's degrees. On the other hand, in terms of Master's degrees, 12% of the colored teachers have Master's degree and 15% of the white teachers hold Master's degrees. The colored teachers average twenty years of experience, and the white teachers nineteen years.

Q. Dr. Speer, what did you find concerning class size and teaching load; would you explain to the Court what teaching load is?

A. Teaching load is the number of pupils which the teacher has each day and, again, here I found not much difference. There is some difference at the kindergarden level where the colored kindergartens are somewhat smaller. I think the white average is 42; the colored aver- [fol. 186] age about 25. But, in grades 1 to 6, the average is very close together; 34 in the white schools and 32 in the colored schools. Again, I would say, I found no significant difference in teacher load or teacher preparation.

Q. In examining the two sets of schools, negro and white, did you find any provisions for special rooms in any of these?

A. I found provision for two special rooms for white children; I found no provision for special rooms for any colored children.

Q. Now, did you study all of the school buildings in Topeka, Dr. Speer?

8—8

114

A. Yes, we examined data in the Board of Education files on all school buildings, and we personally visited, Dr. Buchanan and I and some of my other assistants, we visited about two-thirds of the schools in the city.

Judge Hill: If counsel will let me interrupt, what do you mean by special rooms?

Mr. Greenberg: Well, if I may explain, in the white schools there are rooms for specially retarded or handicapped children, whereas in the negro schools there are none.

Judge Hill: Very well.

By Mr. Greenberg:

Q. Did you examine these schools with regard to their age and their insured value?

A. Yes. We——

[fol. 187] Judge Huxman: With regard to what?

Mr. Greenberg: Regard to their age and insured value.

The Witness: On the revised list furnished by the Board of Education we secured the ages of the buildings and also from the insured values of buildings, as provided by the Board of Education, in the exhibits, we made a study of the current values in terms of the insured values.

By Mr. Greenberg:

Q. Why did you use insurance value rather than construction cost, Dr. Speer?

A. Construction cost back over the sixty-year period dates these buildings would vary a great deal which is obvious. Therefore, we could not make comparisons on construction cost; but we assumed that the Board of Education and their insurance companies have arrived accurately at the current value of buildings, and that those values are reflected in the insurance figures furnished by the board.

Q. Is the total insurance value—does the total insurance value of the building reflect accurately the value of the building as broken down into instructional units?

Mr. Goodell: We object to this testimony from this witness. There is no foundation laid for his expert knowledge about evaluating of physical property. The testimony [fol. 188] shows he is an educator, that is true. That is in the field of engineering and architects.

Judge Huxman: The question presupposes a knowledge he might not have because sometimes you only insure a building for three-fourths of its value and others may be insured for 100%.

Mr. Goodell: Plus the additional reason for the objection is that it stands admitted the physical value of the physical plants on two exhibits.

Judge Huxman: We will let the witness answer.

Mr. Greenberg: May I ask him whether or not, as an educational expert he has been trained in evaluating the physical plants of buildings?

Judge Huxman: On the basis of insurance?

Mr. Greenberg: On the basis of insurance.

Judge Huxman: Mr. Counsel, here's the difficulty with that question: Suppose it is the policy of the board to insure Buildings for 25% of their—75%——

Mr. Greenberg: I intend to bring out an explanation of that particular factor.

Judge Huxman: You don't know the basis of the insurance.

Mr. Greenberg: They insure on the basis of 80%, Your Honor, and I intend to bring that out.

[fol. 189] Judge Hill: That would be hearsay from this witness, wouldn't it?

Mr. Greenberg: It has been admitted in evidence by stipulation.

Judge Hill: All right.

Judge Huxman: They are insured at 80% of their value, is that in the stipulation?

Mr. Greenberg: Your printed sheet of insurance values of each building; the one you have right there.

Mr. Goodell: No, that doesn't mean that. We have got an insurance clause that 80% on total loss is paid; that is the type of insurance, but that doesn't mean that their insurability of the buildings is limited to 80%.

Judge Huxman: I think the objection to the question will be sustained.

By Mr. Greenberg:

Q. Dr. Speer, in making your evaluation, did you take into account the fact that some buildings might have had some unused classrooms?

A. Yes.

Q. What significance did you ascribe to that fact?

A. Well, an unused classroom is very limited value to the school. We assume that as most schools operate one class with one teacher, can profitably use one classroom.

[fol. 190] Q. Now, did you conduct a visual inspection of any of the buildings in Topeka as well as inspecting the records which you have indicated?

A. Yes, we did.

Q. How many schools did you inspect visually?

A. We inspected I think it was fourteen directly.

Q. And what criteria did you use to determine which schools you would evaluate merely on the basis of the records and which schools you would evaluate by a personal visit?

A. We first examined the records on all of them, and then, in order to substantiate our findings, we thought we should visit at least a representative sample and we visited in all two-thirds of them, making sure we got the older buildings and the newer buildings and some of the medium-aged buildings so that we would have a representation of the complete range.

Q. What criteria did you use in your visit?

A. We used the usual criteria that are recognized in this area, such as sight, the nature of the structure, the plan of the building, the classrooms, the service rooms, the kindergartens, library books, the supplies, the safety features, the maintenance features. I might add these are the kind of features that are included by such authorities as Holly and Arnold in their scorecard for elementary school [fol. 191] buildings. Dr. Holly is from the Ohio State University and Dr. Arnold is from the University of Pennsylvania.

Mr. Goodell: We object to this as hearsay, about what some book says about evaluation.

Judge Huxman: He is testifying as to the basis of his

knowledge of works on this. I think it's competent. This is an expert witness. He may testify.

Judge Mellott: There seems to be no unanswered question.

By Mr. Greenberg:

Q. In order to save the time of the Court, Dr. Speer, did you make any general observations that seemed to apply to all of the buildings you visited?

A. Yes, I think I can. First of all, in regard to gymnasiums and auditoriums, the facilities, all in all, seemed to be about equal between the colored schools and the white schools. Three-fourths of the colored schools have a combined gymnasium-auditorium, and we would say approximately that proportion of the white schools have similar facilities. However, I should add that none of the colored schools have anything like the luxurious facilities that we would find in the Oakland building or the State Street building or the Gage Building, for example.

Q. How do the various——

A. I might, if I may——

Q. Go ahead.

[fol. 192] A. —add one or two other general observations to save time. The buildings are all well kept, well preserved, and I think well maintained. Dr. Buchanan and I felt that that was equal throughout the system.

Q. How do the buildings compare as to their ages, Dr. Speer?

A. The ages of the white buildings average twenty-seven years, according to the figures furnished by the board, and the ages of the colored buildings thirty-three years. In other words, the white buildings average six years newer. However, I think we should add another feature here. Inasmuch as the newer buildings tend to be larger, we found this to be the case, that according to last year's enrollment figures, 45% of the white children attend schools that were newer than the newest colored buildings, whereas 14% of the white children attended schools that were older than the oldest colored building. To state another kind of a comparison, 66%, or two-thirds, of all white children attend schools that are newer than the average age of the colored buildings.

Q. Dr. Speer, how do the colored schools compare to the

118

white schools in regard to the insured value per available classroom?

A. The average for the white schools is $10,517, and the average for the colored schools is $6,317. Or, stated another way, the insured value per available classroom is 66% [fol. 193] higher in the white schools.

Q. Dr. Speer, did you examine the curriculum in the schools in the City of Topeka?

A. Yes.

Q. Tell the Court what you mean by "curriculum", also.

A. By "curriculum" we mean something more than the course of study. As commonly defined and accepted now, "curriculum" means the total school experience of the child. Now, when it comes to the mere prescription of the course of study, we found no significant difference. But, when it comes to the total school experience of the child, there are some differences. In other words, we consider that education is more than just remembering something. It is concerned with a child's total development, his personality, his personal and social adjustment. Therefore it becomes the obligation of the school to provide the kind of an environment in which the child can learn knowledge and skills such as the three "R's" and also social skills and social attitudes and appreciations and interests, and these considerations are all now part of the curriculum.

Q. I see, Dr. Speer. Do you have anything further to say?

A. Yes. And we might add the more heterogeneous the group in which the children participate, the better than can function in our multi-cultural and multi-group society. For example, if the colored children are denied the experience [fol. 194] in school of associating with white children, who represent 90% of our national society in which these colored children must live, then the colored child's curriculum is being greatly curtailed. The Topeka curriculum or any school curriculum cannot be equal under segregation.

Q. Dr. Speer, I would like to go through these—through the school system rather rapidly now school by school and have you point out key characteristics you found as to each school.

What did you find concerning the Buchanan School in regard to these?

A. The Buchanan School is thirty years old; the insurance

value per available classroom is $5,623. It has five rooms, all of which are in use, including a double room divided with sliding doors that is used for an auditorium and also for a playroom. The furniture is quite old, reflecting the age of the building. The site and playground is only fairly adequate. The books in the building are generally old and in poor condition. Many titles date back to the 1920's and even some before 1920.

Q. What did you find concerning Gage School, Dr. Speer?

A. The Gage School, a white school, is twenty-three years old and has an insured value per classroom of a little more —of $9,136. It has fifteen classrooms all in use. The building is more crowded than most, although the classes run [fol. 195] about average for the system. It has a good auditorium with—it's combination—it has a kitchenette that adjoins the auditorium and has an attractive kindergarten room with murals, toilet facilities and a fireplace; and also it has some old titles among the books, but a fair proportion of the books in this building are of a newer and better — than we found elsewhere. It has a very excellent and spacious playground.

Q. Concerning Lafayette School, Dr. Speer.

A. Lafayette is forty-eight years old, has an insurance value per classroom of $3,373.

Mr. Goodell: While he is making his testimony, would it be better if he designates which are the white schools.

Mr. Greenberg: Dr. Speer, when you describe a school, tell us also whether it's a negro school or white school.

The Witness: Thus far——

By Mr. Greenberg:

Q. Buchanan is what?
A. Colored.
Q. What about Gage?
A. White.
Q. What about Lafayette?
A. Is white. The Lafayette building is forty-eight years old, insured for $3,373. Although not the oldest, this is [fol. 196] certainly one of the poorest buildings in Topeka. The comprehensive plan suggested in 1942 by the planning commission recommended that it be abandoned but it still

houses 300 pupils. Small, the auditorium is small, and the playground is small. The kindergarten is fair; books are only fair. There are two fire escapes, but the safety factor is somewhat questionable partly due to the number of children who are housed in the building.

Q. Tell us your findings concerning the McKinley School, Dr. Speer.

A. McKinley is a colored school; it's forty-four years old. It's insured value per available classroom is $2,477. The building was well constructed. It has wooden floors and stairs, which make it something of a fire hazard. It has one fire escape. Approximately three-fourths of the books were too old to be suitable for school use. The comprehensive plan for the City of Topeka, prepared by the City Commissioner——

Mr. Goodell: If the Court please, we object to this witness telling about some book comprehensive plan. It's outside the scope of the issues in this case; secondly, it's not the best evidence; it's hearsay as far as this witness is concerned.

Mr. Greenberg: If the Court please, may I ask Dr. Speer whether such city plans and city surveys are things which [fol. 197] an educator customarily studies in making an evaluation.

Judge Huxman: What comprehensive plan are you referring to, Doctor?

The Witness: I am referring, Your Honor——

Judge Huxman: Bartholomew plan?

The Witness: I am referring, Your Honor, to the one that was mentioned in court this morning that was prepared jointly by the Board of Education, the City Commissioners, and, I think——

Mr. Goodell: Now, if the Court please, that is this witness' idea that it was prepared jointly.

Judge Huxman: That plan was ruled out. We haven't received or permitted any evidence concerning that plan. I think the witness should refrain from reference to this comprehensive plan.

The Witness: This—the site of the McKinley building is not at all attractive and hardly adequate for school purposes. In other words, we might say it has very poor aesthetic value.

By Mr. Greenberg:

Q. Would you tell us what you found concerning Monroe School?

A. Monroe. Colored building, is twenty-four years old; it's valued at $9,760. This is, in our judgment, the best of the colored buildings. It's well constructed, has tile floors. [fol. 198] Again, however, many of the books are too old for good school use. The site is rather small, and the building and site are not very attractive.

Q. And tell us about what you found concerning Oakland School, Dr. Speer.

A. The Oakland School is white; it's only one year old. It's insured value per available classroom is $23,906. It's a beautiful structure. It's about the last word in school buildings; has modern furniture, asphalt tile floors, acoustical ceilings, good lighting, good heating, darkroom for audio-visual aids, office vault, public address system for use of radio programs, music programs, has a beautiful, large combination auditorium-gymnasium very suitable for community gatherings and parent meetings, large dining and social room with a kitchen adjoining; well adapted for community meetings; has a beautiful kindergarten room with new equipment; the books still not ideal but they are very good. All in all, it's an excellent building that should provide for one of the best educational opportunities.

Q. And tell the Court what you found concerning the Parkdale School.

A. The Parkdale, white, is age twenty-seven, value $8,016. The building appears to have been rather poorly constructed. It has a stucco exterior for the most part. It is [fol. 199] in rather an attractive location with ample playground area. The kindergarten room is quite dull; the books are just fairly good.

Q. And would you do the same concerning the Polk School.

A. The Polk School, for white children, is sixty-four years old; it's the oldest building in Topeka. It's insured value per room is $2,547. It is the oldest building in Topeka, but it is not, in my judgment, the worst building. It is surprisingly substantial, surprisingly attractive on the inside. Has a nice auditorium, two playrooms in the basement, built

122

of native stone; has two fire escapes; the books in the building are very good.

Q. And what did you find concerning the Potwin School?

A. The Potwin School is white, age two years, value per room, $18,100. It's a beautiful building with very modern features. It has a spacious playground which is surfaced with asphalt. It has a beautiful auditorium, also double playrooms. The books are mostly good, at least dating from the 1930's on, mostly. It has a kitchen, a visual aids room. This building seems to be filled to capacity already although only two years old. It is, all in all, one that should provide an excellent educational opportunity.

Q. And what about the Randolph School, Dr. Speer.

A. The Randolph School, a large school, age twenty-four, [fol. 200] value $6,947. It's a large building which is reasonably good. The desks are old, but the books are fairly good, the majority of them dating in the 1940's. It has a very attractive kindergarten with a fireplace and good decorations. It has an excellent, spacious playground. It has a beautiful row of trees which highlight the landscaping. Although it's a little old, this building is still capable of providing a very good educational opportunity. It has a small combination auditorium-gymnasium which is not adequate for the entire enrollment.

Q. Would you please tell the Court what you found concerning State Street School.

A. State Street is a white school, age eleven years, insured value per classroom, $13,880. It's an excellent building, beautifully located, well landscaped; most of the new features, such as a public address system, beautiful auditorium, adequate gymnasium, excellent playground, has a kitchen, library room; the books are fairly good but not in keeping with the building. All in all, the facilities are available to provide a very good educational opportunity, one of the best.

Q. Would you tell the Court what you found concerning Sumner School.

A. The Sumner School is white, age fifteen years, value $15,936 per room. It's another excellent building; beautiful [fol. 201] auditorium, a large good gymnasium, has its public address system; the books are good; very attractive kindergarten. Again, the facilities are available for an excellent educational opportunity.

Q. Would you do the same concerning the Van Buren School.

A. Van Buren is a white school, age forty-one years, value $6,030 per classroom. Although it's an old building, it has steel stairways which eliminates some fire hazard. It has an auditorium and a playroom; has good pictures and good books. The one fire escape, however, is approached through a window on the second floor which might be locked or hard for children to reach in an emergency. However, the building can still provide a fair educational opportunity.

Q. Would you tell the Court what you found concerning the Washington School.

A. Washington is a colored school, thirty-six years old, valued at $6,284. It's a fairly good building in a rather unattractive setting. One room seemed to be set aside for books. The books were fair; better than in most of the colored buildings. The faculty here—there was evidence to lead us to believe that the faculty here were doing the best to make the most of their facilities.

Q. Are there other buildings that you did not visit, Dr. Speer, but concerning which you have data.

[fol. 202] A. Yes, there are, I think, eight other buildings that I have this data on.

Q. Could you rapidly go down that list and tell the Court what data you found.

A. Yes, I will very quickly read age first and value second, if I may.

Central Park, white, thirty-nine years old, $5,160.

Clay, White, twenty-five years old, $12,750.

Grant, thirteen years old, $15,336. Grant is a white school.

Lincoln, a white school, thirty-five years old, $4,610.

Lowman Hill, a white school, forty-eight years old, $5,220.

Quincy, white building, forty-seven years old, $4,040.

Quinton Heights, thirty-eight years old, $3,024.

I might mention here that there is a new building now under construction to be called the Southwest building which, I presume, will be available sometime during the coming year and, by our formula, the insured value per classroom should be about $26,660.

Q. Now, Dr. Speer, you have gone through all the schools [fol. 203] in the City of Topeka, and I would like to ask you some hypothetical questions which I would like you to answer on the basis of your study of the schools in the City of Topeka and on the basis of your knowledge and experience and study as an educator.

I want you to assume the following set of facts, Dr. Speer: That a negro child who lives in Topeka, where there are racially segregated schools, attends the Buchanan School, although if there were not racial segregation in the City of Topeka, because of where he lives, he would otherwise attend the Randolph School, would you say that on the basis of the evidence you have given above and the other factors which I mentioned, that he obtains the same educational opportunity at Buchanan that he would obtain if he attended Randolph?

Mr. Goodell: To which we object as the hypothetical question assumes a fact not proven, and the fact assumes another fact that is contrary to some evidence. The fact it assumes that if the child lived at Randolph and there wasn't racial segregation he would attend Randolph. It assumes that fact. It isn't necessarily so. The child, even if you didn't have segregation, might not prefer to go to Randolph. He might prefer to go to some school where he wasn't outnumbered by fifty to one. Object to the question in the present form because it assumes a hypothe- [fol. 204] tical fact unsupported by any evidence.

Judge Huxman: You may answer, Doctor.

The Witness: The question, as I understand it——

Mr. Greenberg: (To reporter) Would you read it back, please.

(The last preceding question was read by the reporter.)

By Mr. Greenberg:

Q. What is your answer to that question, Dr. Speer?
A. No, I would say he would not get the same educational opportunity for some of the following reasons: First of

all, the Buchanan building is an older building; it's thirty years old; Randolph is twenty-four years old. The insured value per classroom for Buchanan is $5,623; for Randolph it's $6,947. To look at some of the details of the buildings, Buchanan has no combined gymnasium-auditorium; Randolph has one that is not completely adequate but it will hold several grades at one time. The furniture——

Mr. Goodell: Pardon me, I want to interpose another objection, that this has no probative force to show denial of equal protection of the law on this sort of a comparison because he is now demonstrating that because—that an inequality exists because some physical plants are newer [fol. 205] and bigger and better than other physical plants. He is comparing, it's true, with a colored plant, but he is also in the other part of his testimony—he has shown that the same disparity exists between many white schools as to the newer school where we have very old schools, very low cost per capita per room, classroom, and also the testimony very obviously shows no school system in the world could have buildings equal because newer buildings necessarily incorporate modern facilities not known when they were built twenty or thirty years ago.

Mr. Greenberg: May I answer that, Your Honor?

Mr. Goodell: I address that to the Court, not you.

Mr. Greenberg: I didn't ask you whether I could answer it.

Judge Huxman: The witness may answer.

The Witness: Proceeding, on the other hand, we might say that the Randolph building has these features, a much more attractive kindergarten room, more spacious playground, much more attractive surroundings which adds to its aesthetic educational value, and I would add, if I may consult my notes a moment here——

Mr. Greenberg: Go ahead.

The Witness: That the books in the Randolph School are better than the books in the Buchanan building, in [fol. 206] my judgment. There are better heating and lighting in the Randolph building, and I think I would add, Your Honor, that most important of all the curriculum in the Randolph building provides a much better educational opportunity than the one in the Buchanan building, because, in the Randolph building, the colored child would have opportunity to learn to live with, to work with, to cooperate with, white children who are representative of approximately 90% of the population of the society in which he is to live.

By Mr. Greenberg:

Q. Now, Dr. Speer, rather than asking you the same question again, I would like you to answer the same question, comparing the Gage and the Buchanan Schools.

Judge Huxman: Would your answers be substantially the same, based upon substantially the same reasons?

The Witness: Some of the reasons would be the same, Your Honor. However, I believe this particular comparison the difference is greater.

Judge Huxman: Well, would be a difference of degree, otherwise your answer would be the same.

The Witness: Some of the specific details might be different.

Judge Huxman: Does that satisfy you, Mr.——
[fol. 207] Mr. Greenberg: That is all right; that satisfies us, yes.

By Mr. Greenberg:

Q. I would like to ask you the same question concerning a comparison of Sumner and Monroe Schools, Dr. Speer.

A. Sumner and Monroe. Again I would say for some of the same kinds of reasons that the Sumner building would provide a better educational opportunity.

Judge Huxman: May I ask the doctor a question?
Mr. Greenberg: Yes.

Judge Huxman: To be sure I understand his answer, is one of the reasons which is common to all three of these, your reason that they are by segregation denied in all three of these schools the opportunity to mingle and live with the white children, which they would otherwise have and that, to you, is an important factor, is that part of your answer?

The Witness: Yes, Your Honor, that would enter into all of them.

Judge Huxman: I was quite sure that was it, but I wanted to be clear in my own mind that that was a part of your answer in all of these schools.

By Mr. Greenberg:

Q. Dr. Speer, I would like you to make a similar comparison between State and Washington Schools.
[fol. 208] A. The same curriculum reasons, of course, apply and, in addition, we find, as I stated in earlier testimony, that the State Street School is one of the better schools, and it has many features such as the P. A. system and a beautiful auditorium, an excellent playground, a library room, a kitchen that can be used to provide a considerably better educational opportunity than could be provided in the Washington School.

Mr. Greenberg: Your witness.
Judge Huxman: You may cross examine.

Cross-examination.

By Mr. Goodell:

Q. Dr. Speer, if I understand your testimony correctly, boiled down to—as to the physical facts on the comparison of buildings and facilities feature of it, eliminating the racial feature, is it your opinion that any school, white school, that is considerably older and inferior and a wide disparity as to modern facilities, that that child going to such a white school is likewise being denied an equal opportunity of education?

A. It is unequal in another sense, I would say, if I understand your question correctly. Would you mind repeating the crux of it; I am not sure that I understand you.

Q. What I am trying to say is, eliminating the racial feature and restricting your opinion entirely to comparison of plants, facilities and accessories, will you still [fol. 209] say that a child, a white child, who goes to one of these other schools, such as Lafayette, Quinton Heights, Polk and some of these old schools, and Lowman, are denied equal educational opportunities as against children —as compared to children who live in a territory such as Oakland and Randolph and Potwin and get to go to those new schools.

A. A child might be—might have an inferior educational opportunity in some respects, but he would not have the stigma of segregation, nor be denied the opportunity to mix with the majority group of the population. Also——

Q. I said eliminating that feature of it. Other than that, do you consider that it's an inferior opportunity as far as the white child is concerned so that he is denied an equal opportunity of education, eliminating the racial thing.

A. It might be if all other facilities are equal, but that is an accident of geography.

Q. Well, you made comparisons between some of the best white schools we have here in town to the colored schools, haven't you?

A. Yes, sir.

Q. Now, while we are on that subject, I will ask you to turn to Exhibit "K", which is the Board of Education's record pertaining to the original cost of these buildings [fol. 210] and also, in the same connection——

A. I don't have a copy of that here, sir.

Q. I will step over here and let you see it. What I have marked on my copy here in red are the negro schools; what I have marked in blue pencil are the white schools; you understand?

A. Yes, sir.

Q. Now, I will direct your attention, if the schools that were built about the same time, the white schools, as the colored schools, if this exhibit doesn't show the same—practically—outlay of cost and, in some instances, more money spent for structural, or the school, and land acquisition than there were for white schools that were built at that same period of time.

A. I think that may be possible.

Q. Doesn't the exhibit show that, the records of the Board of Education.

A. Which two buildings do you mean?

Q. Well, compare Quinton Heights, which was built in 1913, at a cost of $12,640.

A. With what?

Q. We will get that in a minute, and McKinley, which was built six years earlier at a cost of $51,000 for the structure.

A. I would say that between 1907 and 1913 building costs might have fluctuated a great deal, and I don't think—
[fol. 211] I would not base a comparison on building—on construction cost with that many years intervening. That is why we used insurance costs which are supposed to be current and accurate as prepared by the Board of Education.

Q. Let's compare Lowman Hill, which is a white school built, according to the exhibit, in 1906, with McKinley.

A. May I correct you? It was built in 1901 and an addition in 1906.

Q. All right. Compare that to McKinley School.

A. McKinley School was built in 1907, six years later; again there may have been considerable difference in construction costs over a six-year period. They sometimes change very rapidly to the best cycle and other things.

Q. Let's look at the exhibit on the insurance values; don't you see disparity between the old white schools and the new white schools?

A. That is possible.

Q. On the present insurance table——

Judge Mellott: What is the exhibit on the insurance?
Mr. Goodell: "L".

By Mr. Goodell:

Q. I call your attention specifically to some schools shown on this exhibit and their present insurance values as shown by this exhibit. Quinton Heights has a total [fol. 212] structure insured value of $14,000, doesn't it?

A. Yes, sir.

Q. Van Buren has an insured value of $46,800, doesn't it?

A. Yes, sir.

Q. That is a white school. Washington has an insured value of $64,800, doesn't it?

A. Yes, sir.

Q. Monroe has an insured value of $112,000, doesn't it?

9—8

A. Yes, sir.

Q. So there you have got three white schools, all of which are lower present value than the colored schools, isn't that right?

A. If I may express my view, my basis, you cannot compare building by building on—even on insured cost because some buildings are larger than others. Therefore, the only basis I was able to arrive at was an insured value per available classroom. You have to have some kind of a common yardstick to use on all buildings. For instance, some of those buildings are twice as big as others and, therefore, their value would naturally be proportionately greater.

Q. Do you know of any school system in the United States—not just Topeka—in the United States, that has buildings that are equal, that there isn't great differences based upon when they were built and the needs of the com-
[fol. 213] munity at the time they were built?

A. That has not—doesn't have great differences as to their value and commodious quarters and characters that are recognized now in modern education and that are applied in modern buildings, that doesn't have great disparities, those types of buildings, in any school system in the United States with buildings built twenty, thirty or forty years ago.

A. I believe there is very likely to be some disparity, may not be great, and may not be great as compared to this group and this group, but between individual buildings, I am sure you would find some disparity if there is more than one building.

Q. You realize that school buildings are built as a community grows up and population trends—where the town grows and which way it grows determines whether buildings are located and newer buildings are added.

A. That is one factor.

Q. Do you know of any way *way* on earth to keep those facilities adequate and at the same time equal in any school system?

A. There are ways that it can be approached.

Q. Well, just tell me how you would approach it.

A. By forming a good cooperative city planning with

the Board of Education and the City Commissioners on [fol. 214] a long-term scale and then following it.

Q. Would you recommend that if we had a building like, say in Topeka, that cost $112,000 and is now a sound and structural safe colored building, that you tear that down because we happen to have a new building built a year ago that cost a half million dollars; would you recommend that?

A. Not merely for that reason, no.

Q. What other reasons would you have for tearing it down?

A. If I found that throughout the community the colored children's buildings were decidedly inferior to the buildings of the white schools, then I would consider that to be an unequal educational opportunity between the groups.

Q. Well, now, let's talk about that subject. Let's talk about Quinton Heights and Polk Street and Lafayette School and Lowman School, all of which have a physical plant value at the time they were built and at the present time, an insurance value less than any of the four colored schools. Do you think that makes the white children get inferior education than to the colored children going to those schools?

A. The colored children are getting an inferior education, I think, for this reason: That, as I cited in my original testimony, 45% of the white children can go to schools that are newer than the newest colored building; only 14% [fol. 215] of the white children have to go to schools that are older than the oldest colored building, so it's a comparison of 14% against 45%.

Q. Let's get back on the track. I asked you whether or not, using an illustration of four white schools, if they are inferior as to value, both at the time they were built and now, to the colored schools, do you consider that alone makes the white child that is attending those schools, Quinton Heights, Polk, Lowman and Lafayette, receive in and of itself, receive an inferior education.

A. Not necessarily.

Q. Well, then, why do you say that when you talk about that element as causing the colored child——

A. Because——

Q. Wait just a minute until I ask my question, will you please? Why do you say that when you are talking about a colored child who goes to one of the four colored schools and you compare the plant and facilities to some of the modern buildings—school buildings—in the last two or three years.

A. Because, in the first instance, we are assuming——

Judge Mellott: The witness must wait until the question is completely asked. The reporter can't get it down when you both talk at the same time.

(The last preceding question was read by the re-
[fol. 216] porter.)

Judge Mellott: Strike out the answer as partially given.

By Mr. Goodell:

Q. Why do you say in such a situation in making the comparison in the case of a negro child going to one of the four negro schools, comparing it to some of the schools built in the Topeka area, in the Topeka school system in the last two or three or four years, such as Randolph, Potwin and Oakland, that that fact alone gives the negro child an inferior educational opportunity, that would not apply in the case of the children going to the white schools that I have previously mentioned in my other question.

A. In the first instance, if I understand you correctly, I was assuming that other things were equal because of the —as we admitted, the faculty preparation is approximately equal, the class size equal, and so forth. But, in the latter instance, other things are not equal primarily because of the difference in the curriculum which is a very important factor.

Q. All right, now, what is present in the case of the Quinton Heights white school, in the curriculum you talk about, that is not present for comparison purposes in any of the four colored schools?

A. Because in Quinton Heights the child has the opportunity to learn his personal adjustments, his social adjust-
[fol. 217] ments and his citizenship skills in the presence of a cross-section of the population.

Q. I asked you to eliminate the racial feature entirely and restrict it to physical things alone; that is what I asked you.

The Witness: If the Court will permit, I don't think that we can answer an educational opportunity purely on physical features. There are too many other elements that are also involved.

Q. Mr. Speer, Professor Speer, I probably misunderstood you. I thought—I understood your testimony to be that because of these physical things that in and of itself, ignoring the racial thing, that that constituted an unequal educational opportunity to the negro child because of these modern buildings that he wasn't allowed to go to; is that correct, or not?

A. It is certainly one of the very important things and, if the other factors are equal, and this one is unequal, then there may be an inequality in the total educational opportunity.

Q. Maybe I am so stupid I can't understand you. Did you not say, is it your opinion, that because of physical factors, and I mean by physical factors differences in plant facilities, of some of the white schools and the four negro [fol. 218] schools, that alone, in and of itself, causes you to give an opinion, and it is your opinion that that child, the negro child, because of that alone, doesn't have equal educational opportunity.

A. That is a contributing factor, but I do not consider that of—that alone.

Q. Then you didn't say that alone caused him to have an unequal opportunity.

A. No, but that coupled with other factors did cause him to have an unequal opportunity.

Q. What are the other factors rather than racial factors.

A. Curriculum factor; there is faculty; there is size of classrooms; there is books——

Q. Let's compare some white schools—let's take Quinton Heights, Lowman, Polk and Lafayette again. What is present as to the faculty, comparing that to the faculty of the four negro schools, that is inferior or that is—there is a disparity.

134

Mr. Carter: I would like—I think that we have listened to this line of questioning—it seems to us that it is now objectionable. What I apparently gather from the line of examination that is being made is that the—Mr. Goodell is attempting to establish that because there are deprivations of white children that he call off the deprivations of the negro child in segregation. We don't think that is [fol. 219] the issue in the case.

Judge Huxman: This is cross-examination of your expert witness where the latitude is a little greater. You may proceed.

By Mr. Goodell:

Q. Restricting now for this question, I will ask you to compare and point out dissimilarities or disparities between the faculty—one thing alone now—the faculty, that is, the teaching in the four white schools, that is, Quinton, Polk—Quinton Heights, Polk Street, Lowman Hill and Lafayette, to the four negro schools that are in issue in this lawsuit.

A. I can't answer that at the moment, sir. I would have to add up the preparation of the faculties of those four particular schools. I do not have that at hand. I added them up for the entire system and took the entire averages, but I do not have them for those four particular schools.

Q. As far as you know, they are perfectly equal then, is that right?

A. I don't think they could be perfectly equal; that would be impossible.

Judge Huxman: Well, now, that is rather quibbling, of course. Perfect equality you can't find in two teachers any place.

Mr. Goodell: I think so.
The Witness: Yes.

[fol. 220] By Mr. Goodell:

Q. What—is the faculty, then, comparing it to the other factor which you mentioned, curriculum, on the four white schools covered by the illustration and the four negro schools——

A. How does the curriculum compare?

Q. Yes.

A. Between the two schools. As far as course of study is concerned, as far as I know, it is probably about equal but as far as the total curriculum is concerned, and that is the only basis on which I can discuss it, it is not equal.

Q. What do you mean by total curriculum?

A. I mean the total school experience of the school child, what the instructions, what the books are, what the surroundings of the buildings are, what his associations with the other children are.

Q. Well, eliminating that feature, the associations with the other children, which is the racial feature, what are the other part of the curriculum which is any dissimilarity or inferior factors present in the case of the negro schools and the white schools that I have used for illustration.

A. In professional circles we have a term called the great "gestalt" which means the sum is greater—the whole is greater than the sum of the parts and, when we start taking into account only the parts one by one, we destroy [fol. 221] our "gestalt", and we cannot make a wise comparison.

Judge Mellott: What was that word?
The Witness: (Spelling) G-e-s-t-a-l-t.

By Mr. Goodell:

Q. Now you come from Missouri, don't you?

A. I at present live in Missouri, yes, sir.

Q. You have segregated schools there, don't you?

A. We have some segregated schools. On the university campus we have a mixed school.

Q. I am talking about the public school system in the State of Missouri.

A. Yes, sir.

Q. And it is mandatory, isn't that right?

A. I presume in some cases it is.

Q. Have you studied any of the various state statutes over the country which we have had for a half century concerning this segregation of students?

Mr. Carter: Your Honor, I can't see how this——
Mr. Goodell. This is preliminary for another question.

Judge Huxman: I think that is an improper question. Well, as long as it is preliminary, you may answer whether you have or have not studied these various statutes.

Mr. Goodell: I will withdraw the question.

[fol. 222]   By Mr. Goodell:

Q. You know in a great many cities and communities of the United States there are statutes similar to the statutes here in Kansas which we have had for a half century or three-fourts of a century, isn't that right?

A. I presume so.

Q. You know, as a practical man, laws get passed by legislators coming from the various parts of their communities over the state, don't you?

A. Yes, sir.

Judge Huxman: Mr. Goodell, what is the purpose of that question? What value does that have to our problem how laws are passed?

Mr. Goodell: I am getting to that. I can't ask it all at once. I am trying to get from this witness the feature as to whether he thinks elimination of racial segregation, if it's unwanted by the community and is out of step with the thinking of the community which the mere existence of the laws have some indication——

Judge Huxman: I think Dr. Speer has made it quite clear from his evidence—he has to me at least, if I understand it—that segregation, racial segregation, is the prime and controlling factor of the equality of the whole curriculum, and that these physical factors are secondary, and that his testimony, as it registered with me, is that aside from [fol. 223] racial segregation he perhaps would not testify that there was any such inequality in the physical properties as would deny anybody an equal educational opportunity. Do I understand your testimony correctly?

The Witness: If I may say, Your Honor, I think I would sum up this way: That there is, in my opinion, some inequality in physical facilities between the groups in Topeka, but, in addition to that, there is also the difference of segregation itself which affects the school curriculum.

Judge Huxman: Let's see if I can get myself straightened

out. Do you not also agree with what Mr. Goodell is trying to bring out here—you haven't gotten together—that if you put it on that fact, that there is inequality in physical facilities as between the white schools and the colored schools, sometimes the greater facilities are with the colored schools against the older white schools.

The Witness: Yes, Your Honor, but they are not as many in that direction as there are in the other direction in this case.

Judge Huxman: It seems to me we are spending a lot of time on that when that is rather, it seems to me, it would be obvious if you have an older white building [fol. 224] than a colored building that perhaps the physical facilities in the older white building would be poorer than the colored building.

The Witness: Yes, I will agree.

Mr. Goodell: I will try to shorten this up.

By Mr. Goodell:

Q. If I understand you correctly, the basis of your opinion on saying that the mere separation—strike that. It's your opinion, then, that you can't have separate schools in any public school system and have equality, is that right?

A. Yes.

Q. And that is predicated on the—on your philosophy or your theory that merely because the two races are kept apart in the educational process, isn't that right, mere separation causes inequality.

A. That is one of the things which causes inequality, yes, sir.

Q. Yes. Now, assuming, Doctor, that we didn't have separate schools and they were altogether, and you still had a social situation in this community which didn't recoignize co-mingling of the races, didn't admit them on free equality, that child would run against those—run up against those things in his practical every-day world, wouldn't he?

[fol. 225] A. I presume so.

Q. Sir?

A. I would think so.

138

Q. Wouldn't that tend to cause more of a tempest and emotional strain or psychological impact if he got used to going to school with white children than when he went downtown and couldn't eat in a white restaurant, couldn't go to a white hotel and couldn't do this and that, wouldn't that make the impact greater and accentuate that very thing.

Mr. Greenberg: This witness is qualified as an expert in the field of education, and I don't believe has testified or is qualified to testify concerning segregation all over the State of Kansas or elsewhere.

Mr. Goodell: Well, I restrict it to Topeka.

Judge Huxman: I think the Court will sustain the objection. That is purely argumentative. I doubt whether the doctor has qualified himself.

By Mr. Goodell:

Q. Assuming, Doctor, we will restrict this to the educational process, assuming that—that we didn't have segregation, for the purpose of this question, and assuming further we had a negro child going to Potwin or Oakland or Randolph and assuming that the population trend appears in the schoolroom as it does in our city, so that he would be outnumbered from twenty to fifty to one, assuming all that, for the purpose of this question as being true, [fol. 226] wouldn't that cause some inferiority feeling on the part of the colored child when he went to such a school where he was outnumbered twenty to fifty to one and caused some sort of mental disturbance and upset.

A. On which basis would you rather for me to—on theory or on personal observation or experience?

Q. I am talking about theory here.

A. And personal observation and experience.

Q. Yes.

A. Let me first mention the latter one; we have adjoining our campus a demonstration school of 210 students in the elementary grades and mixed in with them are about ten negro children, so they are outnumbered in that proportion, and my observation is, and the reports I receive from my assistants are, that those children are very happy, very well adjusted, and they are there voluntarily. They don't have to attend.

Mr. Elisha Scott: I object to that.

Judge Huxman: Mr. Scott, are you entered here as an attorney of record?

Mr. Elisha Scott: I am supposed to be.

Judge Huxman: Go ahead.

Mr. Elisha Scott: I object to that because he is invading the rights, and he is answering a question not based upon [fol. 227] the evidence adduced or could be adduced.

Mr. Goodell: You just got here; you wouldn't know.

Mr. Elisha Scott: Yes I do know.

Judge Huxman: Objection will be overruled. You may answer.

The Witness: Shall I repeat the answer?

By Mr. Goodell:

Q. Have you finished?

A. I think, also, on the basis of our knowledge of child behavior that we can say on a short-range basis there may be occasionally, the first time we jump into water we may be a little bit frightened, but, on a long-range basis, we generally are able to work out our adjustments and make a good situation out of it.

Q. Segregation occurs, doesn't it, Doctor, in any school system among the races. I mean by that, children that come from wealthy families co-mingle with children from poor families; they go off into different cliques; that occurs, doesn't it?

A. It occurs sometimes.

Q. Occurs frequently, doesn't it?

A. Well, it all depends on your definition.

Q. And the child that is left out of the swim, so to speak, he feels inferior or second-class, doesn't he?

A. Yes, and I think we should prevent that in all cases [fol. 228] possible.

Q. You wouldn't make a new social order to prevent social strata of society, would you?

Judge Huxman: Just a minute. The Court will sustain an objection to that question.

By Mr. Goodell:

Q. Have you made a survey of any of the students that have gone to our segregated schools, the negro students, and picked them up to see what effect to their education that you call attention to as being inferior, how it's worked out in every-day life.

A. I have talked to a few of them, but I have not made a survey of them.

Q. Have you heard of anybody getting hired or a professional man having a plant or a businessman having a customer based upon what elementary school he went to in the first grade or the second grade or the sixth grade for that matter?

A. Oh, probably not, but probably there are cases where a person is hired or not hired on the basis of the kind of education he received in the first six grades.

Q. You don't know a thing about our community and how the negro child, when he goes through our school system, how he is received in the business world at all, do you?

A. Oh, I have known Topeka for some years. I may have a little knowledge.

[fol. 229] Q. Do you know anything about that?

A. A little, not too much.

Q. What?

A. I don't know too much about it.

Q. Do you know that in the case of the junior high grades and in the senior high grades that they are not segregated?

A. Yes, sir.

Q. Do you think, getting back to the school system and the illustration of where the negro child would go to a school where he would be outnumbered twenty to fifty to one, and he wasn't recognized because of pure majority rule and wasn't elected head of his class or class officers or recognized in the various school activities, that that would have any impact on such a child.

A. Not as much impact as having been denied even to get into the running.

Q. You think if you got in the school and left out entirely he would feel happy about it, would he?

A. What's that again?

Q. You think if the negro child was simply by edict of

law forced into the white school, whether the white school was ready to receive him or not, and however much he was in the minority and however much he would be left out of things, he would still be happy merely because he had found his way into the white school, is that right?

[fol. 230] A. I think on a long-range plan he would be happier than on the other way.

Mr. Goodell: That's all.

Mr. Carter: Your Honor, may we have a five-minute recess?

Judge Huxman: Yes. The court will take a ten-minute recess.

(The court then, at 2:40 o'clock p. m., stood at recess until 2:50 o'clock p. m., at which time court was reconvened and the following further proceedings were had:)

Mr. Goodell: I would like to recall Dr. Speer for two short questions.

Judge Huxman: Dr. Speer, take the witness stand for a question or two further.

HUGH W. SPEER, having been previously sworn, reassumed the stand and testified further as follows:

Cross-examination (continued).

By Mr. Goodell:

Q. Dr. Speer, in giving your opinion here a moment ago as to the comparison based upon library books—library or books in certain of the negro—in the negro schools to certain of the white schools covered by your testimony, did you consider, in forming that opinion, the fact that the Par- [fol. 231] ent Teachers Association in the various school territories contribute personally and raise the money to buy those books, and they are not furnished by the Board of Education.

A. Yes, I have been informed that that is sometimes the case.

Q. Well, how did you segregate which books have been bought by Parent Teachers Association and the books that have been furnished by the Board of Education?

A. I didn't make that separation. I felt that by neglect the Board of Education permitted an inequality to exist.

Q. Now, did you also—strike that. State whether or not any of the books in any of the libraries or rooms in the schools that you made the investigation concerning books, that at the end of the term the books, some of them, were gone, that is, packed up in boxes.

A. Yes, we understood that, and we also understood that some of the books are regularly kept in the central office of the Board of Education, and we took that into account, knowing that the same—those books are taken out of all the schools and kept in the Board of Education, so that what remained are really the comparable—form the basis for comparison.

Q. So if some of the books were missing, either being packed up or gone, and you didn't know what they were, you are just basing your testimony, your considered opin-
[fol. 232] ion, on what you found, is that right?

A. Sir, the books that were gone are the books that circulate among all the buildings in the course of the year, so we assume that those are equal. It's the books that are left in the building that really belong to that building, and it is on that basis that we made our differential.

Q. Were some of them packed up?

A. Some of them packed up, and we looked into the boxes.

Q. Did you take them all out volume by volume and examine them?

A. We did not examine every book in the Topeka school system, but we sampled it in an unbiased way. We sampled a large number of rooms and a large number of buildings and a large number of boxes, but we did not examine every book.

Q. You mean you took a book out here and there from a box and, from that, made up your mind that they were all alike and, consequently, that is the way you got at your opinion.

A. No, sir. We took sampling in a scientific way.

Q. What do you mean scientific way?

A. We took a sample that was representative and large enough to where we could feel confident in it.

Judge Huxman: Is that all?

By Mr. Goodell:

Q. Which books were bought in the various schools that you gave your opinion about—were bought by the Parent [fol. 233] Teachers Association?

A. I don't know just which books. Some, no doubt, were but not a great many. It is not enough to affect the percentage very much.

Q. If you don't know what books they were, some of the books you didn't even examine, you don't know what quantity they are, how do you get at an opinion as to book facilities at the various schools?

A. On this basis, sir, that it is the books in the school that are responsible for the education of the child, and we examined the books in the school and, on that basis, we made our opinion.

Q. So what you are saying, if I understand you right, the books you found and examined showed less books or inferior quality as to date and so forth in the colored schools than the books you found in the white schools, is that right?

A. Yes, sir.

Mr. Goodell: All right.
Judge Huxman: Step down.

JAMES H. BUCHANAN, having been first duly sworn, assumed the stand and testified as follows:

Direct examination.

By Mr. Greenberg:

[fol. 234] Q. Dr. Buchanan, will you tell the Court your full name, please.
A. James H. Buchanan.

144

Q. Please tell the Court something of your educational background.

A. At the present time I am Director of the Graduate Division, Kansas State Teachers College, and acting head of the Department of Education. The year preceding this year I was associate professor of education at the Kansas State Teachers College. Six years preceding that time, from 1943 to 1949, I was superintendent of schools at Boulder, Colorado. From 1933 to 1943 superintendent of schools in Lamar, Colorado, and, from 1930 to '33, superintendent of schools at La Jara, Colorado, and, from 1928 to 1930, superintendent of schools in Boyero, Colorado.

Q. Dr. Buchanan, what degrees do you hold and where were they earned?

A. I hold an A.B. Degree from Denver University, 1928; Master of Arts Degree, University of Colorado, 1932; I have had three years—three summers of graduate study at Harvard University, 1936, 1938, 1939, and a Doctor of Education Degree from the University of Colorado, 1949.

Q. Have you visited any of the schools in the City of Topeka?

A. Yes.

Q. Did you visit the Buchanan School?

[fol. 235]   A. Yes, I did.

Q. Gage, Lafayette?

A. Yes.

Q. McKinley?

A. Yes.

Q. Monroe?

A. Yes.

Q. Parkdale?

A. Yes.

Q. Polk?

A. Yes.

Q. Potwin?

A. Yes.

Q. Randolph?

A. Yes.

Q. State Street?

A. Yes.

Q. Sumner?
A. Yes.
Q. Van Buren?
A. Yes.
Q. Washington?
A. Yes.

Q. Did you observe the general appearance of the interior, exterior and the surrounding areas about the school? [fol. 236] A. I did.

Q. Would you describe what you noticed with regard to these factors in the Randolph School.

A. Well, I would say that the Randolph School was situated in a very average residential section; perhaps above average. I think the school is a well-constructed building; it shows good signs of being in a very good state of repair, I should say, and the maintenance in it has been excellent. The facilities in it, such as auditorium, the classrooms and so on, are adequate to a good educational program. I would say the grounds are ample for proper play and recreation for the pupils.

Q. Would you tell us what you found concerning these factors at the Buchanan School, Dr. Buchanan.

A. I would say that the Buchanan School is an older school. It has been well constructed. The walls are in a good state of preservation; redecoration seems to have been done within a reasonable time and the maintenance is equally good. I think in the maintenance you have to take into consideration the age of the building, but I would say it was very good at the Buchanan School. The playground, it would seem to me, was ample for recreational facilities. I think there was no auditorium in the Buchanan School, but it was my impression that adequate precautions have been made for prevention of fire or escape from the building [fol. 237] in case of fire.

Q. I don't recall, Dr. Buchanan, did you say anything concerning the surrounding areas of the Buchanan School?

A. Yes, I would say the surrounding area, as I observed it, being a stranger to the city, practically so, was not quite as substantial; certainly not as substantial a residential area as I would say around the Randolph School.

10—8

146

In other words, I would say it would reflect the general community in which it was associated, perhaps both in age and state of preservation of the building.

Q. Would you tell us what you found concerning the Gage School, Dr. Buchanan.

A. Well, the Gage School is a very fine school. I would say, speaking from memory, I would say it's within a few years of the age of the Randolph School. I have the impression it's somewhat larger. It had some very good pictures on the wall; the walls were in a good state of preservation; there was some repair work going on. There were some rooms in which they needed some repair work and were planning on doing it immediately because there were materials placed outside the doors and, in some places, the floors were up. I would say that the playground and the landscaping is quite attractive and quite beautiful; a very nice piece of work.

Q. Would you tell us, now, what you found concerning [fol. 238] the Sumner School.

A. The Sumner School is a newer school than Gage. I think it's perhaps about ten or eleven years old. It has quite ample—very spacious suitable classroom facilities and a nice auditorium. I think the landscaping would be nothing that anyone could take particular objection to. The general appearance of the building, I should say, was in keeping with a good school situation.

Q. Will you now tell us what you found concerning the Monroe School, Dr. Buchanan.

A. I would say the Monroe School would compare fairly well in construction, in appearance, with the Randolph School, I would rather carry them in mind. I think the Monroe School, I woud say, is about twenty-four, twenty-five years of age. It has fireproof stairways. It shows sign of good care and good maintenance and quite serviceable, I should say, for a number of years. The playground and the landscaping in front of the building is about in keeping with the community in which it is located, I should say. In other words, I would say it is a credit to the community.

Q. And would you tell the Court about the State Street School?

147

A. Yes. I saw the State Street School. It is a very good school, I should say; it's more or less in a class with the Sumner School, perhaps a little more modernistic, a [fol. 239] little more in keeping with modern design and the demands of modern education. The playground or the grounds that were vacant, which I assume were available for the children, I thought were quite adequate and quite spacious for a large enrollment. It had auditorium facilities and other features of that kind that make for a good educational situation.

Q. Would you tell us something about the area surrounding the State Street School.

A. I would say that it was quite a creditable residential section.

Mr. Goodell: I didn't hear that.

The Witness: I say it was quite a creditable residential section; very good residential section.

By Mr. Greenberg:

Q. Would you tell us what you found concerning the Washington School, Dr. Buchanan?

A. Well, the Washington School is an older school; I think it is not so old as the Buchanan School; at least that is my impression of it. It has been well cared for. It has an auditorium which, I would assume, for an enrollment of 150, 160 children, would be adequate for them. The maintenance there is quite a creditable thing. I would say that was characteristic of the Topeka schools. There were fourteen I visited; I would say the maintenance and repairs were quite good.

[fol. 240] Q. In your visit to the fourteen schools, Dr. Buchanan, did you make any general observations concerning the areas in which they exist?

A. I think I have already implied that in the answers that I have given. My observation would be that the schools visited, the fourteen of the twenty-two schools, reflect the communities in which they are located, that is, if they are like, well, Polk, perhaps Buchanan, Gage; the varying degrees of the quality of the school is somewhat dependent upon the age of the residential region or section of the city in which they are located. That is, you would find the better schools in the places that are comparatively newer and better developed; that would be my general observation. The poorer schools were perhaps in a region, we might say, have longer been a residential region or area of the city, which is tending, perhaps, to slide down just a bit in quality.

Q. Can you make any general statement concerning the negro schools which you saw and the areas in which they live, Dr. Buchanan.

A. My general statement would be merely to say that they reflect the situation which I have outlined. I think they show a very good care. I think, for instance, the Monroe School, is a school that definitely looks the way you would expect; I think anyone who has had experience [fol. 241] in examining or visiting schools would say that it looks about the way you would expect it to look when you see it from the outside and when you go in. It has been well cared for. All of the schools in Topeka I was impressed by the fact that there was a minimum amount of marking on the walls or disfiguring of the walls or furniture in any way, either in the white schools or the colored schools.

Q. Did you make any general observation concerning the areas in which these colored schools existed, Doctor?

A. I would say, in general, they probably are in the areas which were not the best residential section of the city. I don't know that they would be the poorest, but they were not in the best residential section, and I think there was some variation there. I thought I observed some variation in the quality of the residential section.

Q. Dr. Buchanan, in evaluating the quality of education which a student obtains when attending school, does an educator consider the physical characteristics of the school; I mean their appearance and the appearance which they present to the child, along with the appearance of the area in which the school exists. Is there a direct correlation between that and educational opportunity?

A. Yes, I think that is true. I think the educator—educators do recognize the relationship between the quality [fol. 242] of the building, landscaping of the grounds, the area in which it is placed as an important factor in education.

Q. Now, bearing that criterion in mind, Dr. Buchanan, I would like you to make several comparisons. I want you to assume in the City of Topeka a negro child would attend Randolph School, if there were not racial segregation in the city, but is compelled to attend Buchanan because of racial segregation. Would you say that if all other factors in the City of Topeka and in the schools were equal, except these factors concerning appearance, residential area, and so forth which you have just described in answer to a previous question, if all factors were equal except those factors, would the child attending Buchanan obtain the same educational opportunities that he would obtain if he attended Randolph?

A. I believe no; my answer would be that he would not receive the same educational opportunity.

Q. Well, bearing in mind the correlation which you stated between educational opportunity and physical appearance and area, would you explain the reason for your answer?

A. I believe that education is best facilitated when it is in a beautiful environment, where there is a building which pupils can take pride in and where they have beautiful landscaping and the interior of the building is a place where there are the maximum number of modern facilities [fol. 243] to facilitate a good curriculum.

Q. And to the extent that these are different, you would say that the opportunity to learn is different.

A. Beg pardon; would you——

Q. Would you say that to the extent that these are different, the opportunity to learn is different?

A. Yes, I think it has a relationship to the opportunity, yes.

Q. Is this supported by the authorities in the field of education, Dr. Buchanan?

A. I am certain it is, yes, sir.

Q. Did you say yes?

A. I am certain that it is, yes.

Q. Could you state any authorities who support this view?

A. Well, I think that my number of authorities, for instance, Dr. Reeder of Ohio State University in his recent publication on administration, "Public Education of the United States" which came from the press in 1951, just a few months ago, a revision of his book, makes that very clear. He makes that statement that the quality of a building, its setting, is an important factor in the education of a child. Strayer and Englehart, of Columbia University, who are recognized as the leading authorities in schoolhouse construction, hold that view and numerous others.

Judge Mellott: You drop your voice, and I usually get [fol. 244] most excepting the last two or three words. You drop your voice, and I can't hear you.

The Witness: I am sorry; I thought I had a very strong voice.

Judge Mellott: You do, but you don't keep it up.

By Mr. Greenberg:

Q. Dr. Buchanan, I am going to ask you to make three more comparisons without going into as much detail, if you believe the detail you stated concerning the first comparison applies to the following schools: I would like you to compare Gage against Buchanan with regard to these criteria.

A. I would say that Gage very obviously is a better school than Buchanan.

Q. On the basis of the criterion you stated?

A. Yes.

Q. I would like you to compare Sumner against Monroe.

A. Obviously Sumner is a better school than Monroe; a more up-to-date school, a newer school, as I have indicated.

Q. I would like you to compare State Street School against Washington Street School with regard to these criteria.

A. State Street is a better school than Washington School in terms of age, in the terms of these things we have talked about.

Mr. Greenberg: Your witness.

[fol. 245]   Cross-examination.

By Mr. Goodell:

Q. Dr. Buchanan, if I understand you correctly, you are stating that the plant or the building is a very important factor in the educational opportunity.

A. Yes.

Q. The building a child goes to.

A. Yes, indeed.

Q. And, therefore, where you have one building with shrubbery around it and landscaping, which is pretty, and another building built earlier many years ago which isn't as pretty, even however strong and commodious and sufficient, if it isn't as pretty and big and new and as modern, that educational opportunity is minimized in the child that goes to that building, is that right?

A. That would be—other factors being equal, I would say the better one——

Q. I am restricting it to that factor if I understood your testimony.

A. That's right; I would say that that would be detracting from it.

Q. The only way children in any community could have an equal educational opportunity would be to have buildings all beautiful, built about the same time, all modern, all beautifully landscaped and everything just about alike, [fol. 246] isn't that right?

A. As far as that factor is concerned, that is correct.

Q. As a practical matter, don't you realize that we live in a practical world?

A. I have lived in it for nearly fifty years.

Q. How do you think any Board of Education could have all of their buildings built at the same time, same landscaping——

Judge Huxman: You need not answer that question; that is argumentative, has no probative value.

By Mr. Goodell:

Q. Well, according to your theory, if I understand it right, if I went to a little country schoolhouse, even though I had good teaching and good texts and all other facilities, but not a building as good as Randolph, I was in a bad way, or anybody would be in a bad way, to get an education, is that right?

A. No, that isn't my theory. My theory would be you would get a better education if you had better equipment, but you would not—I wouldn't say you would have a poor education because you went to a poorer building. You might have a very superior teacher or you might have very superior ability yourself.

Q. Buildings don't make the educated child, does it?

A. I wouldn't say entirely, no; they are a contributing factor, but not the entire thing.

[fol. 247] Q. You compared the negro schools to Gage and Randolph and Sumner, I believe those three.

A. I think so.

Q. Now, would you please compare those same schools, I mean those white schools; they are all white schools, aren't they?

A. Yes.

Q. —with the schools of Lafayette and Quinton Heights and Polk and Lowman and Quincy.

A. Well, I didn't visit all you have named, but——

Q. Which did you visit?

A. Lafayette. I visited——

Q. Didn't you know we had those others?

A. Yes, but——

Q. You didn't get around to them.

A. We didn't get around to them. I would say that Lafayette compared with Gage or Randolph or Sumner would be far inferior.

Q. Far inferior.

A. Far inferior to it.

Q. We are discriminating then against a child that lives in that territory if he goes to Lafayette as against a child that lives—goes to Gage.

Judge Huxman: That is immaterial and need not be answered.

[fol. 248] Mr. Goodell: No further questions.

Judge Huxman: Anything else of this witness? Doctor, you may stand aside.

(Witness excused.)

R. S. B. ENGLISH, having been first duly sworn, assumed the stand and testified as follows:

Direct examination.

By Mr. Greenberg:

Q. Will you please tell the Court your full name, Mr. English.

A. Horace B. English.

Q. What is your occupation, Mr. English?

A. I am professor of psychology at the Ohio State University.

Q. Would you tell the Court something about your background and the degrees you hold.

A. I took my Bachelor's Degree at Oxford University, and there I also took a certificate in cultural anthropology. Later I took the Ph.D. Degree at Yale. As for my experience, I have been teaching and doing research work since 1916. I have been a full professor since 1921. During the war I was—during the first war I was psychological examiner and then chief of the re-education service in one of the hospitals. In the second world war I was a consultant on personnel problems part time for the Adjutant General's Office of the Army and then immediately after the surrender [fol. 249] I was a morale analyist in Japan. I then—I have had a number of part-time positions; I was consultant for the Forest Service on human relations. I was consultant to the West Virginia Department of Education on the curriculum in their state teachers colleges. I was chairman of the counsel on human relations appointed by the American Association for the Advancement of Science, for work with the Conservation Departments of the government, and I spent some six months in the study and research in the field of child development under the auspices of the American Council on Education.

Q. Have you ever held office in, or been a member of, any learned societies?

A. Yes, in the American Psychological Association I am a Fellow; I have been a member of the Council of Directors, and I have been chairman of the Committee on Professional Ethics of that association. At the moment I am president

of the Division of Educational Psychology of that association. In 1940 I was president of the American Association for the Advancement of Science—for the American Association for Applied Psychology, and I have been president of the Ohio State Psychologists and the Midwestern Psychological Association. And I am a Fellow of the British Psychological Society and member of the Executive Committee of the Psychology Section of the American As-
[fol. 250] sociation for the Advancement of Science.

Q. Have you ever published any books or articles in the field of education and psychology, Dr. English?

A. Published with Victor Ramey, of the University of Colorado, a book on studying the individual school child. Just this year brought out a textbook on child psychology, and I have published something around 150 articles in professional journals.

Q. Have you ever made any studies bearing on the capacities of different groups to profit by education?

A. Yes. As a matter of fact my first research, which was begun in 1912, was addressed to this very thing; the results were published in 1918. Then I was also on the team which brought out the celebrated alpha test of intelligence in the United States Army, as I helped with the experimental work which lead to that; and I have been continuously occupied in the field of individual differences and of group differences, and I teach that subject at the Ohio State University. Then I also supervise somewhere between 75 and 100 students a year who make case studies of individual children and I may add some of these are always negro children. I have done some research studies in the field of attitudes, including two of them concerning the attitudes of negroes and, finally, in this list I have done a rather prolonged [fol. 251] series of experiments in the field of learning with special reference to how children learn in school, rather than mere laboratory learning.

Q. Dr. English, have you told me all the courses that you now teach at Ohio State University?

A. No; I teach chiefly individual differences, child psychology and the more practical aspects of learning, rather than theoretical, and I also teach the theory of personality. Those are the main courses.

155

Q. Dr. English, at this point I want to ask you a hypothetical question. I want you to assume that in the City of Topeka there is a body of white school children and a body of negro school children, and that there is also racially enforced segregation in the schools. Would you say that on the basis of your learning, experience and study that on the basis of color alone there is a difference in their ability to learn?

A. No, there certainly is not.

Q. Would you tell me, the support for your statement.

A. Well, in the first place, we don't have racial groups learning; we have individuals learning and in both groups, white and negro, we have some persons who are very good learners; we have some persons who are very poor learners, and we have some medium learners. You can break that down to as fine a point as you like; the range is exactly [fol. 252] the same. Well, I say that, as a matter of fact, with regard to school children in respect to the I. Q. which is the best single measure of a child's ability to learn. The best I. Q. on record is that of a negro girl who has no white blood as far as that can be told at all, but right after this child there are four white children, so, you see, it's—at the top it's quite equal and at the bottom it's quite equal and in the middle it's quite equal. It's a matter of individuals and not a matter of groups. So knowing only the color you can't predict at all how well a child can learn. If a child is white you can't tell from that fact alone how well that child will learn in comparison with a group of negro children and, of course, vice versa from the fact that a child is a negro you can't tell how well he will learn with respect to a group of white children. From color alone there is no telling. We know that the negro child, moreover, learns in the same way, that he uses the same process in learning and learns the same things, but I do want to make one exception; it's a notable exception: If we din it into a person that it is unnatural for him to learn certain things, if we din it into a person that he is incapable of learning, then he is less likely to be able to learn.

Q. That difference is not based upon any inherent quality.

A. Not at all. It's a parallel exactly the way it is with [fol. 253] women learning mathematics. There is sort of

156

a supersticion that women are naturally incapable of learning mathematics, and so they don't, most of them, learn it. They can, if they will, and some of them do, but there is a tendency for us to live up to, or perhaps I should say to live down to the social expectation and to learn what we think people say we can learn, and legal segregation definitely depresses the negroes expectancy, and is therefore prejudicial to his learning. If you get a child in the attitude that he is somehow inferior, and he thinks to himself, "Well, I can't learn this very well.", then he is unlikely to learn it very well.

Q. Dr. English, is there any other scientific evidence to support this conclusion which you have stated other than what you have said.

A. Yes, there is a good deal. For example, in the last war we took the people who were illiterates. These, of course—a good many more of them were colored than white, but we put them into schools to teach them fourth-grade literacy and, as a matter of fact, 87% of the negroes and 84% of the whites successfully completed the work of these schools. Now I don't make anything of the difference of 3% in favor of the negroes as compared with the white. That is, of course, within the range of accidental error, but I say these results do show that under favorable conditions [fol. 254] and under conditions of motivation where these men wanted to learn, the negro men proved that they could learn as well as the whites. Most of the scientific evidence concerns intelligence testing, which, as I said a moment ago, is the best single measure of the ability to learn, and the scientific question that we would ask is, "Are there differences in intelligence which we find? Are these differences due to race or are they due to unequal opportunities?" and the whole trend of the evidence, beginning with the work in 1912, but especially beginning after the first world war when we analyzed the scores of the recruits in the first world war, the whole trend of the evidence is this, and there are no real exceptions to this trend, that wherever we try to equalize the opportunities, we minimize or extinguish the differences in learning ability as between the two racial groups. Perhaps the best study of this is Dr. Klineberg's study showing the results of the migration to New York

City of children from the deep south. He found—of course we all know that the schools in the south, and particularly the negro schools in the south, are by and large inferior. There are some cities in the south where the schools are very good, but the general tendency, and especially in the rural regions, is for the educational opportunities in the south to be very bad and particularly bad for negroes. [fol. 255] These things are well known in educational circles. So the negroes then coming out of these very poor school situations had very low ability to learn. They seemed stupid and their intelligence test scores were low. But each year that they were in the more favorable learning opportunities in the north, their intelligence quotient was rising, and the longer they were in that favorable region the more their intelligence rose, so that the conclusion is unavoidable that their previous condition was due to the unfavorable opportunities.

Q. Dr. English, is there any scientific evidence to the contrary?

A. Very little indeed and such little evidence as there is doesn't stand up. Now, for example, there was a study by a man named Tanzer, worked with Canadian negroes in a place in Ontario. They went to the same school with the whites, and the whites were, as a group, somewhat better than the negroes. But in this study when we reanalyze the data we found that the negroes were of lower economic status, and we know that lower economic status affects these things, and we found that the negro children went to school less often. In the white group the attendance was 93 and in the colored group it was 84% of the time. With a loss of schooling like that and coming from an inferior group, the tendency is to think that the difference found was [fol. 256] attributable to these unfavorable factors, rather than the race itself. Certainly these factors that I mention were a contributing cause, and I don't say they are the whole thing; they themselves reflect the whole tissue of social circumstances which somewhat discouraged negro learning, and this is a rather typical sample of the few, the relatively few, studies which even seem to point in the opposite direction. The overwhelming tendency is all in the direction of my first statement. May I summarize that?

It seems to me that what we have here is that the segregation tends to create—first of all, segregation seemingly is based upon a fallacy of a difference and then by the mere fact of segregation it turns around and creates the very difference which it assumes to have been present to begin with, and we get into a vicious circle.

Q. Dr. English, I would like to ask you another hypothetical question now, and I would like you to answer on the basis of your experience and learning as an educational psychologist. I want you to assume that a negro child lives within a few blocks of a school; that he lives a much greater distance from another school, which is a negro school which he is compelled to attend on the basis of race; that he spends perhaps a half hour, perhaps more, perhaps an hour or two a day travelling to and from school, whereas if he were not compelled to attend this negro school he [fol. 257] would spend a few minutes, perhaps fifteen or twenty minutes, a day going to and from school. Would you say that if all other factors were equal that he would receive the same benefits from attending the negro school as he would from attending the white school?

A. Definitely not.

Q. Give us the reasons.

A. May I say—perhaps your question is, you say from attending the negro school. May I broaden it, from his education, if the Court will permit that extension because it's the whole education of the child which is being damaged here. The education of the child is not wholly in the classroom. The education of the child goes on on the playground, in playing with his equals and his fellows, around home. This is one of the most important things for the wholesome development of the child and, when you take an hour a day from a child, you are taking away something very precious to his total education. I have had this in my own home because one of my children had to go to quite a distant school because of a physical handicap, and we could see the results upon his development of this deprivation. It was one of those things we couldn't help. I gather that what you are talking about is something that we could help if it were not for the presence of the law.

[fol. 258] Q. Is there any scientific data supporting this opinion which you have just given, Dr. English?

A. It would be very hard to find it, for me to recall it. It's one of those things which has such universal consent that I can't recall it ever being challenged. I am sure we see in our clinics all the time, as we examine children who are disadvantaged and who are maladjusted, we see all the time the evidence of the children who do not get out and play with others. As a matter of fact, I don't think there is any—I am sure there is no psychologist, no child psychologist in the country who would challenge the statement that there is—that the child's play is of the utmost importance and should not be unnecessarily diminished.

Mr. Greenberg: That is all.

Cross-examination.

By Mr. Goodell:

Q. Dr. English, this opinion you have rendered is somewhat founded upon theory, is it not?

A. No, sir, it is based upon literally thousands of experimental studies.

Q. How many cases have you taken, for example, of children that have gone to segregated schools and followed them through—you yourself—and examined their situation in adult life.

A. Well, now to what answer of mine is that addressed. I [fol. 259] thought you were asking me about the question of individual differences.

Q. No.

A. What are you asking them about.

Q. Have you personally conducted a survey or supervised a survey where you took cases of children that had gone through, negro children, that had gone through segregated schools and examined them in their adult life to determine whether or not the fact that they had gone to segregated schools had any bearing or relation to their success or achievement record.

A. I don't believe that I testified on that point, did I?

Q. I didn't say you did. I am asking you if you have ever done such a thing.

160

A. I have not done such a thing. I am not sure that it's relevant at all to my testimony.

Q. Well, is it possible that you could be in error in some of your conclusions here? Could you be mistaken about some of them?

A. Every man can be mistaken; certainly I can.

Q. You could be mistaken, couldn't you?

A. Oh, yes.

Q. Have you given this expert testimony around the country in cases such as this?

A. No, sir, never before; I teach it.

[fol. 260] Q. Now, Doctor, the ideal state, if I understand your testimony, that you testified in your opinion to, would be where you had no segregation as far as educational process.

A. I don't think I said anything about the ideal state.

Q. Well, it would be better, in other words, is that right?

A. I certainly believe that things would be better if we had no segregation, but that is not an expert opinion; that is my personal opinion. I didn't testify to that.

Q. Well, I mean restricting it to the educational process is what I meant.

A. Yes, without any doubt.

Q. Would you—would it change your opinion any if the facts present in this community were that the child, the negro child, that we are dealing with, if he went to a white school he would be outnumbered ten to one or fifty to one.

A. Not at all. I have seen that happen. I have grown up in schools where that happened myself. I have seen it happen repeatedly. We have it in our own city.

Q. Don't you think there is a general tendency, forgetting the racial thing, for the majority to rule and operate the thing that they belong to.

A. In what sense "majority"?

Q. Well——

A. Racial majority?

[fol. 261] Q. Assuming you had 500 white children going to Randolph School and ten negro children. What would be the natural tendency, taking into account the human element and human equations of whether the negro children would run that school or participate actively in the student activities or whether it would be run by the white students?

A. Well, of course, the majority would generally have a preponderant voice if they divided along racial lines which they tend to do, but which they do not invariably do. I have seen many cases where the colored child receives in a mixed school from the majority group considerable amount of status and honor. You may recall just recently a man was elected captain of the football team in a predominantly white school. I think it was Williams or Amherst, I am not quite sure which, and this is reproduced all the way through our school systems where we do have mixed schools.

Q. And there are some outstanding negroes in different fields of professions and—who have received their—part of their education—in the deep south in segregated schools.

A. That is true.

Q. And yet have achieved great places of importance, isn't that right?

A. Education isn't the whole answer to ability; it is merely one factor. There are men who are big enough, [fol. 262] white or black, to rise above unfavorable circumstances.

Q. Surely. You are familiar, of course, as an educator, with the experience that was had back in the reconstruction days, sometimes referred to as the carpet-bagger days in the south.

A. Very definitely.

Q. You realize that a certain element, radical element I would call it, of the Republican party, perhaps to gain some political advantage, decided to go down in the various states and abolish certain segregation; you realize that was done.

A. Well, there wasn't exactly segregation at that time, but they did go down there and set up some laws of one sort or another, yes.

Q. Which attempted, in one swoop, to eliminate all of their custom and usages of those communities in the south, didn't it?

11—8

A. I am not here as an expert on history, but I read history that way, yes.

Q. Surely. Don't you realize that the experience of that period was that they had a tremendous amount of trouble, tremendous amount of emotional outburst and that it caused a great deal of strife between the races and didn't work at all.

[fol. 263] A. Well, if the Court wants a layman's opinion on history, I will answer that question to the best of my knowledge as a layman on history; I am not here as a historian.

Judge Huxman: It seems to me the question is going far afield.

Mr. Goodell: That is all.

Judge Huxman: Any further questions of the doctor? If not, you may step down, doctor.

(Witness excused.)

WILBUR B. BROOKOVER, having been first duly sworn, assumed the stand and testified as follows:

Direct Examination.

By Mr. Greenberg:

Q. Mr. Brookover, will you please state your full name.
A. Wilbur B. Brookover.
Q. What is your occupation?
A. I am a social psychologist by profession. The position I now hold is professor of social science, sociology, at Michigan State College.
Q. What degrees do you hold, Mr. Brookover?
A. I hold an A.B. Degree from Manchester College, a Master of Arts Degree and a Doctor of Philosophy Degree in sociology and psychology from the University of Wisconsin.
Q. Are you a member of any learned societies, Doctor?
[fol. 264] A. I am a member of the American Sociological Society, Society for Applied Anthropology, Society for the Psychological study of Social Issues, the High Valley

Sociological Society, Michigan Academy of Science, the American Association for the Advancement of Science.

Q. What is your field of special interest, Dr. Brookover?

A. I am particularly concerned in my teaching and research in the field of social psychology with particular reference to the human relations in the school society, or the school as a social institution and in relations between minority groups and majority groups in society.

Q. Are you the author of any books or publications?

A. I am the author of several articles on various topics concerned with social relations between teachers and pupils and other aspects of social factors in education. I am also the author of articles concerned with relation of these social factors to teaching—to pupil achievement. I have published articles on the impact of social stratafication on education, one that is in press at the present time to appear in the Journal of Educational Theory. I am also the author of articles concerning social factors in relation to citizenship education, an article to appear in the 1951 yearbook of the National Council of Social Studies, now in press. I have in preparation a book to be published by the American Book company that will be entitled "The Sociology of [fol. 265] Education." I am a joint author of a book now in preparation; it's a monograph which will report research which—committee of which I was chairman conducted on minority groups in Maple County, which is a midwestern community.

Q. Other than what you have stated, have you devoted any special study to the problem of the effect of racial segregation on the individual?

A. Well, the monograph which I last mentioned grows out of a rather extended project still in process on the analysis of minority group relations in midwestern society. I have inaugurated at the present time, designed a study to analyze the dynamics of prejudices among youth.

Mr. Goodell: I didn't get that.

The Witness: The dynamics of prejudices among youth in a midwestern school community.

Q. Now, Dr. Brookover, I am going to ask you a hypothetical question which I would like to have you answer on the basis of your learning. Assume that in the City of Topeka there is maintained a racially segregated school system. Would you say that the negro child who attends the racially segregated school receives the same benefits as he would receive from attending a racial integrated school, if all other factors were equal?

A. No, I would not.

[fol. 266] Q. On what do you base your opinion?

A. Well, I would say, first of all, that I would want to emphasize the nature of the educational process in this respect: Education is a process of teaching youth to behave in those ways that society thinks is essential. In our society it has long been held that this is a necessary function, to prepare democratic citizens. Now, the child acquires these essential behavior patterns in association with other people. In other words, they are not fixed; they are not inherent in the behavior of the child, but they are acquired in a social situation. Now, in order to acquire the types of behavior that any society may expect and to learn how to behave in various situations, the child must be provided an opportunity to interact with and understand what kinds of behavior are desired, expected, in all kinds of situations. This is achieved only if the child has presented to him clearly defined models.

Q. What do you mean by models, Professor?

A. Examples, illustrations of behavior; persons behaving in the ways that are—that the child is expected to behave and also consistent behavior of this sort. In other words, of an example, one kind of a model, and another time he is expected to behave if at one time he is presented one kind of an example, one kind of model, and another time he is [fol. 267] presented another kind of a model, and there is a constant confusion. Now that, I think, leads us immediately to the situation with regard to segregated schools. In American society we consistently present to the child a model of democratic equality of opportunity. We teach him the principles of equality; we teach him what kind of ideals we have in American society and set this model of behavior before him and expect him to internalize, to take on, this model, to believe it, to understand it. At the same time, in a segregated school situation he is pre-

sented a contradictory or inharmonious model. He is presented a school situation in which it is obvious that he is a subordinate, inferior kind of a citizen. He is not presented a model of equality and equal opportunity and basis of operating in terms of his own individual rights and privileges. Now, this conflict of models always creates confusion, insecurity, and difficulty for the child who can not internalize a clearly defined and clearly accepted definition of his role, so he is faced with situations which he doesn't— he has two or three, at least two in this situation, definitions of how he is expected to behave. This frustration that results may result in a delinquent behavior or otherwise criminal or socially abnormal behavior. Now the negro child is constantly presented with this dual definition of his role as a citizen and the segregated schools perpet-
[fol. 268] uates this conflict in expectancies, condemns the negro child to an ineffective role as a citizen and member of society.

Q. Dr. Brookover, this opinion and the reasons you have just given, are they supported by scientific authority?

A. Yes, there is extensive work been done by psychologists, social psychologists, on the whole theory of role-taking and the question of eternization of patterns of expectancy, such people as George Herbert Meade, Charles Horton Cooley and numerous other people have done extensive work, extensive research in the processes of personality development and learning a situation through social interaction.

Mr. Greenberg: That is all.

Cross-examination.

By Mr. Goodell:

Q. Doctor, I will just ask you one question: Have you ever heard of these people, all negroes: Mary McLeod Bethune of Sumter, South Carolina, who is president of the college there, Bethune-Cookman College, Daytona Beach, Florida.

A. I have heard of someone by the name of Bethune. I am not sure that I know.

Q. Richard Wright, Greenwood, Mississippi and Jackson, Mississippi, author of Native Son, negro.

A. I have.

[fol. 269] Q. Charles Johnson of Bristol, Virginia.

A. Charles Johnson, that I know.

Q. Sociologist and president of Fisk University.

A. I think that is in Tennessee.

Q. Perhaps so. Walter White, of Atlanta, Georgia, Executive Secretary of National Association for the Advancement of Colored People.

A. I have heard of him; don't know him.

Q. George Washington Carver, Neosho, Missouri, residence.

A. I have heard of him.

Q. Langston Hughes, poet and author; I believe from Kansas.

A. I have heard of him; don't know him.

Q. W. E. B. DuBois who was an author, I believe connected with Fisk University at Nashville.

A. I know a DuBois who is an anthropologist. I don't know if this is the one.

Q. Mordecai Johnson, Paris, Tennessee, president of Howard University, Washington, D. C., negro university.

A. I know the name; I don't know him at all.

Q. William Grant Still, a composer of Little Rock, Arkansas.

A. Don't know him.

Q. Negro. A. Philip Randolph, Florida, president of the Sleeping—strike that. Charles Wesley of Baltimore, Maryland, president of the university in Ohio; I don't have the town.

[fol. 270] A. I don't know him.

Q. Frederick Patterson, president of Tuskegee Institute, Washington, D. C.

A. I don't know him.

Q. Some of these men you know. Assuming they were all educated—got their preliminary education in segregated schools, a large part of them in the south, would you—did you consider that in arriving at your opinion here?

A. Certainly did. The fact that occasionally a person is able to overcome, through various readjustments and other experiences, the conflict of roles, the conflict of models, does not disturb the generalization which I make, in the least. Certainly there are individual cases which either through psychotherapy or other experiences, the individual is able to overcome such difficulties. But this is not the general case at all.

Q. Well, there are many illustrations of emotional stress and strain among the white children who go to school and don't get—get sort of left out, don't make the football team or the basketball team or don't get invited to the parties, isn't that right?

A. Sure, there are differences in ability to adjust and there are emotional disturbances. The differences which you cite are not enforced differences. They are not inevitable in terms of the situation in which they come—in which [fol. 271] they operate. The child is not by fiat or legalization required to have presented to him this conflict.

Q. That is your opinion about what the law ought to be, in other words, is that it?

A. I would say on the basis of my testimony that the segregation of schools presents a conflicting set of models inevitably.

Q. This opinion you have given here is largely your own personal view based upon your study.

A. No, I wouldn't say it's my own personal view at all. I would say it's the result of a tremendous amount of research and evidence.

Q. I said study.

A. That is accumulated by social psychologists over a period of years and as I have studied and analyzed this research, I would come to this conclusion.

Q. You think you could be wrong?

A. Of course any scientist always presents the possibility or recognizes the possibility that new evidence and new research may modify to some extent the conclusions of a particular time.

Mr. Goodell: That is all.

(Witness excused.)

[fol. 272] Louisa Holt, having been first duly sworn, assumed the stand and testified as follows:

Direct examination.

By Mr. Carter:

Q. Mrs. Holt, what is you occupation?
A. I am a social psychologist.
Q. Would you indicate to the Court what your educational background is.
A. I received the Bachelor's Degree, Master's Degree and Ph.D. all from Radcliffe College, which is the feminine adjunct of Harvard University. This was in the field of sociology in the Department of Social Relations there, which includes cultural anthropology, clinical psychology, social psychology, as well as sociology.
Q. Mrs. Holt, would you also describe your various job experiences.
A. Well, I started under an arrangement which gave me a kind of internship in public administration where I worked in the Federal Bureau of Prisons.
Q. Where was this?
A. For six months in Alderson, West Virginia; for about nine months in Washington. Following that, I had a year of graduate study concurrent with work in a settlement house in Boston, South End House, and then was appointed an instructor in sociology at Skidmore College and also [fol. 273] director of a college community center in Saratoga Springs. I was then returned to Radcliffe College where I was appointed a teaching fellow and tutor in sociology. Concurrently with that, I held a Sigmund Freud Memorial Fellowship at the Boston Psychoanalytic Institute in 1944 and 1945. Following these other jobs, I participated in some research work for the Family Society of Boston in connection with their vocational counseling service. I was then an educational counselor for the National Institute of Public Affairs in Washington. From 1947 to 1949 I held a part-time appointment in the Menninger Foundation School of Psychiatry and for part of that time in their school of clinical psychology affiliated with the University of Kansas.

Q. That is located in this city.

A. What's that?

A. Is that in Topeka?

A. Yes. In the interim, there was a post-doctorate research fellowship of the National Institute of Mental Health. This past year I have been on the faculty of the University of Kansas in the Psychology Department, teaching courses in social psychology and personality and some of their inter-relations. At the same time I also prepared a long paper for a United States Public Health Service project in connection with the Mid-Century Whitehouse Conference [fol. 274] on Children and Youth dealing with the problems, the methodology of evaluating mental health programs.

Q. What is your major field of interests, Mrs. Holt?

A. It's probably clear that I am interested in the relations between social process and social conditions and personality functioning behavior.

Q. Are you a member of any professional societies?

A. The American Sociological Society, the Society for Applied Anthropology, Society for the Psychological Study of Social Issues, the American Society for Group Psychotherapy and Psychodrama, and I am an associate member of the Topeka Psychoanalytic Society.

Q. Mrs. Holt, are you at all familiar with the school system in Topeka?

A. Yes; I have one child who entered that system this last year and another who enters next September.

Q. You are then aware of the fact that the schools are operated on a segregated basis.

A. I am.

Q. Based upon your experience and your knowledge, taking the segregated factor alone in the school system in Topeka, in your opinion does enforced legal separation have any adverse effect upon the personality development of the negro child?

[fol. 275] A. The fact that it is enforced, that it is legal, I think, has more importance than the mere fact of segregation by itself does because this gives legal and official sanction to a policy which inevitably is interpreted both by white people and by negroes as denoting the inferiority of the negro group. Were it not for the sense that one group is inferior to the other, there would be no basis, and I am not granting that this is a rational basis, for such segregation.

Q. Well, does this interference have any effect, in your opinion, on the learning process?

A. A sense of inferiority must always affect one's motivation for learning since it affects the feeling one has of one's self as a person, as a personality or a self or an ego identity, as Eric Erickson has recently expressed it. That sense of ego identity is built up on the basis of attitudes that are expressed toward a person by others who are important. First the parents and then teachers, other people in the community, whether they are older or one's own peers. It is other peoples reactions to one's self which most basically affects the conception of one's self that one has. If these attitudes that are reflected back and then internalized or projected, are unfavorable ones, then one develops a sense of one's self as an inferior being. That may not be deleterious necessarily from the standpoint of [fol. 276] educational motivation. I believe in some cases it can lead to stronger motivation to achieve well in academic pursuits, to strive to disprove to the world that one is inferior since the world feels that one is inferior. In other cases, of course, the reaction may be the opposite and apathetic acceptance, fatalistic submission to the feeling others have expressed that one is inferior and therefore any efforts to prove otherwise would be doomed to failure.

Q. Now these difficulties that you have described, whether they give a feeling of inferiority which you were motivated to attempt to disprove to the world by doing more or whether they give you a feeling of inferiority and therefore cause you to do less, would you say that the difficulties which segregation causes in the public school system interfere with a well—development of a well-rounded personality?

A. I think the maximum or maximal development of any personality can only be based on the potentialities which that individual himself possesses. Of course they are affected for good or ill by the attitudes, opinions, feelings, which are expressed by others and which may be fossilized into laws. On the other hand, these can be overcome in exceptional cases. The instances I cited of those whose motivation to succeed in academic competition is heightened [fol. 277] may very well not be fulfilling their own most basic, most appropriate potentialities but seeking, rather, to tilt against windmills, to disprove something which there was no valid reason, in my opinion, to think was so anyhow, namely, the feeling of their inferiority. So even when educational success is achieved that still may not denote the most self-realization of the person. I feel, if I may add another word, I feel that when segregation exists, it's not something—although it may seem to be such—that is directed against people for what they are. It is directed against them on the basis of who their parents are, since that is the definition which, according to sociologists and social psychologists analysis of the matter, that is used in determining who shall go to a segregated school, a negro school or a white school; it is not simply skin color. In the case of Walter White, for example, and sociologist Allison Davis, his brother, John Davis, who are negroes, their skin color is lighter than mine; of course, I have been out in the sun—the definition does depend upon who a person's parents were. That appears also if a dark-skinned person had parents who were high potentates in India he is not defined as a negro; therefore he is not required to use segregated facilities. It is not the skin color; it is who the parents were, and my understanding and various sociolo- [fol. 278] gists and psychologists analysis of the American tradition, religious tradition as well as set of values and ethos, determining much of our most valued and significant behavior, hinges upon a belief in treating people upon their own merits and we are inclined to oppose a view which states that we should respect people or reject them on the basis of who their parents were.

Q. Now, Mrs. Holt, you are aware of the fact that segregation is practiced in Topeka only for the first six grades. Thereafter, the child goes to high school and junior high school apparently without regard to race or color. You have described difficulties and interferences with the personality development which occurs by virtue of segregation at the first six grades. Is the integration of the child at the junior high school level, does that correct these difficulties which you have just spoken of, in your opinion?

A. I think it's a theory that would be accepted by virtually all students of personality development that the earlier a significant event occurs in the life of an individual the more lasting, the more far-reaching and deeper the effects of that incident, that trauma, will be; the more—the earlier an event occurs, the more difficult it is later on to eradicate those effects.

[fol. 279] Q. Your opinion would be that it would be more difficult to eradicate those effects at the junior high school level, is that it; merely because you integrate them at the junior high school level——

A. Well, once a trauma has occurred, and I do believe that attending a segregated school, perhaps after the preschool years of free play with others of different skin color, is a trauma to the negro child; that occurs early. There is also evidence emerging from a study now going on at Harvard University that the later achievement of individuals in their adult occupational careers can be predicted at the first grade. If that is true, it means that the important effects of schooling in relation to later achievement are set down at that early age, and I therefore don't think that simply removing segregation at a somewhat later grade could possibly und*ue* those effects.

Cross-examination:

By Mr. Goodell:

Q. You mean, Mrs. Holt, there is a serious study being made now to project in the future whether a child in the first grade is going to be a flop or a success?

A. I do.

Q. You have confidence in that, do you?

A. That study is being directed by Professor Tawkett [fol. 280] Parsons, the head of the Department of Social Relations.

Q. You have a good deal of confidence in that?

A. I certainly do.

Q. You made a comment in your testimony I would like

to call your attention to again; this segregation in some cases would spur, act as a whiplash, on the child to spur him on and make him achieve, and that would be a bad thing.

A. Yes.

Q. You mean it's a bad thing, for example, for a poor boy, because he is poor, the whiplash of poverty makes him work harder to rise higher; that is a bad thing?

A. I mean that that can be at the expense of healthy personality development, self-actualization, self-realization of the most basic fundamental and appropriate kind for that person, and we have plenty of evidence of people who burn themselves out with various emotional or perhaps psychosomatic diseases in whose cases that can be attributed to this overweening striving for competitive success to overcome feelings of inferiority.

Q. Mrs. Holt, more or less educational process has in it competitive features, that is, the children are given tests and examinations and gradecards and the ones that don't make good grades, they get poor grades; at least the teacher gives them their merit grade. You don't believe [fol. 281] in that, do you?

A. I believe in the children being appraised on the basis of their own objective achievement.

Q. You don't believe, then, in any sort of competition in the public school system, do you?

A. I believe competition has its values.

Q. Do you believe in that in the way it's carried on and have competitive examinations and gradecarding and things of that kind?

A. I don't know how else one can operate a society in which individuals are judged primarily on their own merits rather than through connections of who their parents were or who they know which are the alternatives to that system.

Q. Progressive education, that is one of the elements that they believe which has been set up in California and other areas, to abolish all grading, abolish all examinations, let every child go to school and never have to worry about what his grades are; never know what they are, isn't that right?

A. I think a child needs some definiteness in the expectations which the authorities over him, the teachers, have in order to stimulate him to his own maximal productiveness. I think also competition with his peers, if not carried to excessive limits, if not *if not* undue emphasis is placed on it, can also have very beneficial effects.

[fol. 282] Q. These are your personal views you have been giving here largely.

A. They are based on a fair amount of acquaintance with scientific work in this field.

Mr. Goodell: That is all.

If the Court please, at the outset the Court mentioned— I don't care to be objecting about it, but the Court, I thought, suggested a limit on this line of testimony.

Judge Mellott: That is about nine now that we have had on this phase. How many more are there?

Mr. Greenberg: Pardon me, sir, I didn't hear you.

Judge Mellott: You have had several now of the so-called expert testimony; how many will there be?

Mr. Greenberg: We have three or four more, Your Honor, and they are all different.

Judge Huxman: Well, now, we are not disposed to be critical, but it's my opinion from having listened to this testimony, the last four witnesses—that it's all cumulative. I can see no difference, substantial difference, between any of the testimony of the last three or four witnesses. It's fifteen minutes until adjournment time. We are going to have to adjourn this evening at 4:30 on account of a com-[fol. 283] mitment I have. We can, perhaps, finish one more witness in that time. Then I suggest that you gentlemen tonight really appraise your witnesses and appraise this evidence, see whether my statement is warranted that this evidence we are now receiving is all substantially the same and, unless there is more difference in the testimony that you have, we might well have the qualifications of the remaining witnesses read into the record and have a stipulation that their testimony as to the effect of segregation itself upon the mental attitude upon the outlook and life of the student is substantially as testified to by these witnesses. I am just simply suggesting that, saying not that we will enforce that rule in the morning, but it was understood that about five witnesses would be allowed, and then we would examine the subject, and we are reaching that point, so suppose you call your next witness; that will take us to adjournment time.

JOHN J. KANE, having been first duly sworn, assumed the stand and testified as follows:

Direct examination.

By Mr. Greenberg:

Q. What is your full name?
A. John J. Kane.
[fol. 284] Q. What is your occupation?
A. I am an instructor in Sociology at the University of Notre Dame.
Q. What is your educational background?
A. I have a Bachelor of Arts Degree from St. Joseph's College, a Master of Arts Degree in sociology from Temple University, a Doctor of Philosophy Degree in Sociology from the University of Pennsylvania.
Q. What positions have you held?
A. I was an instructor in sociology at St. Joseph's College about two and a half or three years. I have been instructor in Sociology at the University of Notre Dame for three years.
Q. Have you devoted yourself for any of your professional attention to the field of the impact of racial segregation on the individual?
A. I have done two studies in the general field of prejudices, racial—my major interest in the graduate school was in the field of race relations and ethnic relations.
Q. Mr. Kane, on the basis of your educational experience and your studies, I want you to answer the following hypothetical question: Assume that in the City of Topeka there is maintained a racially segregated school system and that a negro child is compelled to attend a racially segregated school because of his race alone; that if this [fol. 285] system did not exist, he would attend a racially

176

integrated school, would you say that if all other factors are equal, that he obtains the same educational opportunities at the former school as at the latter?

A. No, I would not.

Q. Now, would you give us the basis for your opinion, Mr. Kane.

A. I would begin with two points: The first one is that the school, with the exception of the home, is the institution that makes the greatest impact on American youth. You see, the school gets the child early in life, keeps him for a number of years, so that day after day, year after year it is transferring attitudes for him. Now, we have some scientific evidence about the effectiveness of the accumulation of materials in this area. For instance, Professor Thurston's work on changing attitudes through motion pictures shows that when one picture was shown to a group of youngsters it had relatively little influence in changing attitudes; two had a little more, but if he worked in series of three, he discovered cumulative evidence was very powerful in changing attitudes. What I am mentioning this for is the fact that the influence of the segregated school, when a negro child day after day, year after year, does have this cumulative effect. Secondly, I would like to point out that one of the things children get out of education besides cer-
[fol. 286] tain manual skills, spelling, arithmetic and science, is above all, the formation of attitudes. This is what lasts; this is what continues after the school years, and therefore the attitude they get in the particular schools is of great significance. Now, in a school system in which racial segregation is practiced, you have a day after day accumulation of attitudes that the negro child is inferior because segregation is differentiation and distinction. It means, as Professor Newcomb has pointed out, that one group denies to another group, status, privilege and power and so it is borne in upon a negro boy and girl that they are being differentiated not merely because of skin color or physical characteristics, but because there is something inately inferior or subordinate about them and so most of them begin to learn that certain avenues of vertical mobility are closed to them.

Q. What do you mean by vertical mobility?

A. I mean the opportunity of advancing in the world, moving ahead, having a better job than your father had, more social position, and I would point out to you that this concept is fundamental to the American system of values. This is one of the things that we Americans believe in very intensively, and it is something which is denied to negro children. Furthermore, the philosophy of racial segrega-
[fol. 287] gation is supported by rationalizations on the racial myth of inferiority for which we have no adequate scientific evidence. Secondly, segregation cuts down on the communication among people. It erects a barrier. Now, certain barriers will exist whether you have a segregation enforced by law or not, but here's a case where barriers are created and upheld by law. The total effect is to make most of your negro children feel inferior, and I would like to refer to a study that was made by Preston with regard to projected scores on tests. A number of white boys were asked to put down the score they expected to get on a certain test and, when they put down the score, they were told that negro youths had made a higher score. The white boys were allowed to change, and they immediately changed their scores above the negro score. Negro youths were told they were about to take a test and were asked to put down the expected score and, when they put it down, they were told this was higher than the white boys made, and they were asked if they wanted to change it, and they lowered their scores below that of the white group. This is indicative of the expectation of behavior which is engendered in a segregated school among most of your colored students.

Q. Dr. Kane, you mentioned a study that you made.

A. Well——

[fol. 288] Q. —in this field. Could you tell us whether or not that study supports the conclusion which you just stated and describe the study.

A. I studied groups of negro boys, gangs, in West Philadelphia. I think it could be used.

Q. Will you describe what you did in this study.

A. We discovered in this particular area there was a system of social stratafication among negroes. The area

12—8

was roughly split into two sections, one in which the negroes called the "Tops" and the other which they called the "Bottoms." In the "Tops" you had a high degree of homeownership, negro males there, the fathers had better occupations, larger income and a fairly stable family. The "Bottoms" area you never had any area in which as many as 6% of the negroes owned their homes. You had a relatively unstable family; for the most part they were employed in menial jobs. Now you would think that the "Bottoms" area, as a group, represented the lowest level of negro society, but these negroes themselves made a distinction, and they would point out that there was still a lower group than this, and that was the negro from the south and, if you asked them, they said because of segregated education. Now, I want to point out, whether or not that was true, is quite beside the point because, as W. I. Thomas indicated long ago, if men define situations as [fol. 289] real, they are real in their consequences and this is the attitude the negro group itself held, and, of course, this is the way we form attitudes about ourselves; not only what we think, but what we know or believe other people think about us. So, here again, you have an indication of the inferiority that was engendered because of the segregated school system amongst the immigrants from the south.

Mr. Greenberg: That is all.

Cross-examination.

By Mr. Goodell:

Q. Professor, don't you believe a home which has the child, say the first five years without any—where the school doesn't have him at all, in any case whether he is negro or white, don't you think the child has a great deal to do with attitudes, it's race and towards another race and acceptance, and so forth.

A. You are perfectly correct. As a matter of fact, the home is much more important than the school, if it's an adequate home. Now, I should like to point out, if I may——

Q. That answers my question.

Judge Huxman: You may go ahead and give your explanation. This is an expert witness.

The Witness: I should like to point out that when the home facilities are inadequate, as they are in so many [fol. 290] cases of your poor negro family, then the school becomes increasingly important and, in those cases probably, more important than the home since it is exercising little influence.

Mr. Goodell: I have no further questions.

Judge Huxman: It is now five minutes of adjournment time, and we perhaps could not finish another witness, and I just have an appointment I must keep. So we will suspend at this time.

The court will be in recess until tomorrow morning promptly at 9:30.

(The court then, at 4:25 o'clock p. m., adjourned until 9:30 o'clock a. m., the following day, Tuesday, June 26, 1951.)

[fol. 291]   Tuesday, June 26, 1951

(Pursuant to adjournment as aforesaid, the court met, present and presiding as before, and the following proceedings were had:)

Judge Huxman: You may proceed, gentlemen.

Let me inquire of the attorney for plaintiff, how many more of these expert witnesses do you have?

Mr. Carter: Your Honor, we at the present time—we only have one more expert witness to put on.

Judge Huxman: Just one more expert witness.

Do you have any testimony after that or will that conclude your case?

Mr. Carter: We have subpoenaed a number of witnesses, Your Honor, and we are contemplating calling only one other witness to establish one point.

Judge Huxman: All right, you may put on this other witness, expert witness.

180

BETTIE BELK, having been first duly sworn, assumed the stand and testified as follows:

Direct examination.

By Mr. Carter:

Q. Miss Belk, what is your occupation?
A. At the present time I am on the staff of the Workshop in Human Relations at the University of Kansas City, Missouri.

[fol. 292] Q. What is your educational background?
A. I have my Bachelor's Degree from State Teachers College in Worcester, Massachusetts, my Master's Degree from Clark University in Worcester, Massachusetts, and, at the present time, I am working on my Ph.D. in Human Development at the University of Chicago.

Q. Miss Belk, what other than your present employment at the University of Kansas City—what other job experience have you had?
A. I have taught junior and senior high school in Indiana for two years; for ten years I was employed by the Y. W. C. A., first as director of the teen age program in Trenton, New Jersey, and for five years as a member of the national staff as a consultant on the teen age program. In that capacity I did work in the midwest; Kansas was one of the twelve states in the area that I served, and I have worked with the local organization here on their problems of teen age program. At the university I have been employed as a research assistant in the study of developmental tasks of adolescents and, during the past year, I have been on the staff of the Center for Inter-Group Education.

Q. Have you published any books or articles on the problems of adolescents?
A. Yes, for the Y. W. C. A. I published several articles on teen age problems and a pamphlet designed for train-
[fol. 293] ing adult leaders to work with teen agers.

Q. Do you belong to any professional societies?
A. Yes. I am a member of the National Association of Group Workers.

Q. What is your field of major interests?

A. Well, my recent experience has been in training adults to work with groups, and I am particularly interested in this aspect of human development. My work at the present time is in the training of adult leadership for this kind of job.

Q. That is the training of an adult—of adults to work with adolescents and so forth?

A. Yes.

Q. Now, assume, Miss Belk, that the City of Topeka has organized its public school system so that a child enters the first grade at approximately the age of six; goes through the elementary schools, six grades; he would be entering a junior high school at approximately the age of twelve. Assume that for the first six grades the schools in Topeka are maintained on a segregated basis. Thereafter, the junior high schools and high schools, the schools are integrated. Based upon your experience and your knowledge, would you give an opinion as to whether or not it would be harmful—it would have any adverse effect on the child at that stage of his development to move from a segregated educational [fol. 294] pattern into an integrated pattern?

A. I would say that by bringing children together for the first time at this age, the Board of Education is working a real hardship on both the negro and white children, and I would like to explain why, if I may.

Q. Please do so.

A. I think that it is a well established fact that the years just preceding age 12, the years 10 to 12, roughly, for girls and 11 to 13 for boys, are the years during which the important physical and physiological changes take place. The child at age 12 is trying to integrate two to five inches of standing height that he had acquired very rapidly. He is also trying to integrate very important physiological changes. In our society, girls reach puberty at about twelve and a half and boys at about thirteen and a half, and they are adjusting to really a new kind of body for them because of the changes which have taken place. There are social changes that take place also at this age; changes take place within the school system itself. Up until this point the child has been accustomed to a school situation in which he has related to one adult. Now he moves into what we call a departmentalized pattern. He has several teachers; he moves from one classroom to another. In other words, he has a pattern of relationship with many important adults in the school system. Also, at this age the child moves [fol. 295] from a peer society which has been largely made up of members of the same sex, into a heterosexual society. The seventh grade is a crucial one for girls, particularly, because they become interested in boys before boys become interested in them, and this is a very difficult time for them to live through. All in all, these are the years when children are making some of their most important life adjustments, and I would say that having been brought up in a separate system where they can only learn that negroes and white are different, they must at this age then make an adjustment to living with someone that they have learned is different, and I think that this puts an additional adjustment on them at an age when it is very difficult for them to make it.

Cross-examination.

By Mr. Goodell:

Q. Is it Miss or Mrs. Belk?
A. It's Miss Belk.
Q. Are you familiar with the City of Topeka and the customs and usages with respect to inter-racial matters?
A. I have visited the City of Topeka as a consultant for the Y. W. C. A., yes.
Q. Do you realize that for half a century, to some degree, there has been segregation practiced in the business world and in the social strata of this community?
A. I believe that I have heard that there is segregation in [fol. 296] in the community, yes.
Q. Without regard to the merits, if that is a fact, assuming—strike that—that there is segregation practiced in the ordinary workday life of the community in the business world and in the social strata as of our two races here, negro and the white, and assuming further for the purpose of this question that there were no segregation in the first six grades of our public school system, and the negro children were absorbed in the present existing white schools,

183

where they were outnumbered twenty-five to fifty to one and, in some cases, more than that, would you reform your opinion any, taking that into account?

A. No, I would not.

Q. Do you know what the natural tendencies are in a practical world? Would it be customary, where children come from homes—living in a community where segregation is practiced other than in the schools, for those same white children to carry on that same custom and usage in their relations with the race—with the opposite race—the negro.

A. I don't understand your question.

Q. Well, assuming that segregation, as I have just stated, as practiced in this community in Topeka, in the city, outside of the school, and that is a fact, children coming from homes in this community, isn't it very natural that they [fol. 297] would simply carry on that custom and usage in their relations with other negro students of the opposite race?

A. Well, I think our recent studies have shown that children, adolescents particularly, take most of their social pattern from their peers rather than their parents; in fact, it's one of the real problems in our American society today that this is true.

Q. Who are the children, what do you mean by that, that the negro children they would look upon as their peers and therefore they would follow them; what do you mean?

A. I mean that all adolescent children take most of their social patterns from people their own age; they tend to see each other as authorities. It's an age at which they break away completely from parental authority, in fact to the extent that it becomes a difficult problem in home-life, so it is not always the patterns of the parents that they are repeating; in fact, during this time they are forming their own values.

Q. I don't know as I understand it. You consider another child, that a child will look upon another white child as his peer, is that what you are getting at?

A. Yes.

Q. What is there about another child of the same age that would make him a peer as to another child?

A. This is one of the phenomena of development. The child must, in his growing up process, ultimately break [fol. 298] away from the home. Now adolescents in our society are treated at one moment as though they were children and the parents are very authoritarian with them and at another moment they are expected to behave like adults and, consequently, most of them are in some state of confusion as to what their status really is. But they are moving always toward adulthood, toward establishing their own values and, for this reason, they take more of their pattern—you can see it even in their dress. I don't know if you have any adolescent children of your own, but if you do you know they dress alike, they act alike, they talk alike. They get their values largely from each other at this age.

Q. Assuming for the purpose of this question, though, that segregation was abolished and the negro child was absorbed in the white school system and, for illustration, he was outnumbered in the particular school system on the average of thirty to one or twenty to one or any figure of that proportion; taking into account the natural factors of every-day life and the practicabilities of the situation, wouldn't that result in and of itself of him being a very small minority group and being left out of activities and the run of things, the negro child.

A. I do not think that that is necessarily true. In fact, in my own experience I have seen it not to be true.

[fol. 299] Q. Well, isn't that true within the white structure, that some children run things and others tag along; some are leaders and others aren't?

A. This is an individual matter. It is quite true.

Q. And to that extent where you have children that do run things, elected class officers and in all activities, make the teams and so forth, and in their own group, and in the other children that doesn't—aren't given recognition in that sense, that child—this philosophy of yours, this theory of yours, is made to feel second-class and left out of things, isn't that right, of his own group.

A. Of his own group, yes, and most of us who work in

inter-group relations nowadays see this as a total thing. There is no longer any stress on negro-white relations; it's on inter-group relations.

Q. I mean without regard to the racial factor, you have that situation in any organized society, don't you; some people get along better than others, run things, are leaders; others tagging along and are not leaders.

A. This is true and our problem is to work so that everybody has a niche into which he fits.

Q. How would you eliminate that aspect of life in a school system where some children are not the leaders and don't run the show and are sort of left out, so they don't have an inferiority feeling that they are second-[fol. 300] class? How would you get rid of that?

A. As a matter of fact we have been doing some work on that at the center for inter-group education. Our work deals with schools. Well, for example, in one school children said you are separated here according to whether or not you belong to the cashmere sweater set, so this became the problem that we worked on. The way that we usually do it is sitting down with young people themselves and talking about why people do exclude other people and why this is important to them and what are the values in learning to live with people who are different from you and being able to accept them.

Q. Well, without regard to your—adoption of your theories and your opinion here in the school system, you are still going to have that problem considering the practicalities of the situation.

A. The problem of rejection and acceptance is one that will be with all of us all through life.

Q. Surely. Isn't it awfully difficult for you to have the experience of a negro child so that you could expertly say what he feels, a first grader and a third grader, and so forth, how he feels about anything.

A. Is it difficult for me?

Q. Certainly, to put your mind—I mean to—for you to assume the feelings of a negro child that is in these elemen-[fol. 301] tary grades? How do you do that?

A. It is difficult for me really to understand the experiences of anyone else, but this is part of my job.

Q. Well, I grant all that, but how do you do it; how can you tell what I feel and react and my reactions, and so forth, to a set of facts or my social relations.

A. How do I actually do it?

Q. How do you tell it, yes.

A. Well, I try to put myself in the other person's place.

Q. Well, I know that, but I mean is it like a mathematical problem that we have got in algebra so that you can add it up and prove it.

A. We do have techniques for doing this sort of thing and the technique is known as role-playing, and I would be glad to describe it to you.

Q. If some of your assumptions are wrong, then your whole conclusions you reach are wrong too, aren't they; isn't that right? That's all.

A. Well——

(Witness excused.)

Mr. Carter: We were going to call our next witness, Mrs. Dorothy Crawford, but I don't believe she is here, and so we will rest.

Judge Huxman: You will rest.

Mr. Carter: Yes, sir.

[fol. 302] Judge Huxman: Plaintiff rests.

Mr. Goodell: If the Court please, I would like to be given about ten minutes. There were some members of the school system I couldn't reach last night and, because you started at 9:30, I couldn't get hold of them in time. I won't take over ten minutes.

Judge Huxman: That was too early for the school members to be out?

Mr. Goodell: No, I couldn't get in touch with them.

Judge Huxman: You want a ten-minute recess?

Mr. Goodell: If it isn't imposing, yes.

Judge Huxman: Court will be in recess.

(The court then, at 9:45 o'clock a. m., stood at recess until 9:55 o'clock a. m., at which time the following proceedings were had:)

Mr. Goodell: Does the Court want all my witnesses sworn at one time?

Judge Huxman: We will follow the same procedure.

Mr. John Scott: If the Court please, we have a witness that just arrived, and we would like to put her on; just a short witness.

Judge Huxman: All right.

Mr. John Scott: And we would also like to invoke Rule [fol. 303] 43(b), that is, on hostile witnesses. This witness will testify pertaining to transportation, and she also has a financial interest in it and, therefore, we would like to invoke that rule.

Mr. Goodell: Who is the witness?

Mr. John Scott: Mrs. Dorothy Crawford.

Judge Huxman: The hostile witness rule is rather a flexible rule, and it depends upon whether the witness shows any hostility, so suppose you proceed in the regular way of examination, and we will then be guided by what follows.

Mr. John Scott: All right.

DOROTHY CRAWFORD, having been first duly sworn, assumed the stand and testified as follows:

Direct Examination.

By Mr. John Scott:

Q. State your name to the Court, please.
A. Mrs. Dorothy Crawford.
Q. Where do you live?
A. 835 Clay.
Q. Here in the City of Topeka?
A. Topeka.
Q. Defendants' Exhibit "B"(1) that has been admitted into evidence indicates that you are engaged in the pro- [fol. 304] fession of teaching, is that correct?
A. That's right.
Q. And you also teach at Buchanan School.
A. That's right.
Q. And you also teach the first and part of the second grade, is that right?
A. That's right.

188

Q. And also Defendants' Exhibit "D" states that you receive $272.19 for transportation, is that correct?

A. I don't remember the exact amount.

Q. I want you to explain to the Court, if anybody, that you transport, what persons and of what grades that you transport.

Mr. Goodell: We object to that as incompetent, irrelevant and immaterial; don't see the purpose of it.

Judge Hill: What is the purpose of it?

Mr. John Scott: The purpose of this testimony is to show that she transports kindergarten children and she dismisses her grade for the purpose of transporting children, and those children are sent to another classroom during the time that she is conveying these children.

Judge Huxman: You may answer.

(The last preceding question was here read by the reporter.)
[fol. 305]

By Mr. John Scott:

Q. —if any.

A. I do transport kindergarten children after dismissing the first grade at 11:30 and the second grade at 11:45.

Q. Now, when you dismiss your class at 11:30, where does—where do the second-grade children go?

A. I stay in the building and teach the second-grade children until 11:45. I do not dismiss the second grade until 11:45.

Q. Now, Mrs. Crawford, you say you transport the children at 11:30, is that correct?

A. No, I did not say that. I said that I transport the children after dismissing the first grade at 11:30 and the second grade at 11:45. I do not leave the building until after I dismiss the second grade at 11:45.

Q. Isn't it a matter of fact that you take the kindergarten children home at 11:30, and you send the second-grade class into another classroom?

A. No, I do not.

Q. During the time that you have undertaken these duties

of transporting the kindergarten children, haven't you done that?

A. I have not.

Judge Mellott: Didn't your witness testify it was 11:45 that this transportation began?
[fol. 306]   Mr. John Scott: No, 11:30.
Judge Mellott: I don't agree.
Mr. John Scott: I think the testimony yesterday indicated it was 11:30.
Judge Mellott: No, the testimony yesterday was as she has given, after the dismissal of the second class at 11:45 that she transported the children.
Mr. John Scott: I don't think the record shows that, Your Honor.
Judge Mellott: I think it does, but you may proceed.

By Mr. John Scott:

Q. Well, during the year of 1950 and '51 can you state to the Court the approximate number of children that you transported, that is, each day.
A. The number varied according to the attendance, daily attendance, and also according to the transfer of children from one district to another and according to some children going out of town and some coming in town and also some parents on some days elected to come for their children; so it's hard to tell the exact number each day.
Q. Well, use your best judgment, Mrs. Crawford.

Judge Huxman: What's the purpose of this? What are you trying——
Mr. John Scott: It's to ascertain the number of children she transports daily, and I am going to ask her the type
[fol. 307] of vehicle she is driving, Your Honor.
Mr. Goodell: If the Court please, this isn't an accounting procedure. Do they claim she's overpaid or what is it?
Mr. John Scott: We are not claiming anything such.
Judge Huxman: You are trying to establish the buses are overcrowded, is that it?
Mr. John Scott: Trying to establish the number of children she's transporting daily and the type of vehicle.

190

Judge Huxman: What is the purpose of that when you establish it?

Mr. John Scott: The fact that these children are transported under crowded conditions.

Judge Huxman: Well——

By Mr. John Scott:

Q. What type of vehicle do you drive, Mrs. Crawford?
A. I drive a Ford two-door.
Q. What model?
A. A two-door.
Q. Well, I mean——

Mr. Goodell: Year model he means.

By Mr. John Scott:

Q. Year model.
A. 1938.
[fol. 308] Q. Just give your best judgment the number of children that you take in that car each day; is it six, eight, nine, ten or twelve?
A. Well, I take no more than five at a time. When there are more than five children I make two trips.
Q. You make two trips.
A. Yes.
Q. I see. Do you have any special coverage for liability of these children that you carry?

Mr. Goodell: Now, we submit, if the Court please, we object to that as incompetent, irrelevant and immaterial, has no probative force in this case.

Judge Huxman: The objection will be sustained. It is collateral and can't go to any due process, has no bearing on this matter.

Mr. John Scott: I believe that is all.

Cross-examination.

By Mr. Goodell:

Q. Are you neglecting your teaching job by hauling some kids wholly during the noon hour?
A. I am not.

Mr. Goodell: That is all.

Judge Huxman: Are you through now? Plaintiff rests?

Mr. Carter: Yes.

[fol. 309] Judge Huxman: You may proceed with the defense.

CLARENCE G. GRIMES, having been first duly sworn, assumed the stand and testified as follows:

Direct examination.

By Mr. Goodell:

Q. State your name for the record and for the Court.

A. Clarence G. Grimes.

Q. You are commonly known around town here as "Cap" Grimes.

A. That's right.

Q. Were you an officer in World War I?

A. I was.

Q. Have you had for many years the contract with the Topeka Board of Education for the transporting of pupils to the negro schools?

A. Thirty-five years.

Q. Are you familiar then with all the details of the actual carrying out of that mission or the transportation of——

A. I am.

Q. There has been some testimony here offered in the plaintiffs' case to the effect that they had to wait long periods of time at scheduled bus stops. State what the facts are about these buses running on schedule, and so forth.

A. I plan my schedule on clock time to reach the corners at a certain time and, if they are waiting much longer [fol. 310] than what they say here, they are there before the bus is supposed to get there.

Judge Hill: I can't hear the witness.

Judge Mellott: It's difficult to hear you, Mr. Grimes; if you will talk a little louder.

192

By Mr. Goodell:

Q. Repeat that.

A. I say I run my bus on the scheduled time by the clock and, if there is children at the corners that have to wait any length of time, they are there long before the bus should be able to get there. They know what time the bus is supposed to get to the corner.

Q. There is some testimony here in the case given yesterday relating to scheduled stop where a child or parent, perhaps both, testified they had to go seven blocks down here to get to the bus at First and Quincy. Are you familiar with that?

A. Yes, I am.

Q. Is that correct?

A. No.

Q. What are the facts about it?

A. This child lives four blocks and three houses west of First and Kansas Avenue and the bus sets seventy-five feet east of First and Kansas Avenue.

Q. Were you present in court when the testimony was given about the time of the morning that they left in [fol. 311] order to get to the bus stop?

A. I was.

Q. So that would be thirty minutes to go four blocks.

A. That's right.

Q. Do you have, as a practical matter, do you have instances of colored children, negro children, going farther from their home than a scheduled bus stop in order to get to ride longer?

A. I used to have, but I don't have that anymore.

Q. What—do you know the proximity—some of the children have you pick them up—how far away?

A. I think the longest distance is five blocks.

Q. And the closest?

A. The closest distance, some of them are right by their houses.

Q. How far from school?

A. Oh, some of the Washington children are eight or nine blocks from school when I pick them up.

Q. What are some of the closest you pick up and take?

A. From the school?

Q. From many of the schools, yes.

A. That is about the distance—Sixth and Chandler is the closest.

Q. Yes. Now there was some testimony given yesterday [fol. 312] to the effect by one parent—I don't have his name—lives out here in the east part of town, around Chandler in that neighborhood—he had his child ride on the city bus because he had observed children leaning out the windows and their arms out the windows, and so forth. How are these buses built?

A. According to the state regulations on buses, school buses, you have to have half windows in your buses and my windows let down from the top, not any farther than that distance, and they can't get their heads out.

Q. It's impossible.

Judge Mellott: Indicating what, six inches?
The Witness: About six inches.

By Mr. Goodell:

Q. Now, do you try to maintain some decorum in those buses so that it's orderly and the children——

A. —the principal to put a patrol on each one of these buses.

Q. You mean the principals of the schools have a school patrol on each bus.

A. That's right.

Q. And they ride the buses, do they?
A. They do.

Mr. Goodell: I believe that is all.
Judge Huxman: You may cross-examine.

[fol. 313] Cross-examination.

By Mr. Carter:

Q. Mr. Grimes, how many buses do you operate?
A. Just one.
Q. And to how many schools do you take children?
A. Two.
Q. I show you this exhibit, would you indicate to me what

13—8

194

the bus schedule you follow on that exhibit—the exhibit is marked "G"——

Judge Mellott: "G"?

Mr. Carter: "G".

The Witness: I follow the Washington and Monroe schedules.

By Mr. Carter:

Q. Now you have looked at this schedule and this is correct?

A. That is the time the bus arrives at certain places.

Q. I note on this schedule which you have indicated is correct that at 8:29 you unload the rest of the group at the Monroe School; that is, your first load is taken to the Monroe School, and you get there 8:29, is that correct?

A. That varies on account of traffic sometimes; sometimes it's after that and sometimes a little before that.

Q. The schedules—the schedule indicates—I think your testimony indicated that you arrived at a certain time per day and that there was no waiting because of the sched-
[fol. 314] ule. Now you tell me that here when it says you are supposed to get to the Monroe School at 8:29 you cannot say that is correct because it varies due to the traffic. Now is this or is this not a correct time schedule for your buses?

A. I didn't say I got to the Monroe School at 8:29.

Q. Your schedule says it does.

A. I know, but that is not my schedule.

Judge Huxman: It seems to me—I don't want to restrict the opportunity to present this evidence—but this goes to a very minor matter. In the first place, there is a schedule and, in the second place, I think I would take judicial knowledge that maybe buses sometimes are a little bit late and sometimes children get there a little ahead of time. I doubt if there ever was a bus that ran exactly on the second. I don't want to restrict you in your cross-examination, but I wouldn't pursue that too far.

Mr. Carter: Well, the only reason that I raised it is that the testimony which has been established, attempted to be established by the defendants, is that the schedule is followed and that the bus arrives on time.

Judge Huxman: Suppose you established that the schedule varied or the bus wasn't always there on time, do you think that would have a weighty bearing on the question [fol. 315] of whether the due process clause of the Fourteenth Amendment was thereby violated. It might be an insignificant——

Mr. Carter: I don't believe it would be crucial.

Judge Huxman: Let's not pursue it too far. This case isn't going to turn on whether this schedule is strictly adhered to or whether there is a variance in it.

Mr. Carter: All right, sir, I will follow your suggestion.

Judge Huxman: In the first place, I think the buses are late. I have never seen a bus yet that wasn't late.

By Mr. Carter:

Q. What is the maximum capacity on your buses?

A. My bus has a seating capacity of thirty-six.

Q. And you indicated that there are monitors on the bus.

A. Yes.

Q. Who are they?

A. I don't know them by name. I don't know hardly any of the children by last names; some of the first names, I believe, the older boys and girls of the different schools.

Q. Is this only on your return from school?

A. No, going to and coming.

Q. Going to and coming.

[fol. 316] A. Yes, sir.

Q. Every day there is a different person.

A. No, it isn't a different person; it's the same child.

Q. You don't know who it is.

A. I know who they are by looking at them. I can't tell you their names because I am not familiar with all their names.

Redirect examination.

By Mr. Goodell:

Q. Mr. Grimes, you mentioned that only Monroe and Washington were the only ones you personally transported.

196

Do you know how the other schools are handled, who transports them?
A. The Topeka Transportation Company.
Q. The city bus system.
A. The city bus system.
Q. They use their own ordinary equipment.
A. That's right.
Q. They contract that with the Board of Education.
A. That's right.

Mr. Goodell: That's all.
Judge Huxman: Step down.

(Witness excused.)

[fol. 317] THELMA MIFFLIN, having been first duly sworn, assumed the stand and testified as follows:

Direct examination.

By Mr. Goodell:

Q. State your name to the Court and for the record.
A. Thelma Mifflin.
Q. What official position do you hold in the city schools?
A. I am the clerk of the Board of Education.

Judge Huxman: I didn't get the answer.
The Witness: I am the clerk of the Board of Education.

By Mr. Goodell:

Q. How long have you been in such administrative capacity?
A. I have been in Topeka in that capacity for nine years; twenty-seven years total in other school systems.
Q. Are the records then that have been furnished the Court here that are exhibits in this case, were they made under your supervision and direction?
A. Yes, sir.
Q. They are true and accurate records?
A. They are.
Q. And reflect correctly the matters which are covered by them?

A. That's right.

[fol. 318] Q. Did you bring with you this morning at my direction an exhibit or list of the number of colored, negro, students transported?

A. Yes, sir, four copies.

Q. I will hand you what has been marked Defendants' Exhibit "O" and is that a list of the—broken down by schools—of the negro students that are transported in the City of Topeka to the negro schools?

A. That's right.

Q. And it's true and correct?

A. It is.

Mr. Goodell: We offer the same in evidence.
Judge Huxman: What is the exhibit number?
Judge Mellott: "O".
Judge Huxman: Exhibit "O" will be received.

Defendants' Exhibit "O", having been offered and received in evidence, is contained in the case file.

By Mr. Goodell:

Q. Mrs. Mifflin, do you attend all board meetings in your capacity as clerk for the Board of Education?

A. Yes, sir, I do.

Q. You are present then when discussions of policy and administrative policy and the running of the schools comes up for discussion by the board and Dr. McFarland.

[fol. 319] A. Yes, sir.

Q. You are familiar, then, and have been all these years, with that policy.

A. Yes, sir.

Q. Are you familiar then with the actual policy with respect to the operation of the entire school system which includes the eighteen elementary schools and the four negro schools?

A. Yes, sir, I am.

Q. State whether or not you know the policy that has been adopted and carried out by the Board of Education with respect to the negro schools concerning the right of a child, if he so elects or his parents, to attend any one of the four negro schools of his own selection; do you know the policy about that?

198

A. Yes, it is the policy of the board to allow the child to attend the school which he wishes to attend in the colored division.

Q. Do you recall of any instances when that election was made which wasn't acceded to?

A. No.

Q. Are you likewise familiar with the course of study that is prescribed by state law and whether or not it's been adopted and used in the city schools, elementary schools, both negro and white schools.

A. The same course of study is used in all schools.

[fol. 320] Q. That would mean then, of course, the same textbooks.

A. That's right.

Q. There was some testimony given here yesterday by Dr. Speer concerning his examination of books and comparisons that he made from books found in negro schools, comparing the books found in certain of the white schools, that he made such a similar examination. Do you know whether or not, as far as the Board of Education is concerned, there is any distinction or differences in the furnishing of books to the different schools on the basis of their color, whether negro or white schools.

A. There is no distinction made. The number of books isn't—the number of books sent is determined by the number of children in the school.

Q. Well, I mean do you have any policy to send old-style books down to the negro schools and new books to the white schools?

A. No, there is no policy like that. I am sorry that Dr. Speer didn't see the schools when they were in operation. He saw them after they were closed. If a principal had "put his school to bed" as we say correctly, the good books would have been packed in boxes and packed away. The books that are left out on the shelf are books that could be eliminated, really.

Q. Obsolete books.

A. That's right.

[fol. 321] Q. But the modern up-to-date books that are actually used in the operation of the schools, your policy has been as soon as school is out to box them up and put them away.

A. Put them away very carefully so they won't be dusty when school starts.

Q. Now, Miss Mifflin, state, if you know, whether or not additional books, not furnished by the Board of Education, are sometimes furnished by the Parent Teachers Association made up of parents of children living in the various territories in the city?

A. Yes. P. T. A.'s very frequently have money to spend, and they do buy books for various schools.

Q. Buy it with their own money, not public funds.

A. That's right.

Q. And put it in that particular school where the P. T. A. decides to make that purchase, is that correct?

A. That's right.

Q. And that is no different, whether it's negro or white, is that right?

A. That's right.

Q. The board doesn't spend its money or have any control over that.

A. No.

Q. Other than that dissimilarity wherein the Parent Teachers Association in some territory might buy more—might have more money to spend, is there any dissimilarity [fol. 322] by reference books or books furnished by the board in any of the schools in the elementary system?

A. There is no difference.

Q. Now, I want to direct your attention, Miss Mifflin, to what has been introduced in evidence as Exhibit "A" and which I want—first, I will ask you if all of the territories are named and designated on this Exhibit "A", both white and negro?

A. Yes, sir.

Q. Of the entire school system?

A. That's right.

Q. Are school territories also shown on Exhibit "A" which are outside the city limits of Topeka?

A. Yes; the school district is on that map.

Q. In other words, you have some areas shown on Exhibit "A" which are in the City of Topeka for school purposes alone, is that right?

A. That's right.

Q. Does that appear colored in blue?

A. That's right.

Q. I will ask you whether or not in each, if you know, according to the records of the Board of Education, if you have children attending from all of these areas shown in the territory, school territory, or put it another way, from [fol. 323] the blue, what is marked blue.

A. Yes, we do have.

Q. Is any transportation furnished to any of the white children from any part of town?

A. None at all.

Q. Do some of them live as much as thirty blocks away?

A. Yes, sir.

Q. Well, in those cases, if they ride a bus, do they ride a city bus?

A. Yes, they would have to furnish their own transportation.

Q. Now, do you furnish a convoy with any of these children, people to go with them to get them across the streets, and so forth.

A. No, sir.

Q. White children.

A. No.

Q. Do you have any control—state, if you know, whether you have any control—I mean by you, the Board of Education, over selection of traffic lights or blinker lights at any territory in the City of Topeka?

A. No; that is the business of the city.

Q. And how—and do you know how they make that decision?

A. I think they——

Judge Huxman: Mr. Goodell, that would have to be hearsay on her part.

[fol. 324] Mr. Goodell: Yes, it would be.

By Mr. Goodell:

Q. Miss Mifflin, Exhibit "E" and "J" that have been introduced in evidence have to do or set out in a portion of the exhibits the facilities of each school in the whole City of Topeka and, particularly, it shows on that exhibit —those exhibits—whether they have a gymnasium or auditorium and, in some cases, where they are combined, is that accurate, true and correct?

A. Yes, sir.

Q. Those exhibits.

A. That's right.

Q. Do you have some white schools where you have that combination where you turn one room into one, using it——

Judge Huxman: Mr. Goodell, haven't those exhibits been agreed to?

Mr. Goddell: I believe so. I have a note that it wasn't entirely agreed to as to that particular feature.

Judge Huxman: There were only two questions about it at all. The exhibits were admitted.

Mr. Goodell: Except it was held up because they claim inaccuracies in the case of one school. I have a note to that effect.

Judge Huxman: You might ask her about that one inaccuracy.

By Mr. Goodell:

Q. I believe Dr. Speer was the witness who testified [fol. 325] pertaining to four schools which I will direct your attention to, as being Buchanan, Lafayette, Polk and Potwin—in other words the data contained in this data as being true with respect to auditoriums and gymnasiums, will you examine now particularly those schools I have indicated. I will take it one by one and ask you a question: Potwin, for example, you have the record shows that it has an auditorium but no gymnasium, is that correct?

A. That's right, it has a playroom but all schools have playrooms.

Q. Is that true of the negro schools?

A. They all have rooms that they do not use; any room that is not used can be called a playroom.

Q. I notice Polk Street now, the next one that Dr. Speer mentioned in his testimony, it's marked auditorium room

202

used for auditorium purposes but no **gymnasium**, is that correct?

A. That's right; there is no **gymnasium** there.

Q. I notice the same before **Lafayette**, that your records show it has an auditorium room, facilities for an auditorium, but no **gymnasium**, is that right?

A. That's right.

Q. And I direct your attention to the same matter on Buchanan; your record shows it has an auditorium but [fol. 326] no gymnasium, is that correct?

A. That is correct.

Judge Mellott: Is the difference of opinion, take, for instance, Buchanan School, purely one of terminology? Now she refers to it as having an auditorium. As I understood it, counsel's statement was that there were two rooms capable of being thrown together for an assembly room, but they object to calling it an auditorium, is that the point of difference?

Mr. Goodell: That perhaps is the point of difference.

By Mr. Goodell:

Q. That is correct in some of these older schools, white schools, for example, like Lafayette and Polk and some of the others.

A. We have made auditoriums by remodeling in a number of schools. Now the auditorium, what we call auditorium at Buchanan, has a stage; it has seating. The only difference, if they do not wish to have the whole room included in the auditorium, they may pull a sliding door closed and not use the entire auditorium.

Q. Now, are you familiar and is it part of your job and are you familiar with the ordinary maintenance and operation of the school system with respect to furnishing of supplies upon requisition, accessories and needed supplies to properly make the school function?

[fol. 327] A. Yes, sir; I am the business manager of the schools; purchase all the supplies.

Q. You are familiar, then, with the practice and policy that actually has been adopted and used by the board in that respect in the furnishing of supplies.

A. Yes, sir.

Q. State, if you know, as a matter of policy, whether there has ever been any distinction shown between furnishing supplies when requested to negro schools as compared to white schools in the elementary system?

A. There is no distinction made between colored and white schools.

Q. They are operated, in other words, the whole thing is operated as a school system, is it?

A. That's right; it's a school system, and we operate entirely on the need of the school.

Q. And do you know what factors—strike that. Are you familiar with the factors, by reason of board policy and administrative practice, that Dr. McFarland and the board uses actually in fixing teachers' salaries in the entire school system, inclusive of these elementary schools.

A. Yes, sir.

Q. What are those factors?

A. Salaries—you mean the salaries?

Q. How are they arrived at?

[fol. 328] A. Salaries are determined by education, by experience and how well the job is being done.

Q. Teaching experience, educational attainments?

A. That's right.

Q. And actual manner in which the teacher has performed his duties, is that right?

A. That's right.

Q. If I understand you correctly, then, you might have a teacher with the same number of years experience and the same educational attainments, but one that didn't have as good performance record; in the case of one that had a good performance record might get more money than another one having all the other qualities except that one.

A. He might; he also might have extra duties.

Q. Extra duties.

A. That's right.

Q. State whether or not the Board, as a matter of policy by Dr. McFarland and the board, in fixing these salaries there has ever been any other factors applied to the negro school teachers not applied to the white teachers in fixing those salaries?

204

Mr. Carter: Your Honor, all the things brought out, I think, so far have been stipulated to, particularly the salaries.

Mr. Goodell: They wouldn't stipulate on that, and I [fol. 329] have it in my stipulation and I have it marked they wouldn't stipulate.

Judge Huxman: She may answer. I didn't think there was any issue made on it. There is no evidence whatever to show anything to the contrary, but she may answer.

By Mr. Goodell:

Q. Are the same factors used, in other words, in fixing salaries in teachers contracts—I mean the same factors observed and actually followed in fixing salaries for both negro and white teachers?

A. Yes, sir, exactly the same.

Mr. Goodell: I believe that is all.

Cross-examination.

By Mr. Carter:

Q. Miss Mifflin, you said you were the clerk of the Board of Education?

A. That's right.

Q. I think you testified that—as to an exhibit with regard to the school program that this program was carried out throughout the school system, is that correct?

A. That's right.

Q. Among your duties as clerk of the board, are you the person who goes and visits the schools and examines them and inspects them; are those—is that included in your duties?

A. Yes, it is; I call on all schools.

[fol. 330] Q. I see. Now, with regard to the books that are held, if there is any difference between the books that are held by the white schools and those that are held by the negroes, if I understand your testimony correctly, you would attribute that to donations by the P. T. A. organization, is that right?

A. That's right.

Q. Is it or is it not a fact that if these books do—if they are donated by the P. T. A. they belong to the school or the Board of Education or what happens?

Mr. Goodell: We object to that as calling for a conclusion, legal conclusion, of this witness, where title is in the books.

Judge Huxman: She said she's in charge of the school system for that purpose. She may answer.

The Witness: They are usually gifts to the school. If they are a gift, then they become the property of the school.

By Mr. Carter:

Q. They become the property of the school to which they are given.

A. However, we wouldn't feel that we could go—if a gift would go to a certain school, we wouldn't feel that we should go in and remove it to another school.

Q. I understand that. They become the property of the school to which it's given, and they remain there, is that correct?

[fol. 331] A. That's right.

Judge Huxman: You may step aside, please.

(Witness excused.)

KENNETH McFARLAND, having been previously sworn, assumed the stand and testified as follows:

Direct examination.

By Mr. Goodell:

Q. State your name again for the record.
A. Kenneth McFarland.
Q. And you are the superintendent of schools of the City of Topeka.
A. Yes.
Q. How long have you held that post?
A. Nine years; since 1942.
Q. How long have you been in educational work?

206

Judge Huxman: Wasn't all of that gone into yesterday. I thought the doctor was asked his qualifications.

The Witness: No.

Mr. Goodell: I don't recall it.

Judge Huxman: Proceed.

Mr. Goodell: I will dismiss it, though, if the Court doesn't want to hear it. I will make this very brief.

[fol. 332] By Mr. Goodell:

Q. What is your educational background?

A. Bachelor's Degree from Pittsburgh Teachers College here in Kansas and a Master's Degree from Columbia University and doctorate degree from Stanford University.

Q. How long have you been in education work, Doctor?

A. Twenty-four years.

Q. When you came to Topeka, state whether or not the elementary schools were being operated, separated as to negro and whites in the first six grades.

A. Yes, sir.

Q. You understand, do you, that the statute of Kansas is a permissive one, that the Board of Education may— it's up to their discretion—according to statute.

A. Yes.

Q. —to so operate the elementary schools.

A. Yes, I understand that.

Q. Has it ever been your policy that you recommended to the board to change that operation actually?

A. We have—no; we have never recommended that we change the fundamental structure of the elementary schools.

Q. Why not.

Judge Huxman: Mr. Goodell, what would that establish in this lawsuit?

Mr. Goodell: Well, I think he, as an administrator—I am leading to something. I can't ask more than one question [fol. 333] at a time.

Judge Huxman: I know, but what's the purpose? If the statute gives the city permission to operate the schools, and he testified they are operating separate schools, what difference would it make whether they had or had not considered changing?

Mr. Goodell: It might make some difference. We had a lot of expert testimony here on a hypothetical community or hypothetical situation, and I want to show the human factor in the custom and usage in this community, whether he knows it and whether or not it had something to do with the operation of the schools, why they operated——

Judge Huxman: Whether the city authorities had considered discarding what they had a right under the statute to do or hadn't considered, wouldn't prove any issue in this case.

By Mr. Goodell:

Q. Have you ever, as an administrator of schools, considered it part of your business to formulate custom and—social customs and usage in the community?

A. Mr. Goodell, I think that point is extremely significant; in fact, it's probably the major factor in why the Board of Education is defending this lawsuit, and that is that we have never considered it, and there is nothing in the record historically, that it's the place of the public school system to dictate the social customs of the people [fol. 334] who support the public school system.

Q. Do you say that the separation of the schools that we have is in harmony with the public opinion, weight of public opinion, in this community?

A. We have no objective evidence that the majority sentiment of the public would desire a change in the fundamental structure.

Q. Now, we will get on to the actual operation. Have there been any distinction in the question of fixing salaries, furnishing accessories or supplies to the negro schools as opposed to the white schools?

A. No. I think we found what we thought were some discrepancies when we first came here in salaries. Those were corrected; we adopted a minimum salary of $2400 for inexperienced teachers with degrees; that was the basis where we started and, from that point on, there has been no discrepancy of any kind.

Q. Do you take into account, as head of the schools, as recommending to the Board of Education the matter of the

208

color of the teacher at all in fixing that teacher's contract salary?

A. No.

Q. You have heard Mrs. Mifflin testify to the factors that are considered, is that correct?

A. The three factors plus the total responsibilities in-
[fol. 335] volved in the job.

Q. Some teachers have more responsibilities than others.

A. That's right.

Q. Of course a principal, that would be naturally true. Now, in respect to furnishing, honoring requisitions and furnishing all supplies, are the same factors considered by you and the Board of Education in respect to that, without regard to whether the school is white or negro school?

A. Oh, yes, no difference.

Q. There has been some testimony here about curriculum. Is the same curriculum followed in both the negro and white schools, elementary schools.

A. Yes, they are all under the same director of elementary schools, same supervisor of elementary schools and same special supervisors, no difference.

Q. Your administrative set-up is entirely one for the operation of the entire school system, is it not?

A. Yes, it's considered twenty-two elementary schools.

Q. Yes. In any particular, whether I have asked you or not, is there the slightest difference in the actual operation and maintenance of the school system between the negro and the white schools the way it's carried on?

A. Nothing done on the basis of color. They are merely treated as individuals.

Q. Do you know whether or not this operation has been
[fol. 336] well received in this community?

A. Well, I feel that it has, in the main, been well received.

Q. State whether or not the school system has been commented on by national authorities, educational authorities.

Judge Huxman: Doctor, you need not answer that question. Mr. Goodell, that is not an issue in this case, has nothing to do with the problems concerning the Court.

Mr. Goodell: I thought they were trying to show we had some poor schools. Maybe not. That is all.

Judge Huxman: You may cross-examine.

Cross examination.

By Mr. Carter:

Q. Mr. McFarland, I think you said that you didn't consider it the function of the Board of Education to go against the prevailing opinion with regard to the maintenance of public schools.

A. I said the social customs of the people. I didn't think it was the purpose of the school system to dictate the social customs of the people who support the schools. That has been our policy.

Q. Now, how do you know that social customs of Topeka require the maintenance of separate schools at the elementary school level?

A. I said we had no objective evidence that the majority [fol. 337] of the people wishes to change in the fundamental structure which we don't have.

Q. Would you say that there is a difference in the social or public opinion or social customs with regard to the maintenance of segregated schools above the elementary school level?

A. I didn't say that.

Q. Would you say, I am asking you a question.

A. I don't know; I wouldn't pass on that. You see, we are operating the schools under essentially the same structure that we took them over in 1942.

Q. But you are operating schools that have a mixed characteristic, mixed characteristics, rather, do you not? You are operating schools that are segregated at the elementary school level, integrated beyond. Now why does the Board of Education feel that they are maintaining their —they are in accord with public opinion by maintaining that type of operation?

A. Well, we have——

Mr. Goodell: Just a minute. Object to this question because it assumes as a part of the question—assumes that

14—8

part of this integration is caused by public policy of the board. The Supreme Court decision in the case of Graham vs. Board of Education, decided that there couldn't be a separation in the seventh and eighth grade where we had [fol. 338] a junior and senior set up. There is a policy set up on it of cities of the first class, all except Kansas City, which is controlled by another statute, so it isn't a matter of policy of the board.

Judge Huxman: I doubt if there is very much value to this whole line of questions.

Mr. Goodell: My point is that the law compels them to have integrated system as to junior high and high school.

Judge Huxman: The witness may answer the question.

(The last preceding question was read by the reporter.)

Mr. Goodell: If the Court please, I insist again my objection is proper. He is asking the doctor to distinguish the board forming a policy, saying in the elementary grades they will be separate and in the others it won't; it isn't a matter of choice with them as to junior high and high school. It's fixed by law.

Judge Huxman: The objection will be overruled.

The Witness: The answer is essentially that given by the attorney. The board has had no vote upon whether or not they would segregate the schools above the sixth grade [fol. 339] nor have the people—the public that they represent.

By Mr. Carter:

Q. I see. So, actually, you are not maintaining—you can't really say you are maintaining the schools in accord with social custom. You merely have kept consant the status quo as you found it when you came here. You are maintaining segregated schools merely because they were here when you arrived; that's all you can say, isn't that true?

A. We have, as I stated, no objective evidence that there is any substantial desire for a change among the people that the board represents.

Judge Huxman: May I ask counsel on both sides, assuming that is true, assuming the schools are maintained in accordance with social customs and the wishes of the people, or that they are not, what bearing does that have on the right to so maintain them under the Fourteenth Amendment?

Mr. Goodell: Judge Parker in his opinion that was handed down by that court of South Carolina, goes into that very, very carefully.

Judge Huxman: Presently we are not interested in that. I am asking—this is——

Mr. Goodell: Our theory of the equal protection of the laws——

Judge Huxman: Mr. Goodell, the question is what the [fol. 340] Fourteenth Amendment warrants and what it doesn't. We don't care what social customs provide. That is the reason I can't see any use in pursuing this line of argument unduly—this line of questioning.

Mr. Carter: I agree with that, Your Honor, but——

Judge Huxman: Then let's not pursue it too far. I don't want to cut you off because Mr. Goodell opened it up, but don't pursue it unnecessarily.

Mr. Carter: I am not going to pursue it any further, but I thought I shouldn't allow it to remain in the record unchallenged. That is the only reason I have asked the question.

By Mr. Carter:

Q. Now, I have just a few more questions, Mr. McFarland. Are you familiar with J. Murray Lee, who is the dean of the School of Education of the State of Washington; are you familiar with him; do you know him?

A. No, I don't know him.

Q. Do you know his wife, Doris Mae Lee, who is the co-author of "Learning to Read Through Experience"?

A. Do I know her?

Q. Are you familiar——

A. I just know there is such a person.

Q. In a book which both of them collaborated on——

[fol. 341] Mr. Goodell: What did you say? I didn't hear you.

Mr. Carter: Collaborated in writing.

212

By Mr. Carter:

Q. This statement appears, and I would like to get your views on this: "No longer is the curriculum to be considered a fixed body of subject matter to be learned. We realize only too well that the curriculum for each child is the sum total of all of his experiences which are in any way affected by the school. However rich or valuable any printed course of study may seem to be, the child benefits not at all if he does not have those experiences in classroom."

Now, would you agree or disagree with that statement?

A. Well, you lift one statement like that out of its context in an educational philosophy—it's a little difficult to say whether you would agree with the single statement or not. We would have to know the background of that, what lead up to it.

Q. The statement is—follows a philosophy that the sum total of a child's experience throughout the school—is the curriculum, not merely the subjects in the school. Now, do you or do you not agree with that?

A. I would agree with that in principle, but, of course, you understand when you go to that theory of education that the child is in the public schools a small percentage of [fol. 342] his total living hours. That puts the curriculum over into a field that is largely out of control of the schools.

Q. It puts the curriculum certainly out of control of the school but insofar as the school provides the atmosphere and everything that is part of the curriculum, not only the books but everything else that goes into the—into his experience in the schools, is that right?

A. Anything that would have to do with motivation of learning.

Mr. Carter: That is all.
Judge Huxman: Is that all.
Mr. Carter: That is all.
Judge Huxman: You may step down.
Mr. Goodell: The defendant rests.
Judge Huxman: The defendant rests. Any rebuttal testimony?
Mr. Greenberg: Yes, Your Honor.

Ernest Manheim, having been first duly sworn, testified on behalf of the plaintiffs in rebuttal as follows:

Direct examination.

By Mr. Greenberg:

Q. Would you please state your full name to the Court.
A. Ernest Manheim.
Q. What is your occupation, Mr. Manheim?
A. Professor of Sociology at the University of Kansas City.
[fol. 343] Q. What degrees do you hold and where were they earned?
A. A Ph.D. in sociology at the University of Leipzig, a Ph.D. in anthropology from the University of London.
Q. What is your field of special interest, Professor Manheim?
A. Social organization, juvenile delinquency and social theory.
Q. Have you published any articles in this particular field? Or any books?

Mr. Goodell: We don't want to interfere but we object to this if this is a repetition, simply cumulative of more expert opinion.

Mr. Greenberg: It is not, Your Honor.

Judge Huxman: What do you propose to rebut by the testimony of this witness? I take it you are qualifying him as an expert. Now just what testimony offered by the defendants are you proposing to rebut?

Mr. Greenberg: The clerk of the School Board stated that to the extent that there was a difference of library holdings between the colored and white schools, it was attributable to P. T. A. donations to the white schools. We intend to show that the maintenance of a segregated school system in Topeka has caused this difference in P. T. A. and community support of the colored as against the white schools.

Mr. Goodell: We object to that.
[fol. 344] Mr. Greenberg: Directly rebuts——

Judge Huxman: Just a minute. The doctor isn't a residet of this community, is he?

214

Mr. Greenberg: The doctor is not a resident of this community.

Judge Huxman: How could he know whether that is what caused this condition in Topeka?

Mr. Greenberg: Well, the doctor is a man who has studied social forces in nearby communities and, in qualifying as an expert, we believe that he will be competent to generalize from his studies and his experience.

Judge Huxman: How would that qualify him to testify that segregated schools in Topeka is what caused certain voluntary and independent groups to make donations of books to certain schools?

Mr. Greenberg: I don't want to give the doctor's testimony, but——

Judge Huxman: How could it tend to establish that?

Mr. Greenberg: I believe the doctor is going to testify that studies have shown that the distance which community support—the distance that community support is from a particular school determines the force of the community effectiveness of the community support.

Judge Huxman: How long is this testimony going to [fol. 345] take?

Mr. Greenberg: Perhaps five or ten minutes.

Judge Huxman: Frankly, the Court doubts if it is rebuttal testimony. If it's brief, we will give you the benefit of the doubt and let you go ahead. I don't think it rebuts anything.

(The last question was here read by the reporter.)

The Witness: Yes, I have published in my field in sociology six books; one of them deals with juvenile delinquency in Kansas City.

By Mr. Greenberg:

Q. Have you ever made any studies which would enable you to form a conclusion concerning the community support which a community gives to a school?

Mr. Goodell: We object to this as calling not for any fact, pure conjecture and guesswork and conclusion on the part of the witness.

215

Judge Huxman: He may answer.

The Witness: Inasmuch as I can generalize from experience in Kansas City, I would tend to say that a school which is far from the clientele's residence, from their parents, is weakened in its position to supervise the conduct of the children, and is—and it is the cooperation between the teachers and the parents tend to be weaker.

[fol. 346] Mr. Goodell: We object to this for the further reason it's not rebuttal. If anything, it's part of their case in chief and, for the further reason, that is opinion——

Judge Huxman: The objection to that question will be sustained. It isn't responsive; it doesn't rebut anything that has been offered in the case.

Mr. Greenberg: Well, Your Honor, I believe that the clerk of the Board of Education did testify that the discrepancy between the white and colored schools was attributable to discrepancies in P. T. A. support. We are trying to show that——

Judge Huxman: Didn't so testify. She testified that these additional books or extra books were the result of donations by P. T. A. organizations; that is what she testified to and——

Mr. Greenberg: I hope to establish by this witness that a weakened P. T. A. is caused by having children and parents great distance from the school which the children attend.

Mr. Goodell: Object to it for the further reason it's outside the scope of the pleadings; it's not an issue raised by the pleadings as being one or any of the grounds of inequality, so it's outside the scope of the issues.

[fol. 347] Judge Huxman: The majority of the Court feels that this testimony is not proper rebuttal testimony from the very nature of the explanation that you have given. The doctor could not testify that the discrimination, if you want to so refer to it, which results in the donation of books in Topeka to one school and not to another is caused by segregation. He could only give that as his theory that that will flow and result from segregation generally. But he knows nothing about Topeka. The objection will be sustained. We will receive no further evidence along this line.

Anything further?

216

Mr. Carter: We have nothing further.
Judge Huxman: Both parties rest?
Mr. Goodell: Yes, Your Honor.
Mr. Carter: Yes.

Colloquy Between Court and Counsel

Judge Huxman: We perhaps should take a short recess. We would like to ask counsel, is there a desire to argue this case orally?

Mr. Goodell: I would personally, my notion about it, I believe the Court has heard all the testimony, that we could perhaps aid the Court more in a written brief. I would like to submit a written brief, and I can have it ready inside of a week.

Judge Huxman: Does plaintiff desire to argue the case [fol. 348] to the Court?

Mr. Carter: Yes, we do, Your Honor.

Judge Huxman: You shall be afforded that opportunity. Will the defendant then want to argue the case?

Mr. Goodell: We will make a short argument.

Judge Huxman: How much time do you feel you would want to argue this case?

Mr. Carter: We would think, Your Honor, just about a half hour on opening, and we would like to have time for rebuttal.

Judge Huxman: How much time for rebuttal?

Mr. Carter: I should think approximately fifteen minutes.

Judge Huxman: Forty-five minutes, of which you take thirty minutes in the opening argument and fifteen in the closing; and how much does the defendant want?

Mr. Goodell: Twenty or thirty minutes, I think, will be sufficient.

Judge Huxman: We will take a five or ten-minute recess before we start into that phase.

(The court then, at 11:05 o'clock a. m., stood at recess until 11:15 o'clock a. m., at which time the following further proceedings were had:)

[fol. 349] Judge Huxman: Do you gentlemen desire the Court to keep a record of your time or will you do that yourselves?

Mr. Carter: I will do that, Your Honor.

Judge Huxman: All right, forty-five minutes, thirty for opening, fifteen for closing and, of course, the defendant, while they have only asked for twenty, if they should want not to exceed that, they will be given the same amount.

You may proceed.

Opening Argument on Behalf of Plaintiff

Mr. Carter: Involved in this case is a question of the constitutionality of the state statute, Section 72-1724, of the General Statutes of the State of Kansas which purports to give to the Boards of Education of cities of certain class the power to organize and maintain separate schools for the education of white and colored children, and I think that the reading of the wordage of the statute is very interesting. The statute says that such power as "to organize and maintain separate schools for the education of white and colored children, including the high schools in Kansas City, Kansas; no discrimination on account of color shall be made in high schools, except as provided herein; * * *."

Now, I think, that that is very interesting verbiage because, I think, there is a recognition, certainly the lan-[fol. 350] guage is a recognition by the framers of the statute, that the separation at the elementary school level was discrimination and is discrimination.

Now we rest our case on the question of the power of the state. We feel, one, that the state has no authority and no power to make any distinction or any classification among its citizenry based upon race and color alone. We think that this has been settled by the Supreme Court of the United States in a long line of cases which hold that in order for a classification to be constitutional it must be based on a real difference, a real and substantial difference which has pertinence to the legislative objective. The Supreme Court has also held in a series of cases that race and ancestry and color are irrelevant differences and cannot form the basis for any legislative action. The only exception to this provision has been in the cases involving the Japanese war cases which included—involved rights under the Fifth Amendment and the exception has been repeated by the Supreme Court of the United States after

218

Hirabayashi vs. U. S. and other cases that were decided, Korematsu vs. United States, and the Supreme Court has repeated again and again when it has struck down a legislative or governmental action because it said it was based on race and race alone, the Supreme Court has said that there is absence of compelling necessity to support the [fol. 351] constitutionality of this statute and the only compelling necessity that we have found in the cases is a national emergency which, in the Hirabayashi case, the court decided even though it questioned the constitutionality of the Exclusion Act of the Japanese because of their ancestry; the Supreme Court felt that national interests were of such a nature that they could not interfere with the judgment of the War Department. But that is the only exception to this general theory which I think the Court is familiar with and the principle of law established by the Supreme Court that there can be no distinction, no classification, unless it is based upon a real and substantial difference, and race is not a real and substantial difference.

The other trend of the law is that the rights under the Fourteenth Amendment are individual rights. You cannot take away the individual's rights by classifying him or putting him in a group and therefore saying that we, on the average, treat the group well, therefore the individual, if he suffers he has to suffer because he is a member of the group. The Supreme Court of the United States has taken care of that in a series of cases which I think I need not mention but one particularly is Missouri ex rel Gaines vs. Canada; the other is the recent Sweatt vs. Painter, involving the admission of a negro to the University of Texas. [fol. 352] Another is the Henderson vs. U. S. which involved the right of negroes to eat any place on a dining car without the curtains or signs or distinctions based on race and color.

Now, in all of those cases the argument raised was that we are providing for negroes as a group about as much as we can. We are meeting the demand. It just happens that this individual—if this individual wants to eat in the dining car and the space we have reserved for him is filled, then even though there are vacant seats in the outer part of the dining car, the fact that he has to wait, he is no more disadvantaged than a white person who comes into the dining car and the place is filled, and he has to wait. The Supreme Court said in those cases that the Fourteenth Amendment granted individual rights, rights to the individual, and it was no answer to say that because the person was a member of a group or because of his number, because of the numbers of the group, that therefore he should not be accorded this right which the Fourteenth Amendment gives.

Now, I think that those two trends of the law—those are the two trends of the law which presently exist, and those two trends, I think, make it clear that no other conclusion can be reached in this case other than that this statute is unconstitutional.

[fol. 353] I realize that there is a body of law which is classified under the separate but equal doctrine of Plessy vs. Ferguson which would seem to give authority to a state to maintain segregation, but it is our contention, and I will attempt to show—I will attempt to demonstrate to the Court that whatever potency that doctrine may have had that by virtue of the present classification doctrine which has been established by the Supreme Court of the United States by the emphasis and reemphasis of the individual right under the Fourteenth Amendment, the Plessy vs. Ferguson doctrine of separate but equal has been whittled away.

Now, it is interesting, in examining the cases under this doctrine, in the field of education to find that in none of the Supreme Court cases has this doctrine been applied. It was mentioned—the nearest case in which it came to being applied, rather, was a case which was decided sometime ago, I think about 1925, Gong Lum vs. Rice. In that case Mr. Chief Justice Taft assumed that the Supreme Court of the United States had followed and had made as to law the separate but equal doctrine of Plessy vs. Ferguson, but the real problem in that case was not the application of the separate but equal doctrine; the real problem in Gong Lum vs. Rice is whether a person of Chinese extraction who was classified by the state as a negro had [fol. 354] a right to being so classified. The petitioner, the Chinese child, did not question the power of the state to make a classification; it questioned the use of the power in putting her, as a Chinese, being classified as a negro for purposes of education, so that the problem which we here present as to whether or not the state has the power to classify on the basis of race, was not presented in Gong Lum vs. Rice and certainly was not passed upon. The Gaines case, the Sipuel case, Sweatt case, the McLaurin case, the McKissick vs. Carmichael, and I will merely mention it because it is a more recent case and it may well be that the Court hasn't read it; I am sure that you are familiar with the other cases that I will not have to go into, but in McKissick vs. Carmichael involves the right of a negro to attend the University of North Carolina School of Law. The state maintained a separate and segregated school at the North Carolina College for Negroes. The case was lost in the lower court on the grounds that it would be better for negroes to go to a segregated school than it would be for them to go to the university—to the University of North Carolina. On appeal to the United States Court of Appeals for the Fourth Circuit the judgment of the court below was reversed on authority of the U. S. Supreme Court in Sweatt vs. Painter, and the Supreme Court, on June 4, 1951, refused to review the case. Now, the interesting [fol. 355] thing about that case, if the Court please, is that here in North Carolina one of the oldest negro law schools in the country had been operated. It had been established and had been operating since 1939—the oldest school. It was conceded that the state was making an effort to maintain a school for the education of negroes but, because of the segregation, because that school was segregated, the Court of Appeals held, consistent with the case of Sweatt vs. Painter, the state had no power to make any such distinctions.

Now I think that, if anything, the only argument that can be made with regard to this problem is not whether the law, as it now stands, is for the proposition that the maintenance of separate schools can be maintained by the state. I think that the law, as it now stands with the classification cases, with the individual right under the Fourteenth Amendment, I think that the inevitable conclusion must be that segregation, the maintenance by the state of segregated facilities on the basis of race, is unconstitutional.

The question sometimes may arise with regard to whether or not even though this is the law, it is expedient for the Court to reach a decision at this time, and I think that that seems to me to probably be apparently the trend of [fol. 356] the present cases. The United States Supreme Court recently also handled a case involving interstate travel and, in this case, in which it denied to review on May 28, 1951, the Fourth Circuit held that Jim Crow coaches— the separate coaches for negroes and whites on a north-south journey was unconstitutional. The Supreme Court refused to review this. Now I see no distinction between Jim Crow coaches on a north-south journey than between Jim Crow coaches on a south-north journey. The Court made the distinction, and the law as I understand it at the present time, applies only to north-south journies. I think that the distinction was made because the Court felt that it could and should strike down illegal regulations involving racial distinctions of a person who comes from an area in which they do not have to submit to that, going into an area in which they do, even though they pass the imaginary Mason-Dixon Line.

Now, however, I think the facts show that here in Topeka the time is now ripe for decision and for this court to use its power to strike down this statute. The system in Topeka is operated with eighteen schools for white children and four schools for negroes. The white children attend the schools in the territories in which they live. Negroes attend four schools that are located in I think for the most part in the center of town, with one in an area which I believe is called North Topeka. A number of negro children have to be [fol. 357] transported to these schools in buses. We have submitted testimony to show that insofar as the time spent on the bus takes away from the child the opportunity to play and to learn, to play rather, that he is being deprived of something of value to his education, and he is being deprived of this in this instance because the state says that the City of Topeka can, and the City of Topeka has decided to maintain separate schools at the elementary school level.

222

Now also in the City of Topeka there is a school system which is different from that at the elementary school level. At the junior high school level and the high school level we have mixed schools. Now, defendants have indicated, and I realize that this is because the statute says that there can be no discrimination at the high school level; however, in this type of mixed situation where on one hand you have for only six grades of the same public school system you maintain segregation, with the other six grades you do not maintain segregation, then certainly the interest, whatever interest the state may have in the maintenance of segregation, if it could be argued that it has such an interest, and therefore a court should withhold its authority to strike down that power, whatever interest it has, it seems that the picture of it maintaining in one end of the system for most of the system and not maintaining it in another, in-
[fol. 358] dicates that if there is such an interest, it is of minor importance and should be disregarded.

We maintain, of course, that the state has no power in this area. But this case, I think, is as close to McLaurin vs. The Board of Regents of Oklahoma as any other case that we have been familiar with. If the Court will remember, in that case a negro, or a group of negroes, were admitted to the University of Oklahoma. They were given the same teachers, the same textbooks; they apparently got the same education, that is, in terms of subject matter. But, because they were negroes, they were forced in the classroom to sit at separate seats; they were forced to sit at separate benches in the library; they were forced to eat at separate tables in the cafeteria. In reviewing this case, the United States Supreme Court felt that here was an area in which it was apparent that this type of segregation was ridiculous and meaningless. If McLaurin could be admitted into the classroom, necessarily he should be able to be permitted into the classroom without distinction or difference based upon race and color. The Court found that these arbitrary distinctions, putting him aside, stigmatized him and interfered with his ability to learn and with the learning process.

Now we contend the same thing here. We contend that
[fol. 359] this statute, one, that the state has no power to enforce the statute in the first place, and, two, that if it has

such power, that by making a difference at the high school level and the junior high level, whatever interest it may have, that interest is not now of any importance because it is clear that there is no distinction between maintaining a power to maintain segregation in the first six grades of school and the power to maintain segregation at the junior high and the high school level. So that with this mixed situation we think that it's even more important that the power of this Court should be exercised in striking down this statute.

We have introduced testimony to show that there are differences, substantial differences, between various of the white schools as contrasted to the negro schools. We have shown that on the average in terms of teacher preparation, subject matter taught, buildings, and so forth, that on the average the school system here, as between the negro and the white schools, there is not too much difference except for this factor: We have shown that 45% of the white children attend schools newer than the newest colored schools and that 66% of them attend in buildings newer than the average age of the negro school, and that on the average the insured value per classroom of the negro school is approximately $4,000 below that of the white school. We have also [fol. 360] shown that in terms of books which are held by the various schools that the white schools maintain a newer supply of books; that the white schools have better books and that therefore the book holdings of the schools, as between negro and white, is substantially different.

Now, the defendants attempt to defend this on the grounds that the P. T. A. is the cause of this difference. It is our contention that in spite of where the books come from and it has been testified that when they get into the school they belong to that particular school; that without regard to where they come from, the fact that they belong to the school and are held by the school is really the factor which makes for the difference and that has to be considered.

We have submitted testimony also to show that the separation of negroes and whites in the elementary school of the school grades of Topeka is harmful to the development of the child, although it has been conceded that the subject-matters taught are the same, and in our definition of what is a school curriculum we have attempted to point out in the record that the school curriculum is the sum total of the child's experience from the time he leaves home to go to school until the time that he returns, and therefore the fact that negroes have to ride buses, those [fol. 361] who do, and cannot go to the school which is within walking distance of them, therefore they cannot come home for hot lunches, that they are required to travel across the town merely because they are negroes and attend a segregated school and makes it impossible for us to say that the curriculum at the segregated negro schools are equal to those at the white schools.

We have also attempted to establish that, if anything, the maintenance of the segregated system at the first six grades and then integration at the high school, junior high school level, places an added burden upon the child because that is the time that he is meeting the problems of adolescence and attempting to develop into a man or into a woman and that with those additional burdens upon him, we think this is an additional hardship which makes this statute, in our view, unreasonable.

Now, with that in mind we feel that we have sufficiently established that the separation of negroes and whites in the public schools of Topeka is a denial of equal protection because of the Fourteenth Amendment, that this statute which the city or Board of Education under which it purports to operate, is unconstitutional and should be so declared by this Court, and we also contend that by virtue of the facts which we have set in the record with regard to the stigma on the negro child because of race and color [fol. 362] at what is considered the most crucial age of his development, that the injuries which are established here, we have put on evidence to show that these injuries are likely permanent and that they cannot be corrected merely by introducing them into the junior high school at a later age. In fact, we show that it probably by making this introduction to the junior high school on an integrated basis at the adolescent age, probably compounds the injury which has been suffered at the elementary school level and, for these reasons, we think we have established the rights of the plaintiffs for the issuance of the injunction for which

225

we have prayed and we submit that this Court should declare this statute to be unconstitutional and order the Board of Education of Topeka to admit all persons into its schools without regard to race or color.

Judge Huxman: In assigning time for argument, we overlooked the State of Kansas represented by the attorney general. That was unintentional. How much time, Mr. McQueary, if any, do you desire to argue in behalf of the constitutionality of the state statute which you are defending here.

Mr. McQueary: If the Court please, I think we can explain our position very fully and amply well in a brief [fol. 363] on the matter of the constitutionality of the statute.

Judge Huxman: All right. You may proceed with the argument.

Do you desire the Court to keep track of your time, or are you going to keep track of your time?

Mr. Brewster: Perhaps you better keep track, Your Honor.

Judge Huxman: How much time do you desire to take in the opening argument, Mr. Brewster?

Mr. Brewster: I would say twenty, twenty-five minutes.

Judge Huxman: Well, now, you say which? I can't keep——

Mr. Brewster: Twenty-five minutes.

ARGUMENT ON BEHALF OF DEFENDANTS

Your Honor, I would like to touch on one point mentioned by counsel for the plaintiffs, and that is attempting to lay some stress on the fact that the distance traveled by a pupil in attending school has some bearing upon the question before this Court.

There are a number of cases to the effect that the mere fact that certain colored school children must travel farther to reach a colored school than any white child is required to travel to reach the white school, is not necessarily a deprivation of equal advantages. There are a lot of cases on that. They are collected in an annotation in A. L. R. [fol. 364] Then, going to a United States Supreme Court

15—8

decision of Gong Lum vs. Rice, in there the Court pointed out that there was no colored school within the district in which this—school for other than whites; that involved a Chinese girl being declared as ineligible to attend a white school; but they did point out in that case that there was a school in the county in which this particular school district was located where she could attend and therefore there could be no objection made on constitutional ground. The distance you travel is immaterial, and I would say that that is especially true in our situation where the entire city of Topeka constitutes a school district and where the evidence, testimony, shows that there are a number of white students who are required to walk to school a greater distance than these colored children who are furnished transportation, and we have the Kansas case in which this question was raised, Reynolds vs. The Board of Education—well, I believe it's the Wright case, and there the Supreme Court pointed out that the question was raised that they had to attend Buchanan School which was twenty blocks farther than a white school they could attend, and our court pointed out the fact that transportation was furnished and therefore the question of distance traveled would have no bearing on the proposition. Now that is all I want to say right [fol. 365] now on distance traveled.

The plaintiffs in this case, of course, are by these cases attempting to have the courts abandon the separate but equal doctrine which was enunciated in the case of Plessy vs. Ferguson, which appears in 163 U. S. 537. It has been mentioned by counsel for the plaintiff, and they mention or contend that the more recent descisions have whittled away the effect of that decision and, of course, in that connection, they rely upon the case of Sweatt vs. Painter, which is the most recent case on this point. I will come to that in just a minute. First, I would like to call attention to the fact that there have been a number of decisions to the effect that establishing separate schools for white and colored children does not violate the constitutional right to equal privileges and immunities if equal advantages are afforded for each class.

Now, defendants admit that there has been engrafted upon this separate but equal doctrine the requirement that you must afford equal opportunity, and it's our position that under the facts stipulated to here and the evidence, that there is no real question but what we do afford equal educational opportunities to the colored folks, and we finally get down to there one point and that is that segregation in and [fol. 366] of itself constitutes a discrimination.

School segregation statutes have been before the United States Supreme Court in a number of cases and at no time have they held that these state statutes are unconstitutional.

Now, getting down to the case of Sweatt vs. Painter, we have here the opinion of the District Court of the United States for the Eastern District of South Carolina. This is the opinion of the court and, while it is not published, it is, of course, authority—Harry Briggs, Jr., et al, Plaintiff, vs. R. W. Elliott, et al.

Judge Mellott: You mean that is the last case that came down a year or two ago.

Mr. Brewster: That is correct. This is the opinion of the court, and it was decided June 23, 1951. I would like to first call attention to this Sweatt case. In the opening paragraph of the opinion of that case the Court said this:

"This case and McLaurin vs. Oklahoma State Regents" and cites "present different aspects of this general question: To what extent does the Equal Protection Clause of the Fourteenth Amendment limit the power of a state to distinguish between students of different races in professional and graduate education in a state university?"

[fol. 367] In other words, the Court specifically restricted that to professional and graduate education in a state university. Then the Court pointed out that broader issues had been urged for their consideration, but adhering to the rule that constitutional questions are made as narrow as possible, and the Court says that was—is not necessary to consider, and the point I am making is that the Sweatt and the McLaurin cases do not in anyway detract from the effect of Plessy vs. Ferguson which is still the law.

Now, reviewing Plessy vs. Ferguson, that is the case which involved the state statute providing for separate railway carriages for white and colored races, and it was a Louisiana statute, and it provided that the passengers be assigned to the coaches according to their race by the conductor, and the Court held that it did not violate—deprive a colored person of any rights under the Fourteenth Amendment to the federal constitution. That is the case from which stems this separate but equal doctrine which the defendants think is still applicable and which the plaintiffs, of course, are seeking to overturn.

Here's one thing the Court said:

"So far, then, as a conflict with the Fourteenth Amendment is concerned, the case reduces itself to the question [fol. 368] whether the statute of Louisiana is a reasonable regulation, and with respect to this there must necessarily be a large discretion on the part of the legislature. In determining the question of reasonableness it is at liberty to act with reference to the established usages, customs and traditions of the people, and with a view to the promotion of their comfort, and the preservation of the public peace and good order. Gauged by this standard, we cannot say that a law which authorizes or even requires the separation of the two races in public conveyances is unreasonable, or more obnoxious to the Fourteenth Amendment than the acts of Congress requiring separate schools for colored children in the District of Columbia, the constitutionality of which does not seem to have been questioned, or the corresponding acts of state legislatures.

"We consider the underlying fallacy of the plaintiff's argument to consist in the assumption that the enforced separation of the two races stamps the colored race with a badge of inferiority. If this be so, it is not by reason of anything found in the act, but solely because the colored race chooses to put that construction upon it. The argument necessarily assumes that if, as has been more than once the case, and is not unlikely to be so again, the colored race should become the dominant power in the state legislature, [fol. 369] and should enact a law in precisely similar terms, it would thereby relegate the white race to an inferior position. We imagine that the white race, at least, would not acquiesce in this assumption. The argument also assumes that social prejudices may be overcome by legislation, and that equal rights cannot be secured to the negro except by an enforced commingling of the two races. We cannot accept this proposition. If the two races are to meet upon terms of social equality, it must be the result of natural affinities, a mutual appreciation of each other's merits and a voluntary consent of individuals."

Judge Huxman: Mr. Brewster, I don't know——
Mr. Brewster: I am about through with that.

Judge Huxman: I was going to say that on the Circuit Court we do not care to have reading from an opinion.

Mr. Brewster: I want to point out that Plessy vs. Ferguson, which establishes the separate but equal doctrine and the basis upon which they go, and that is that this regulation that this is a part of the police power of the state. Now, it has been repeatedly held, and that is part—that is the basis of the decision in the South Carolina case, that each state determines for itself, subject to the observ-
[fol. 370] ance of fundamental rights and liberties guaranteed by the federal constitution, how it shall exercise the police power and that the power to legislate with respect to safety, morals, health and general welfare and that in no field—in no field is this right of the several states more clearly recognized than in that of public education.

Well, now, the case—the South Carolina case—bases their decision, and I won't quote a great deal from it on the proposition that it's within the police power of the state to segregate these schools if they want to, but they must provide equal educational facilities.

Now, speaking of the Sweatt vs. Painter case which, of course, it will be found the plaintiffs rely on that to a great extent; that dealt with a professional or graduate school. We are here dealing with an elementary school system which, assuming that the student goes through high school and college, this segregation exists in less than one-half of the normal educational, formal educational, period. "At this level" I would like to quote just briefly from this opinion, "At this level as good education can be afforded in negro schools as in white schools and the thought of establishing professional contacts does not enter into the picture. Moreover, education at this level is not a matter of voluntary choice on the part of the student, but of compulsion by the [fol. 371] state."

Now, I would like to also call attention to the fact that in Sweatt vs. Painter the Supreme Court of the United States specifically refused to overrule Plessy vs. Ferguson and, in that respect, I think it strengthens the opinion and shows that the present segregation and separation and equality is still recognized.

Now, there has been testimony to the effect that mixed schools would give a better education. But, on the other hand, it's been indicated that mixed schools might result in additional racial friction due to the fact that the colored student would be greatly outnumbered and you'd still have that inferior feeling.

I would like to, with the Court's permission, quote just a little more from this South Carolina opinion; I just got it this morning or I would have tried to give it without quoting it:

"The federal courts would be going far outside their constitutional function were they to attempt to prescribe educational policies for the state in such matters, however desirable such policies might be in the opinion of some sociologists or educators. For the federal courts to do so, would result not only in interference with local affairs by an agency of the federal government, but also in the substitution of the judicial for the legislative process in what [fol. 372] is essentially a legislative matter." In other words continuing the theory that this is a matter of the police power, and the state has the right to make this regulation.

We submit that under the facts which are stipulated, there is established—it is established that there is no inequality of educational facilities and, furthermore, that it is within the province of the state to determine what regulations necessary under its police power which, of course, is to promote the peace and the welfare of the people of that state, and, as far as the opinions of some sociologists or educators are concerned, we are in agreement with what the Court decided in South Carolina that it would not be within the province of a federal court or any federal agency to adopt those views regardless of what the state might consider to be the proper regulation under the police powers.

Judge Huxman: You may proceed, Mr. Goodell.

Mr. Goodell: I prefer to—if we are given authority to file briefs, I will waive argument.

Judge Huxman: You will waive your argument. All right, the plaintiff may close the argument, then.

CLOSING ARGUMENT ON BEHALF OF PLAINTIFF

Mr. Carter: Your Honor, I just have a few comments to make.

[fol. 373] I remember the last point that counsel for the defendants made about the statements of sociologists and educators. I would like to point the Court's attention again to the decision in McLaurin vs. The Board of Regents where what was considered in that case to be crucial to the decision was the mental attitude of the negro and the impact of segregation upon him mentally, and therefore it was held that he was deprived of the equal protection of the laws in the segregated educational system.

Now, I have to congratulate the attorneys for the Board of Education on being much more efficient than, at least, I am, because I had hoped that we could have the South Carolina opinion ourselves and that we could quote from the dissent, but we were unable to get it.

Judge Mellott: We have a copy of it.

Mr. Carter: No, thank you. But, at any rate, if the Court please, I think that although these two decisions certainly, McLaurin and Sweatt, were limited, as counsel indicated, to the graduate and professional schools, it was not necessary for the Court to have made any such limitation because that would have been obvious because they applied to graduate and professional schools anyway, but the United States Supreme Court, in a recent case, Rice vs. Arnold, which I don't remember the exact date of the decision, I think it was about October 16, 1950; I don't [fol. 374] believe it's yet reported—that case involved a question of the separate days for the use of a golf course in Miami; negroes were given certain days of the week and whites were given the rest of the time. The matter was appealed through the Florida Supreme Court to the U. S. Supreme Court, and the question raised was whether or not the separation and giving of this separate time to negroes and not permitting them to use the golf course without discrimination based on race or color was a denial of the equal protection clause, the golf course being municipally owned. The Supreme Court took the case, granted certiorari, reversed and remanded in the light of the McLaurin and Sweatt opinions.

Now, I think that that is clear evidence at least that the Supreme Court realized and certainly feels that the decisions and the principles which it enunciated in Sweatt and McLaurin have wide application and cannot be limited in the narrow scope of a professional school or a law school. I believe that what the Supreme Court, of course, in Plessy vs. Ferguson—the Supreme Court refused to overrule Plessy vs. Ferguson, refused to apply it or refused to re-examine it, but I don't believe that counsel for the defendants can take too much hope in that in view of the decision which was reached. The two decisions reached were to the effect that segregation, at least at the level at [fol. 375] which the decision was handed down, were unconstitutional in the law school and in the graduate schools and I might also add that Plessy vs. Ferguson applied to railroads and not to education and, although it has somehow been taken over into the educational field, it is really a railroad case. However, I think that actually what—with the trend of the law, I think that the trend of the law is to such an extent that it is impossible to reach any other decision except that the State of Kansas has no power to order segregation. I think also that here this is no situation—this is not applicable to South Carolina; the two states are entirely different. There is not the vested interest in the maintenance of segregation in Kansas as there is in South Carolina or in Georgia. This is clear, by virtue of the fact that the state forbids it at one level even though it permits it at another, and I think that what should be applied in this case is the rule that at least if the segregation is unconstitutional, and I think that the Supreme Court cases inevitably point to that end, that a declaration of unconstitutionality should be made in an area in which it is ripe. The time is ripe for such a decision to be reached, and I think that certainly in Kansas, with the situation as it is, that the time is now ripe for this Court to strike down the statute here in issue and to declare [fol. 376] that the State of Kansas has no power to maintain segregation in its public school system.

Judge Huxman: Before the Court adjourns, the Court wants to compliment the parties on both sides for their fairness in the presentation of this case, the spirit of cooperation exhibited by all, to have a speedy determination of the issues in the trial of the case. I think this case was tried within less than ten days after the issues were made up and concluded, and we feel that we want to have as speedy a determination by the Court as can be handed down, giving counsel an opportunity to file briefs because, if this law is declared unconstitutional, certainly the City of Topeka is—wants to have it done as soon as possible before the beginning of the fall school term and all those matters. So we are all interested in having the matter determined just as expeditiously as it can be done, affording everybody an opportunity to prepare and file their briefs.

Now, the questions are comparatively simple to state and quite difficult to answer. There are only two questions in the case; one is, are the facilities, as I see them, are the facilities which are afforded by Topeka in its separate schools, comparable; that is one question, and the other is, granting that they are, is segregation unconstitutional notwithstanding, in light of the Fourteenth Amendment. As [fol. 377] I get it, those are the two points in the case, is that right?

Mr. Carter: Yes, sir.

COLLOQUY BETWEEN COURT AND COUNSEL.

Judge Huxman: There is nothing else.

Now, ordinarily, of course, the plaintiffs prepare and file their briefs and the defendants have a certain time to reply thereafter, which, of course, would take additional time. I am wondering if you want to invoke that rule or whether, in view of the fact that these two issues are so clear, and the testimony is clear in the minds of all of us, whether you would be willing or feel that you would prefer to proceed without waiting to receive the briefs on the part of the plaintiff. What do you say, Mr. Goodell?

Mr. Goodell: Subject only to this, Your Honor: If coun-

234

sel chooses to argue points of evidence, I would be a little handicapped to answer them when I didn't know what he was going to argue.

Judge Huxman: You would be given the right for reply brief.

Mr. Goodell: With that exception, I would be perfectly willing to hand mine in at the same time.

Judge Huxman: How much time do you think you need to prepare and file your brief?

[fol. 378] Mr. Goodell: I think a week we can do it in.

Judge Huxman: Well, no need of rushing you to that extent.

Mr. Goodell: Ten days.

Judge Huxman: What do plaintiffs—of course, you have done a lot of work; you have practically got your material assembled on the law, naturally. How long does plaintiff feel that you need to prepare and file your brief?

Mr. Carter: Well, Your Honor, we could, of course, do it within a week, but we would like to have, say, a week from next Monday, which would give us about ten days.

Judge Huxman: Well, let's give the parties—do you want to wait in the preparation of your brief until you receive the record? Of course it will take approximately ten days to get the record. I presume each side will want a record, because, irrespective of the outcome of this litigation, it's headed for the Supreme Court anyway. Do you prefer to wait with your brief until you have a copy of the record? What do you say?

Mr. Goodell: That depends on the turn it takes. As I understand counsel, you are relying now entirely on the question of segregation in itself is discriminatory.

[fol. 379] Mr. Carter: We are relying—of course we are relying on that. I think, Your Honor, that we would not need the record. I think we have our testimony in mind that has been presented.

Mr. Goodell: If that is your point, of course, then——

Judge Huxman: Mr. Goodell, I do not understand the attorneys for plaintiff waive the one point and rely on the other alone.

Mr. Goodell: I——

Judge Huxman: I understand from what they have said

they practically indicate they do not lean too heavily on this discrimination in the facilities which are furnished.

How much time from today does plaintiff want to file their brief, assuming the record will be ready for you in ten days. We will put it that way. How much time do you want from today?

Mr. Carter: We would like to have ten days, Your Honor.

Judge Huxman: We will give you fifteen days. You understand what I asked was assuming that it will take ten days from now to get the record, how much time from now do you want to file your brief? If you want ten days after the record is furnished, you may take twenty days, of [fol. 380] course, from now.

Mr. Goodell: The time, Your Honor, while I am on that subject——

Mr. Carter: Fifteen days will be ample.

Mr. Goodell: If it's going to be appealed, and I think it will be perhaps, either way this decision goes, the time lag would be such that we couldn't have a determination, I don't believe, by September in the appellate court.

Judge Huxman: Of course there are these factors: Judge Mellott and Judge Hill, both, have heavy schedules left and myself, my schedule isn't as heavy as theirs is for the remaining portion of the summer, but if we defer this matter too long, it runs into the fall when our new terms of court take place, and then it would be difficult for any of us to devote our time to it. We don't want to cut the parties short, but, on the other hand, there is no need of granting more time than you need for the preparation.

Mr. Goodell: It seems to me if he is going to go into evidence, it's pretty awkward to write a brief about evidentiary matters without having a transcript, and it's not satisfactory.

Judge Huxman: We will give you twenty days from today for the filing of your brief, and the reporter has told us [fol. 381] it would be about a week for the preparation of the record so, in any event, if you wanted the record, you will have ten or twelve days, and I will say this: If your briefs don't get in on the twentieth day, you will not be out of court.

Mr. Goodell: That will be satisfactory.

Judge Huxman: Are the parties going to order a copy of the record, each of you; I presume that is your intention.

Mr. Goodell: Yes, we will.

Mr. Carter: Yes, sir.

Judge Huxman: All right.

Mr. Goodell: Your Honor, do I understand we are given the privilege of a reply brief if we desire.

Judge Hill: Certainly.

Judge Huxman: Now, there is one other suggestion that the Court has in mind that you could be very helpful to the Court, and that may take a little additional time; that when you file your brief, to go with it each side file suggested findings or requested findings of fact, on the theory that you are going to prevail in the lawsuit, and conclusions of law.

Judge Mellott: We are required to make them under Rule 52.

Judge Huxman: Yes. We must make them, of course, and [fol. 382] it will be helpful to the Court if we had in mind when we come to consider this case, the idea and the theories of both sides as to the findings of fact; if we have both of them, then we will make our own findings, of course.

You also understand that there are three of us, that we all live in separate cities and if you would file your briefs in triplicate so that each judge can have a copy of the brief, it will expedite matters.

One thing I would like to inquire of my two associates of the district bench, what is your practice with regard to requiring printed or typewritten briefs in cases such as these? Of course in the Circuit Court, as you know, briefs must be printed, but my associates tell me that typewritten briefs are the practice here so that will be the practice in this case.

Judge Mellott: Use some good carbon paper because carbons are hard to read.

Mr. Goodell: We will do that.

Judge Huxman: Judge Hill makes this suggestion, which I have found valuable in my work on the appellate bench: If, when you prepare and submit a requested finding of fact, if you will alongside of it have the page of the record that you claim sustains that request, it will save us a tremendous amount of work; otherwise we have to go [fol. 383] through the whole record to see whether there is any warrant in the record for that request. So, if you will do that, that will help the Court.

Judge Mellott: I would like to have you get copies of the court's rules of practice, which are printed, and that will call your attention to the way we want the brief prepared; give us a table of cases and your citations.

Judge Huxman: My associates are more familiar with those rules than I am. It's their court, and they know what the practice is.

Now, I suppose Judge Mellott and Judge Hill, that we should make the same order with respect to all of these requests for brief amicus curiae, that they be filed within the same length of time, within twenty days from today: anybody that has appeared here that wants to file a brief as amicus curiae.

Mr. Goodell: Our notion, if it doesn't interfere with the rules of the court, would be to have the other lawyers join with us in a certain section of the brief.

Judge Huxman: Well, I would certainly prefer—frankly, I have never been very much impressed with this amicus curiae theory of the law. There just isn't such a thing anyhow because an amicus curiae has an active interest on [fol. 384] one side or the other of the litigation and if you could get—that is, however, for you defendants to arrange—if you could get all the parties who have entered an appearance amicus curiae to join with you in the brief, it would save a lot of duplication.

Mr. Goodell: That is what I thought.

Judge Huxman: These issues are sharply drawn. There is a certain line of cases, and it's just a question of analyzing and distinguishing those cases, but, however, I doubt whether we could order that—whether we can order amicus curiae to join with you in a brief.

Mr. Goodell: If it's satisfactory, I meant, I think that is what we will do.

Judge Huxman: That would be much simpler. Anything that the parties have to request? The court will be adjourned subject to further call.

238

(The court then, at 12:15 o'clock p. m., stood adjourned until further call.)

* * *

REPORTER'S CERTIFICATE (omitted in printing)

[fol. 385] Clerk's Certificate to foregoing transcript omitted in printing.

[fol. 386] IN UNITED STATES DISTRICT COURT

OPINION OF THE COURT—Entered August 3, 1951.

HUXMAN, Circuit Judge, delivered the opinion of the Court.

Chapter 72-1724 of the General Statutes of Kansas, 1949, relating to public schools in cities of the first class, so far as material, authorizes such cities to organize and maintain separate schools for the education of white and colored children in the grades below the high school grades. Pursuant to this authority, the City of Topeka, Kansas, a city of the first class, has established and maintains a segregated system of schools for the first six grades. It has established and maintains in the Topeka School District eighteen schools for white students and four schools for colored students.

The adult plaintiffs instituted this action for themselves, their minor children plaintiffs, and all other persons similarly situated for an interlocutory injunction, a permanent injunction, restraining the enforcement, operation and execution of the state statute and the segregation instituted thereunder by the school authorities of the City of Topeka and for a declaratory judgment declaring unconstitutional the state statute and the segregation set up thereunder by the school authorities of the City of Topeka.

As against the school district of Topeka they contend that the opportunities provided for the infant plaintiffs in the separate all negro schools are inferior to those pro-

239

vided white children in the all white schools; that the respects in which these opportunities are inferior include the physical facilities, curricula, teaching resources, student personnel services as well as all other services. As against both the state and the school district, they contend that apart from all other factors segregation in itself constitutes [fol. 387] an inferiority in educational opportunities offered to negroes and that all of this is in violation of due process guaranteed them by the Fourteenth Amendment to the United States Constitution. In their answer both the state and the school district defend the constitutionality of the state law and in addition the school district defends the segregation in its schools instituted thereunder.

We have found as a fact that the physical facilities, the curricula, courses of study, qualification of and quality of teachers, as well as other educational facilities in the two sets of schools are comparable. It is obvious that absolute equality of physical facilities is impossible of attainment in buildings that are erected at different times. So also absolute equality of subjects taught is impossible of maintenance when teachers are permitted to select books of their own choosing to use in teaching in addition to the prescribed courses of study. It is without dispute that the prescribed courses of study are identical in all of the Topeka Schools and that there is no discrimination in this respect. It is also clear in the record that the educational qualifications of the teachers in the colored schools are equal to those in the white schools and that in all other respects the educational facilities and services are comparable. It is obvious from the fact that there are only four colored schools as against eighteen white schools in the Topeka School District, that colored children in many instances are required to travel much greater distances than they would be required to travel could they attend a white school, and are required to travel much greater distances than white children are required to travel. The evidence, however, establishes that the school district transports colored children to and from school free of charge. No such service is furnished to white children. We conclude that in the maintenance and operation of the [fol. 388] schools there is no willful, intentional or substantial discrimination in the matters referred to above between the colored and white schools. In fact, while plaintiffs' attorneys have not abandoned this contention, they did not give it great emphasis in their presentation before the court. They relied primarily upon the contention that segregation in and of itself without more violates their rights guaranteed by the Fourteenth Amendment.

This contention poses a question not free from difficulty. As a subordinate court in the federal judicial system, we seek the answer to this constitutional question in the decisions of the Supreme Court when it has spoken on the subject and do not substitute our own views for the declared law by the Supreme Court. The difficult question as always is to analyze the decisions and seek to ascertain the trend as revealed by the later decisions.

There are a great number of cases, both federal and state, that have dealt with the many phases of segregation. Since the question involves a construction and interpretation of the federal Constitution and the pronouncements of the Supreme Court, we will consider only those cases by the Supreme Court with respect to segregation in the schools. In the early case of Plessy v. Ferguson, 163 U. S. 537, the Supreme Court said:

> "The object of the amendment was undoubtedly to enforce the absolute equality of the two races before the law, but in the nature of things it could not have been intended to abolish distinctions based upon color, or to encorce social, as distinguished from political equality, or a commingling of the two races upon terms unsatisfactory to either. Laws permitting, and even requiring, their separation in places where they are liable to be brought into contact do not necessarily [fol. 389] imply the inferiority of either race to the other, and have been generally, if not universally, recognized as within the competency of the state legislatures in the exercise of their police power. The most common instance of this is connected with the establishment of separate schools for white and colored children, which has been held to be a valid exercise of the legislative power even by courts of States where

the political rights of the colored race have been longest and most earnestly enforced."

It is true as contended by plaintiffs that the Plessy case involved transportation and that the above quoted statement relating to schools was not essential to the decision of the question before the court and was therefore somewhat in the nature of dicta. But that the statement is considered more than dicta is evidenced by the treatment accorded it by those seeking to strike down segregation as well as by statements in subsequent decisions of the Supreme Court. On numerous occasions the Supreme Court has been asked to overrule the Plessy case. This the Supreme Court has refused to do, on the sole ground that a decision of the question was not necessary to a disposal of the controversy presented. In the late case of Sweatt v. Painter, 339 U. S. 629, the Supreme Court again refused to review the Plessy case. The Court said:

> "Nor need we reach petitioner's contention that Plessy v. Ferguson should be reexamined in the light of contemporary knowledge respecting the purposes of the Fourteenth Amendment and the effects of racial segregation."

Gong Lum v. Rice, 275 U. S. 78, was a grade school segregation case. It involved the segregation law of Mississippi. Gong Lum was a Chinese child and, because of color, was required to attend the separate schools provided for colored children. The opinion of the court assumes that the educational facilities in the colored schools were adequate and equal to those of the white schools. Thus the court said: "The question here is whether a Chinese citizen of the [fol. 390] United States is denied equal protection of the laws when he is classed among the colored races and furnished facilities for education equal to that offered to all, whether white, brown, yellow or black." In addition to numerous state decisions on the subject, the Supreme Court in support of its conclusions cited Plessy v. Ferguson, supra. The Court also pointed out that the question was the same no matter what the color of the class that was required to attend separate schools. Thus the Court said: "Most of the cases cited arose, it is true, over the establishment of separate schools as between white pupils and black pupils, but we cannot think that the question is any different or that any different result can be reached, assuming the cases above cited to be rightly decided, where the issue is as between white pupils and the pupils of the yellow race." The court held that the question of segregation was within the discretion of the state in regulating its public schools and did not conflict with the Fourteenth Amendment.

It is vigorously argued and not without some basis therefor that the later decisions of the Supreme Court in McLaurin v. Oklahoma, 339 U. S. 637, and Sweatt v. Painter, 339 U. S. 629, show a trend away from the Plessy and Lum cases. McLaurin v. Oklahoma arose under the segregation laws of Oklahoma. McLaurin, a colored student, applied for admission to the University of Oklahoma in order to pursue studies leading to a doctorate degree in education. He was denied admission solely because he was a negro. After litigation in the courts, which need not be reviewed herein, the legislature amended the statute permitting the admission of colored students to institutions of higher learning attended by white students, but providing that such instruction should be given on a segregated basis; that the instruction be given in separate class rooms or at separate times. In compliance with this statute McLaurin [fol. 391] was admitted to the university but was required to sit at a separate desk in the ante room adjoining the class room; to sit at a designated desk on the mezzanine floor of the library; and to sit at a designated table and eat at a different time from the other students in the school cafeteria. These restrictions were held to violate his rights under the federal Constitution. The Supreme Court held that such treatment handicapped the student in his pursuit of effective graduate instruction.[1]

---

[1] The court said: "Our society grows increasingly complex, and our need for trained leaders increases correspondingly. Appellant's case represents, perhaps, the epitome of that need, for he is attempting to obtain an

In Sweatt v. Painter, 339 U. S. 629, petitioner, a colored student, filed an application for admission to the University of Texas Law School. His application was rejected solely on the ground that he was a negro. In its opinion the Supreme Court stressed the educational benefits from commingling with white students. The court concluded by stating: "We cannot conclude that the education offered petitioner in a separate school is substantially equal to that which he would receive if admitted to the University of Texas Law School." If segregation within a school as in the McLaurin case is a denial of due process, it is difficult to see why segregation in separate schools would not result [fol. 392] in the same denial. Or if the denial of the right to commingle with the majority group in higher institutions of learning as in the Sweatt case and gain the educational advantages resulting therefrom, is lack of due process, it is difficult to see why such denial would not result in the same lack of due process if practiced in the lower grades.

It must however be remembered that in both of these cases the Supreme Court made it clear that it was confining itself to answering the one specific question, namely: "To what extent does the equal protection clause limit the

advanced degree in education, to become, by definition, a leader and trainer of others. Those who will come under this guidance and influence must be directly affected by the education he received. Their own education and development will necessarily suffer to the extent that his training is unequal to that of his classmates. State imposed restrictions which produce such inequalities cannot be sustained."

"It may be argued that appellant will be in no better position when these restrictions are removed, for he may still be set apart by his fellow students. This we think irrelevant. There is a vast difference—a Constitutional difference—between restrictions imposed by the state which prohibit the intellectual commingling of students, and the refusal of individuals to commingle where the state presents no such bar. * * * having been admitted to a state supported graduate school, [he] must receive the same treatment at the hands of the state as students of other races."

244

power of a state to distinguish between students of different races in professional and graduate education in a state university?", and that the Supreme Court refused to review the Plessy case because that question was not essential to a decision of the controversy in the case.

We are accordingly of the view that the Plessy and Lum cases, supra, have not been overruled and that they still presently are authority for the maintenance of a segregated school system in the lower grades.

The prayer for relief will be denied and judgment will be entered for defendants for costs.

[fol. 393] IN UNITED STATES DISTRICT COURT

FINDINGS OF FACT AND CONCLUSIONS OF LAW—Entered August 3, 1951.

FINDINGS OF FACT

I

This is a class action in which plaintiffs seek a decree, declaring Section 72-1724 of the General Statutes of Kansas 1949 to be unconstitutional, insofar as it empowers the Board of Education of the City of Topeka "to organize and maintain separate schools for the education of white and colored children" and an injunction restraining the enforcement, operation and execution of that portion of the statute and of the segregation instituted thereunder by the School Board.

II

This suit arises under the Constitution of the United States and involves more than $3,000 exclusive of interest and costs. It is also a civil action to redress an alleged deprivation, under color of State law, of a right, privilege or immunity secured by the Constitution of the United States providing for an equal rights of citizens and to have the court declare the rights and other legal relations of the interested parties. The Court has jurisdiction of the subject matter and of the parties to the action.

III

Pursuant to statutory authority contained in Section 72-1724 of the General Statutes of Kansas 1949, the City of Topeka, Kansas, a city of the first class, has established and maintains a segregated system of schools for the first six grades. It has established and maintains in the Topeka School District, eighteen schools for white children and four [fol. 394] for colored children, the latter being located in neighborhoods where the population is predominantly colored. The City of Topeka is one school district. The colored children may attend any one of the four schools established for them, the choice being made either by the children or by their parents.

IV

There is no material difference in the physical facilities in the colored schools and in the white schools and such facilities in the colored schools are not inferior in any material respects to those in the white schools.

V

The educational qualifications of the teachers and the quality of instruction in the colored schools are not inferior to and are comparable to those of the white schools.

VI

The courses of study prescribed by the State law are taught in both the colored schools and in the white schools. The prescribed courses of study are identical in both classes of schools.

VII

Transportation to and from school is furnished colored children in the segregated schools without cost to the children or to their parents. No such transportation is furnished to the white children in the segregated schools.

[fol. 395]

VIII

Segregation of white and colored children in public schools has a detrimental effect upon the colored children.

The impact is greater when it has the sanction of the law; for the policy of separating the races is usually interpreted as denoting the inferiority of the negro group. A sense of inferiority affects the motivation of a child to learn. Segregation with the sanction of law, therefore, has a tendency to retain the educational and mental development of negro children and to deprive them of some of the benefits they would receive in a racial integrated school system.

IX

The court finds as facts the stipulated facts and those agreed upon by counsel at the pre-trial and during the course of the trial.

Conclusions of Law

I

This court has jurisdiction of the subject matter and of the parties to the action.[1]

II

We conclude that no discrimination is practiced against plaintiffs in the colored schools set apart for them because of the nature of the physical characteristics of the buildings, the equipment, the curricula, quality of instructors and [fol. 396] instruction or school services furnished and that they are denied no constitutional rights or privileges by reason of any of these matters.

III

Plessy v. Ferguson, 163 U. S. 537, and Gong Lum v. Rice, 275 U. S. 78 upholds the constitutionality of a legally segregated school system in the lower grades and no denial of due process results from the maintenance of such a segregated system of schools absent discrimination in the maintenance of the segregated schools. We conclude that the above cited cases have not been overruled by the later cases of McLaurin v. Oklahoma, 339 U. S. 637, and Sweatt v. Painter, 339 U. S. 629.

---

[1] Title 28 U.S.C. § 1331; idem § 1343; idem Ch. 151. Title 8 U.S.C. Ch. 3. Title 28 U.S.C. Ch. 155.

IV

The only question in the case under the record is whether legal segregation in and of itself without more constitutes denial of due process. We are of the view that under the above decisions of the Supreme Court the answer must be in the negative. We accordingly conclude that plaintiffs have suffered no denial of due process by virtue of the manner in which the segregated school system of Topeka, Kansas, is being operated. The relief sought is therefore denied. Judgment will be entered for defendants for costs.

>Walter A. Huxman, Circuit Judge, Arthur J. Mellott, Chief District Judge, Delmas C. Hill, District Judge.

[fol. 397] IN UNITED STATES DISTRICT COURT

DEGREE—Entered August 3, 1951.

Now on this 3rd day of August, 1951 this cause comes regularly on for hearing before the undersigned Judges, constituting a three-judge court, duly convened pursuant to the provisions of Title 28 U. S. C. 2281 and 2284.

The Court has heretofore filed its Findings of Fact and Conclusions of Law together with an opinion and has held as a matter of law that the plaintiffs have failed to prove they are entitled to the relief demanded.

Now, therefore, it is by the court, considered, ordered, adjudged and decreed that judgment be and it hereby is entered in favor of the defendants.

>Walter A. Huxman, Circuit Judge, Arthur J. Mellott, Chief District Judge, Delmas C. Hill, District Judge.

[fol. 398] IN UNITED STATES DISTRICT COURT

[Title omitted]

PETITION FOR APPEAL—Filed October 1, 1951

Considering themselves aggrieved by the final decree and judgment of this court entered on August 3, 1951, Oliver Brown, Mrs. Richard Lawton, Mrs. Sadie Emanuel, Mrs. Lucinda Todd, Mrs. Iona Richardson, Mrs. Lena Carper, Mrs. Shirley Hodison, Mrs. Alma Lewis, Mrs. Darlene Brown, Mrs. Shirla Fleming, Mrs. Andrew Henderson, Mrs. Vivian Scales, Mrs. Marguerite Emmerson, and Linda Carol Brown, an infant by Oliver Brown, her father and next friend; Victoria Jean Lawton and Carol Kay Lawton, infants, by Mrs. Richard Lawton, their mother and next friend; James Meldon Emanuel, an infant, by Mrs. Sadie Emanuel, his mother and next friend; Nancy Jane Todd, an infant, by Mrs. Lucinda Todd, her mother and next friend; Ronald Douglas Richardson, an infant, by Mrs. Iona Richardson, his mother and next friend; Katherine Louise Carper, an infant, by Mrs. Lena Carper, her mother and next friend; Charles Hodison, an infant, by Mrs. Shirley Hodison, his mother and next friend; Theron Lewis, Martha Jean Lewis, Arthur Lewis and Frances Lewis, infants, by Mrs. Alma Lewis, their mother and next friend; Saundria Dorstella Brown, an infant, by Mrs. Darlene Brown, her mother and next friend; Duane Dean Fleming and Silas Hardrick Fleming, infants, by Mrs. Shirla Flem-
[fol. 399] ing, their mother and next friend; Donald Andrew Henderson and Vicki Ann Henderson, infants, by Mrs. Andrew Henderson, their mother and next friend; Ruth Ann Scales, an infant, by Mrs. Vivian Scales, her mother and next friend; Claude Arthur Emmerson and George Robert Emmerson, infants, by Mrs. Marguerite Emmerson, their mother and next friend, plaintiffs herein, do hereby pray that an appeal be allowed to the Supreme Court of the United States from said final decree and judgment and from each and every part thereof; that citation be issued in accordance with law; that an order be made with respect to the appeal bond to be given by said plaintiffs, and that the amount of security be fixed by the order allowing the

appeal, and that the material parts of the record, proceedings and papers upon which said final judgment and decree was based duly authenticated be sent to the Supreme Court of the United States in accordance with the rules in such cases made and provided.

Respectfully submitted, Charles E. Bledsoe, 330 Kansas Avenue, Topeka, Kansas, John J. Scott, Charles S. Scott, 410 Kansas Avenue, Topeka, Kansas, Robert L. Carter, Jack Greenberg, Thurgood Marshall, 20 West 40th Street, New York 18, New York, Counsel for Plaintiffs-Appellants.

[fol. 400] IN UNITED STATES DISTRICT COURT

[Title omitted]

ASSIGNMENT OF ERRORS AND PRAYER FOR REVERSAL—
filed October 1, 1951.

Oliver Brown, Mrs. Richard Lawton, Mrs. Sadie Emanuel, Mrs. Lucinda Todd, Mrs. Iona Richardson, Mrs. Lena Carper, Mrs. Shirley Hodison, Mrs. Alma Lewis, Mrs. Darlene Brown, Mrs. Shirla Fleming, Mrs. Andrew Henderson, Mrs. Vivian Scales, Mrs. Marguerite Emmerson, and Linda Carol Brown, an infant by Oliver Brown, her father and next friend; Victoria Jean Lawton and Carol Kay Lawton, infants, by Mrs. Richard Lawton, their mother and next friend; James Meldon Emanuel, an infant, by Mrs. Sadie Emanuel, his mother and next friend; Nancy Jane Todd, an infant, by Mrs. Lucinda Todd, her mother and next friend; Ronald Douglas Richardson, an infant, by Mrs. Iona Richardson, his mother and next friend; Katherine Louise Carper, an infant, by Mrs. Lena Carper, her mother and next friend; Charles Hodison, an infant, by Mrs. Shirley Hodison, his mother and next friend; Theron Lewis, Martha Jean Lewis, Arthur Lewis and Frances Lewis, infants, by Mrs. Alma Lewis, their mother and next friend; Saundria Dorstella Brown, an infant, by Mrs. Darlene Brown, her mother and next friend; Duane Dean Fleming and Silas Hardrick Fleming, infants, by Mrs. Shirla Fleming, their [fol. 401] mother and next friend; Donald Andrew Henderson and Vicki Ann Henderson, infants, by Mrs. Andrew Henderson, their mother and next friend; Ruth Ann Scales, an infant, by Mrs. Vivian Scales, her mother and next friend; Claude Arthur Emmerson and George Robert Emmerson, infants, by Mrs. Marguerite Emmerson, their mother and next friend, plaintiffs in the above-entitled cause, in connection with their appeal to the Supreme Court of the United States, hereby file the following assignment of errors upon which they will rely in their prosecution of said appeal from the final judgment of the District Court entered on August 3, 1951.

The District Court erred:

1. In refusing to grant plaintiffs' application for a temporary and permanent injunction restraining the defendants from acting pursuant to Chapter 72-1724 of the General Statutes of Kansas under which they are maintaining separate public elementary schools through the first six grades for Negro children solely because of their race and color.

2. In refusing to hold that the State of Kansas is without authority to promulgate Chapter 72-1724 of the General Statutes of Kansas in that such statute constitutes a classification based upon race and color which is violative of the Constitution of the United States.

3. In refusing to enter judgment in favor of plaintiffs, after the court found that plaintiffs suffered serious harm and detriment in being required to attend segregated elementary schools in the City of Topeka, and were deprived thereby of benefits they would have received in a racially integrated school system.

Wherefore, plaintiffs pray that the final decree of the [fol. 402] District Court be reversed, and for such other relief as the Court may deem fit and proper.

    Charles E. Bledsoe, 330 Kansas Avenue, Topeka, Kansas, Charles S. Scott, John Scott, 410 Kansas Avenue, Topeka, Kansas, Robert L. Carter, Jack Greenberg, Thurgood Marshall, Counsel for Plaintiffs-Appellants.

Dated: September 28, 1951.

[fol. 403] IN UNITED STATES DISTRICT COURT

[Title omitted]

ORDER ALLOWING APPEAL—Entered October 1, 1951.

Oliver Brown, Mrs. Richard Lawton, Mrs. Sadie Emanuel, Mrs. Lucinda Todd, Mrs. Iona Richardson, Mrs. Lena Carper, Mrs. Shirley Hodison, Mrs. Alma Lewis, Mrs. Darlene Brown, Mrs. Shirla Fleming, Mrs. Andrew Henderson, Mrs. Vivian Scales, Mrs. Marguerite Emmerson, and Linda Carol Brown, an infant by Oliver Brown, her father and next friend; Victoria Jean Lawton and Carol Kay Lawton, infants, by Mrs. Richard Lawton, their mother and next friend; James Meldon Emanuel, an infant, by Mrs. Sadie Emanuel, his mother and next friend; Nancy Jane Todd, an infant, by Mrs. Lucinda Todd, her mother and next friend; Ronald Douglas Richardson, an infant, by Mrs. Iona Richardson, his mother and next friend; Katherine Louise Carper, an infant, by Mrs. Lena Carper, her mother and next friend; Charles Hodison, an ingant, by Mrs. Shirley Hodison, his mother and next friend; Theron Lewis, Martha Jean Lewis, Arthur Lewis and Frances Lewis, infants, by Mrs. Alma Lewis, their mother and next friend; Saundria Dorstella Brown, an infant, by Mrs. Darlene Brown, her mother and next friend; Duane Dean Fleming and Silas Hardrick Fleming, infants, by Mrs. Shirla Fleming, their mother and next friend; Donald Andrew Henderson and [fol. 404] Vicki Ann Henderson, infants, by Mrs. Andrew Henderson, their mother and next friend; Ruth Ann Scales, an infant, by Mrs. Vivian Scales, her mother and next friend; Claude Arthur Emmerson and George Robert Emmerson, infants, by Mrs. Marguerite Emmerson, their mother and next friend, having made and filed their petition praying for an appeal to the Supreme Court of the United States from the final judgment and decree of this court in this cause entered on August 3, 1951, and from each and every part thereof, and having presented their assignment of errors and prayer for reversal and their statements as to the jurisdiction of the Supreme Court of the United States on appeal pursuant to the statutes and

252

rules of the Supreme Court of the United States in such cases made and provided,

Now, therefore, it is hereby ordered that said appeal be and the same is hereby allowed as prayed for.

It is further ordered that the amount of the appeal bond be and the same is hereby fixed in the sum of $500 with good and sufficient surety, and shall be conditioned as may be required by law.

It is further ordered that citation shall issue in accordance with law.

Walter A. Huxman, U. S. Circuit Judge.

Dated: October 1, 1951.

[fol. 405] Citation in usual form showing service on Lester M. Goodell and George Brewster omitted in printing.

[fol. 406] NOTE RE COST BOND

Cost bond in the sum of $500.00, with Fidelity & Deposit Company of Maryland, as surety, was approved by the Clerk and Filed October 1, 1951.

[fols. 407-408] Statement required by Paragraph 2, Rule 12 of the Rules of the Supreme Court of the United States (omitted in printing).

[fols. 409-411] Acknowledgment of service (omitted in printing).

[fols. 412-413] PRAECIPE—Filed October 5, 1951 (omitted in printing).

[fol. 414]   IN UNITED STATES DISTRICT COURT

ORDER EXTENDING TIME TO FILE AND DOCKET RECORD ON APPEAL IN THE SUPREME COURT OF THE UNITED STATES—Entered November 5, 1951

Now, on this 5 day of November, 1951, upon the application of Charles S. Scott, one of the attorneys for the plaintiffs, and for good cause shown,

It is hereby ordered that the time within which to file and docket the record on appeal in above action in the Supreme Court of the United States be and it is hereby extended twenty days from November 9, 1951.

   Walter A. Huxman, United States Circuit Judge.

[fol. 415] Clerk's Certificate to foregoing transcript omitted in printing.

[fols. 416-417] IN THE SUPREME COURT OF THE UNITED STATES, OCTOBER TERM, 1951, No. 436

[Title omitted]

STATEMENT OF POINTS TO BE RELIED UPON AND DESIGNATION OF PARTS OF RECORD TO BE PRINTED—Filed November 27, 1951

A. Appellants adopt for their statement of points upon which they intend to rely in their appeal to this Court the points contained in their Assignment of Errors heretofore filed.

B. Appellants designate the entire record, as filed in the above-entitled case, for printing by the Clerk of this Court.

   Robert L. Carter, Counsel for Appellants.

[File endorsement omitted.]

254

[fol. 418] SUPREME COURT OF THE UNITED STATES

No. 436, OCTOBER TERM, 1951

ORDER NOTING PROBABLE JURISDICTION—June 9, 1952

The statement of jurisdiction in this case having been submitted and considered by the Court, probable jurisdiction is noted.

(2734)

HEART OF ATLANTA MOTEL VS. THE UNITED STATES OF AMERICA

The Heart of Atlanta Motel refused service to an African American, thus violating Title II of the Civil Rights Act of 1964 (page 460 of this book)

'1/31/64

No. 515

TRANSCRIPT OF RECORD

Supreme Court of the United States

OCTOBER TERM, 1964

HEART OF ATLANTA MOTEL, INC., A GEORGIA CORPORATION, ~~PLAINTIFF~~, *Appellan*

vs.

THE UNITED STATES OF AMERICA AND ROBERT F. KENNEDY AS THE ATTORNEY GENERAL OF THE UNITED STATES OF AMERICA.

SUPREME COURT OF THE UNITED STATES
OCTOBER TERM, 1964

HEART OF ATLANTA MOTEL, INC., A GEORGIA CORPORATION, ~~PLAINTIFF~~, *appellant,*

vs.

THE UNITED STATES OF AMERICA AND ROBERT F. KENNEDY AS THE ATTORNEY GENERAL OF THE UNITED STATES OF AMERICA.

INDEX

	Original	Print
Record from the United States District Court for the Northern District of Georgia, Atlanta Division		
Docket entries	1	1
Complaint for declaratory judgment	4	5
Order to show cause	11	10
Summons and return	12	11
Amendment to complaint for declaratory judgment	13	13
Order allowing amendment to complaint	15	15
Plaintiff's statement of issues	17	15
Stipulation of facts	20	17
Defendants' notice of motion and motion for preliminary injunction	22	18
Defendants' notice of motion and motion to dismiss	25	19
Certificate and request for three-judge court	27	20
Answer and counterclaims	28	21
Answer to counterclaims and response to motion for preliminary injunction	34	24
Motion to dismiss second counterclaim and order allowing	39	27

RECORD PRESS, PRINTERS, NEW YORK, N. Y., AUGUST 26, 1964

ii   INDEX

	Original	Print
Record from the United States District Court for the Northern District of Georgia, Atlanta Division—Continued		
Transcript of proceedings, July 17, 1964	42	29
Appearances	42	29
Stipulation of counsel	48	32
Testimony of Albert Richard Sampson—		
direct	49	33
cross	53	35
Charles Edward Wells—		
direct	56	37
cross	59	39
Argument on behalf of plaintiff by Mr. Rolleston	62	41
Argument on behalf of defendant by Mr. Marshall	86	56
Closing argument on behalf of plaintiff by Mr. Rolleston	110	71
Reporter's certificate (omitted in printing)	114	73
Opinion of the Court and order	115	74
Permanent injunction	121	79
Notice of appeal	123	80
Amended notice of appeal	125	81
Amendment to notice of appeal as amended	130	84
Clerk's certificate (omitted in printing)	132	84

[fol. 1]
IN THE UNITED STATES DISTRICT COURT FOR THE NORTHERN DISTRICT OF GEORGIA

3-Judge Case
9017
(Tuttle, Hooper & Morgan)

Jury Trial Demanded
Docket Closed

HEART OF ATLANTA MOTEL, INC., a Georgia Corporation,

vs.

THE UNITED STATES OF AMERICA and ROBERT F. KENNEDY, as the Attorney General of the United States of America.

Basis of action:

Complaint for declaratory judgment, for temporary and permanent injunction—Civil Rights Act of 1964
Jury trial claimed by Plaintiff on July 7, 1964

For Plaintiff:

Moreton Rolleston, Jr.
1103 C & S Nat'l Bk Bldg.
Atlanta, Ga. 30303
(JA 3-1566)

For Defendant:

Chas. L. Goodson, U.S. Atty.
Robert F. Kennedy, Atty. Gen.
Burke Marshall, Asst. Atty. Gen.
St. John Barrett, Atty.,
  Depart. of Justice

J.S. 5 Card—7-2-64
J.S. 6 Card—7-22-64

7-22-64 Opinion denying complaint and issuing injunction in favor of deft.

[fol. 2]

Docket Entries
Jury Trial Demanded
Closed

DATE	FILINGS—PROCEEDINGS
July 2, 1964	Complaint filed.
July 6, 1964	Summons issued and delivered to U.S. Marshal.
July 6, 1964	Order that defendant Robert F. Kennedy show cause on 7-17-64 at 10:00 A.M., filed. Served with complaint. Notice to JSW.
July 6, 1964	Per FAH, set for hearing on Friday, July 17, 1964 at 10:00 A.M., counsel and parties advised by notice.
July 7, 1964	Letter to Judge Hooper advising this is a three judge case. (Per Judge Tuttle)
	Order of Hon. Elbert P. Tuttle, Chief Judge of the Fifth Circuit, U.S.C.A., designating three judge court composed of Judges Tuttle, and Hooper and Morgan, U.S. District Judges—filed. Copy of order and complaint to three judges.
	Pltf's. Demand for Jury Trial—filed. Copy to 3 judges.
July 8, 1964	Marshal's return on service of complaint executed 7-7-64 as to both defts., filed.
July 10, 1964	Defts.' notice of motion and motion for preliminary injunction, notice of motion and motion to dismiss, with memorandum of points and authorities in support of above two motions; certificate and request for three-judge court; Answer, including first and second counterclaims—filed. Marshal's return of service of

DATE	FILINGS—PROCEEDINGS
	above notice, 2 motions, certificate and answer on pltf.—filed. (Copy of above to 3 judges)
	Order that each party herein file with Clerk before 4:30 P.M. on 7-15-64 a brief statement containing such party's understanding of the issues of fact that will be involved in hearing for injunction set for 9:30 A.M. 7-17-64; suggesting that deft. file response to motion for injunction at same time—filed. Copy to counsel. Copy to 3 judges.
July 15, 1964	Statement of issues of fact by defts., pursuant to order of 7-10-64—filed. Copy to 3 judges.
	Motion of defts. to dismiss SECOND COUNTERCLAIM in its answer—filed. To FAH by counsel (Milano) for order.
	Amendment to complaint, and order allowing same, subject to objections—filed. Copy to 3 judges.
	Pltf's. answer to counterclaims and response to motion for preliminary injunction—filed. Copy to 3 judges.
	Pltf's. statement of issues, pursuant to order of 7-10-64—filed. Copy to 3 judges.
July 16, 1964	Order by Judges Tuttle, Hooper and Morgan allowing defts. to withdraw second counterclaim and Paragraph (c) of its prayer for relief—filed. Copy to counsel. Copy to 3 judges.
	Brief of pltf. in support of complaint and prayers and in opposition to defts.' motion to dismiss complaint—filed. (copy to 3 judges by Mr. Rolleston).
July 27, 1964	Came on for hearing pursuant to Rule Nisi on preliminary injunction. Stipulation of facts, filed. Memo of law of the deft.,

DATE	FILINGS—PROCEEDINGS
	filed. Court took the matter under consideration for a permanent injunction.
July 20, 1964	Supplemental statement of plaintiff, filed. (Copy to 3 judges by plft)
July 22, 1964	Deft's supplemental memorandum of law, filed. Copy to 3 judges.
July 22, 1964	Opinion of court and order enjoining plfts. from refusing to accept Negroes as guests in the motel by reason of their race and make available the goods, services, facilities, privileges and advantages to the guests of the motel; the injunction shall become effective 20 days from hereof, to-wit, August 11, 1964, filed.

[fol. 3]

July 22, 1964	Plaintiff's notice of appeal, filed. Copies to counsel and Supreme Court.
July 23, 1964	Order that plft. is enjoined from refusing to accept Negroes as guests and making any distinction upon the basis of race or color in the availability of goods, services, facilities, privileges, advantages or accommodations offered or made available to the guests; this injunction shall become effective 20 days from 7-22-64, to-wit, 8-11-64, filed. Copies to counsel.
July 24, 1964	Transcript of proceedings of July 17, 1964, filed.
July 30, 1964	Plaintiff's amended notice of appeal, filed. Copy to counsel.
July 31, 1964	Amendment to notice of appeal as amended, filed. Copy to counsel.

DATE	FILINGS—PROCEEDINGS
Aug. 12, 1964	Certified copy of opinion rendered 8-10-64 by Mr. Justice Black denying applications for stay—received.

A True Certified Copy

August 12, 1964

B. G. Nash, Clerk

By: Sammy Godsey
    Deputy Clerk

(Seal)

[fol. 4] [Handwritten notation—Filed in Clerk's Office July 2nd, 1964. 8.55 P.M. by B. G. Nash, Clerk]

In the United States District Court

For the Northern District of Georgia

Atlanta Division

Civil Action No. 9017

Heart of Atlanta Motel, Inc., a Georgia Corporation, Plaintiff,

vs.

The United States of America and Robert F. Kennedy, as the Attorney General of the United States of America, Defendants.

Complaint for Declaratory Judgment—Filed July 2, 1964

Jurisdiction and Venue

1. Plaintiff is a Georgia Corporation whose only place of business is in Fulton County, State of Georgia. This action is for a declaratory judgment pursuant to the provisions of the Declaratory Judgment Act set forth in 28 USCA Sections 2201 and 2202. This is also an action seeking a temporary and permanent injunction to prevent the Attorney General from exercising the powers granted unto

him under Section 2004 of the Revised Statutes (42 U.S.C. 1971), as amended in 1957 and 1960 and as further amended by the "Civil Rights Act of 1964", Section 206 (a).

Nature of Plaintiff's Business

2. Plaintiff corporation owns and operates a motel which has facilities for sleeping, eating, drinking, swimming and other activities usually carried on in a motel. The name of said motel is Heart of Atlanta Motel and it is located in the city block bounded by Courtland Street, Harris Street, [fol. 5] Piedmont Avenue and Baker Street in Fulton County, Atlanta, Georgia. Plaintiff corporation operates no other business except at this location and owns all of the land on which said motel is built. Said motel's activity is so intermingled with wholly local business and so essentially local in character as to be outside the stream of interstate commerce.

3. Heart of Atlanta Motel rents sleeping accommodations to persons desiring them. Some of the guests of Heart of Atlanta Motel live in Georgia and rent sleeping accommodations from said motel when they come to Atlanta. Some of the guests of Heart of Atlanta Motel live in other states and rent sleeping accommodations from said motel when they visit Atlanta.

4. When Heart of Atlanta Motel rents sleeping accommodations to a guest who has come from another state, that guest has literally and legally "come to rest"; his interstate movement is completed by the time he reaches the premises of the Motel; and he has ceased to be in the stream of interstate commerce when he crosses the threshold of Heart of Atlanta Motel.

5. Heart of Atlanta Motel has refused and intends to refuse to rent sleeping accommodations to persons desiring said accommodations, for several different reasons, one of which is based on the ground of race, unless ordered by this Court to comply with the provisions of the Civil Rights Act of 1964.

Controversy

6. Heart of Atlanta Motel has never rented sleeping accommodations to members of the Negro race, is not now renting sleeping accommodations to members of the Negro [fol. 6] race and does not intend to do so unless ordered by this Court to comply with the provisions of the Civil Rights Act of 1964. Plaintiff contends and shows to this Court that said Civil Rights Act of 1964 is unconstitutional and that, even if said Civil Rights Act of 1964 be held to be constitutional, plaintiff corporation is not engaged in interstate commerce and its operations do not affect interstate commerce.

7. Section 206 (a) of said Civil Rights Act of 1964 provides as follows:

> "Whenever the Attorney General has reasonable cause to believe that any person or group of persons is engaged in a pattern or practice of resistance to the full enjoyment of any of the rights secured by this title, and that the pattern or practice is of such a nature and is intended to deny the full exercise of the rights herein described, the Attorney General may bring a civil action in the appropriate district court of the United States by filing with it a complaint (1) signed by him (or in his absence the Acting Attorney General), (2) setting forth facts pertaining to such pattern or practice, and (3) requesting such preventive relief, including an application for a permanent or temporary injunction, restraining order or other order against the person or persons responsible for such pattern or practice, as he deems necessary to insure the full enjoyment of the rights herein described."

Plaintiff corporation shows to the Court that the President of the United States has stated that the Civil Rights Act of 1964 shall be enforced by the United States and that unless the Attorney General of the United States, one [fol. 7] of the defendants herein, is restrained and enjoined from enforcing said unconstitutional act and from interfering with plaintiff's trade and business, plaintiff corporation will suffer irreparable damages.

8. Before the Civil Rights Act of 1964 became law, plaintiff corporation owned the fee simple title to Heart of Atlanta Motel and the land upon which it is located. Before the adoption of said Act, plaintiff corporation operated its motel in any way it deemed fit, provided it complied with local ordinances and statutes of the State of Georgia pertaining to the protection of the health of the guests of said motel. Before the adoption of said Act, plaintiff corporation made use of its land in any way it saw fit in its own discretion, subject only to local laws pertaining to health and pertaining to zoning. Before the adoption of said Act, plaintiff corporation picked and chose its guests from those people it considered to be compatible with the other guests of said motel and excluded Negro guests because plaintiff corporation determined that such exclusion was in the best interest of plaintiff's business and was necessary to protect plaintiff's property, trade, profits and reputation.

9. The Civil Rights Act of 1964 prohibits plaintiff corporation from exercising and enjoying the full rights inherent in the private ownership of private property in that said Act prohibits plaintiff corporation from doing now those things enumerated hereinabove in paragraph eight which it had the right to do before said Act became law. Said Civil Rights Act of 1964 deprives plaintiff corporation of liberty and property without due process of law, in violation of the Fifth Amendment to The Constitution of the United States. Defendant United States of America has taken for public use part of the rights of plaintiff corporation in and to its private property, without any compensa-
[fol. 8] tion, in violation of the Fifth Amendment to The Constitution of the United States, which reads in part as follows:

> "... nor (shall any person) be deprived of life, liberty or property, without due process of law; nor shall private property be taken for public use, without just compensation."

10. Section 201 (a) of the Civil Rights Act of 1964 appropriates and takes for public use by all persons part of the private rights of plaintiff corporation in and to its private property, the Heart of Atlanta Motel. Said Section 201 (a) reads as follows:

"All persons shall be entitled to the full and equal enjoyment of the goods, services, facilities, privileges, advantages, and accommodations of any place of public accommodation, as defined in this section, without discrimination or segregation on the ground of race, color, religion, or national origin."

11. The Civil Rights Act of 1964, Section 201 (b) provides that said Act applies to any motel "if its operations affect commerce". Section 201 (c) defines an establishment whose operations affect commerce as being, among other types of business, "any motel". Taking both of said sections together, said Act declares that the operations of any motel affect commerce and in doing so said Act unconstitutionally exceeds the grant to Congress by Article I, Section 8, Clause 3 of the Constitution of the United States of America, which is set forth hereinafter, of the power to regulate commerce among the several states, to wit:

"*Powers of Congress*. The Congress shall have Power.

3. *Commerce*. To regulate Commerce with foreign Nations, and among the several States, and with the Indian Tribes;"

[fol. 9] 12. The value of the liberty taken by the defendant United States of America from plaintiff corporation is priceless, but this plaintiff corporation shows that it should be compensated in an amount of not less than Ten Million ($10,000,000.00) Dollars. The value of the rights of plaintiff corporation in and to its private property, which have been taken by the United States of America, without any compensation, is One Million ($1,000,000.00) Dollars.

13. More than ninety-five (95%) percent of all the past guests of Heart of Atlanta Motel prefer not to rent sleeping accommodations at said motel if members of the Negro

race also rent sleeping accommodations at said motel. A majority of the guests at said motel, who account for more than fifty (50%) percent of the income to said motel, are guests who have previously rented sleeping accommodations at said motel, said guests being referred to as "repeat guests". Plaintiff corporation shows and contends that if the Attorney General of the United States, one of the defendants herein, is permitted to enforce the provisions of the Civil Rights Act of 1964 as to the plaintiff corporation and its motel, plaintiff corporation will lose a large percentage of its customers, income and good will and will suffer irreparable damages.

Wherefore, Plaintiff prays and demands:

1. That Robert F. Kennedy, as the Attorney General of the United States of America, be temporarily and permanently restrained and enjoined from enforcing said Civil Rights Act of 1964 against plaintiff corporation, Heart of Atlanta Motel, Inc.

[fol. 10] 2. Judgment in the sum of Eleven Million ($11,000,000.00) Dollars against the United States of America, together with reasonable attorney fees for the prosecution of this action, and all costs.

>Moreton Rolleston, Jr., 1103 Cit. & Sou. National Bank Building, Atlanta, Georgia 30303, JAckson 3-1566, Attorney for Plaintiff.

[fol. 11] [File endorsement omitted]

In the United States District Court

For the Northern District of Georgia

Atlanta Division

Civil Action No. 9017

[Title omitted]

Order to Show Cause—July 6, 1964

The petition in the above and foregoing complaint having been read and considered, it is hereby ordered that

(~~Robert F. Kennedy, as the Attorney General for the United States of America, be and he is hereby restrained from enforcing the provisions of the Civil Rights Act of 1964 against Heart of Atlanta Motel, Inc. until further order of this Court; and that~~) said Robert F. Kennedy, as the Attorney General of the United States of America, is hereby ordered to show cause before me on the 17th day of July at 10:00 A.M., 1964 why the prayers of the plaintiff corporation for permanent injunction should not be granted.

This 6th day of July, 1964.

 Frank A. Hooper, Judge, United States District Court for the Northern District of Georgia.

[fol. 12]

In the United States District Court
For the Northern District of Georgia
Atlanta Division

Civil Action File No. 9017

Heart of Atlanta Motel, Inc.,
a Georgia Corporation, Plaintiff,

v.

The United States of America and Robert F. Kennedy, as the Attorney General of the United States of America, Defendants.

Summons and Order to Show Cause

To the above named Defendants:

You are hereby summoned and required to serve upon Moreton Rolleston, Jr. plaintiff's attorney, whose address is 1103 C & S National Bank Building, Atlanta, Georgia an answer to the complaint which is herewith served upon you, within 60 days after service of this summons upon you, exclusive of the day of service. If you fail to do so,

12

judgment by default will be taken against you for the relief demanded in the complaint.

 B. G. Nash, Clerk of Court, Forrest L. Martin, Deputy Clerk.

[Seal of the Court]

Date: July 6th, 1964

Note.—This summons is issued pursuant to Rule 4 of the Federal Rules of Civil Procedure.

[fol. 12a]

I hereby certify and return that I have this July 7th, 1964 mailed by certified mail a copy of the within Summons & Complaint and Order to the Attorney General, Washington, D. C.

 W. J. Andrews, U. S. Marshal, By: Rosalie Rich.

Return on Service of Writ

I hereby certify and return, that on the 7th day of July 1964, I received this summons and served it together with the complaint and order herein as follows:

and on July 7th 1964 I served United States of America and Robert F. Kennedy as the Attorney General of the United States of America by handing to and leaving with Gus Wood Assistant U. S. Attorney a true copy of the within Summons and Complaint and order at his office in Federal Bldg., Atlanta, Ga. this 7th day of July 1964.

 W. J. Andrews, United States Marshal, By Joe M. Allen, Deputy United States Marshal.

Marshal's Fee
Travel .... $.........
Service 6.00
      ———
     $6.00

Subscribed and sworn to before me, a .... this .... day of ...., 19.....

[Seal]

[Stamp—Filed in Clerk's Office, July 8, 1964, B. G. Nash, Clerk, By: S G Deputy Clerk]

By: S G Deputy Clerk.

8436

Note.—Affidavit required only if service is made by a person other than a United States Marshal or his Deputy.

[fol. 13]   [File endorsement omitted]

IN THE UNITED STATES DISTRICT COURT

FOR THE NORTHERN DISTRICT OF GEORGIA

ATLANTA DIVISION

Civil Action No. 9017

HEART OF ATLANTA MOTEL, INC.,
a Georgia corporation, Plaintiff,

vs.

THE UNITED STATES OF AMERICA and ROBERT F. KENNEDY, as the Attorney General of the United States of America, Defendants.

AMENDMENT TO COMPLAINT FOR DECLARATORY JUDGMENT—
Filed July 15, 1964

Now Comes Heart of Atlanta Motel, Inc., the corporate plaintiff in the above styled case, and with leave of Court having first been obtained, amends its Complaint heretofore filed in the following manner:

1.

By adding the following paragraph which shall be known as Paragraph 14, as follows:

The Civil Rights Act of 1964 is unconstitutional in that it imposes involuntary servitude upon the corporate plaintiff in violation of the thirteenth amendment to the Constitution of the United States which reads as follows:

"Neither slavery nor involuntary servitude, except as a punishment for crime whereof the party shall have been duly convicted, shall exist within the United States, or any place subject to their jurisdiction."

[fol. 14] 2.

By adding the following paragraph which shall be known as Paragraph 15, as follows:

The Civil Rights Act of 1964 is unconstitutional in that it deprives the plaintiff corporation of its freedom to contract in violation of that portion of the Fifth amendment to the Constitution of the United States which is quoted hereinabove in paragraph 9 of the original complaint.

Wherefore, Plaintiff prays:

1.

That this amendment be allowed, subject to the objections of the defendants.

2.

That the Civil Rights Act of 1964 be declared unconstitutional.

> Moreton Rolleston, Jr., 1103 Cit. & Sou. Bank Building, Atlanta, Georgia 30303, JAckson 3-1566, Attorney for Plaintiff.

[fol. 15] [File endorsement omitted]

In the United States District Court
For the Northern District of Georgia
Atlanta Division
Civil Action No. 9017

[Title omitted]

Order Allowing Amendment to Complaint—
July 15, 1964

The foregoing amendment to the original Complaint filed in the above styled case is hereby allowed, subject to the objections of the defendants.

This 15th day of July, 1964.

>Frank A. Hooper, Judge, United States District Court for the Northern District of Georgia, Atlanta Division.

[fol. 16] Certificate of Service (omitted in printing).

[fol. 17] [File endorsement omitted]

In the United States District Court
For the Northern District of Georgia
Atlanta Division
Civil Action No. 9017

[Title omitted]

Plaintiff's Statement of Issues—Filed July 15, 1964

In response to the Order of this Court, dated July 10, 1964, that the parties file a brief statement of the issues of fact that will be involved in the hearing for injunction now set for 9:30 o'clock AM, July 17, 1964, the corporate plaintiff respectfully submits the following:

1.

The answer of the defendants, by paragraph 3, admitted all well pleaded allegations of fact contained in the Complaint, except the following sentence set forth in paragraph 2 of the complaint:

"Said motel's activity is so intermingled with wholly local business and so essentially local in character as to be outside the stream of interstate commerce."

and the following portion of paragraph 9 of the Complaint:

"Defendant United States of America has taken for public use part of the rights of plaintiff corporation in and to its private property."

[fol. 18]
2.

Plaintiff corporation intends to show that there is located within the Heart of Atlanta Motel a restaurant, which is owned and operated by Interstate Hosts, Inc. whose address is 11255 West Olympic Boulevard, Los Angeles 64, California, and that it is not the policy and practice of this restaurant to refuse to sell food and provide service in the restaurant to Negroes because of their race and color and that, since the Civil Rights Act of 1964 became law, this restaurant has served all Negroes who have asked for service. Furthermore, plaintiff corporation intends to show that it leases the restaurant space to Interstate Hosts, Inc. and has no legal control over whom the restaurant shall serve and that it has agreed in principle with Interstate Hosts, Inc. that Negroes shall be served in the restaurant.

> Moreton Rolleston, Jr., 1103 Citizens & Southern Nat'l Bk. Bldg., Atlanta, Georgia 30303, JAckson 3-1566, Attorney for Plaintiff.

[fol. 19] Certificate of Service (omitted in printing).

[fol. 20] [File endorsement omitted]

In the United States District Court
For the Northern District of Georgia
Atlanta Division
Civil Action No. 9017

[Title omitted]

Stipulation of Facts—Filed July 17, 1964.

It is stipulated by and between the Plaintiff and the Defendants that:

1.

Plaintiff owns and operates the Heart of Atlanta Motel in Atlanta, Georgia. The motel has 216 rooms for lease or hire to transient guests.

2.

Through various national advertising media, including magazines having national circulation, the Plaintiff solicits patronage for the motel from outside the State of Georgia.

3.

The Plaintiff accepts convention trade from outside the State of Georgia.

4.

Approximately 75% of the total number of guests who register at the motel are from outside the State of Georgia.

[fol. 21]   5.

Plaintiff maintains over fifty billboards and highway signs advertising the motel on highways in Georgia.

Signed: This 16th day of July, 1964, By: Moreton Rolleston, Jr., On Behalf of Plaintiff.

Signed: This 16th day of July, 1964, By: St. John Barrett, On Behalf of Defendants.

[fol. 22] [File endorsement omitted]

In the United States District Court
For the Northern District of Georgia
Atlanta Division
Civil Action No. 9017

[Title omitted]

Defendants' Notice of Motion and Motion for Preliminary Injunction—Filed July 10, 1964

To Heart of Atlanta Motel, Inc., Plaintiff, and Moreten Rolleston, Jr., Attorney for Plaintiff:

Please take notice that on July 17, 1964, at 10:00 a.m., or as soon thereafter as counsel may be heard, in the courtroom of the United States District Court for the Northern District of Georgia in the United States Post Office and Courthouse, Atlanta, Georgia, the defendants will move the Court for a preliminary injunction, pending the trial upon their first and second counterclaims, enjoining the Heart of Atlanta Motel, Inc., its successors, officers, attorneys, [fol. 23] agents and employees, together with all persons in active concert or participation with them, from:

(a) Refusing to accept Negroes as guests in the motel by reason of their race or color;

(b) Making any distinction whatever upon the basis of race or color in the availability of the goods, services, facilities, privileges, advantages or accommodations offered or made available to the guests of the motel or to the general public within or upon any of the premises of the Heart of Atlanta Motel; and

(c) Failing or refusing to sell food and meals in the restaurant or to provide service to Negroes in the restaurant upon the same basis and in the same manner as food, meals and service are made available to white patrons; and,

(d) Otherwise violating in any manner or by any means the provision of Title II of the Civil Rights Act of 1964 with respect to the operation of the motel or of any facilities located within the premises of the motel.

This motion will be based upon all of the pleadings and other documents on file in this case and upon oral testimony and other evidence to be offered at the hearing.

[fol. 24] United States of America and Robert F. Kennedy, Attorney General of the United States, Defendants, By: Burke Marshall, Assistant Attorney General, Charles L. Goodson, United States Attorney.

[fol. 25] [File endorsement omitted]

In the United States District Court

For the Northern District of Georgia

Atlanta Division

Civil Action No. 9017

Heart of Atlanta Motel, Inc.,
a Georgia Corporation, Plaintiff,

v.

The United States of America and Robert F. Kennedy, as the Attorney General of the United States of America, Defendants.

Defendants' Notice of Motion and Motion to Dismiss—Filed July 10, 1964

To Heart of Atlanta Motel, Inc., Plaintiff and Moreten Rolleston, Jr., Attorney for Plaintiff:

Please take notice that on July 17, 1964, at 10:00 a.m., or as soon thereafter as counsel may be heard, in the courtroom of the United States District Court for the Northern District of Georgia, in the United States Post Office and Courthouse, Atlanta, Georgia, the defendants will move the Court for an order dismissing the complaint in this case upon the following grounds:

[fol. 26] 1. The complaint fails to state facts upon which relief can be granted.

2. The United States of America has not consented to be sued.

3. The Court lacks jurisdiction of a claim against the United States in excess of $10,000.

> United States of America and Robert F. Kennedy, Attorney General of the United States, Defendants, By: Burke Marshall, Assistant Attorney General, Charles L. Goodson, United States Attorney.

[fol. 27] [File endorsement omitted]

IN THE UNITED STATES DISTRICT COURT

FOR THE NORTHERN DISTRICT OF GEORGIA

ATLANTA DIVISION

Civil Action No. 9017

[Title omitted]

CERTIFICATE AND REQUEST FOR THREE-JUDGE COURT—
Filed July 10, 1964

Robert F. Kennedy, Attorney General of the United States, requests, pursuant to Section 206(b) of the Civil Rights Act of 1964, that a court of three judges be convened to hear and determine the above-captioned case.

The Attorney General of the United States certifies that in his opinion the above-captioned case is one of general public importance.

> Robert F. Kennedy, Attorney General of the United States.

[fol. 28] [File endorsement omitted]

In the United States District Court
For the Northern District of Georgia
Atlanta Division
Civil Action No. 9017

[Title omitted]

Answer and Counterclaims—Filed July 10, 1964

The United States of America and Robert F. Kennedy, defendants, answer the complaint as follows:

1. The defendants deny the allegation contained in the last sentence of paragraph 2 of the complaint that the activity of the Heart of Atlanta Motel is so intermingled with solely local business and so essentially local in character as to be outside the strain of interstate commerce.

2. The defendants deny the allegation contained in paragraph 9 of the complaint that the United States of America has taken for public use part of the rights of the plaintiff in and to its private property.

3. The defendants admit all other well pleaded allegations of fact contained in the complaint.

[fol. 29] First Defense

The complaint fails to state a claim against the defendants upon which relief can be granted.

Second Defense

The United States has not consented to be sued by the plaintiff.

Third Defense

This Court lacks jurisdiction to entertain the plaintiff's claim for damages against the United States in excess of $10,000.

First Counterclaim

The United States of America and Robert F. Kennedy allege as a counterclaim against the plaintiff:

1. This counterclaim is asserted by the Attorney General and the United States pursuant to Section 206(a) of the Civil Rights Act of 1964 and Rule 13 of the Rules of Civil Procedure.

2. This Court has jurisdiction of this counterclaim under Section 207(a) of the Civil Rights Act of 1964 and under 28 U.S.C. 1345.

[fol. 30] 3. The Heart of Atlanta Motel, which is owned and operated by the plaintiff as alleged in paragraph 2 of the complaint, provides lodging for transients and has over two hundred rooms for rent or hire. It is a place of public accommodation within the meaning of Section 201(b) of the Civil Rights Act of 1964 and its operations affect commerce within the meaning of Section 201(c) of the Act.

4. Plaintiff has refused, is refusing and has announced that, unless enjoined by this Court, it will continue to pursue its policy of refusing accommodations in the Heart of Atlanta Motel to Negroes on account of their race or color.

5. The acts and practices set forth in the preceding paragraph constitute a pattern and practice of resistance to the full enjoyment by Negroes of the right, secured by Title II of the Civil Rights Act of 1964, to the full and equal enjoyment of the goods, services, facilities, privileges, advantages, and accommodations of the Heart of Atlanta Motel, without discrimination or segregation on the ground of race or color, and such pattern or practice is of such a nature and is intended to deny the full exercise of such right.

[fol. 31] ## Second Counterclaim

The United States of America and Robert F. Kennedy allege as a second and further counterclaim against the plaintiff:

6. The defendants re-allege each of the facts and matters set forth in paragraphs 1 through 5 of their first counterclaim.

7. Physically located within the premises of the Heart of Atlanta Motel is a restaurant, owned and operated by the plaintiff, which serves the public and holds itself out as serving patrons of the Heart of Atlanta Motel.

8. The restaurant described in paragraph 7 herein is principally engaged in selling food for consumption on its premises and it serves and offers to serve interstate travelers and a substantial portion of the food and other products which it sells has moved in commerce.

9. The restaurant described in paragraphs 7 and 8 is a place of public accommodation within the meaning of Section 201(b) of the Civil Rights Act of 1964, and its operations affect commerce within the meaning of Section 201(c) of the Act.

10. It is the policy and practice of the plaintiff to refuse to sell food and provide service in the restaurant to Negroes because of their race and color.

11. The acts and practices set forth in the preceding paragraph constitute a pattern and practice of resistance to the full enjoyment by Negroes of the right, secured by Title II of the Civil Rights Act of 1964, to the full [fol. 32] and equal enjoyment of the goods, services, facilities, privileges, advantages, and accommodations of the Heart of Atlanta Motel, without discrimination or segregation on the ground of race or color, and such pattern or practice is of such a nature and is intended to deny the full exercise of such right.

Wherefore, the defendants pray that this Court enter an order enjoining the Heart of Atlanta Motel, Inc., its successors, officers, attorneys, agents and employees, together with all persons in active concert or participation with them, from:

(a) Refusing to accept Negroes as guests in the motel by reason of their race or color;

(b) Making any distinction whatever upon the basis of race or color in the availability of the goods, services, facilities, privileges, advantages, or accommodations offered or made available to the guests of the motel or to the general public within or upon any of the premises of the Heart of Atlanta Motel;

(c) Failing or refusing to sell food and meals in the restaurant or to provide service to Negroes in the restaurant upon the same basis and in the same manner as food, meals and service are made available to white patrons; and,

[fol. 33] (d) Otherwise violating in any manner or by any means the provision of Title II of the Civil Rights Act of 1964 with respect to the operation of the motel or of any facilities located within the premises of the motel.

Plaintiffs further pray for their costs of suit and for such further and additional relief as the interest of justice may require.

> United States of America, and Robert F. Kennedy, Attorney General of the United States, Defendants, By: Robert F. Kennedy, Attorney General, Burke Marshall, Assistant Attorney General, Charles Goodson, United States Attorney, St. John Barrett, Attorney, Department of Justice.

[fol. 34]   [File endorsement omitted]

In the United States District Court

For the Northern District of Georgia

Atlanta Division

Civil Action No. 9017

[Title omitted]

Answer to Counterclaims and Response to Motion for Preliminary Injunction—Filed July 15, 1964

Heart of Atlanta Motel, Inc., plaintiff, answers the First Counterclaim of the defendants as follows:

1.

The allegations of paragraphs 1 and 2 of the First Counterclaim are denied and plaintiff further shows that this honorable Court has already acquired jurisdiction by virtue of the Complaint filed by the plaintiff.

2.

Plaintiff denies the allegations of paragraph 3 of the First Counterclaim which reads as follows:

"It is a place of public accommodation within the meaning of Section 201(b) of the Civil Rights Act of 1964 and its operations affect commerce within the meaning of Section 201(c) of the Act."

[fol. 35] **3.**

Plaintiff denies the allegations contained in paragraph 4 of the First Counterclaim where it is alleged that "the plaintiff is refusing" accommodations to Negroes on account of their race or color.

4.

Plaintiff admits the allegations of paragraph 5 of the First Counterclaim except the reference to that portion of paragraph 4 of said First Counterclaim pertaining to "is refusing" and except that plaintiff also denies that Title II of the Civil Rights Act of 1964 secures to Negroes the right to use any of the goods, services, facilities, privileges, advantages and accommodations of Heart of Atlanta Motel. Plaintiff further denies that the restaurant located within Heart of Atlanta Motel, if construed to be a facility of Heart of Atlanta Motel, is refusing to serve Negroes on the grounds of race or color.

Answer to Second Counterclaim

5.

The plaintiff denies the allegations of paragraph 6 of the Second Counterclaim in the same manner, and verbatim, as it denied the allegations of paragraphs 1, 2, 3, 4 and 5 of the First Counterclaim.

6.

Plaintiff denies that it owns and operates a restaurant in Heart of Atlanta Motel and shows to the Court that said restaurant is owned and operated, under a lease from plaintiff corporation, by Interstate Hosts, Inc., whose address is 11255 West Olympic Boulevard, Los Angeles 64, California.

7.

Plaintiff admits the allegations of paragraph 8 of the [fol. 36] Second Counterclaim except it shows to the Court that it can neither admit nor deny, for lack of information, the following quoted portion of said paragraph 8:

> " . . . it serves and offers to serve interstate travelers and a substantial portion of the food and other products which it sells has moved in commerce."

8.

Plaintiff denies the allegations of paragraphs 9, 10 and 11 and plaintiff further shows to the Court that said restaurant has served all Negroes, being three in number upon information and belief, who have applied for service since the Civil Rights Act of 1964 became law.

First Defense

The First and Second Counterclaims fail to state a claim against the plaintiff upon which relief can be granted in that the Civil Rights Act of 1964 is unconstitutional and violates the Fifth and Thirteenth Amendments to the Constitution of the United States as well as Article I, Section 8, Clause 3 of the Constitution of the United States of America.

In Response to the Motion for Preliminary Injunction Plaintiff Shows to the Court as Follows:

9.

Defendants are entitled to no injunction of any kind against the operation of the restaurant in Heart of Atlanta

Motel, even if the Civil Rights Act of 1964 is constitutional, in that the restaurant is not refusing service to Negroes and has in fact served Negroes on an equal basis with other guests.

[fol. 37] 10.

Defendants are not entitled to a preliminary injunction against the plaintiff corporation because the Civil Rights Act of 1964, upon which the defendants rely, is unconstitutional.

Wherefore, plaintiff prays:

1.

That the First Counterclaim and the Second Counterclaim of the defendants be dismissed.

2.

That the Motion of the defendants for a Preliminary Injunction be denied.

> Moreton Rolleston, Jr., 1103 Cit. & Sou. Bank Building, Atlanta, Georgia 30303, JAckson 3-1566, Attorney for Plaintiff.

[fol. 38] Certificate of Service (omitted in printing).

[fol. 39] [File endorsement omitted]

IN THE UNITED STATES DISTRICT COURT

FOR THE NORTHERN DISTRICT OF GEORGIA

ATLANTA DIVISION

Civil Action No. 9017

[Title omitted]

MOTION TO DISMISS SECOND COUNTERCLAIM—
Filed July 15, 1964

The United States of America and Robert F. Kennedy move to dismiss their second counterclaim in the above entitled case and to withdraw its prayer for relief in Paragraph (c) of its answer and counterclaim.

 United States of America, and Robert F. Kennedy, Attorney General of the United States, Defendants, By: Charles L. Goodson, United States Attorney.

[fol. 40]   [File endorsement omitted]

ORDER—Filed July 16, 1964

This Court having read and considered the attached motion of the United States of America and Robert F. Kennedy to withdraw its second counterclaim and Paragraph (c) of its prayer for relief, that motion is hereby granted and it is Ordered that the second counterclaim of the defendants be dismissed.

This the .... day of July, 1964.

 Elbert P. Tuttle, Frank A. Hooper, Dist. Judge, Lewis R. Morgan.

[fol. 41] Certificate of Service (omitted in printing).

[fol. 42]

IN THE UNITED STATES DISTRICT COURT
FOR THE NORTHERN DISTRICT OF GEORGIA
ATLANTA DIVISION
Civil Action No. 9017

HEART OF ATLANTA MOTEL, INC.,

vs.

THE UNITED STATES OF AMERICA and ROBERT F. KENNEDY, as The Attorney General of The United States of America.

Transcript of Proceedings—Atlanta, Georgia; July 17, 1964

Before Honorable Elbert P. Tuttle, Honorable Frank A. Hooper, Honorable Lewis R. Morgan, Judges.

APPEARANCES:

For the Plaintiff: Moreton Rolleston, Jr., 255 Courtland Street, N.E., Atlanta, Georgia.

For the Defendants: Burke Marshall, St. John Barrett, Harold Green, Department of Justice, Washington 25, D. C.; Charles L. Goodson, U. S. Attorney, Atlanta, Georgia.

[fol. 44] Judge Tuttle: The Court will call two cases this morning to get responses as to whether the parties are ready to proceed. The first case is Moreton Rolleston, Junior—excuse me—Heart of Atlanta Motel, Incorporated, against The United States and Kennedy, Attorney General. Are you ready to proceed?

Mr. Rolleston: Plaintiff's ready, Your Honor.

Mr. Goodson: If it please the Court, the Attorney General and the Government will be represented in this case by Mr. Burke Marshall, the Assistant Attorney General in charge of the Civil Rights Division, and Mr. St. John Barrett of the Civil Rights Division of the Justice Department.

Judge Tuttle: Glad to have you here, Mr. Marshall.

Mr. Marshall: The Government is ready, Your Honor.

Judge Tuttle: The next case set to be heard this morning is George Willis, Jr., and others against Pickrick Corporation and Lester Maddox, and Attorney General of the United States, Intervenor. Are you ready for the plaintiffs in that case?

Mr. Alexander: The plaintiffs are ready, Your Honor. The plaintiffs will be represented by Mr. Jack Greenberg, Mrs. Connie Baker Motley and myself, William Alexander.

Mr. Marshall: The intervenors are ready.

Judge Tuttle: The defendant, Pickrick Corporation, [fol. 45] Mr. Maddox, represented in Court?

Mr. Schell: Yes, sir.

Judge Tuttle: We were just calling your case, Mr. Schell.

Mr. Schell: We're ready, sir.

Judge Tuttle: For the convenience of the parties and counsel, it would appear that there'll be some element of time, some element of delay before the second case is reached. It's impossible for me to tell now unless—I'll call on the parties in the first case and maybe they can give me an indication. Mr. McRae, we just called the case. I guess we were a minute early.

Mr. McRae: Well, we had a little trouble getting in. There was a kind of blockade and they were separating the wheat from the chaff, so to speak, and—

Judge Tuttle: You mean the lawyers and the parties from those who are not in the case?

Mr. McRae: Yes, sir; that's right. They had a blockade out there.

Judge Tuttle: Yes, sir. You are ready for the plaintiff?

Mr. McRae: We are ready, Your Honor.

Judge Tuttle: In the first case, Mr. Rolleston, will you give us an estimate of about how long you think it necessary for you to take? Are the facts—

[fol. 46] Mr. Rolleston: Your Honor, the facts have been stipulated and I think the government has two witnesses, and I don't anticipate my argument to last over a half hour. I have no witnesses.

Judge Tuttle: Right. Mr. Barrett?

Mr. Barrett: I don't believe that the testimony will take more than twenty or thirty minutes, and perhaps twenty minutes for argument. I would say forty-five minutes for —to an hour for the government's case.

Judge Tuttle: Let's see. That's 9:30 to 11:30. Counsel's estimates are usually rather optimistic. The Court will run through till 12:00 o'clock and take a recess for lunch; and then proceed in the second case. The second case may be excused until one-thirty.

Mr. Barrett: Thank you, sir.

Mr. McRae: Thank you, sir.

Mr. Greenberg: Excuse me, Your Honor. May we be permitted to sit here? Since this is the first case under the Act, I think we might—

Judge Tuttle: Oh, yes. Yes.

Mr. Greenberg: —be able to profit by it.

Judge Tuttle: Yes. Of course. You may proceed then with the first case. Mr. Rolleston, you are the moving party.

Mr. Rolleston: I did want to inquire of the Court if [fol. 47] I am the moving party since they had a motion to dismiss pending. It doesn't make any difference to me.

Judge Tuttle: We take it as the Court normally does as a motion for preliminary injunction and let the movant for the injunction proceed, and then we'll hear from the other side.

Mr. Rolleston: Thank you. If it please the Court, in this case the government has filed an answer in which they have admitted all of the actual facts pleaded in the complaint. They have denied what amounts to two conclusions, legal conclusions in the petition, so in view of that admission, we have no evidence to offer to the Court at this time.

Mr. Barrett: If the Court please, I have a written—

Judge Tuttle: Excuse me a minute, Mr. Barrett.

Mr. Barrett: Yes, sir.

Judge Tuttle: Of course, this doesn't go at all to your contention to being entitled to damages against the United States, does it?

Mr. Rolleston: No, sir; I take it that the real issue before the Court—

Judge Tuttle: Yes.

Mr. Rolleston: —is the legal question of the constitutionality.

Judge Tuttle: All right.

[fol. 48]   Stipulation of Counsel

Mr. Barrett: If the Court please, I have a written stipulation that has been entered into by counsel on both sides.

Judge Tuttle: Will you read it in the record or have it read in the record, please?

Mr. Barrett: Yes; if I may.

It is stipulated by and between the plaintiff and the defendants that,

One, Plaintiff owns and operates the Heart of Atlanta Motel in Atlanta, Georgia. The Motel has 216 rooms for lease or hire for transient guests.

Two, Through various national advertising media, including magazines having national circulation, the plaintiff solicits patronage for the Motel from outside the State of Georgia.

Three, Plaintiff accepts convention trade from outside the State of Georgia.

Four, Approximately 75% of the total number of guests who register at the hotel are from outside the State of Gergia.

Five, Plaintiff maintains over fifty billboards and highway signs advertising the Motel on highways in Georgia.

If I may, I will file the original with the clerk and pass the Court a copy. If the Court please, in view of the defendants by reason of the stipulation, the only issue [fol. 49] of fact remaining as raised by the pleadings is whether or not the plaintiff is refusing accommodations to Negroes; and the testimony which we will offer will be directed solely to that issue.

Judge Tuttle: I understood that Mr. Rolleston asserted that, alleged that in his complaint. Do you conceive that there is still an issue of fact with respect to that matter?

Mr. Barrett: Yes, Your Honor. As I understand the position of the plaintiff, he concedes that it his purpose to refuse accommodations to Negroes; but that he is not refusing and has not refused Negroes on the basis of their race since the enactment of the statute. And inasmuch as that could have a bearing on whether or not there is a pattern or practice of resistance in terms of the Act, we believe that evidence is appropriate on that point.

Judge Tuttle: Well, you may put on your evidence.

Mr. Barrett: The defendants will call Albert Richard Sampson.

ALBERT RICHARD SAMPSON, having first been duly sworn and called as a witness in behalf of the defendants, testified as follows:

Direct examination.

By Mr. Barrett:

Q. Would you state your full name, please?
[fol. 50]   A. Albert Richard Sampson.

Q. Where do you live, Mr. Sampson?

A. 339 Holly Street, Apartment 2-B, Northwest, Atlanta, Georgia.

Q. What is your occupation?

A. Executive Secretary of the Atlanta Branch of the NAACP; Associate Editor of the ATLANTA ENQUIRER NEWSPAPER.

Q. Are you a Negro, Mr. Sampson?

A. Yes, I am.

Q. Mr. Sampson, on July 7th of this year, did you take any steps to make a hotel reservation?

A. Yes, I did.

Q. Would you tell the Court what you did?

A. Well, on July 7th in the afternoon, I telephoned the Heart of Atlanta Motel and made a reservation for Wednesday evening commitment. I then drove to South Carolina with some friends of mine who had to take a car to the Naval Base in Charleston, South Carolina to ship it overseas. I left Atlanta that Tuesday evening and I went to Charleston. And while in Charleston, I wired twelve dollars and thirty-six cents because the man on the phone told me that that's what the price of the room was. I wired it from a Western Union office, twelve dollars and thirty-six cents.

Q. Do you have any receipt for that wire?

A. Yes, I do.

Q. May I see it, please?
[fol. 51]   A. From—

Mr. Barrett: If—pardon me—if the Court please, may this be marked for identification?

Clerk: Respondent's Exhibit Number 1 marked for identification is a receipt to Western Union Telegraph Company.

By Mr. Barrett:

Q. Mr. Sampson, I'll show you Respondent's Exhibit Number 1 for identification and ask you if that is the receipt you received from the Western Union—
A. That's correct.
Q. —Telegraph Company?
A. Yes; in Charleston, South Carolina.
Q. Did you return—
A. There was a message on the telegram, "Arriving at seven o'clock."
Q. Did you return to Atlanta?
A. Yes. I flew—
Q. How did you return?
A. I flew in on a Delta Flight 450—I mean at 4:50, Flight 620. This is my baggage stub.
Q. Where did you go when you got into the Atlanta Airport?
A. I got on a shuttle bus and the shuttle bus took us to several hotels, and my ultimate, my final destination was the Heart of Atlanta Motel.
[fol. 52] Q. Did you go in?
A. Yes.
Q. Did you go to the desk?
A. That's correct.
Q. Who was at the desk?
A. A dark haired fellow and a light haired fellow. I don't know their names. I just know that they were at the registration desk.
Q. Will you tell the Court what happened when you got to the desk, what you said and what the men at the desk said?
A. When I got to the desk, I said, "I'm here for the, for the express purpose of getting my room reservation. I wired the money ahead of time." And so they went, and they were looking for my wire. Then the dark haired fel-

low came out and he said to me, "I'm very sorry; but I don't have your wire." Meanwhile, the light haired fellow was taking someone else's reservation, and at that time I saw my name on the list, and I said, "There's my name." And the light haired fellow snatched it away. And then the dark haired fellow saw the Western Union telegram, and at that time he told me that he wouldn't be able to accommodate me because of the fact that they have a suit pending before the courts on this basic issue. And I pointed out to him that "you don't have an argument with me; you have an argument with the Federal Government. [fol. 53] The only thing I know is that I confirmed the reservation you took over the phone, and you have my receipt." And at that point, he said, "I'm very sorry. We can't accommodate you." And I said, "Will you give me my money back?" And he said, "No, I'm not qualified to give you your money back." He said, "I just can't give it to you over the counter." And I said, "I'm not leaving until I get it." I said, "I'll have to call the police because of the fact I've paid you and I think you should give me my money back." So at that time, this gentleman came in and—

Q. Who do you mean when you say "this gentleman?"

A. Mr. Rolleston. He came in and he pointed out to me— he checked both the guest list, my telegram receipt, and he took me over to the side and he pointed out to me that they had, that he had a suit against the Federal Government on this same basic situation and he said that if the courts decide for me to open up, I'll open up; but until then, I can't accommodate any Negroes. And at that time, he gave me my money back and I left the hotel.

Mr. Barrett: No further questions.

Cross examination.

By Mr. Rolleston:

Q. Mr. Sampson, were you treated in a polite, courteous manner when you were there?
[fol. 54] A. Yes.
Q. When you got there, you talked to two men who were in red coats, did you not, who were on the front desk?

A. No—one of them had on a red coat. The other one did not. The light—the dark skinned fellow had on a red coat.

Q. And when I got there, I asked you your name and address, did I not?

A. That's correct.

Q. And what did you tell me?

A. I told you my name was Albert Richard Sampson.

Q. Where did you say you were from?

A. I was from Massachusetts.

Q. But you are from Atlanta?

A. No, I'm from Massachusetts.

Q. Well, where do you live in Atlanta?

A. I live at 339 Holly Street. See, I'm a—I was a student here in Atlanta. Because of financial difficulties, I'm not able to return to school. But my permanent address has always been in Massachusetts.

Q. You were born and raised in Massachusetts?

A. Born and raised, and I maintain my permanent address there. My voter registration is in Massachusetts.

Q. But you are now living in Atlanta?

A. I reside here in Atlanta.

[fol. 55] Q. Was it not also explained to you by myself that we had two policies, Number 1, that as a general rule we took no people of any kind or class who lived in Atlanta; and the other policy which you were explained, that we would not take members of the Negro race until this suit was disposed of?

A. You—your latter statement is correct; but your former statement isn't.

Q. You don't remember me telling you—

A. No.

Q. —that we didn't take people from Atlanta?

A. No, for the simple reason that I didn't tell you I was from Atlanta, because I came in from Charleston, and I was from Massachusetts.

Q. But you didn't tell me you were from Atlanta?

A. You didn't ask me where I was from.

Q. All right.

A. You asked me where I resided. I am from Massachusetts. If you want, I can show you my identification.

Q. I just wanted to know where you were from.
A. Thank you.

Mr. Rolleston: That's all.
Judge Tuttle: You may step down.
Mr. Barrett: Charles Wells.

[fol. 56] CHARLES EDWARD WELLS, having first been duly sworn and called as a witness in behalf of the defendants, testified as follows:

Direct examination.

By Mr. Barrett:

Q. Would you state your full name, please?
A. Charles Edward Wells, Senior.
Q. Where do you live, Reverend Wells?
A. I live at 1096 Main Street, Macon, Georgia.
Q. Where are you living at the present time? Where are you residing?
A. Presently I am residing at 641 Beckwith Street.
Q. In Atlanta?
A. That's correct.
Q. But Macon is your permanent address, permanent residence?
A. That's correct.
Q. Are you employed?
A. Yes, I am employed.
Q. By whom?
A. I'm employed by the United States Post Office.
Q. In what capacity?
A. I'm employed as a clerk.
Q. Are you also a minister?
A. That's correct.
Q. What education have you had, Reverend Wells?
A. I'm a graduate of West Virginia State College, re-
[fol. 57] ceiving a Bachelor of Arts Degree in Psychology and Sociology; presently pursuing a Bachelor of Divinity Degree.
Q. Reverend Wells, I'd like to call your attention to July 11th of this year and ask you if you went to the Heart of Atlanta Motel here in Atlanta on that day?

A. Yes, I did.

Q. Was anyone with you?

A. Yes, a minister friend of mine was with me.

Q. What is his name?

A. The Reverend John H. Gillison.

Q. About what time did you go to the motel?

A. Approximately one o'clock.

Q. What was your purpose in going there?

A. The purpose for going to the motel was to seek accommodations in the motel; a room.

Q. Did you go to the desk?

A. Yes, I did.

Q. Two of you together at that time?

A. That's correct.

Q. Would you just tell the Court what happened when you went to the desk, what you said and what others said while you were there?

A. Well, I went to the desk. I believe I approached the clerk first. And I asked him if he had any vacancies. He told me he would not be able to rent me a room. And I asked him why, and I believe he told me that it was the [fol. 58] policy of the motel not to rent rooms to Negroes until such time as a decision was made on the suit which was pending in the Federal Courts. I then asked to see the manager, and asked him the same question. He gave me the same answer. At that time, the, I assumed it was the owner, appeared and I asked him about the matter and he told me that the motel had adopted a policy not to serve Negro guests until such time—not to rent rooms to Negro guests until such time as a decision was made on the suit that was pending in the Federal Courts. I then asked him if he was telling me that he was failing to comply with the civil rights law that had been passed, and he told me that he wasn't—he told me that the only thing that he was saying is what he had said before, and he repeated that he wasn't renting guests—renting rooms to Negro guests until such time as a decision had been made on the suit that was pending in, in Federal Court.

Q. Have you since learned the name of the person that you spoke to on that occasion?

A. I believe his name is Mr. Morty Rolleston, or something of that nature.

Q. The plaintiff in this case who is seated here at the table?

A. That's correct.

Mr. Rolleston: If it please the Court, I would like to correct counsel. The plaintiff is a corporation.

Mr. Barrett: Yes. I beg your pardon. Yes.

[fol. 59] Judge Tuttle: You don't object to his assumption that you are president of the corporation, do you?

Mr. Rolleston: No, sir.

Judge Tuttle: I believe you allege that, don't you?

Mr. Rolleston: No, sir; I didn't allege that.

Judge Tuttle: You didn't allege that.

Mr. Barrett: No further questions.

Cross examination.

By Mr. Rolleston:

Q. Reverend Wells, when you came to the motel, who else was with you?

A. I believe I answered that question before. The Reverend John H. Gillison.

Q. And when I was talking to you two gentlemen, were you treated courteously and politely?

A. Yes, we were.

Q. Did I not ask each of you your names and addresses and write them down on a piece of paper?

A. Yes, you did.

Q. And you gave me your name and address as 1096 Main Street, Macon; and Reverend Gillison gave his address as 671 Beckwith Street, Atlanta?

A. That's correct.

Q. After I got your names and addresses, isn't it true I told Reverend Gillison that it was a policy of the motel [fol. 60] not to accept people in general of any race from Atlanta for previous reasons of policy of the motel, and that since he said he was from Atlanta, he would be turned down on that basis?

40

A. I don't believe that was the exact wording of your statement.

Q. What did you understand I said?

A. My understanding of what you said was that "as far as you are concerned, Reverend Gillison, it's the policy of the motel not to rent rooms to any resident of Atlanta." You didn't mention the word "race."

Q. No resident of Atlanta we would rent rooms to?

A. That's correct.

Q. And I turned him down on the basis of him being a resident?

A. That was your—that was the reason you stated.

Q. Now you were turned down on the basis that you mentioned, that we had a suit pending in Federal Court and we wanted to await the outcome of that suit?

A. That's the reason you gave.

Q. Now Reverend Wells, how long have you lived in Atlanta?

A. How long have I lived where?

Q. In Atlanta.

A. My home is Macon, Georgia. I've lived in Macon, Georgia, for seven years.

Q. I'll ask you another way. How long have you worked [fol. 61] with the United States Post Office Department in Atlanta?

A. I have been in the United States Post Office approximately fourteen months.

Q. While you are working for the Post Office Department, you stay in Atlanta, I presume?

A. Yes. I'm—

Q. You don't commute every day, do you?

A. I'm in transit from Macon to Atlanta. My home is there. My church is there. My family is there.

Q. I ask you again, do you commute every day from Macon to Atlanta?

A. No, I don't commute every day from Macon to Atlanta.

Q. As a matter of fact, the day you came to the motel, you went to work for the Post Office Department about 4:30 that afternoon, didn't you?

A. That's correct.

Q. And you went to work for the Post Office Department at—the next day on Sunday about 4:30, didn't you?

A. That is incorrect. I don't work on Sundays. I'm a minister.

Q. You don't work Sunday?

A. I'm a minister. I don't work Sundays.

Q. If your job requires you to work on Sunday, do you work?

A. My job does not require me to work on Sundays. I'm a minister.

[fol. 62] Q. But you worked Saturday three hours after you came to the motel, didn't you?

A. That's correct.

Mr. Rolleston: That's all.

Judge Tuttle: You may go down. Any other witnesses, Mr. Barrett?

Mr. Barrett: No further witnesses.

Judge Tuttle: You may proceed with your argument, Mr. Rolleston. I understood you to say you had no witnesses.

ARGUMENT ON BEHALF OF PLAINTIFF BY MR. ROLLESTON

Mr. Rolleston: No witnesses.

May it please the Court, of course we filed a brief in this case and I certainly don't intend to go through the whole brief, in accordance with the rules of Court. I would like to state briefly our position without even arguing it as far as their motion is concerned. We have brought this suit in court under the declaratory judgment act, and under that act we believe the provisions are broad enough to include all of the prayers in the petition because the act says that in the case of an actual controversy—and we submit there is a controversy because of nothing else, regardless of the testimony, because of our announced intention—within this jurisdiction except in the case of federal taxes any court of the United States upon the filing of appropriate pleadings may declare the rights and other legal relations of any [fol. 63] interested party seeking such declaration whether or not further relief is or could be sought. And the fact that they have brought in their motion to dismiss the question of the amount of damages we sought and limit of ten thousand dollars, should go to the Court of Claims, is one basis of their argument I'm sure, and they say we have no controversy.

Judge Tuttle: Let me—let me—

Mr. Rolleston: Yes, sir.

Judge Tuttle: —clarify one point. Of course, their motion to dismiss does go to the point of your including or undertaking to include a suit against the United States for damages. You don't, I believe, reach that point in your, in your brief that you filed.

Mr. Rolleston: No, sir; I didn't even touch on it.

Judge Tuttle: Well, it may help you to get a little—at least in my thinking on the matter it does appear to me that you cannot join a suit against the United States for damages on any theory with your suit for injunction because it's perfectly clear that even though your theory be right that your property is taken without just compensation, the Tucker Act does limit the District Court's jurisdiction to ten thousand dollars. You might file written briefs on that if you will, because I would hardly think it necessary to have further oral argument on that.

[fol. 64] Mr. Rolleston: Yes, sir. Of course, the other part of the act says that if the court takes jurisdiction and makes a decision in the declaratory judgment suit, they can render such other relief that is necessary. And that is the basis on which we are travelling. Of course, they have raised the point of sovereignty immunity. On that particular issue I'll simply state that if there has been a taking of property without just compensation, we don't have to ask permission of the United States Government to sue them because they are violating the Constitution, if they are.

Judge Tuttle: The Government is giving you that permission by giving you the right to sue in the Court of Claims if it exceeds ten thousand dollars.

Mr. Rolleston: As to the facts, Your Honor, before I get to the legal end of it—

Judge Tuttle: Yes.

Mr. Rolleston: —it is our position, and I'd like to state it very clearly, Number 1, whatever the order of this Court or any other court is, Federal, State or any other court, this plaintiff corporation will obey.

Number 2, our policy had been to exclude Negroes on the basis of race from this motel before the passage and before the Act became law. Our policy since that time, we announced that, our policy since that time, we have announced that we would not take guests, because we filed [fol. 65] a suit within two hours after the law was signed into law, and on the theory that even though we recognize that any law is valid and, until declared to the contrary, once the matter is in the breast of the court, it was our interpretation that we could stand on whatever the court decided, and there was an early hearing set, and that was what we were standing on.

As far as the testimony of these witnesses, both of them actually live in Atlanta, Georgia. They may maintain their domicile somewhere else, but they are living in Atlanta, Georgia.

Judge Tuttle: Of course, you didn't take the witness stand to testify that you don't accept Atlanta residents in your motel; so this fact issue that you asked them about, one of them denied and the other said yes, as to one man it applied.

Mr. Rolleston: Yes.

Judge Tuttle: Does this become an issue in the case?

Mr. Rolleston: No, sir; but I want to make the point that, and I, it's important to me as a lawyer, that in my opinion the plaintiff corporation hasn't as yet been confronted with a situation where it had to make the choice whether it was obeying the law at this time because these people wouldn't have qualified anyway. We don't take white people from Atlanta except under very unusual [fol. 66] circumstances.

Judge Tuttle: Now isn't it undisputed evidence, and this is all there is so far, that one of the witnesses, that is, the first witness, that he was not asked—stated by you anything about the Atlanta policy. That's his testimony.

Mr. Rolleston: His testimony; yes, sir.

Judge Tuttle: That's undisputed.

Mr. Rolleston: But the other witness said that was made to him. That that statement was made to him.

44

Judge Tuttle: Yes, he did.

Mr. Rolleston: So you've got two witnesses; at least one heard it.

Judge Tuttle: Not testifying about the same situation, though.

Mr. Rolleston: Well, all—the only point I want to make, Your Honor, is I think we have been complying with the law up until now and just haven't had to be in the embarrassing position to make a decision.

As to the law in the case, and this is the important thing, the constitutionality of the Civil Rights Act of 1964 is, is really the only and the basic issue that this Court really needs to decide.

Judge Tuttle: This is why I'm wondering if you really just don't state that and say that the facts do bring you [fol. 67] within it and therefore the legal question is all we have to decide. You don't go quite that far as I understand it.

Mr. Rolleston: I think—I had hoped our petition brought us within the actual controversy part of the declaratory judgment act and I would like to state that that is our position so there won't be any conflict in the record.

Judge Tuttle: All right.

Mr. Rolleston: Of course, this act was put forth by the executive part of our government, two administrations. It's been debated at least by a number of really good lawyers who represent us in Congress. It is now the act of Congress; the legislative branch has passed on it; and the real question now is whether or not those two departments of the government have acted wisely and in accordance with the Constitution in passing this law.

Judge Tuttle: We don't deal with whether it's—

Judge Morgan: Whether it's wise?

Judge Tuttle: —wise or not, do we?

Mr. Rolleston: Well, I will go further and say "accurate and just," and a judicial interpretation has got to be put on it by the third party, this judicial branch of the government. No, they—they have the question of determining whether it's wise or not. This Court, I'll submit, has [fol. 68] only one question to determine, and that is whether it's in accordance with the law. But the courts can best effect justice for all people by carefully preserving and observing our legal processes.

Really, there's only one issue that I'm—would rely on today, although I would like to discuss it briefly—discuss briefly all of the issues, and that is that where a United States Supreme Court decision on a subject has been handed down and still valid and unreversed, no court, State, local or any other, has the right under our Anglo-Saxon jurisprudence and judicial proceedings to reverse that other decision of the United States Supreme except the United States Supreme Court itself. That's really the basis. Of course, there's a lot of things been changed in the law. But when I was in law school, and every freshman law school man now, I think every member of the bar right now, and most every court, knows of that simple principle, that no court can reverse the United States Supreme Court except the Supreme Court itself, if, if it's a decision that is valid and fits the facts of the case before the court.

There's an old principle that we lawyers hear about, or adage anyway, "Beware of a man that comes into court with one case." I'm really here with one case.

Judge Tuttle: What you call a "white horse" case.

Mr. Rolleston: A "white horse" case. Whatever you want to call it. But I'm riding this "white horse," and that's [fol. 69] the civil rights case decided 109 U.S. Page 3 in 1883 involving the Civil Rights Act of 1875. I submit that this Court, regardless of how it will decide the constitutionality of the present law, is bound by that case.

Judge Tuttle: I think I should make it plain, when I said "white horse" case, of course lawyers know what I meant by it. The law students speak of a "white horse" case as a case that fits the facts and the law precisely.

Mr. Rolleston: Yes, sir. Yes, sir. You don't come in on a black horse, as the fellow said, on the front or back of it; you come in on a whole "white horse."

And this Court can't presume either, I submit, that the United States Supreme Court will reverse itself. That's up to them, whatever they want to do about it.

Now our act, if I may read just one paragraph of that previous act, previous Act of 1875 had only two sections and the second section, the penal section was about, if—if it had been passed today it would really be a subject of controversy because it was a strong penal section. But the first section of the act is almost verbatim, the hundred some-odd years apart, to the act that was passed in the present Congress. And it reads that "all persons within the jurisdiction of the United States shall be entitled to the full and equal enjoyment of accommodations, advantages, [fol. 70] facilities and privileges of inns, public conveyances on land or water, theatres and other places of public amusement subject only to the conditions and limitations established by law and applicable alike to citizens of every race and color, regardless of any previous condition of servitude." And that's my one "white horse" case, because they have decided the same issue exactly which is presented by the Civil Rights Act of 1964.

Judge Tuttle: Now, of course, if you read that opinion carefully as I know you have, you'll find this language or something like this in it, "Neither party contends that this Act may be sustained by anything other than the Fourteenth Amendment to the Constitution," which of course means the court there stated that no one then contended that it could be sustained by the commerce clause. Now what has the Supreme Court of the United States done with the commerce clause since that time?

Mr. Rolleston: They have distorted it, may it please the Court.

Judge Tuttle: So that without doing violence to that decision, the court has now made it really inapplicable for anyone to argue that this Act, which is ostensibly placed, based on the commerce clause cannot be supported by the commerce clause rather than the Fourteenth Amendment.

Mr. Rolleston: Well, I have read the whole case, of [fol. 71] course, and I've cited a good portion of the decision in my brief,—

Judge Tuttle: You don't—

Mr. Rolleston: —but I—

Judge Tuttle: You don't recall that language?

Mr. Rolleston: Oh, yes; I recall the language referring to the commerce clause. As a matter of fact, the court in that part of the decision said, "We're not saying that it could not be decided on the commerce clause," but the decision held, the first part of it asked the question, "Has Congress constitutional power to make such a law?" And they made this statement, "Of course"—using the words "of course"—of course, this is a long time ago—"no one will contend that the power to pass it was contained in the Constitution before the adoption of the last three amendments"—meaning the Thirteenth, Fourteenth and Fifteenth Amendments. The commerce clause was in the Constitution and the Fifth Amendment was in the Constitution at that time.

Judge Tuttle: So the Court there did not pass on whether it could be sustained under the commerce clause. It said no one has contended it was supported under the commerce clause.

Mr. Rolleston: But here's the interesting part of the language which is the basis for what is said in the decision. "Such legislation cannot properly cover the whole domain [fol. 72] of rights appertaining to life, liberty and property, defining them and providing for their vindication. That would be to establish a code of municipal law regulative of all private rights between man and man in society. It would be to make Congress take the place of the State legislatures and to supersede them." And we say that this really is the basis of this, of this Act. But the Court is not responsible for the consequences of its judgment, as to what happens to what you decide. It's only responsible it seems to me to uphold our judicial processes.

Now the commerce clause which is now the basis of the present act is the interesting thing, because this is an innocuous and simple little clause and all it said was, in the third clause, it says, "Congress shall have the power to regulate commerce with foreign nations among the several states and with the Indian tribes." That's all it said, and on that one little sentence we are about to change the government of the United States. We have a Fifth Amendment in the Constitution which guarantees that no person shall be deprived of life, liberty or property without due process. We have a Thirteenth Amendment in the Constitution that says there will be no slavery or involuntary servitude. We have a Fourteenth Amendment in the Constitution that says no state shall pass a law abridging the equal rights of people of any color for any reason. And [fol. 73] yet, the Congress didn't rely on any of these amendments to the Constitution in passing this bill. It specifically relies on interstate commerce.

Judge Morgan: Don't you think a motel such as yours is in interstate commerce, Mr. Rolleston?

Mr. Rolleston: No, sir, I don't; and I'll proceed to say why. As a matter of fact, this bill—

Judge Morgan: Under the decisions of the Supreme Court?

Mr. Rolleston: Well, I've got three decisions in here that say to the contrary. This bill really, instead of being called the Civil Rights Act of 1964 should really have been called, named—and it's the biggest misnomer in history—The Extension of the Interstate Commerce Clause to eradicate State Legislatures. What commerce is now and what it was way back yonder are entirely different. But there are three cases cited in our brief. One involves taxicabs. One involves the Howard Johnson Restaurant. And one involves a bowling alley.

In the taxicab case, the facts were that people from out of the state—whether they were domiciled in Massachusetts and lived in Atlanta or not—people from out of the state came to the railroad station in Chicago, got off the train, got in a taxicab and either went to a hotel, office building or home. And the other part of the facts were the [fol. 74] very reverse, they started at their homes and office buildings and hotels, and went to the railroad station. And under the Anti-Trust Act which they were tried under, they held that the taxicab transporting that man to the railroad station or going vice versa, the taxicab company was not in interstate commerce. In the Howard—this was some time ago—but in the Howard Johnson Case, which was decided in the Fourth Circuit Court of Appeals, it's not the United States Supreme Court—and my theory, may it please the Court, as far as the controlling case on this issue in my first legal theory, of course, doesn't apply to interstate commerce or these other parts of my argument. But in the Howard Johnson case in 1959, they brought, a Negro attorney for the Internal Office—Internal Revenue Office brought a suit against Howard Johnson and said, "You serve—you sit here on an interstate highway; you serve guests who are travelling in interstate commerce; and therefore you are in interstate commerce." And they held that the Howard Johnson Restaurant was not in interstate commerce.

Judge Tuttle: Of course, there's no congressional act there being construed by the court.

Mr. Rolleston: No, sir; but Judge asked me did I think we were in interstate commerce. We've got other decisions on similar facts—

Judge Morgan: What I based it on, isn't there a number [fol. 75] of NLRB cases that have gone to the courts holding that hotels or motels except those residential motels were under the, subject to the NLRB wage and hour—

Mr. Rolleston: I don't remember whether they have gone to the Supreme Court or not, Judge Morgan. Of course, you can find a case on any subject.

Judge Morgan: One went from the circuit court of appeals I believe to the Supreme Court, and certiorari, it was sent back to the court of appeals,—

Mr. Rolleston: Yes, sir.

Judge Morgan: —and since that time it's been accepted, hadn't it?

Mr. Rolleston: I'm sure you can find cases in the circuit court and in the Supreme Court to the contrary of these cases. There's no question about it. But here are these cases, too.

Judge Morgan: All right. You go ahead. I didn't mean—

Mr. Rolleston: Then there's a case decided in 1963 in the State of New York by the Supreme Court of New York regarding a bowling alley. And in that case the bowling alley drew trade from interstate commerce; they advertised in interstate commerce, which they stipulated in the facts as we have; and they received equipment in interstate commerce. And they held that just because interstate travellers went to that bowling alley, the bowling alley was not [fol. 76] in interstate commerce. And the Howard Johnson Restaurant was not in interstate commerce. And the hotels that the people went to by taxicabs was not, could not be in my opinion in interstate commerce, if the man in the taxicab had ceased to be in interstate commerce when he got in the taxicabs. That's the substance of it. But the trouble about this thing, and the reason I'm talking about interstate commerce so much is that what is the final conclusion if you are adopting the theory that Congress has now put on the word "commerce among the states?"

I will give you my example again. Suppose a man comes to Atlanta by airplane. That's the usual means of transportation now. He catches a cab into Atlanta; goes to the First National Bank and arranges for a construction loan. He goes to a local real estate company and signs a contract to buy a piece of land to build a building for his company on. The right usual thing happening today. He goes to a local contractor that doesn't ever step out of Fulton County hardly and makes a contract to build the building. He goes to the Commerce Club down the street and eats lunch. He is entertained at the Driving Club. At night he goes to the Wits End, and finally he gets to the Heart of Atlanta Motel. Do you mean to tell me that every one of those local businesses, except the First National Bank of Atlanta, every one of those local businesses has now become in inter-
[fol. 77] state commerce because of the stretching of the word "commerce among the states?" I call it interstate commerce by infection, because it's just like a malaria mosquito jumping from one man to the next one; every victim is infected. And the logical conclusion—

Judge Tuttle: I think the malaria mosquito has one bite and then he dies.

Mr. Rolleston: I wish this man had just one bite. He would have bitten somebody long before he got to me. But in this case, if you drag that out to its conclusion, that because he is a man in interstate commerce, a traveller, if you can say the restaurant is in interstate commerce and the bowling alley and the taxicab and our motel, you can take every corner drugstore and put him in interstate commerce. You can take every lawyer who buys a pencil to run his business with, and he can't run his business without one; you can take every doctor who buys an instrument from Connecticut. You can take anybody who buys anything from another part of the country. That's what they are trying to do with "interstate commerce." And they'll put them all in interstate commerce. And the legislature might as well go home and forget about reapportionment and don't ever come back because whatever they pass would be of no value and no good, if Congress has appropriated that field of legislation. As long as they don't, they haven't. But why [fol. 78] would you expect Congress not to? Has any government in our history ever had power to exert over legal situations and abandoned that power and given it up? If they ever got it, they keep on taking more.

Judge Tuttle: Since you asked that question, let me answer it for you. Congress in the Fair Labor Standards Act expressly saved out of the operation of the Fair Labor Standards Act retail establishments, local retail establishments, which is of course complete congressional restraint. The large retail establishments undoubtedly under decisions of the Supreme Court could be held by Congress to be within the stream of interstate commerce. But they have kept out of that by exempting local retail establishments.

Mr. Rolleston: Well, there's another case of it, Your Honor. Congress has kindly kept the hotel and restaurant industry out of the wage and hour law too, so far. But every time Congress meets—

Judge Tuttle: Not Congress, but the Labor Board.

Mr. Rolleston: Well, I was going to say every time Congress gets—every time Congress meets, Your Honor, they have a law, and have one pending right now, to put these other industries under wage and hour. And the only reason we are not there now, frankly, is that they bring in a great big act that covers everybody, and whoever puts up the biggest opposition they drop them out one time, and pass [fol. 79] the law. And next year, they've only got those two to work on and they get one of them; and then the next year, they get the last one, and finally they've got all of them, in interstate commerce, and under the wage and hour law, and under the Sherman Anti-Trust Law, and under NLRB; and then they've got everything that used to be private rights. This is really the gravamen of the case. This is the guts of it. This is really the reason we brought the lawsuit. We could get along with Negro guests. They would hurt our business as we've alleged, and it's true. We could get along with them. But the next step after this act, there may just be one more step, that's taking over all legislation by Congress, so setting up the stage for a dictatorship in this country. I'm telling you, this extension of the commerce act to every man, woman and child in this room and in the United States, business and personal affairs, is not authorized by the Constitution.

The Fifth Amendment we've claimed is violated also. The Fifth Amendment says you can't take a man's liberty or property without due process; and you can't take it, his property without just compensation. Have they taken our liberty at the Heart of Atlanta Motel? We used to could say who could come there and who could not come there and we would turn them away for whatever reason we wanted. We don't have that liberty under the prohibitions of this [fol. 80] act if the act is good. We say that the taking of our liberty has been done by an act of Congress. It's the same liberty any other local individual has to run his business.

Judge Tuttle: Does the innkeeper traditionally have that same privilege?

Mr. Rolleston: Under, Your Honor, under the common law, the innkeeper did not have it, that privilege. But where the common law has been changed by statute—

Judge Tuttle: He had to take them all, did he not?

Mr. Rolleston: That's right. Under the common law he had to take everyone. But where the common law, as the Court know, prevails unless changed by statute. In Georgia the statute has changed the common law. In the 52nd—Chapter 52-101 defines what an inn is, and they say, "An inn includes all taverns, hotels" and so forth, and then the next chapter, it says, "Persons entertaining only a few individuals are not"—"Persons entertaining only a few individuals, or simply for the accommodation of travellers" —and the stipulation of facts in this case are that we take transient guests—"are not innkeepers, but depositaries for hire, bound to ordinary diligence." And then in another code section, Chapter 52-3 under "Tourist Courts" they define, it says, "This Chapter shall not apply to hotels and inns within the definition of" the previous chapter, and that [fol. 81] "Every person, firm or corporation engaged in the business of operating outside the corporate limits of any city or town in this State a tourist court, cabin, tourist home, roadhouse, public dancehall or other similar establishment by whatever name called, where travellers and transient guests are entertained are not innkeepers." And they have another chapter, which says that a—52-401, which says that a tourist court shall include among other things motor hotels. And then they have a penal section in this chapter which says that motor hotels, for failing to do so and so about health are subject to penal things. All through this whole chapter motels and motor hotels are treated differently; they have to get a different license; there are different penal sections; and they are taken out of the definition of the innkeeper because the very act says so.

As to the Fifth Amendment, not only has our liberty been taken we claim, but part of our property rights. Any proprietary interest in the ownership of private property if interfered with where the owner can thereafter not exercise their right, if it is the result of a taking by a government, it is a taking of property under the law. The Fifth Amendment says property cannot be taken without due process. Certainly this Circuit Court, Fifth Circuit Court of Appeals has defined the due process just recently in the Hornsby Case this year and set up, as the Court is very [fol. 82] familiar with, that there must be a responsible hearing, based on evidence taken at a hearing where notice is given, witnesses there and witnesses to be cross examined, and only based on the evidence adduced at the trial. Has there been a hearing on the taking of our property, if there has been a taking?

Judge Tuttle: Well, you are talking about procedural due process and of course the passage by Congress of a constitutional law is due process. You are speaking of procedural due process in an administrative procedure, which is quite a different thing. You would not—

Mr. Rolleston: Your Honor,—

Judge Tuttle: You would not argue against the proposition that a statute which is constitutional complies with due process, substantive due process.

Mr. Rolleston: That is true. But I would say that a statute could be unconstitutional because it violates the

Fifth Amendment by taking private property without procedural due process. There's no procedural due process set up in the statute, and therefore it's void.

The other part of the statute says that property shall not be taken without just compensation. Of course, there's no compensation set up in the statute for the taking, if there is a taking. And I cite recent cases to the Court in the decisions, one of them from the—they are not Supreme Court cases, but in 1961 the Supreme Court of the State [fol. 83] of Washington, way out on the West Coast, held "this constitutional right of the individual not to be dominated as a private affair is predicated upon the theory that the greatest good for the greatest number can be best achieved by permitting the individual to choose his own course of action, conforming of course to the reciprocal rights of others." And in the other case, decided in 1959 in Washington, in the Cinderella Case, no truer words were ever spoken than these in that case when it says, "In dealings between men, both cannot be free unless each acts voluntarily; otherwise, one is subjugated to the will of the other.

As to the Thirteenth Amendment which we have attacked by amendment, the Thirteenth Amendment provided there be no slavery and no involuntary servitude. In our case, how can we say that we are subject to involuntary servitude? We say that we had the right to run the motel like we wanted to before the act was passed. We now have the right to run the motel like the Government says. Sure, we have the alternative of quitting and giving up a four million dollar business; but can that be required of a business by law? In the Hodges versus United States in 1906, some time ago, they held concerning the Thirteenth Amendment that slavery and involuntary servitude is denounced by the Thirteenth Amendment, meaning a condition of enforcement of compulsory service one to another. And while [fol. 84] the cause in citing that amendment was the emancipation of the colored race, it reaches every individual and every race.

In this Fifth Circuit Court of Appeals in 1944 in the Heflin Case, they say, Well, if you got paid for it, that's all right; that takes it out of the Thirteenth Amendment.

The case held whether the parent was paid little or nothing is not the question. It is not uncompensated service but involuntary servitude which is prohibited by the Thirteenth Amendment. Compensation for service may cause consent, but unless it does, unless it does, it is no justification for forced labor.

And the United States Supreme Court has held it requires no argument to show that the right to work for a living is, in the common occupation of the community, is the very essence of the personal freedom and opportunity that it was the purpose of the Fourteenth Amendment to secure.

May it please the Court, our legal position is that there has been a case decided which is controlling on facts that are in this case and on a law which is almost exactly the same, and that the Court is bound in following our legal procedures to follow it and throw this case to the United States Supreme Court to do what they may. But at this stage of the game, it ought to go up there. And we claim, of course, that it violates the Fifth Amendment by the taking [fol. 85] of property and liberty without due process of law and without compensation; violates the Thirteenth Amendment involving involuntary servitude.

I would like to say one other thing, may it please the Court. The name of Kennedy will be, go down in history of all times regarding civil rights.

Judge Tuttle: Mr. Rolleston,—

Mr. Rolleston: John F. Kennedy—

Judge Tuttle: —is this proper argument?

Mr. Rolleston: Yes, sir; I think so. Just—

Judge Tuttle: We are not disposed to cut you off, but actually, what—what's proper about it?

Mr. Rolleston: Well, sometimes in the affairs of men it takes more than one individual to express a thing, and I want to quote a man. Mr. Robert Kennedy, the defendant in this case, wrote in the prefaced word to the Memorial Edition of the PROFILES IN COURAGE that the one thing that President Kennedy admired was courage. It took courage to pass this law. It took a little courage maybe to file a suit against the Federal Government. And I know this Court will follow the motto over the Supreme Court of Georgia's bench which says in Latin, when translated, "Let justice be done though the heavens may fall." And I know this Court, if it agrees with our legal interpretation will do that in spite of the consequences which could arise out of [fol. 86] such a decision. And I thank you.

ARGUMENT ON BEHALF OF DEFENDANT BY MR. MARSHALL

Judge Tuttle: Mr. Marshall.

Mr. Marshall: May it please the Court, the United States has prepared a memorandum on the constitutional—

Judge Tuttle: I think you might almost call it a brief without exaggerating.

Mr. Marshall: Memorandum of points and cases. I've given a copy to Mr. Rolleston. We captioned the brief in the case involving Pickrick Restaurant as well as in this case for the sake of convenience.

Clerk: Have you got an extra copy, sir?

Mr. Marshall: Yes, sir. I think I can be relatively brief about this, may it please the Court.

The first point made by Mr. Rolleston turns on the civil rights cases which involve the constitutionality of a bill passed in 1875. As you mentioned, Judge Tuttle, it shows on the face of those cases that they were not deciding any question about the power of Congress to pass a law under the commerce clause. In addition to the language which you referred to, I would like to call the Court's attention to the later case of Butts against Merchant and Miners Transportation Company, which is 230 U.S. 126. It involved a private suit for damages under the 1875 Act, and it was based—argued that, that the act was unconstitutional under the commerce clause. The Supreme Court said in that case [fol. 87] that the civil rights act had not been passed under the commerce clause. The question of the constitutional validity of those sections was passed on only under the Fourteenth Amendment, and that it was held, they say, that the act received no support from the power of Congress to regulate interstate commerce because as is shown by the preamble and by their terms, they were not enacted in the exertion of that power. That case is cited in the brief. There are a number of leading—

Judge Tuttle: Do you deduce from that, the statement by the Supreme Court that an act may or may not be found valid by it according to the theory or basis on which Congress sees fit to enact it?

Mr. Marshall: Well, Your Honor, I think under the commerce clause, Congress has to be regulating interstate commerce.

Judge Tuttle: Because that's the power that the Constitution gives to Congress, to regulate commerce.

Mr. Marshall. To regulate; that's right.

Judge Tuttle: Unless the Congress is actually seeking to regulate commerce, then it can't be said that the act would fit under that commerce clause.

Mr. Marshall: That's right. I think that's what the court meant, that Congress wasn't seeking to do that; therefore, the act couldn't be sustained under whatever power Congress had in attempting to do that. The 1875 acts were [fol. 88] based solely on the Fourteenth Amendment and to some extent on the Thirteenth and Fifteenth Amendments.

Judge Morgan: This civil rights act for this year is based on the commerce clause.

Mr. Marshall: There are provisions of it, Judge Morgan, which are not involved in this case, that are based on the Fourteenth Amendment.

Judge Morgan: Well, I was actually referring to those provisions,—

Judge Tuttle: Title II.

Judge Morgan: —public accommodations.

Mr. Marshall: No, not Title II. There are parts—

Judge Tuttle: Or both.

Mr. Marshall: —that are based on the Fourteenth Amendment. If you look at 201-B of the Act, you'll see that it says each of the following establishments which serves the public, if its operations affect commerce or if the discrimination or segregation by it is supported by State action, that was an exercise of power under the Fourteenth Amendment in terms of the sit-in cases where the Supreme Court has held that if the State requires segregation by private establishments,—

Judge Tuttle: I don't mean—I don't understand you to say that any part of it is not, is not based on the commerce clause, but it is also in certain respects sought to be based [fol. 89] on the Fourteenth Amendment. Is that what—

Mr. Marshall: That's right, Judge Tuttle. But that's a very limited application. It's an application which is really designed to eliminate state compulsory segregation. The cases which I would refer the Court to that held generally on the power of the Congress under the commerce clause are four. There are others that are cited in our brief, but I think that four cases, starting in 1936, really set the bounds of the power of Congress to regulate commerce. One is the Jones and Laughlin Steel Corporation Case, 301 U.S. 1, decided in 1936 upholding the Wagner Act which in many ways had similarities to this piece of legislation in the sense that it was intended to deal with a national problem that had been marked by a good deal of emotion and controversy and even violence in the streets. The court said in that case that to regulate, in the course of regulation of commerce the Congress was not limited just to the regulation of institutions which are in the stream of commerce or which themselves move in commerce, like railroads and buses, and that kind of thing, but that it can regulate and pass legislation to eliminate burdens and obstructions due to injurious actions springing from other sources. That the Wagner Act of course regulated the relationships between employers and their employees within the plants where the plants, the operations of the plants affected com- [fol. 90] merce. And that, as you noted, Judge Morgan, has been recently in many cases applied to hotels, retail stores and other establishments that are local in the same sense that the Heart of Atlanta Motel is local.

Judge Tuttle: The Jones-Laughlin Case was the first decision by the Supreme Court that went so far as to hold that what had theretofore been considered purely local, like manufacturing, mining and farming and the like, might still be under congressional regulation. Is that—

Mr. Marshall: Well, Judge Tuttle, you say the first case. I think that the history of the commerce clause goes back to Gibbons against Ogden. I think that the decision in Jones and Laughlin and the following ones after that were in the keeping of the spirit and the view of congressional power which goes back to Justice Marshall's opinion in Gibbons against Ogden. There was a case in 1922 involving the

Packers and Stockyards Act which related to regulation of the stockyards in Chicago, and of course, that was local in a sense that it all happened in Chicago. The hogs came in and meat went out. But what was regulated was local activity.

There are three cases which held also that Congress also has the power to regulate intrastate activity if that is necessary to complete regulation of interstate commerce. Those are United States against Rock Royal Corporation, 307 U.S. 533. The United States against Darby, 312 U.S. 100, [fol. 91] involving the Fair Labor Standards Act. And Wickard against Filburn, involving the Agricultural Adjustment Act. The last case, if you will recall, involved the regulation of a farmer who grew wheat on his own farm for consumption on his own farm, and the Supreme Court held that Congress had the power to reach that operation because of its involvement with the problem of wheat surpluses generally.

Judge Morgan: Wasn't it the old Schecter Case, wasn't that the Schecter Case and the court has been more or less distinguishing or, as you say, whittling at the doctrine laid down in 1935 or '36 in the Schecter Case since that time?

Mr. Marshall: I would say, Judge Morgan,—

Judge Tuttle: The Wickard Case—

Mr. Marshall: Wickard against Filburn. Also the Jones and Laughlin Case narrowed the Schecter Case very much; and there was a milk case I think involving Wrightwood Dairy, which referred to the Schecter Case and said something to the effect that its continuing validity was in doubt.

Judge Tuttle: The Schecter Case—

Mr. Marshall: I would say the Schecter Case is effectively overruled.

Judge Tuttle: I went—

Mr. Marshall: And I think also—

[fol. 92] Judge Tuttle: It went largely as I recall it on the Supreme Court's decision that Congress was illegally giving legislative power to, to an administrative board.

Mr. Marshall: That's right, Judge Tuttle. It held that the—

Judge Tuttle: But in Butler—

Mr. Marshall: That the NIRA was an unlawful delegation of legislative power, which is also a doctrine which has been abandoned.

Judge Tuttle: I think every student recognizes that about 1936 in January after the Butler Case where they knocked out the Agricultural Adjustment Act, there was really a complete turn-around from that point on, the erosion if you would like to speak of it that way, was very effectively commenced. And this Jones-Laughlin Case was the first important decision after the United States lost the Butler Case.

Mr. Marshall: That's right, Judge Tuttle. I believe with the exception of the Jones and Laughlin Case, the other cases that I referred to as basic decisions, the Darby Case, the Rock Royal Case and Wickard and—Wickard against Filburn were unanimous. And of course in recent years since then there have been a number of decisions under the National Labor Relations Act and the Labor-Management Relations Act which have been unanimous; and—and mostly per curiam, upholding exertions of [fol. 93] jurisdiction by the National Labor Relations Board over what are effectively local businesses because what happens to these local businesses affects the interstate commerce.

Judge Morgan: The case I was referring to was the—I believe it was the Floridian Case. I don't know whether that went to the Supreme Court, but it was in regard to the Fair Labor Standards Act, and then went up, is my recollection.

Mr. Marshall: Is that case cited in your opinion?

Judge Morgan: I don't believe it's cited in any of the briefs. I read it recently.

Mr. Marshall: These cases hold that Congress has the power to regulate commerce not only in the sense that they can regulate things that move in interstate commerce generally, but that they can pass legislation that deals with problems that affect interstate commerce. Our brief sets forth four—and there may be more—but it sets forth four ways in which the problem dealt with in Title II could reasonably be considered by Congress to have affected interstate commerce so that it required congressional action. And of course, as you noted, Judge Tuttle, it is not for this Court to decide whether Congress was wise in making that decision. It's a question of whether it had the power to make that decision.

Judge Hooper: Mr. Marshall, to what extent do the courts have the right to say when Congress has said a [fol. 94] certain act does affect commerce, what right do the courts have or do not have to say whether that factual assumption is correct? Now in the Jones and Laughlin Case, the court said this, among other things: Undoubtedly the scope of this power must be considered in the light of our dual system of government and may not be extended so as to embrace effects upon interstate commerce so indirect and remote that to embrace them in view of our complex society would effectually obliterate the distinction between what is national and what is local and create a completely centralized government.

Now what I'm interested in is whether under the Civil Rights Act, Congress says that a certain thing does affect commerce, is that conclusive on the court or is it, is it not?

Mr. Marshall: Judge Hooper, I do not think that any constitutional opinion of Congress is conclusive on the court. It's the responsibility of the courts to repass on the constitutionality of statutes the Congress thinks are constitutional. But I think that the findings of Congress in a matter like this are entitled to very very great weight, and that at least—

Judge Tuttle: Substantial fact findings.

Mr. Marshall: That's right, Judge Tuttle. It is fact findings, and they are based on the record and hearings. The matter was under consideration by Congress for over [fol. 95] a year. It was debated at great length. It is an issue and a problem that involves great emotions. There are great political problems with it. And all of that went into the determination by the Congress to deal with it, Judge Hooper. The decision of Congress on that was made by men that included very conservative men as well as very liberal men. And I think that that kind of a decision is entitled to great weight and has been given great weight by the Supreme Court except for a very brief period really extending maybe ten years from around 1925 to 1935.

Judge Hooper: Well, you see, in the instant case it's stipulated that the Heart of Atlanta, 75% of its business is transient, which is right substantial. But suppose you later have a case where it's almost negligible, the number of people who are in commerce who go there is almost negligible. In that type of case—I was just thinking about the precedent of this case—in that kind of a case, where would the courts draw a line between what is substantial and what is not substantial?

Mr. Marshall: Judge Hooper, the—in dealing with a hotel, which this case does, the Act does not require the court to draw that. Congress has made that determination. It defines the hotels covered by that Act in Section 201-B-1 and 201-C Subsection 1. And it includes all inns, hotels, motels or other establishments which provide lodgings to [fol. 96] transient guests. All of them. It is not a question substantially under the Act. Now the question is, can Congress do that? Can Congress make that factual determination that in order to deal with the problem they have to regulate all hotels,—

Judge Hooper: Sir, do not all hotels furnish lodgings to transient guests?

Mr. Marshall: I would think so, Judge Hooper, or virtually all of them.

Judge Tuttle: Do you have ready reference to any Supreme Court Case that I think states this proposition, something along these lines, that when a determination is made by Congress on—of this nature, the courts are required to support it if there's any reasonable relation to the determination by Congress to the problem that it seeks to legislate on?

Mr. Marshall: I think that's right, Judge Tuttle. I think that—

Judge Tuttle: I think that's the principle. I don't have the case.

Mr. Marshall: I think the principle goes gack to Gibbons against Ogden. I think—

Judge Tuttle: So that what—

Mr. Marshall: I think that language can be found in Gibbons against Ogden.

Judge Tuttle: So that what we are required to do is [fol. 97] to determine whether there was any reasonable basis for Congress to ascertain that the hotel industry reasonably affects interstate commerce.

Mr. Marshall: Yes. And this problem I think, Judge Tuttle, not only the hotel industry, but this problem within the hotel industry of racial discrimination,—

Judge Tuttle: Yes.

Mr. Marshall: —could Congress reasonably have made that determination. I think that's the question.

Judge Tuttle: That this would be and have an adverse effect on interstate commerce.

Mr. Marshall: That's right. In the Darby Case, Judge Hooper—no, I'm sorry. It's in Wickard against Filburn, where there is no question but that the activities of the farmer who was regulated, that particular farmer, were intrastate. He grew wheat on his own farm for consumption on his own farm. He grew more wheat than the quota that was allowed him under the Agricultural Adjustment Act. The question was whether Congress had the power to regulate that farmer, that particular farmer and the court held unanimously that he did—that Congress did. And among other things, it said, the court pointed out, citing Gibbons against Ogden, that effective restraints on the exercise of this power must proceed from political rather than from judicial process. I think our system works that way. If Congress is arbitrary and unreasonable [fol. 98] and the court can make that determination that there is an arbitrary or unreasonable relationship between what Congress was trying to do and some, some commercial problem affecting interstate commerce, then I think it would be the court's duty to strike down the act. But unless it can make that determination, I think it's up to Congress to—

Judge Hooper: You are saying that it is not necessary under this statute as to hotels to show that they take any transients moving in commerce, in interstate commerce.

Mr. Marshall: It has to be shown they take transients, Judge Hooper.

Judge Hooper: Transients.

Mr. Marshall: But it does not have to be shown that the transients in a particular case moved in interstate commerce.

Judge Hooper: Oh, no. We are not talking about the same thing. I realize that, but—

Mr. Marshall: But transients, Judge Hooper,—

Judge Tuttle: Because the definition in this act—

Mr. Marshall: In this act.

Judge Tuttle: —is interstate commerce.

Mr. Marshall: In this act.

Judge Hooper: Any number, any amount of transients.

Mr. Marshall: Yes, that's right.

[fol. 99] Judge Hooper: Transients, that means people who are moving in interstate commerce.

Mr. Marshall: No, Judge Hooper. Not necessarily. It means people that are moving, it means that the hotel is, the hotel caters to transients. That is, it isn't a residential hotel. The people that stay there don't live there as residents. It takes in people that usually come from some other place, but the some other place does not under the Act, Judge Hooper, have to be shown to have been another state.

Now as I said, these cases, the Darby Case, the Rock Royal Case, and Wickard against Filburn expressly hold that Congress has the power to reach some activities that are completely intrastate if they have to do that in order to control a problem, deal with a problem that they properly can deal with under the commerce clause. And those holdings of those cases in turn go back to the Shreveport Rate Cases in 1914 where the question of the validity of an order of the Interstate Commerce Commission over purely intrastate rates in Texas was involved. And that was upheld by the Supreme Court in the Rate Cases in 1914. And these cases carry that on, Judge Hooper.

Our brief sets forth and suggests four ways in which Congress could reasonably have made a determination that this was a commercial problem that they should deal with under their power to regulate interstate commerce. One is [fol. 100] simply the burden on Negro travellers. This is a problem that Congress has dealt with before, dealt with it in the Interstate Commerce Act and dealt with it in the Federal Aviation Act. And those have been upheld unanimously. This Court upheld the, the validity of Interstate Commerce Commission rules that were to deal just with that problem in restaurants in bus stations. The problem of the discrimination against Negro travellers moving through the country. So that is one thing by itself that I think Congress had the legitimate, reasonable power to deal with and to determine that in order to deal with that they had to deal with all hotels.

Judge Tuttle: Let's say then, do you take the position then on that point that if it is, if we find that Congress could have determined that the mere interference with the travel of Negroes by reason of these restrictions, it would be sufficient to sustain the Act on that ground?

Mr. Marshall: I think so, Judge Tuttle.

Judge Tuttle: And that is because the courts have held, including this court, or three-judge court I guess, it's a local—

Judge Morgan: Same court.

Judge Tuttle: It's a local district court,—

Mr. Marshall: I think it was this court.

Judge Morgan: Same court.

Mr. Marshall: I think it's the same court.

[fol. 101] Judge Tuttle: That the, that the interstate commerce rule prohibiting discrimination between white and Negro passengers in a bus station, and including the restaurant, would in no—would be justified—

Mr. Marshall: That's right.

Judge Tuttle: —because that would be a burden on interstate commerce.

Mr. Marshall: Judge Tuttle, you will recall those rules weren't limited to interstate travellers.

Judge Tuttle: That's right.

Mr. Marshall: In fact, the court had that, the Fifth Circuit had that up in Baldwin against Morgan involving the Birmingham—

Judge Tuttle: Involving the Birmingham railroad station.

Mr. Marshall: It applied to anyone that comes into the bus station, and it was reasonable for Congress to feel that that was the way they had to deal with bus stations in order to deal with the problem of discrimination against Negro travellers.

Judge Morgan: Of course, in that—in those cases we dealt with the franchise—I mean the bus companies and so forth had a franchise. I know the principle was intrastate affected interstate. I think that's the way the State of Georgia brought the petition, as I recall.

Mr. Marshall: That's right, Judge Morgan. I mean this [fol. 102] is different, but this goes further; but the type of regulation by Congress going back to 1887 is exactly the same. It was the prohibiting of discrimination in local restaurants because the local restaurants were connected with an interstate bus system and therefore served at least some interstate travellers.

Judge Morgan: That's right.

Mr. Marshall: Another reason that Congress couldn't —could choose to deal with this under its interstate power, interstate commerce power is to move artificial, remove artificial restrictions on markets. And it has regulated essentially local businesses for that reason before. One that occurred to me is in the, under the antitrust laws. There have been a number of cases involving movie theatres and the question of movie threatres allocating runs between themselves and fixing admission prices on tickets. Now that's a, an artificial restriction on who can see a movie when in the local theatre. The movie goes—moves through interstate commerce. So that these restrictions in hotels and in this case in restaurants, and in theatres, is something which restricts the market for goods that move in interstate commerce. The food that goes into a restaurant, if the market is limited to white, that restricts the market artificially. Same thing with a film that moves in interstate commerce. If it is shown in the theatres and Negroes are [fol. 103] not permitted in the theatre, that is an artificial restriction on the market for that commodity that moved in interstate commerce. As I say, under the anti-trust laws, under the Federal Trade Commission Act, Congress has dealt, regulated with this sort of artificial restriction on markets. In this case, in terms of race, but it's the power of Congress to deal with it.

Another one which I think is analogous as I said before to the Wagner Act is to deal with the causes of disputes that affect interstate commerce. The hearings before the Commerce Committee of the Senate included a great deal of material on the economic effect of disputes over discrimination in places of public accommodations. The City of Birmingham, even here in Atlanta, in many many cities while Congress was considering this, there were economic effects on the business generally in those cities developing from the disputes over this. And Congress chose to deal with that through law, through regulation in the same way that it chose to deal with labor disputes under the Wagner Act in the Thirties.

And finally, and it's sort of a corollary point, I think that these disputes and the discrimination generally could reasonably be decided by Congress to have affected arbitrarily in some adverse system against Southern States particularly, the allocation of resources within the country, the decision of where to put industrial plants, the decision [fol. 104] of where to locate hotels, that kind of decision which affects the commerce of the United States very deeply and particularly in some of the states in the United States; it's also a problem I think Congress felt it had to deal with and reasonably felt that it should deal with.

There are a couple of specific cases I wanted to call the Court's attention to by the Supreme Court on this question of regulating local business. One is the Sullivan Case, 332 U.S. 689. That held a drugstore violated the Food, Drug and Cosmetics Act by taking pills out of one box and putting them into other boxes, inside the store, and then selling these other boxes without the labels, properly. That was a very local operation. He bought the pills, and they stopped in the store, and they were reboxed in the store and then they were sold, all in the store. And that—

Judge Tuttle: The Food and Drug Act is entirely dependent upon the commerce clause, isn't it?

Mr. Marshall: Yes, it is, Judge Tuttle. I think in one of these cases, I believe it's in the Darby Case, that—that the courts, court said that Congress may exercise the commerce power to prevent injuries to the public health, morals or welfare. That the fact that they are doing something else, that they are advancing the cause of justice or meeting a [fol. 105] problem of health, morality or public welfare by regulating commerce doesn't make the regulation invalid.

Judge Hooper: Well, has the Supreme Court said on several occasions that the general welfare clause is a matter of state law and not the federal law; that the welfare clause has to be construed in the light of the specific powers which are given to Congress?

Mr. Marshall: Well, Judge Hooper, I did not intend to put any emphasis on the separate power of Congress under the general welfare clause. I said that in regulating commerce, in regulating commerce and in their exercise of that power, their purpose—this is what they said in Darby—could include such purposes as to promote public health, promote—

Judge Hooper: Oh, surely.

Mr. Marshall: —public morals or promote public welfare.

Judge Hooper: Right.

Mr. Marshall: And the fact is that a great deal of legislation passed under the commerce clause does that. The Food and Drug Act, that's mainly a health measure. I mean it's done by regulation of commerce, but it is dealing with the problem of health. The Meat Inspection Act; the Poultry Products Inspection Act; the Plant Quarantine Act; Packers and Stockyards Act as I mentioned before which was held up—upheld in 1922; Fair Labor Standards [fol. 106] Act; the whole Wagner Act; and of course, the Mann Act and other things that are more direct, on that sort.

The—I think that these cases, the other two cases I particularly wanted to call the Court's attention to on this question of local businesses was the Chevrolet Dealer Case, which is an NLRB case, which is cited in our brief, regulation of a Chevrolet dealer who bought his cars from a plant inside the same state; and the Reliance Fuel Oil Corporation Case, which is a recent case, unanimous case by the Supreme Court in 371 U.S. 224. Shubert Case under the anti-trust laws which regulates legitimate theatres through anti-trust laws, but it's local cases. There are others, but—and there are others cited in our brief including a number of cases that deal with regulation of hotels and this kind of establishments, hotels and restaurants.

That brings me to the question of whether there's some limitation in the Fifth Amendment or the Thirteenth Amendment on this power of Congress under the commerce clause, I think it's really the same question, that if Congress has the power under the commerce clause to regulate and the regulation doesn't involve the taking under the Fifth Amendment and isn't prohibited by the Thirteenth Amendment, the, I just want to suggest to the Court some of the implications of the argument that this is a taking. [fol. 107] In the first place, it seems to me that the same argument would apply to the ICC rules, to the Boynton Case, to the Federal Aviation Act, to all the regulation under those statutes which have already been passed on.

Judge Morgan: The Food and Drug Act.

Mr. Marshall: The Food and Drug Act. But these are the same kind, Judge Morgan, is my point. The Boynton Case involves exactly the same kind of regulation. If it's a taking of the Heart of Atlanta, it must be a taking of that restaurant in Virginia that was involved in the Boynton Case. The same thing is true of a restaurant in an airport. That's regulated in the same fashion under the Federal Aviation Act and I don't see how you could make the distinction based on the Fifth Amendment between that and this. And, you could say maybe commerce power doesn't extend to this and it does to that, but that's a different argument. This is that the Fifth Amendment itself is a limitation.

The Thompson Restaurant Case in the District of Columbia, if the Fifth Amendment prohibits this sort of regulation by the Federal Government, then the Thompson Restaurant Case which was unanimously decided by the Supreme Court upholding a prohibition against racial discrimination in restaurants and hotels in the District of Columbia must have been wrongly decided. The Fifth Amendment is applicable in the District of Columbia. The [fol. 108] practice prohibited or regulated by Congress is exactly the same. The kinds of establishments covered are exactly the same. The cases that deal with this are mostly cited in our brief, but the point I wanted to make, in addition to that there are thirty states that have laws that impose this sort of regulation.

The Fourteenth Amendment also prohibits the taking of property without due process, and if it is a taking under the Fifth Amendment, it seems to me that the argument goes to all of these state laws.

Judge Tuttle: Have any of the state supreme courts held invalid this kind of open, open accommodations statutes under the Fourteenth Amendment except the Washington decision?

Mr. Marshall: Well, Judge Tuttle, the Washington decision dealt with an open occupancy housing statute.

Judge Tuttle: I understand.

Mr. Marshall: I believe that the, the opinion that is cited in the plaintiff's brief is a concurring opinion that the—

Judge Tuttle: But they did—

Mr. Marshall: —decision—

Judge Tuttle: —knock out the statute?

Mr. Marshall: They did, Judge Tuttle; but I think it was in terms of the distinction made in the statute between publicly financed housing and other housing.

[fol. 109] Judge Tuttle: Do you know of any supreme court in—any supreme court in any of the states of the United States that have held unconstitutional open accommodation statutes?

Mr. Marshall: No, I do not, Judge Tuttle. A number of them have been upheld, and there's a decision by the Supreme Court of the United States, unanimous, that upholds the validity of the Michigan Statute. That's the Bob-Lo Excursion Company, which is in 333 U.S.

In addition, this point that I have been making about the Fifth Amendment not being an additional limitation but sort of the other side of the coin is made in the case called Bowles against Willingham which involves the price regulation, which was argued in the taking of property under the Fifth Amendment. In that case, the court said this: A member of the class which is regulated may suffer economic losses not shared by others. His property may lose the utility and depreciate in value as a result—as a consequence of regulation; but that has never been a barrier to the exercise of the police power, citing some state cases, and the restraints imposed on the national government in this regard by the Fifth Amendment are no greater than those imposed on the States by the Fourteenth Amendment. And then they cite some other cases involving federal regulations.

Our brief also cites a case called Central Eureka Min-
[fol. 110] ing Company decided in 1958 in which the argument was made that the closing of a gold mine under regulations on the sale and use of gold in this country was a taking, and the court held that that closing of the mine was not a taking under the Fifth Amendment, in view of the power of the Congress to deal with the problem.

That's all.

Closing Argument on Behalf of Plaintiff
by Mr. Rolleston

Judge Tuttle: Mr. Rolleston?

Mr. Rolleston: If the Court please, I believe I have the closing,—

Judge Tuttle: Yes, sir.

Mr. Rolleston: —and I'll be very brief.

Judge Tuttle: Yes, sir.

Mr. Rolleston: Judge Hooper asked about the Act and what is really said. I'd like to point this out, that the Title II says that the Act covers any described establishment if it affects commerce. And then it says in the next wording, it says any of the ones listed in these subparagraphs One through Four affect commerce. So you have to look at the subsection, and it says any inn, hotel or motel or other establishment which provides lodging for transient guests. So under that interpretation I would say that any motel in the United States that takes a transient guest is covered by the Act.

Judge Tuttle: Unless it has less than five.

Mr. Rolleston: Unless it has less than five. Yes, sir.
[fol. 111] Now the facts in the case stipulated that the Heart of Atlanta Motel takes transient guests, and seventy-five percent of them, Judge Hooper, come from outside of

Georgia; and that the rest of the transients, they can be transients even in Georgia if they come from Savannah to Atlanta.

Judge Tuttle: So more than 75% are transients.

Mr. Rolleston: You can almost say under our announced policy practically a hundred percent of them are transients. But 75%, the part that we are trying to stipulate, came from outside of Georgia. So this Act then must be, must be taken to mean that any motel except the one the man lives in and has only five rooms, which isn't a motel; that's just a house where they take lodgers; that any motel as such or any hotel—and there are sixty thousand motels in the United States, if they take one transient guest, they are covered by this Act. And I'm, I'll state to the court, and I'm, I'm sure the Court will almost take judicial notice, there isn't a motel or hotel in the United States that doesn't take transient guests, so they are all covered by the Act. What it amounts to.

Now I would like to call the Court's attention also, it says for the purposes of this Act, which is Section II, commerce, in quotes, means travel, trade, traffic, commerce, transportation and communication among the several states. [fol. 112] Taken literally, that could mean that the Congress of the United States can control communications of individuals between the States. You say that's a far-fetched conclusion? When the commerce clause historically was put in the Constitution, it was put there because under the confederation that this government operated under for twelve years after the War of Independence before the Congress adopted—before the Constitution was adopted in the Constitutional Convention, for twelve years there was practically no trade between these States that had any order, and that is the reason the commerce clause was, as I understand it, put in the Constitution, to regulate trade between the States. That's the history of it. Now we have seen the commerce clause by all the cases I have cited and other counsel have cited for the Government in the various ways they have nibbled and nibbled and nibbled until they have taken the whole piece of cheese. And this is the last step. There isn't anything left of inter-

—intrastate commerce if this Act can be valid and enforced to the full extent, and it will be literally followed, I'll urge on the Court.

The one other point, counsel mentioned that the United States Supreme Court has recently upheld a Michigan decision upholding the Michigan public accommodations law. They did so, though, on the grounds that a state may pass such legislation, pass such valid law, but not the Congress. [fol. 113] Under the Fourteenth Amendment—it follows the ruling in the civil rights case which said the Fourteenth Amendment didn't prohibit a state from doing it, but the Congress couldn't do it.

Thank you.

Judge Tuttle: Anything further on either side? Well, for once counsel were not overly optimistic. We have a little time to spare. But we've announced the next case will be called at one o'clock—

Judge Morgan: One-thirty.

Judge Tuttle: Did we say one-thirty?

Judge Morgan: I believe so.

Judge Tuttle: One-thirty. The Court will take this case under advisement and announce the decision as promptly as possible. I'll ask this question, although this is a motion I guess for preliminary injunction, is there anything further to be proved or further argument to be made? Could this not be considered a final motion and trial on the permanent injunction? What do counsel have to say about that?

Mr. Rolleston: As far as the plaintiff is concerned, there's nothing else, Your Honor.

Mr. Marshall: We are in agreement on that, Judge Tuttle. I think the whole case is before the Court now.

Judge Tuttle: The Court will stand in recess until one-thirty.

[fol. 114] (Whereupon, Court was recessed at 11:10 a.m.)

Reporter's Certificate to foregoing transcript (omitted in printing).

[fol. 115] [File endorsement omitted]

In the United States District Court
For the Northern District of Georgia
Atlanta Division
Civil Action No. 9017

Heart of Atlanta Motel, Inc., a Georgia corporation,
Plaintiff,

—versus—

The United States of America and Robert F. Kennedy as the Attorney General of the United States, Defendant.

Opinion—July 22, 1964

This is a complaint filed by Heart of Atlanta Motel, a large downtown motel in the city of Atlanta, regularly catering to out of state guests, praying for a declaratory judgment and injunction to prevent the Attorney General of the United States from exercising powers granted to him under the Civil Rights Act of 1964, 42 U. S. C. A., Section 1971, as amended. The suit also attempts to obtain recovery from the United States for substantial damages alleged to result from a partial taking of the complainant's property without just compensation.

Conceding, as it does, that it is regularly engaged in renting sleeping accommodations to out of town guests, seventy-five percent of whom come from without the state of Georgia, and that it "has refused and intends to refuse to rent sleeping accommodations to persons desiring said accommodations, for several different reasons, one of which is based on the grounds of race, unless ordered by this Court to comply with the provisions of the Civil Rights Act of 1964," the suit attacks the constitutionality of the public accommodations sections of the Civil Rights Act as applied to such a motel.

Since this is a suit seeking an injunction against the enforcement of a Federal statute on the alleged grounds that it is in violation of the United States Constitution, a three-judge court was convened as provided for in 28 U. S. C. A., Section 2282.

[fol. 116] The Attorney General filed a counterclaim seeking, on behalf of the United States, a temporary and permanent injunction against future violation of the Civil Rights Act by the plaintiff. The case was set down for hearing, and after the introduction of oral testimony on behalf of the United States, the signing of stipulations between the parties, and oral statements made by counsel for the plaintiff in open court, it appeared that no factual issues remained. The parties also conceded in open court that the matter might be treated as a hearing on the petition for the final permanent injunction.

In the first place, the claim of the plaintiff for damages against the United States on the alleged ground of deprivation of property without just compensation alleges no grounds for relief, entirely aside from the question whether such alleged deprivation would be justified by reason of the power of Congress to enact this particular legislation. This is so, because such a claim for damages or recovery for value of property taken by the Federal Government must be asserted in the United States Court of Claims unless the amount sought is not in excess of $10,000. However, in the view we take of the law, such a suit is not maintainable in any event.

The real question presented by this complaint and counterclaim is whether Section 201(a), (b), (1) and (c) is constitutional.[1]

---

[1] "Sec. 201.(a) All persons shall be entitled to the full and equal enjoyment of the goods, services, facilities, privileges, advantages, and accommodations of any place of public accommodation, as defined in this section, without discrimination or segregation on the ground of race, color, religion or national origin.

"(b) Each of the following establishments which serves the public is a place of public accommodation within the meaning [fol. 117] In substance, this section of Title II declares the right of every person to full and equal enjoyment of the goods, services and facilities of any hotel or motel which provides lodging to transient guests if it contains more than five rooms for rent or hire. The section is a congressional ascertainment and declaration of the fact that such "an establishment affect(s) commerce within the meaning of this Title."

Article I, Section 8, of the Constitution provides:

> "Clause 1: The Congress shall have power ... Clause 3: to regulate commerce with foreign nations and among the several states, and with the Indian tribes;" and Clause 18 "to make all laws which shall be necessary and proper for carrying into execution the foregoing powers . . . ."

In United States v. Darby, 312 U.S. 100, 118, the Supreme Court said:

> "The power of Congress over interstate commerce is not confined to the regulation of commerce among the states. It extends to those activities intrastate which so affect interstate commerce or the exercise of the power of Congress over it as to make regulation of them appropriate means to the attainment of a legitimate end, the exercise of the grant of power of Congress to regulate interstate commerce. See McCullough v. Maryland, 4 Wheat 316, 421."

---

of this title if its operations affect commerce, or if discrimination or segregation by it is supported by State action:

> (1) any inn, hotel, motel, or other establishment which provides lodging to transient guests, other than an establishment located within a building which contains not more than five rooms for rent or hire and which is actually occupied by the proprietor of such establishment as his residence; . . . . .

> "(c) The operations of an establishment affect commerce within the meaning of this title if (1) it is one of the establishments described in paragraph (1) of subsection (b); . . . ."

Thus, it need not be decided whether the outlawing of racial discrimination by a hotel accepting transient guests may be justified on the ground that it is actually in the stream of commerce. The power of Congress, when that body seeks to occupy the full extent of its powers under the Constitution, "extends to those activities intrastate which so affect interstate commerce . . . as to make regulation of them appropriate means to . . . the exercise of the granted power of Congress to regulate interstate commerce." Of course, the initial determination of whether the challenged regulation is such "appropriate means" is for Congress. Courts may not overturn such determination unless they conclude that under no reasonable theory could Congress find them "appropriate to the attainment" of its power to regulate commerce.

This Court, as recently as July 10, 1964, in the case of Marriott Hotels of Atlanta, Inc. v. Heart of Atlanta Motel, Inc., C.A. No. 8832, held that the operations of Heart of Atlanta Motel (1) are in the stream of commerce, and that, in any event, (2) such operations affect commerce so as to [fol. 118] subject it to Congressional regulation under the Sherman Antitrust Act. It being undisputed that in the adoption of the Civil Rights Act of 1964, Congress has seen fit to exercise its full power as granted it under the Constitution the scope of its operation in this field must, therefore, be taken to be at least as broad as that which it exercised in the adoption of the Sherman Act. Its scope is, therefore, also as broad as in the legislation affecting labor relations under the National Labor Relations Act. It is broader that that exercised by Congress in its regulation of wages and hours of services under the Wage and Hour laws.

In the specific field of hotel operations, the Supreme Court has ruled that the National Labor Relations Board could not lawfully follow a policy of refusing to take jurisdiction over unfair labor practices and other labor disputes in hotels and motels as a class. Hotels Employees Local No. 255 v. Leedom, 358 U.S. 99. Following that decision, the Court of Appeals of this judicial circuit in N.L.R.B. v. Citizens Hotel Co., 5 Cir., 313 F. 2d 708, overruled a contention by the Citizens Hotel Company, operator of the Texas Hotel in Forth Worth, Texas, that its operations did not fall within the constitutional reach of the National Labor Relations Act because it was not either engaged in commerce, nor did its operations affect commerce. In arriving at that decision the court referred to the Supreme Court's opinion in National Labor Relations Board v. Reliance Fuel Oil Corp., 371 U.S. 224. That case dealt with an attack by the local fuel oil corporation on the jurisdiction of the Labor Board because, while most of the products sold by Reliance had been acquired from Gulf Oil Corporation and had been delivered to it from without the state of New York, they nevertheless had been received and stored in the state before sales were made to Reliance. It was thus contended that Reliance was not engaged in commerce nor were its operations such as to affect commerce within the constitutional sense. The Supreme Court said:

> "That activities such as those of Reliance affect commerce and are within the constitutional reach of Congress is beyond doubt. See e.g. Wickard v. Filburn, 317 U.S. 111."

The opinion also significantly quoted from the court's earlier decision in Polish Alliance v. Labor Board, 322 U.S. where, at page 648, it had said:

> [fol. 119] "Congress has explicitly regulated not merely transactions or goods in interstate commerce but activities which in isolation might be deemed to be merely local, but in the interlacings of business across state lines adversely affect such commerce."

It is clear that the attack by the complainant on the constitutionality of these sections of the Civil Rights Act must fail. It is equally clear that the United States is entitled to the injunction prayed for by it in its counterclaim. An injunction will issue in the following terms:

[fol. 120]   ORDER—July 22, 1964

The plaintiff, Heart of Atlanta Motel, Inc., a corporation, its successors, officers, attorneys, agents and employees, together with all persons in active concert or participation with them, are hereby enjoined from:

(a) Refusing to accept Negroes as guests in the motel by reason of their race or color;

(b) Making any distinction whatever upon the basis of race or color in the availability of the goods, services, facilities, privileges, advantages or accommodations offered or made available to the guests of the motel, or to the general public, within or upon any of the premises of the Heart of Atlanta Motel, Inc.

So that the plaintiff may have an opportunity to prepare its record for appeal and, if so advised, seek a stay of this order, it is Ordered that the foregoing injunction shall become effective twenty (20) days from the date hereof, on, to-wit, the 11th day of August, 1964.

This 22nd day of July, 1964.

> Elbert P. Tuttle, United States Circuit Judge, Frank A. Hooper, United States District Judge, Lewis R. Morgan, United States District Judge.

[fol. 121]   [File endorsement omitted]

IN THE UNITED STATES DISTRICT COURT

FOR THE NORTHERN DISTRICT OF GEORGIA

ATLANTA DIVISION

Civil Action No. 9017

[Title omitted]

PERMANENT INJUNCTION—July 23, 1964

Pursuant to Order and Directions by the Three-Judge Court in the above stated case, and pursuant to Rule 58 of the Rules of Civil Procedure as amended January 21, 1963, the following Order in the above stated case on the prayers for temporary injunction is hereby entered.

Order

The plaintiff, Heart of Atlanta Motel, Inc., a corporation, its successors, officers, attorneys, agents and employees, together with all persons in active concert or participation with them, are hereby enjoined from:

(a) Refusing to accept Negroes as guests in the motel by reason of their race or color;

(b) Making any distinction whatever upon the basis of race or color in the availability of the goods, services, facilities, privileges, advantages or accommodations offered or made available to the guests of the motel, or to the general [fol. 122] public, within or upon any of the premises of the Heart of Atlanta Motel, Inc.

So that the plaintiff may have an opportunity prepare its record for appeal and, if so advised, seek a stay of this Order, it is Ordered that the foregoing injunction shall become effective twenty (20) days from July 22, 1964, to-wit, the 11th day of August, 1964.

This the 23rd day of July, 1964.

B. G. Nash, Clerk of Court.

[fol. 123] [File endorsement omitted]

United States District Court
For the Northern District of Georgia
Atlanta Division

Civil Action No. 9017

[Title omitted]

Notice of Appeal—Filed July 22, 1964

Notice of Appeal of the decision of this Court in the above styled case dated July 22, 1964, to the Supreme Court of the United States is hereby given.

This 22nd day of July, 1964.

Moreton Rolleston, Jr., Attorney for Plaintiff.

[fol. 124] Certificate of Service (omitted in printing).

[fol. 125]   [File endorsement omitted]

IN THE UNITED STATES DISTRICT COURT
FOR THE NORTHERN DISTRICT OF GEORGIA
ATLANTA DIVISION
Civil Action No. 9017

[Title omitted]

AMENDED NOTICE OF APPEAL—Filed July 30, 1964

On July 22, 1964, plaintiff in the above styled case filed a Notice of Appeal. Plaintiff amends said notice as follows:

A.

1. Heart of Atlanta Motel, Inc., plaintiff in the above styled case, is the party taking the appeal.

2. On July 22, 1964, the three-judge court consisting of Judge Elbert P. Tuttle, Judge Frank A. Hooper and Judge Lewis R. Morgan, rendered a judgment in the above styled case and said judgment was entered of record on July 23, 1964 by B. G. Nash, Clerk of Court. This appeal of the plaintiff in the above styled case is from said judgment of said Court.

3. This appeal to the Supreme Court of the United States is taken under the statute known as the Civil Rights [fol. 126] Act of 1964. Section 101, sub-section (h) provides as follows:

"An appeal from the final judgment of such Court (a three-judge court referred to in said sub-section), will lie to the Supreme Court" (parentheses added).

B.

4. The following portions of the record should be certified by the Clerk of the U.S. District Court, Northern District of Georgia, Atlanta Division, as necessary for this appeal:

(1) The Complaint for Declaratory Judgment, filed by the plaintiff on July 2, 1964.

(2) Amendment to Complaint for Declaratory Judgment, filed by the plaintiff on July 15, 1964.

(3) Statement of Issues, filed by plaintiff on July 15, 1964.

(4) Stipulation of Facts, agreed to by attorneys for plaintiff and defendants on July 16, 1964 and submitted to the Court at the hearing on July 17, 1964.

(5) Answer of the defendants, including Defenses and Counter-claims.

(6) Answer to Counter-claims and Response to Motion for Preliminary Injunction, filed by plaintiff on July 15, 1964.

(7) Certificate and Request for Three-Judge Court, filed by defendants.

(8) Notice of Motion and Motion for Preliminary Injunction, filed by defendants.

(9) Motion to Dismiss Second Counter-claim, filed by defendants.

(10) Notice of Motion and Motion to Dismiss, filed by defendants.

[fol. 127] (11) Judgment of the Court, dated July 22, 1964.

(12) Transcript of the hearing on July 17, 1964 from the fifteenth line on page 31, beginning with "Judge Tuttle", through the 17th line on page 41, said transcript containing all of the evidence presented to the Court at that hearing.

C.

5. The sole question presented by the appeal is the constitutionality of the Civil Rights Act of 1964. The Complaint, the Amendment to the Complaint, the Answer of the defendants, the Stipulation of Facts and the testimony of two witnesses, set forth hereinabove as part of the record, clearly describe the existing controversy and the contentions of the plaintiff. Briefly, the plaintiff contends that the Civil Rights Act of 1964 is unconstitutional because:

(1) Said Act violates the Thirteenth Amendment to the Constitution of the United States, in that, by requiring plaintiff to serve Negroes at plaintiff's motel against plaintiff's will, it subjects plaintiff to involuntary servitude, which is expressly prohibited by the Thirteenth Amendment.

(2) Said Act violates the Fifth Amendment to the Constitution of the United States in that it results in a taking of liberty and property without due process and for public use without just compensation, because it deprives plaintiff of its right to choose its customers and to operate its business as it sees fit, which was the right of the plaintiff possessed prior to the effective date of said Act.

[fol. 128] (3) Said Act exceeds the power to regulate commerce granted to Congress by Article I, Section 8, Clause 3, of the Constitution of the United States.

This 30th day of July, 1964.

 Moreton Rolleston, Jr., 1103 Citizens & Southern Bank Bldg., Atlanta, Georgia 30303, Area 404 523-1566, Attorney for Plaintiff.

[fol. 129] Acknowledgment of Service (omitted in printing).

[fol. 130]   [File endorsement omitted]

IN THE UNITED STATES DISTRICT COURT
FOR THE NORTHERN DISTRICT OF GEORGIA
ATLANTA DIVISION
Civil Action No. 9017

HEART OF ATLANTA MOTEL, INC., a Georgia Corporation, Plaintiff,

vs.

THE UNITED STATES OF AMERICA and ROBERT F. KENNEDY, as the Attorney General of the United States of America, Defendants.

AMENDMENT TO NOTICE OF APPEAL, AS AMENDED—
Filed July 31, 1964

The Notice of Appeal, as previously amended on July 30, 1964, is further amended by deleting from paragraph A sub-paragraph 3 of the Amended Notice the words "Section 101, sub-section (h)" and substituting therefor "Section 206 (b)".

> Moreton Rolleston, Jr., 1103 Citizens & Southern Bank Bldg., Atlanta 3, Georgia, JAckson 3-1566, Attorney for Plaintiff.

[fol. 131] Affidavit of Service (omitted in printing).

[fol. 132] Clerk's Certificate to foregoing transcript (omitted in printing).

LOVING VS. VIRGINIA

The state of Virginia intended to prevent certain marriages based solely off race, thus violating the 14th ammendment and leading to this court case

TRANSCRIPT OF RECORD

Supreme Court of the United States

OCTOBER TERM, 1966

No. 395

RICHARD PERRY LOVING, ET UX., APPELLANTS,

vs.

VIRGINIA.

APPEAL FROM THE SUPREME COURT OF APPEALS OF VIRGINIA

FILED JULY 29, 1966
PROBABLE JURISDICTION NOTED DECEMBER 12, 1966

SUPREME COURT OF THE UNITED STATES

OCTOBER TERM, 1966

No. 395

RICHARD PERRY LOVING, ET UX., APPELLANTS,

vs.

VIRGINIA.

APPEAL FROM THE SUPREME COURT OF APPEALS OF VIRGINIA

INDEX

	Original	Print
Record from the Supreme Court of Appeals of Virginia	A	1
Writ of error and supersedeas awarded	1	1
Record from the Circuit Court of Caroline County	2	2
Commonwealth warrant	2	2
Commonwealth warrant	3	3
Indictment	5	5
Judgment	6	6
Motion to vacate judgment and set aside sentence	6	7
Opinion	8	8
Order denying motion to vacate judgment	14	17
Notice of appeal and assignments of error	15	18
Opinion, Carrico, J.	19	19
Mandate	33	28
Motion for stay and order thereon (omitted in printing)	34	28
Notice of appeal to the Supreme Court of the United States	37	29
Order noting probable jurisdiction	41	32

RECORD PRESS, PRINTERS, NEW YORK, N. Y., DECEMBER 23, 1966

[fol. A]
IN THE SUPREME COURT OF APPEALS OF VIRGINIA AT RICHMOND

Richard Perry Loving, et al.,

v.

Commonwealth of Virginia.

FROM THE CIRCUIT COURT OF CAROLINE COUNTY

[fol. 1]
In the Supreme Court of Appeals of Virginia

Richard Perry Loving and Mildred Jeter Loving, Plaintiffs in Error,

against

Commonwealth of Virginia, Defendant in Error.

From the Circuit Court of Caroline County
Leon M. Bazile, Judge

Writ of Error and Supersedeas Awarded—June 11, 1965

Upon the petition of Richard Perry Loving and Mildred Jeter Loving a writ of error and *supersedeas* is awarded them to a judgment rendered by the Circuit Court of Caroline County on the 22nd day of January, 1965, in a prosecution by the Commonwealth against the said petitioners for a felony; but said *supersedeas*, however, is not to operate to discharge the petitioners from custody, if in custody, or to release their bond if out on bail.

[fol. 2]   Record

COMMONWEALTH WARRANT—July 11, 1958

To the Sheriff or any Police Officer of the said County:

Whereas, Bernard Mahon, Com. Atty., of the said County, has this day made complaint and information on oath before me, Robert W. Farmer, Justice of the Peace of the said County that Richard Loving (a white person) and in the said County did on the 2nd day of June, 1958, unlawfully and feloniously did go out of this State for the purpose of being married to Mildred Jeter a Negro and with the intention of returning and was married out of State to the said Mildred Jeter, and afterward, returned to and resided in it, cohabiting as man & wife against the peace and dignity of the Commonwealth of Virginia.

These are, Therefore, to command you, in the name of the Commonwealth, to apprehend and bring before the Judge of the said County the body of the said Richard Loving to answer the said complaint, and to be further dealt with according to law. And you are directed to summon .... as witnesses.

Given under my hand and seal this 11th day of July, 1958.

Robert W. Farmer, J. P.

State of Virginia,
County of Caroline, to-wit:

I, J. L. Webb, Justice of the Peace in and for the County aforesaid, State of Virginia, do certify that Richard Loving and Eleanor A. & John Koons, by, Robert E. Buchanan, attorney in fact as his suret ...., have this day acknowledged themselves indebted to the Commonwealth of Virginia in the sum of one thousand & no/100 Dollars ($1,000.00, to be made and levied of their respective goods and chattels, upon this condition: That the said Richard Loving shall appear before the County Court of the said County, on the 17th day of July 1958, at 10 A. M., at Bowling Green, Va., and not leave hence without the leave of the said Court, and that he appears before the Court to answer the charge in this warrant, and/or any continuance thereof, and/or abide the judgment of said Court, and/or any appeal therefrom, or to [fol. 3] await the action of the Grand Jury upon the within charges, at such time or times as may be prescribed by the Court and at any time or times to which the proceedings may be continued or further heard, and to remain in full force and effect until the charge is finally disposed of or until it is declared void by order of a competent Court.

Given under my hand, this 14th day of July, 1958.

J. L. Webb, J. P.

(on back)

COMMONWEALTH,

v.

RICHARD LOVING.

Warrant of Arrest

Executed this, the 13th day of July, 1958.

Garnett Brooks, Sheriff.

Upon the defendant's plea of not guilty to the within charge, and upon examination of the witnesses, I find probable cause to charge the accused with a felony and it is ordered that he be held for the action of the grand jury. 7-17-58.

Edward Stehl, III, Judge.

COMMONWEALTH WARRANT—July 11, 1958

To the Sheriff or any Police Officer of the said County:

Whereas Bernard Mahon, Com. Atty., of the said County, has this day made complaint and information on oath before me, Robert W. Farmer, Justice of the Peace of the said County that Mildred Jeter a Negro in the said County did on the 2nd day of June, 1958, unlawfully and feloniously [fol. 4] did go out of this State for the purpose of being married to Richard Loving, a white person, and with the intention of returning, and was married to the said Richard Loving out of State, and afterwards, returned to and resided in it, cohabiting as man & wife against the peace and dignity of the Commonwealth of Virginia.

These are, Therefore, to command you, in the name of the Commonwealth, to apprehend and bring before the Judge of the said County the body of the said Mildred Jeter to answer the said complaint, and to be further dealt with according to law. And you are directed to summon .... as witnesses.

Given under my hand and seal this 11th day of July, 1958.

Robert W. Farmer, J. P.

State of Virginia,
County of Caroline, to-wit:

I, Edward Stehl III, Justice of the Peace in and for the County aforesaid, State of Virginia, do certify that Mildred Jeter and Ronnie W. Catlett, as his surety, have this day acknowledged themselves indebted to the Commonwealth of Virginia in the sum of one thousand Dollars ($1,000.00), to be made and levied of their respective goods and chattels, upon this condition: That the said Mildred Jeter shall appear before the Circuit Court of the said County, on the 13th day of October 1958, at 10:00 A. M., at Bowling Green, Va., and not leave hence without the leave of the said Court, and that he appears before the Court to answer the charge in this warrant, and/or any continuance thereof, and/or abide the judgment of said Court, and/or any appeal therefrom, or to await the action of the Grand Jury upon the within charge, at such time or times as may be prescribed by the Court and at any time or times to which the proceedings may be continued or further heard, and to remain in full force and effect until the charge is finally disposed of or until it is declared void by order of a competent Court.

Given under my hand, this 24th day of July, 1958.

Edward Stehl III, Judge.

Ronnie W. Catlett

(on back)

[fol. 5]

COMMONWEALTH,

v.

MILDRED JETER.

Warrant of Arrest

Executed this, the 17 day of July, 1958.

Garnett Brooks, Sheriff.

Upon the defendant's plea of not guilty to the within charge, and upon examination of the witnesses, I find probable cause to charge the accused with a felony and it is ordered that she be held for the action of the grand jury 7-17-58.

Edward Stehl III, Judge.

IN THE CIRCUIT COURT OF CAROLINE COUNTY

INDICTMENT

The grand jurors of the Commonwealth of Virginia, in and for the body of the County of Caroline, and now attending the said court at its October, 1958 term upon their oath present that Richard Perry Loving and Mildred Delores Jeter on the 2nd day of June, 1958, in the said County of

Caroline, the said Richard Perry Loving being a White person and the said Mildred Delores Jeter being a Colored person, did unlawfully and feloniously go out of the State of Virginia, for the purpose of being married, and with the intention of returning to the State of Virginia and were married out of the State of Virginia, to-wit, in the District of Columbia on June 2, 1958, and afterwards returned to and resided in the County of Caroline, State of Virginia, cohabiting as man and wife, against the peace and dignity of the Commonwealth.

(on back)

A True Bill.

Mrs. Gladys Livermon, Foreman.

[fol. 6]

In the Circuit Court of Caroline County

Judgment—January 6, 1959

This day came the attorney for the Commonwealth and the accused, who were represented by counsel, appeared in court upon their own recognizance. Upon being arraigned the accused both plead "not guilty" to the charges in the indictment and waived trial by jury and the Commonwealth by its attorney doth agree to the waiving of trial by jury and the court doth consent thereto. Whereupon the court proceeded to hear the evidence and argument of counsel. After the court heard the evidence and argument of counsel, the accused doth change their plea from "not guilty" to "guilty". The court doth accept the pleas of "guilty" and fix the punishment of both accused at one year each in jail. The court doth suspend said sentence for a period of twenty-five years upon the provision that both accused leave Caroline County and the state of Virginia at once and do not return together or at the same time to said county and state for a period of twenty-five years. Whereupon the court asked the accused if they had anything to say before the court pronounced sentence and when they answered "no" the court proceeded to sentence the prisoners. After the prisoners were sentenced they paid the costs of these proceedings into court and the court ordered them released from custody and further recognizance.

Leon M. Bazile, Judge.

6 January 1959.

Filed 6 Nov. '63.

L. M. B.

IN THE CIRCUIT COURT OF CAROLINE COUNTY

MOTION TO VACATE JUDGMENT AND SET ASIDE SENTENCE

Comes Now the defendants, through counsel, and moves this honorable court to vacate the judgment against them and set aside the suspended sentence, declaring:

[fol. 7] 1. That on January 6, 1959, judgment was rendered and entered by this court in the above-entitled action, by which it was adjudged that the punishment of both defendants be fixed at one year in jail, such sentence to be suspended for a period of twenty-five (25) years upon the condition that both leave Caroline County, Virginia, at once and do not return together or at the same time to said county and state for a period of twenty-five (25) years. A copy of the record entry of said judgment is attached hereto and marked Exhibit "A".

2. That the defendants have complied with and abided by said judgment, and have thereby been banished from the state and county aforesaid.

3. That said judgment be vacated and said suspended sentence be set aside on the grounds that:

A. Said sentence constitutes cruel and unusual punishment, within the meaning of Section 9 of the Virginia Constitution.

B. Said sentence exceeds the reasonable period of suspension permitted by Sec. 53-272 of the Code of Va., 1950, as amended.

C. Said sentence constitutes banishment, and is thus a violation of constitutional due process of law.

D. Said sentence is improper because it is based on a statute which is unconstitutional on its face, in that it denies the defendants the equal protection of the laws and denies the right of marriage which is a fundamental right of free men, in violation of Section 1 of the Virginia Constitution, and the 14th Amendment of the Federal Constitution.

E. Said statute and said sentence are unconstitutional burdens upon interstate commerce.

F. Such sentence has worked undue hardship upon the defendants by preventing them from together visiting their families from time to time as may be desireable and necessary, to promote domestic tranquility.

Wherefore, defendants pray that said judgment be vacated and sentence set aside.

  Richard Perry Loving, Mildred D. Jeter Loving,
   By Bernard S. Cohen, Counsel.

[fol. 8]

IN THE CIRCUIT COURT OF CAROLINE COUNTY

OPINION

The Petitioners here was indicted in this Court at the October term, 1958, the indictment charging that on the 2nd day of June, 1958, "that Richard Perry Loving being a white man and the said Mildred Delores Jeter being a colored person did unlawfully go out of the State of Virginia for the purpose of being married and with the intention of returning to the State of Virginia, and were married out of the State of Virginia, to-wit in the District of Columbia on the 28th day of June, 1958 and afterwards returned to and resided in the County of Caroline, State of Virginia, cohabiting as man and wife against the peace and dignity of the Commonwealth."

On the 6th day of January, 1959, the accused were arraigned and after pleading not guilty withdrew said plea and pleaded guilty; thereupon the Court fixed their punishment at one year in jail; and then suspended said sentence for twenty-five years "upon the provision that both accused leave Caroline County and the State of Virginia at once and do not return together at the same time to said County and State for a period of twenty-five years." After they paid the costs they were released from custody and further recognizance.

The Court file contains his birth certificate which shows that he is white and her birth certificate which shows that she is colored.

On the 6th day of November, 1963, they filed a motion to vacate the judgment and set aside the sentence.

1st It is contended the said sentence constitutes a cruel and unusual punishment within Section 9 of the Constitution of Virginia.

Section 9 of George Mason's Bill of Rights made a part of the Constitution of 1776 is in the identical same words as Section 9 of the Bill of Rights to the present Constitution (9 Henrys Statutes 111; Code of 1950, page 443).

In *Hart* v. *Commonwealth*, 131 Va., 726, 741, 109 S. E. 582, the Court said: "It has been uniformly held by this Court that the provisions in question which have remained the same as they were originally adopted in the Virginia Bill of Rights of 1776, must be construed to impose no limitation upon the right to determine and prescribe by statute the quantum of punishment deemed adequate by the legislature. That the only limitation so imposed is upon the mode of punishments, such punishments only being prohibited by such constitutional provision as were re-[fol. 9] garded as cruel and unusual when such provision of the Constitution was adopted in 1776, namely, such bodily punishments as involve torture or lingering death, such as are inhumane and barbarous, as for example, punishment by the rack, by drawing and quartering, leaving the body hung in chains, or on the gibbet, exposed to public view, and the like. *Aldridge's case,* 2 Va. Cas. 447, 449-450; *Wyatt's Case,* 6 Rand (27 Va.) 694; *Bracey's Case,* 119 Va. 867, 862, 89 S. E. 144.

See also *Buck* v. *Bell,* 143 Va. 310, 319, 130 S. E. 516 (1925).

In *Aldridge's Case* (2 Va. Case 447, 448) (1824) a free person of color was convicted of the larceny of bank notes. He was sentenced to be whipped, sold and transported beyond the bounds of the United States. The Court said "as to the ninth section of the Bill of Rights, denouncing cruel and unusual punishments, we have no notion that it has any bearing on this case."

In *Wyatt's Case* (6 Rand 694) (1825), the law provided "that when any person was convicted of any crime or offense now punishable by imprisonment in the penitentiary the Court could sentence such person to be imprisoned not exceeding two years in the jail of the County or Corporation where such conviction shall have taken place, for a period not exceeding six months, nor less than one month and he shall be punished by stripes at the discretion of the Court to be inflicted at one time provided the same do not exceed thirty-nine at any one time."

"The Court said the punishment of offenses by stripes is certainly odious, but cannot be said to be unusual."

The Court said 6 Rand 763 "This Court if of the opinion and doth decide that the motion in arrest of judgment and also the motion for a new trial ought to be overruled and the judgment should be rendered against the defendant of imprisonment and strips according to law.

In *Buck* v. *Bell,* 143 Va. 310, 130 S. E. 516 (1925) a case in which it had been ordered that Buck be sterilized, it was contended that it violated the Federal Constitution and Sections 9, 11 of the Virginia Constitution and the 11th Amendment to the Federal Constitution. The Court held that the Sterilization Act did not violate any section of the Constitution of Virginia or any sections of the Federal Constitution.

In Re Kemmler, 136 U. S. 436, 34 *Fed.* 519 (1889) it was held that punishments are cruel when they involve torture or a lingering death but the punishment of death is not within the meaning of that word in the Constitution.

The Court said that cruel and unusual punishments are "such as burning at the stake, crucifixion, breaking on the wheel or the like." (34 Fed. 524)

And the Supreme Court of the United States has held in [fol. 10] *Onell* v. *Vermont* that whether a punishment is cruel and unusual within the provisions of a State Constitution does not present a Federal question.

In U. S. Supreme Court Enc. of U. S. Supreme Court Volume 4 p. 513, it is said "The provision of the 8th Amendment that excessive fines shall not be imposed nor cruel and unusual punishment inflicted applies to National and not to State legislation.

It is next said that the sentence exceeds a reasonable period of suspension within the meaning of Section 53-273 of the Code of 1950.

The Court has examined this Section with care and it sees nothing in this statute which limits the time that the person may be put on probation.

It is said that the sentence constitutes banishment and thus is a violation of due process of law.

Section 20-58 provides that "If any white person and colored person shall go out of this state for the purpose of being married and with the intention of returning and be married out of it, and afterwards return to and reside in it, cohabiting as man and wife, they shall be punished as provided in Section 20-59, and the marriage shall be governed by the same law as if it had been solemnized in this State. The fact of this cohabitation here as man and wife shall be evidence of their marriage."

Intermarriage between white and colored persons is prohibited by Section 20-54 of the Code.

Section 20-57 of the Code provides "all marriages between a white person and a colored person shall be absolutely void without any decree of divorce or other legal process."

And Section 20-58 of the Code provides "if any white person and colored person shall go out of this State for the purpose of being married and with the intention of returning and be married out of it, and shall afterwards return to reside in it, cohabiting as man and wife, they shall be punished as provided in Section 20-20 and the marriage shall be governed by the same law as if it had been solemnized in this State. The fact of their cohabitation here as man and wife shall be evidence of their marriage."

These laws were held valid in *Kinney v. Commonwealth*, 30 Gratt, 858 (1878) Judge Christian who wrote the opinion said (30 Gratt 870): "If the parties desire to maintain the relations of man and wife, they must change their domicile and go to some State or Country where the laws recognizes the validity of such marriages."

Their marriage being absolutely void in Virginia they [fol. 11] cannot cohabit in Virginia without incurring repeated prosecutions for that cohabitation.

It is next contended that these statutes are unconstitutional in violation of Section 1 of the Virginia Constitution and the 14th Amendment of the U. S. Constitution.

There is nothing in Section 1 of the Constitution of Virginia which relates to this matter, nor is there anything in the 14th Amendment which has anything to do with the subject here under consideration.

Marriage is a subject which belongs to the exclusive control of the States.

In *State* v. *Gibson,* 16 Ind. 180, 10 Am. Rep. 42 a statute prohibiting the intermarriage of negroes and white persons was held not to violate any provisions of the 14th Amendment or Civil Rights Laws in the course of a well-reasoned and well-supported discussion of the powers retained by and inherent in the States under the Constitution said:

" * * * In this State marriage is treated as a civil contract, but it is more than a mere civil contract, it is a public institution established by God himself, is recognized in all Christian and civilized nations and is essential to the peace, happiness, and well being of society. * * * "

" * * * The right in the States to control, to guard, protect and preserve this God-giving, civilizing and Christianizing institution is of inestimable importance, and cannot be surrendered, nor can the States suffer or permit any interference therewith. If the Federal Government can determine who may marry in a State, there is no limit to its power * * * " (36 Ind. at p. 402-3)

In *Naim* v. *Naim,* 196 Va. 80, 87 S. E. (2nd) 749 (1953) the Court of Appeals in a well considered opinion held that the Virginia statutes were constitutional and concluded its opinion as follows: "Regulation of the marriage relation is, we think, distinctly one of the rights guaranteed to the States and safeguarded by that bastion of States' rights, somewhat battered perhaps but still a sturdy fortress in our fundamental law, the tenth section of the Bill of Rights, which declares 'The powers not delegated to the United States by the Constitution, nor prohibited by it to the States, are reserved to the States respectively, or to the people.'"

In *Pace* v. *Alabama,* 106 U. S. 583, 1 S. Ct. 637, 27 L. ed. 207, a prosecution for a white person marrying a colored person was upheld. Pace, the negro, contended that the

Statute violated the Equal Protection of the 14th Amendment.

In *Jackson* v. *State,* 37 Ala. App. 519, 72 So. (2d) 114, as the party had been convicted under the miscegenation [fol. 12] statute, the conviction was affirmed against the contentions that the right and privilege of marrying a white person violated the Due Process and Equal Protection clauses of the 14th Amendment the Supreme Court of the United States denied a writ of certiorari (1954).

In *Greenhow & Als.* v. *James' Executor,* 80 Va. 636 (1885) the Court held that the children of a marriage contracted in the District of Columbia between a white person and a colored person could take under a will of a relative.

Such on marriage the Court said (80 Va. 61) " * * * Yet that it can have application to a marriage contract entered into a foreign country in contravention of the public statutes of the country of their domicile which *pronunces* a marriage between them not only absolutely void but criminal. In the very nature of things every *soverign* state must have the power to prescribe what incapacities for contracting marriage shall be established as the law among her own citizens, and it follows therefore that when the state has once pronounced an incapacity on the part of any of its citizens to enter into the marriage relationship with each other that such incapacity attaches itself to the person or parties and although it may not be enforceable during the absence of the parties, it at once revives with all its prohibitive power upon their return to place of domicile. * * * "

In *Toler* v. *Oakwood Smokeless Coal Corporation,* 173 Va. 425, 430 the Court speaking through Mr. Justice Spratley said:

"One state, however, cannot force its own marriage laws, or other laws, on any other state, and no state is bound by comity to give effect in its Courts to the marriage laws of another state, repugnant to its own laws and policy. Otherwise, a state would be deprived of the very essence of its sovereignty, the right of supremacy within its own borders.

Such effect as may be given by a state to a law of another state is merely because of comity, or because justice and policy may demand recognition of such law. Such recognition is not a matter of obligation. Minor on conflict laws Sec. 4, 5, 6 and 126."

In 6 Am. Eng. Enc. of Law 2nd Ed. P. 967 it is said "The right to marry is not such a privilege and immunity but a social institution of great importance subject to state regulation and a statute prohibiting intermarriage between white person and negroes is not a discrimination or unequal law contrary to the terms of the constitutional provisions."

[fol. 13] It is next said that the sentence and the statute are unconstitutional as burdens on interstate commerce.

Marriage has nothing to do with interstate commerce. There is nothing more domestic than marriage; and this contentive is without merit.

It is next said such sentence has involved undue hardships upon the defendants by preventing them from together visiting their families from time to time as may be necessary to promote domestice tranquility.

This complaint relates to the terms of the suspension of this sentence, which is as follows:

"And the Court doth suspend said sentence for twenty-five years upon the provision that both accused leave Caroline County and the State of Virginia at once and do not return together at the same time to said County and State for a period of twenty-five years."

The Court knew that if they come to Caroline County or to the State of Virginia together that they would be subject to prosecution for unlawful cohabitation and therefore permitted each are to separately visit his or her people, but not together. If it works a hardship on them not to visit their people together it is the law that they cannot cohabit together in Virginia. Each one of them can come to Caroline separately to visit his or her people as often as they please.

Section 53-272 of the Code of Virginia provides in part:

"In any case wherein the Court is authorized to suspend the imposition or execution of sentence, such Court may fix the period of suspension for a reasonable time having due regard to the gravity of the offense, without regard to the gravity period for which the prisoner might have been sentenced."

The parties were guilty of a most serious crime. As said by the Court in *Kinney's Case* 30 Gratt 865: "It was a marriage prohibited and declared absolutely void. It was contrary to the declared public law, founded upon motives of public policy—a public policy affirmed for more than a Century, and one upon which social order, public morality and the best interests of both races depend. This unmistakable policy of the legislature founded, I think, on wisdom and the moral development of both races, has been shown by not only declaring marriages between whites and negroes absolutely void, but by prohibiting and punishing such unnatural alliances with severe penalties. The laws enacted to further and uphold this declared policy would be futile and a dead letter if in fraud of these salutary [fol. 14] enactments, both races might, by stepping across any imaginary line bid defiance to the law by immediately returning and insisting that the marriage celebrated in another state or county should be recognized as lawful, though denounced by the public law of the domicile as unlawful and absolutely void."

Almighty God created the races white, black, yellow, malay and red, and he placed them on separate continents. And but for the interference with his arrangement there would be no cause for such marriages. The fact that he separated the races shows that he did not intend for the races to mix.

The awfulness of the offense is shown by Section 25-57 which declares: "All marriages between a white person and a colored person shall be absolutely void without any decree of divorce or other legal process.

Then Section 20-59 of the Code makes the contracting of a marriage between a white person and any colored person a felony.

Conviction of a felony is a serious matter. You lose your political rights; and only the government has the power to restore them (Constitution Sec. 73). And as long as you live you will be known as a felon.

> "The moving finger writes and moves on
> and having writ
>
> Nor all your piety nor all your wit
> Can change one line of it."

Leon M. Bazile, Judge.

In the Circuit Court of Caroline County

Order Denying Motion to Vacate Judgment—
January 22, 1965

This day came the defendants, by counsel, and moved the Court to vacate the judgment and set aside the sentence heretofore entered in this cause.

Upon consideration thereof, for reasons stated in an opinion heretofore filed, it is Adjudged and Ordered that the said motion is hereby denied.

It is further ordered that the Clerk of this Court send an attested copy of this order to Bernard S. Cohen, Lainof, Cohen & Cohen, Attorneys at Law, 1513 King Street, Alexandria, Virginia, and J. Peyton Farmer, Commonwealth's Attorney of Caroline County.

Enter 22 January 1965.

Leon M. Bazile, Judge.

[fol. 15]

IN THE CIRCUIT COURT OF CAROLINE COUNTY

NOTICE OF APPEAL AND ASSIGNMENTS OF ERROR

To the Clerk of the Circuit Court of Caroline County:

Please take notice that the defendants herein, Richard Perry Loving and Mildred Delores Jeter, intend to appeal for a Writ of Error and *Supersedeas* from a final order entered herein on January 22, 1965, which order denied the defendants' motion to vacate the judgment and set aside the sentence previously entered herein. The defendants assign the following errors:

1. The Court erred in holding that the anti-miscegenation statutes did not violate the due process and equal protection clauses of Section 1 of the Constitution of Virginia and the fourteenth amendment to the Federal Constitution.

2. The Court erred in holding that the sentence and suspension was not a violation of due process of law.

3. The Court erred in holding that Section 53-272 of the Code of Virginia of 1950, does not proscribe reasonable limits upon the period of suspension of sentence.

  Richard Perry Loving and Mildred Delores Jeter Loving, by Counsel.

Lainof, Cohen & Cohen, Counsel for Defendants, 1513 King Street, Alexandria, Virginia, By B. S. Cohen, By Philip J. Hirschkop.

[fol. 19]

IN THE SUPREME COURT OF APPEALS OF VIRGINIA

Record No. 6163

Present: All the Justices

RICHARD PERRY LOVING, et al.,

—v—

COMMONWEALTH OF VIRGINIA.

OPINION BY JUSTICE HARRY L. CARRICO—March 7, 1966
From the Circuit Court of Caroline County
Leon M. Bazile, Judge

On January 6, 1959, Richard Perry Loving and Mildred Jeter Loving, the defendants, were convicted, upon their pleas of guilty, under an indictment charging that "the said Richard Perry Loving being a White person and the said Mildred Delores Jeter being a Colored person, did unlawfully and feloniously go out of the State of Virginia, for the purpose of being married, and with the intention of returning to the State of Virginia and were married out of the State of Virginia, to-wit, in the District of Columbia on June 2, 1958, and afterwards returned to and resided in the County of Caroline, State of Virginia, cohabiting as man and wife." (Code, § 20-58.)[1]

---

[1] "§ 20-58. *Leaving State to evade law.*—If any white person and colored person shall go out of this State, for the purpose of being married, and with the intention of returning, and be married out of it, and afterwards return to and reside in it, cohabiting as man and wife, they shall be punished as provided in § 20-59, and the marriage shall be governed by the same law as if it had been solemnized in this State. The fact of their cohabitation here as man and wife shall be evidence of their marriage."

[fol. 20] The trial court fixed "the punishment of both accused at one year each in jail." (Code, § 20-59.)[2] The court suspended the sentences "for a period of twenty-five years upon the provision that both accused leave Caroline County and the state of Virginia at once and do not return together or at the same time to said county and state for a period of twenty-five years."

On November 6, 1963, the defendants filed a "Motion to Vacate Judgment and Set Aside Sentence" alleging that they had complied with the terms of their suspended sentences but asserting that the statute under which they were convicted was unconstitutional and that the sentences imposed upon them were invalid.

The court denied the motion by an order entered on January 22, 1965, and to that order the defendants were granted this writ of error.

There is no dispute that Richard Perry Loving is a white person and that Mildred Jeter Loving is a colored person within the meaning of Code, § 20-58. Nor is there any dispute that the actions of the defendants, as set forth in the [fol. 21] indictment, violated the provisions of Code, § 20-58.

The sole contention of the defendants, with respect to their convictions, is that Virginia's statutes prohibiting the intermarriage of white and colored persons are violative of the Constitution of Virginia and the Constitution of the United States. Such statutes, the defendants argue, deny them due process of law and equal protection of the law.

The problem here presented is not new to this court nor to other courts, both state and federal, throughout the country. The question was most recently before this court in 1955, in *Naim* v. *Naim*, 197 Va. 80, 87 S. E. 2d 749, remanded

---

[2] "§ 20-59. *Punishment for marriage.*—If any white person intermarry with a colored person, or any colored person intermarry with a white person, he shall be guilty of a felony and shall be punished by confinement in the penitentiary for not less than one nor more than five years."

350 U. S. 891, 100 L. ed. 784, 76 S. Ct. 151, affd. 197 Va. 734, 90 S. E. 2d 849, app. dism. 350 U. S. 985, 100 L. ed. 852, 76 S. Ct. 472.

In the *Naim* case, the Virginia statutes relating to miscegenetic marriages were fully investigated and their constitutionality was upheld. There, it was pointed out that more than one-half of the states then had miscegenation statutes and that, in spite of numerous attacks in both state and federal courts, no court, save one, had held such statutes unconstitutional. The lone exception, it was noted, [fol. 22] was the California Supreme Court which declared the California miscegenation statutes unconstitutional in *Perez* v. *Sharp*, 32 Cal. 2d 711, 198 P. 2d 17 (sub nom. *Perez* v. *Lippold*).

The *Naim* opinion, written for the court by Mr. Justice Buchanan, contains an exhaustive survey and citation of authorities, both case and text from both state and federal sources, upon the subject of miscegenation statutes. It is not necessary to repeat all those citations in this opinion because the defendants concede that the *Naim* case, if given effect here, is controlling of the question before us. They urge us, however, to reverse our decision in that case, contending that the decision is wrong because the judicial authority upon which it was based no longer has any validity. Our inquiry must be, therefore, whether a change in the *Naim* decision is required.

The defendants say that the *Naim* opinion relied upon *Plessy* v. *Ferguson*, 163 U. S. 537, 41 L. ed. 256, 16 S. Ct. 1138, but argue that the United States Supreme Court reversed the *Plessy* decision in *Brown* v. *Board of Education*, 347 U. S. 483, 98 L. ed. 873, 74 S. Ct. 686.

The *Plessy* case, decided in 1896, involved an attack upon the constitutionality of a Louisiana statute requiring [fol. 23] separate railway carriages for the white and colored races. The statute was upheld by the Supreme Court under the "separate but equal" doctrine there enunciated by the court.

In the *Brown* case, decided in 1954, the Supreme Court ruled "that in the field of public education the doctrine of 'separate but equal' has no place" and that "Any language in *Plessy* v. *Ferguson* contrary to this finding is rejected." 98 L. ed., at p. 881.

The *Plessy* case was cited in the *Naim* opinion to show that the United States Supreme Court had made no decision at variance with an earlier holding by the Tenth Circuit Court of Appeals in *Stevens* v. *United States*, 146 F. 2d 120, that "a state is empowered to forbid marriages between persons of African descent and persons of other races or descents. Such a statute does not contravene the Fourteenth Amendment."

The *Naim* opinion contained a quotation from the *Plessy* case that "Laws forbidding the intermarriage of the two races . . . have been universally recognized as within the police power of the state." Nothing was said in the *Brown* case which detracted in any way from the effect of the language quoted from the *Plessy* opinion. As Mr. Justice Buchanan pointed out in the *Naim* opinion, the holding in [fol. 24] the *Brown* case, that the opportunity to acquire an education "is a right which must be made available to all on equal terms," cannot support a claim for the intermarriage of the races or that such intermarriage is a "right which must be made available to all on equal terms."

The United States Supreme Court itself has indicated that the *Brown* decision does not have the effect upon miscegenation statutes which the defendants claim for it. The *Brown* decision was announced on May 17, 1954. On November 22, 1954, just six months later, the United States Supreme Court denied certiorari in a case in which Alabama's statute forbidding intermarriage between white and colored persons had been upheld against the claim that the statute denied the Negro appellant "her constitutional right and privilege of intermarrying with a white male person," and that it violated the Privileges and Immunities, the Due Process and the Equal Protection Clauses of the Fourteenth Amendment. *Jackson* v. *State*, 37 Ala. App.

519, 72 So. 2d 114, 260 Ala. 698, 72 So. 2d 116, cert. denied 348 U. S. 888, 99 L. ed. 698, 75 S. Ct. 210.

The defendants also say that the *Naim* opinion relied upon *Pace* v. *Alabama,* 106 U. S. 583, 27 L. ed. 207, 1 S. Ct. 637, but contend that the United States Supreme Court overruled the *Pace* decision in *McLaughlin* v. *Florida,* 379 [fol. 25] U. S. 184, 13 L. ed. 2d 222, 85 S. Ct. 283.

The *Pace* case, decided in 1883, involved an attack upon the constitutionality of an Alabama statute imposing a penalty for adultery or fornication between a white person and a Negro. Another statute provided a lesser penalty "If any man and woman live together in adultery or fornication." A white woman and Pace, a Negro, were convicted and sentenced under the first statute "for living together in a state of adultery or fornication." Pace appealed, claiming that the statute under which he had been convicted was violative of the Fourteenth Amendment. The court rejected this claim, holding that "Whatever discrimination is made in the punishment prescribed in the two sections is directed against the offense designated and not against the person of any particular color or race." 27 L. ed., at p. 208.

In the *McLaughlin* case, decided in 1964, the Supreme Court had under review a Florida statute which made it unlawful for a white person and a Negro, "not married to each other," to "habitually live in and occupy in the night time the same room." The statute in dispute provided for a different burden of proof and a different penalty than were provided by other statutes relating to adultery and fornication generally. Florida sought to sustain the [fol. 26] validity of the statute under the holding in *Pace* v. *Alabama*. The court, however, ruled the Florida statute invalid, saying of *Pace* v. *Alabama* that it "represents a limited view of the Equal Protection Clause which has not withstood analysis in the subsequent decisions of this Court." 13 L. ed. 2d, at p. 226.

The *Pace* case, like the *Plessy* case, was cited in the *Naim* opinion to show that the United States Supreme Court had made no decision at variance with the rule that a state may validly forbid interracial marriages. The *McLaughlin* decision detracted not one bit from the position asserted in the *Naim* opinion.

Both parties to the *McLaughlin* controversy cited Florida's miscegenation statute, making it unlawful for a white person to marry a Negro. McLaughlin contended that the miscegenation statute was unconstitutional because it prevented him from asserting, against the cohabitation charge, the defense of common law marriage. Florida argued that it was necessary that its cohabitation statute be upheld so as to carry out the purposes of its miscegenation statute which, it contended, was "immune from attack under the Equal Protection Clause." The court ruled that it was [fol. 27] unnecessary to consider McLaughlin's contention in this respect because the court was holding in his favor on the cohabitation statute. As for Florida's contention, the court said that, for purposes of argument, the constitutionality of the miscegenation statute would be assumed and that it was deciding the case "without reaching the question of the validity of the State's prohibition against interracial marriage." 13 L. ed. 2d, at p. 230.

The defendants direct our attention to numerous federal decisions in the civil rights field in support of their claims that the *Naim* case should be reversed and that the statutes under consideration deny them due process of law and equal protection of the law.

We have given consideration to these decisions, but it must be pointed out that none of them deals with miscegenation statutes or curtails a legal truth which has always been recognized—that there is an overriding state interest in the institution of marriage. None of these decisions takes away from what was said by the United States Supreme Court in *Maynard* v. *Hill*, 125 U. S. 190, 31 L. ed. 654, 657, 8 S. Ct. 723:

> "Marriage, as creating the most important relation in life, as having more to do with the morals and [fol. 28] civilization of a people than any other insti-

tution, has always been subject to the control of the Legislature."

The defendants also refer us to a number of texts dealing with the sociological, biological and anthropological aspects of the question of interracial marriages to support their argument that the *Naim* decision is erroneous and that such marriages should not be forbidden by law.

A decision by this court reversing the *Naim* case upon consideration of the opinions of such text writers would be judicial legislation in the rawest sense of that term. Such arguments are properly addressable to the legislature, which enacted the law in the first place, and not to this court, whose prescribed role in the separated powers of government is to adjudicate, and not to legislate.

Our one and only function in this instance is to determine whether, for sound judicial considerations, the *Naim* case should be reversed. Today, more than ten years since that decision was handed down by this court, a number of states still have miscegenation statutes and yet there has been no new decision reflecting adversely upon the validity of such statutes. We find no sound judicial reason, therefore, to depart from our holding in the *Naim* case. [fol. 29] According that decision all of the weight to which it is entitled under the doctrine of *stare decisis*, we hold it to be binding upon us here and rule that Code, §§ 20-58 and 20-59, under which the defendants were convicted and sentenced, are not violative of the Constitution of Virginia or the Constitution of the United States.

We turn now to the other contention of the defendants —that the sentences imposed upon them are unreasonable and void.

It will be recalled that the trial court suspended the sentences of the defendants for a period of twenty-five years upon the condition that they leave the county and state "at once and do not return together or at the same time to said county and state for a period of twenty-five years."

The defendants first say that the effect of the sentences was to banish them from the state. They refer us to the case of *State* v. *Doughtie,* 237 N.C. 368, 74 S. E. 2d 922, where it was held that "banishment . . . is impliedly prohibited by public policy . . . A sentence of banishment is undoubtedly void."

Although the defendants were, by the terms of the suspended sentences, ordered to leave the state, their sentences did not technically constitute banishment because they [fol. 30] were permitted to return to the state, provided they did not return together or at the same time.

Thus, we do not agree with the defendants' contention that the sentences are void because they constitute banishment. We do agree with their further contention, however, that the conditions of the suspensions are so unreasonable as to render the sentences void.

The trial court acted under the authority of Code, § 53-272 in suspending the sentences of the defendants. The purpose of this statute is to secure the rehabilitation of the offender, enabling him to repent and reform so that he may be restored to a useful place in society. *Marshall* v. *Commonwealth,* 202 Va. 217, 219, 116 S. E. 2d 270; *Slayton* v. *Commonwealth,* 185 Va. 357, 365-366, 38 S. E. 2d 479; *Wilborn* v. *Saunders,* 170 Va. 153, 160-161, 195 S. E. 723.

To effect this statutory purpose, the courts are authorized to impose conditions upon the suspension of execution or imposition of sentence. But such conditions must be reasonable, having due regard to the nature of the offense, the background of the offender and the surrounding circumstances. *Dyke* v. *Commonwealth,* 193 Va. 478, 484, 69 S. E. 2d 48.

[fol. 31] Here, the real gravamen of the offense charged against the defendants, under Code, § 20-58, was their cohabitation as man and wife in this state, following their departure from the state to evade Virginia law, their marriage in another jurisdiction and their return to Virginia. Without such cohabitation, there would have been no offense for which they could have been tried, notwithstanding their other actions.

When the defendants' sentences were suspended, the purpose which the trial court should reasonably have sought to serve was that the defendants not continue to violate Code, § 20-58. The condition reasonably necessary to achieve that purpose was that the defendants not again cohabit as man and wife in this state. There is nothing in the record concerning the defendants' backgrounds or the circumstances of the case to indicate that anything more was necessary to secure the defendants' rehabilitation and to accomplish the purposes envisioned by Code, § 53-272.

It was, therefore, unreasonable to require that the defendants leave the state and not return thereafter together or at the time time. Such unreasonableness renders the sentences void and they will, accordingly, be vacated and set aside. The case will be remanded to the trial court with [fol. 32] directions to re-sentence the defendants in accordance with Code, § 20-59, attaching to the suspended sentences, to be imposed upon the defendants, conditions not inconsistent with the views expressed in this opinion.

In this connection, although it has not been alluded to by either side to this controversy, it should be noted that Code, § 20-59 provides for a sentence in the penitentiary, and not in jail, as called for in the sentencing order of the trial court.

That portion of the order appealed from upholding the constitutionality of Code, §§ 20-58 and 20-59, and the convictions of the defendants thereunder, is affirmed; that portion of said order upholding the validity of the sentences imposed upon the defendants is reversed, and the case is remanded for further proceedings.

Affirmed in part, reversed in part and remanded.

[fol. 33]

IN THE SUPREME COURT OF APPEALS
OF THE SUPREME COURT OF APPEALS

Record No. 6163

RICHARD PERRY LOVING and MILDRED JETER LOVING, Plaintiffs in error,

against

COMMONWEALTH OF VIRGINIA, Defendant in error.

MANDATE—March 7, 1966

Upon a writ of error and supersedeas to a judgment rendered by the Circuit Court of Caroline County on the 22nd day of January, 1965.

This day came as well the plaintiffs in error, by counsel, as the Attorney General on behalf of the Commonwealth, and the court having maturely considered the transcript of the record of the judgment aforesaid and arguments of counsel, is of opinion, for reasons stated in writing and filed with the record, that there is error in part in the judgment complained of. It is therefore adjudged and ordered that the said judgment, in so far as it upholds the constitutionality of Code, §§ 20-58 and 20-59, and the convictions of the plaintiffs in error thereunder, be, and the same is hereby, affirmed; and in so far as it upholds the validity of the sentences imposed upon the plaintiffs in error, be, and the same is hereby, reversed and set aside, and the case is remanded to the said circuit court for further proceedings in accordance with the views expressed in the said written opinion of this court.

Which is ordered to be forthwith certified to the said circuit court.

[fol. 34] Motion for stay and order thereon (omitted in printing).

[fol. 37]

IN THE SUPREME COURT OF APPEALS OF THE COMMONWEALTH OF VIRGINIA

Record No. 6163

RICHARD PERRY LOVING and MILDRED JETER LOVING, Appellants,

v.

COMMONWEALTH OF VIRGINIA, Appellee.

NOTICE OF APPEAL TO THE SUPREME COURT OF THE UNITED STATES—Filed May 31, 1966

I. Notice is hereby given that Richard Perry Loving and Mildred Jeter Loving, the appellants above named, hereby appeal to the Supreme Court of the United States from the final Order of this, the Supreme Court of Appeals of Virginia, entered herein on March 7, 1966, affirming the decision of the Circuit Court of Caroline County entered on January 22, 1965, which decision denied the appellants' motion to vacate the judgment and set aside the sentence, and further, affirming the judgment of conviction originally entered by the Circuit Court of Caroline County on January 6, 1959.

This appeal is taken pursuant to 28 U.S.C. § 1257 (2).

Appellants, Richard Perry Loving, a White person, and Mildred Jeter Loving, a Negro person, were convicted for "unlawfully and feloniously go[ing] out of the State of Virginia, for the purpose of being married, and with the intention of returning to the State of Virginia . . . [and] cohabiting as man and wife against the peace and dignity of the Commonweath". §§ 20-58, 20-59 of the 1950 Code [fol. 38] of Virginia as amended. They were each sentenced to one year in jail, which sentences were suspended "for a period of twenty-five years upon the provision that both accused leave Caroline County and the State of Virginia at once and do not return together or at the same time to said County and State for a period of twenty-five years". The convictions were affirmed, but the sentences were reversed by the Virginia Supreme Court of Appeals as part of the judgment appealed from herein. Your appellants are presently free because the execution of the judgment of the Virginia Supreme Court of Appeals has been stayed by that Court until the final determination of their convictions by the United States Supreme Court.

II. The clerk will please prepare a transcript of the record in this cause for transmission to the Clerk of the Supreme Court of the United States, and include in said transcript the following:

1. Both of the Warrants of Arrest for Criminal Dockets No. 928 and 929.

2. The True bill returned by the grand jurors of the Commonwealth of Virginia at the October 1958 term.

3. The Order which carries the heading "Indictment for a Felony" which is signed by Leon M. Bazile, Judge, and dated the 6th of January, 1959 and which is entered in Common Law Order Book 14, page 161.

4. The motion to vacate judgment and set aside sentence filed on the 6th of November, 1963.

5. The ten page undated written opinion signed by Leon M. Bazile, Judge.

[fol. 39] 6. The Order entered on 22 January 1965, signed by Judge Leon M. Bazile.

7. The Notice of Appeal and Assignments of Error, filed on March 3, 1965.

8. The Writ of Error and Supersedeas granted in this matter on June 11, 1965, together with the clerk's certificate thereof on June 14, 1965.

9. The Opinion by Justice Harry L. Carrico rendered in this matter on March 7, 1966.

10. Appellants' Motion for Stay of March 24, 1966.

11. The Order Staying Execution of Judgment of March 28, 1966.

12. This Notice of Appeal.

III. The following questions are presented by this appeal:

1. Do the Virginia anti-miscegenation laws (§ 20-50 et seq. of the 1950 Code of Virginia as amended) violate the due process and equal protection clauses of the 14th Amendment to the United States Constitution?

2. Does a state statute which proscribes marriage between members of different races violate constitutional rights of privacy?

3. Does a state statute which proscribes marriage between members of different races violate a constitutional right of freedom to marry?

4. Is a state law valid under our Constitution which makes the color of a person's skin the test of whether his marriage constitutes a criminal offense?

[fol. 40] 5. Do the Virginia anti-miscegenation statutes deprive the appellants of the civil rights guaranteed by § 1981 of Title 42 of the U.S. Code?

>Richard Perry Loving and Mildred Jeter Loving, By Counsel;
>Bernard S. Cohen, Philip J. Hirschkop, Lainof, Cohen & Cohen, Esqs.;
>Attorneys for Appellants, 1513 King Street, Alexandria, Virginia, By: Bernard S. Cohen.

Of Counsel:

Melvin Wulf, Esq., American Civil Liberties Union, 156 Fifth Avenue, New York, New York.

Proof of Service

I, Bernard S. Cohen, one of the attorneys for Richard Perry Loving and Mildred Jeter Loving, appellants herein, and a member of the Bar of the Supreme Court of the United States, hereby certify that on the 27th day of May, 1966, I served a copy of the foregoing Notice of Appeal to the Supreme Court of the United States, on the Commonwealth of Virginia, by mailing copies in duly addressed envelopes, with first-class postage prepaid, to Robert Y. Button, the Attorney General for the Commonwealth of Virginia and to R. D. McIlwaine, III, Assistant Attorney General for the Commonwealth of Virginia.

> Bernard S. Cohen, Attorney for Richard Perry Loving and Mildred Jeter Loving, 1513 King Street, Alexandria, Virginia.

[fol. 41]

SUPREME COURT OF THE UNITED STATES

No. 395—OCTOBER TERM, 1966

RICHARD PERRY LOVING, et ux., Appellants,

v.

VIRGINIA.

Appeal from the Supreme Court of Appeals of the Commonwealth of Virginia.

ORDER NOTING PROBABLE JURISDICTION—December 12, 1966

The statement of jurisdiction in this case having been submitted and considered by the Court, probable jurisdiction is noted.

Emancipation Proclamation

January 1, 1863 by President Abraham Lincoln

Whereas, on the twenty-second day of September, in the year of our Lord one thousand eight hundred and sixty-two, a proclamation was issued by the President of the United States, containing, among other things, the following, to wit:

That on the first day of January, in the year of our Lord one thousand eight hundred and sixty-three, all persons held as slaves within any State or designated part of a State, the people whereof shall then be in rebellion against the United States, shall be then, thenceforward, and forever free; and the Executive Government of the United States, including the military and naval authority thereof, will recognize and maintain the freedom of such persons, and will do no act or acts to repress such persons, or any of them, in any efforts they may make for their actual freedom.

That the Executive will, on the first day of January aforesaid, by proclamation, designate the States and parts of States, if any, in which the people thereof, respectively, shall then be in rebellion against the United States; and the fact that any State, or the people thereof, shall on that day be, in good faith, represented in the Congress of the United States by members chosen thereto at elections wherein a majority of the qualified voters of such State shall have participated, shall, in the absence of strong countervailing testimony, be deemed conclusive evidence that such State, and the people thereof, are not then in rebellion against the United States.

Now, therefore I, Abraham Lincoln, President of the United States, by virtue of the power in me vested as Commander-in-Chief, of the Army and Navy of the United States in time of actual armed rebellion against the authority and government of the United States, and as a fit and necessary war measure for suppressing said rebellion, do, on this first day of January, in the year of our Lord one thousand eight hundred and sixty-three, and in accordance with my purpose so to do publicly proclaimed for the full period of one hundred days, from the day first above mentioned, order and designate as the States and parts of States wherein the people thereof respectively, are this day in rebellion against the United States, the following, to wit:

Arkansas, Texas, Louisiana, (except the Parishes of St. Bernard, Plaquemines, Jefferson, St. John, St. Charles, St. James Ascension, Assumption, Terrebonne, Lafourche, St. Mary, St. Martin, and Orleans, including the City of New Orleans) Mississippi, Alabama, Florida, Georgia, South Carolina, North Carolina, and Virginia, (except the forty-eight counties designated as West Virginia, and also the counties of Berkley, Accomac, Northampton, Elizabeth City, York, Princess Ann, and Norfolk, including the cities of Norfolk and Portsmouth[)], and which excepted parts, are for the present, left precisely as if this proclamation were not issued.

And by virtue of the power, and for the purpose aforesaid, I do order and declare that all persons held as slaves within said designated States, and parts of States, are, and henceforward shall be free; and that the Executive government of the United States, including the military and naval authorities thereof, will recognize and maintain the freedom of said persons.

And I hereby enjoin upon the people so declared to be free to abstain from all violence, unless in necessary self-defence; and I recommend to them that, in all cases when allowed, they labor faithfully for reasonable wages.

And I further declare and make known, that such persons of suitable condition, will be received into the armed service of the United States to garrison forts, positions, stations, and other places, and to man vessels of all sorts in said service.

And upon this act, sincerely believed to be an act of justice, warranted by the Constitution, upon military necessity, I invoke the considerate judgment of mankind, and the gracious favor of Almighty God.

In witness whereof, I have hereunto set my hand and caused the seal of the United States to be affixed.

Done at the City of Washington, this first day of January, in the year of our Lord one thousand eight hundred and sixty three, and of the Independence of the United States of America the eighty-seventh.

Amendment XIII

January 31 1865

Section 1

Neither slavery nor involuntary servitude, except as a punishment for crime whereof the party shall have been duly convicted, shall exist within the United States, or any place subject to their jurisdiction.

Section 2

Congress shall have power to enforce this article by appropriate legislation.

Amendment XIV

July 9, 1868

Section 1

All persons born or naturalized in the United States, and subject to the jurisdiction thereof, are citizens of the United States and of the state wherein they reside. No state shall make or enforce any law which shall abridge the privileges or immunities of citizens of the United States; nor shall any state deprive any person of life, liberty, or property, without due process of law; nor deny to any person within its jurisdiction the equal protection of the laws.

Section 2

Representatives shall be apportioned among the several states according to their respective numbers, counting the whole number of persons in each state, excluding Indians not taxed. But when the right to vote at any election for the choice of electors for President and Vice President of the United States, Representatives in Congress, the executive and judicial officers of a state, or the members of the legislature thereof, is denied to any of the male inhabitants of such state, being twenty-one years of age, and citizens of the United States, or in any way abridged, except for participation in rebellion, or other crime, the basis of representation therein shall be reduced in the proportion which the number of such male citizens shall bear to the whole number of male citizens twenty-one years of age in such state.

Section 3

No person shall be a Senator or Representative in Congress, or elector of President and Vice President, or hold any office, civil or military, under the United States, or under any state, who, having previously taken an oath, as a member of Congress, or as an officer of the United States, or as a member of any state legislature, or as an executive or judicial officer of any state, to support the Constitution of the United States, shall have engaged in insurrection or rebellion against the same, or given aid or comfort to the enemies thereof. But Congress may by a vote of two-thirds of each House, remove such disability.

Section 4

The validity of the public debt of the United States, authorized by law, including debts incurred for payment of pensions and bounties for services in suppressing insurrection or rebellion, shall not be questioned. But neither the United States nor any state shall assume or pay any debt or obligation incurred in aid of insurrection or rebellion against the United States, or any claim for the loss or emancipation of any slave; but all such debts, obligations and claims shall be held illegal and void.

Section 5

The Congress shall have power to enforce, by appropriate legislation, the provisions of this article.

Amendment XV

February 3, 1870

Section 1

The right of citizens of the United States to vote shall not be denied or abridged by the United States or by any state on account of race, color, or previous condition of servitude.

Section 2

The Congress shall have power to enforce this article by appropriate legislation.

Misc.

POLICE DEPARTMENT
CITY OF MONTGOMERY

Date 12-1-55   19

Complainant   J.F. Blake   (wm)

Address   27 No. Lewis St.   Phone No.

Offense   Misc.   Reported By   Same as above

Address   Phone No.

Date and Time Offense Committed   12-1-55   6:06 pm

Place of Occurrence   In Front of Empire Theatre (On Montgomery Street)

Person or Property Attacked

How Attacked

Person Wanted

Value of Property Stolen   Value Recovered

Details of Complaint (list, describe and give value of property stolen)

We received a call upon arrival the bus operator said he had a colored female

sitting in the white section of the bus, and would not move back.

We (Day & Mixon) also saw her.

The bus operator signed a warrant for her. Rosa Parks, (cf) 634 Cleveland Court.

Rosa Parks (cf) was charged with chapter 6 section 11 of the Montgomery City Code.

Warrant #14254

THIS OFFENSE IS DECLARED:
UNFOUNDED ☐
CLEARED BY ARREST ☐
EXCEPTIONALLY CLEARED ☐
INACTIVE (NOT CLEARED) ☐

Officers   F. B. Day
           D. W. Mixon

Division   Patrol   Time   7:00 pm
                                        12-1-55

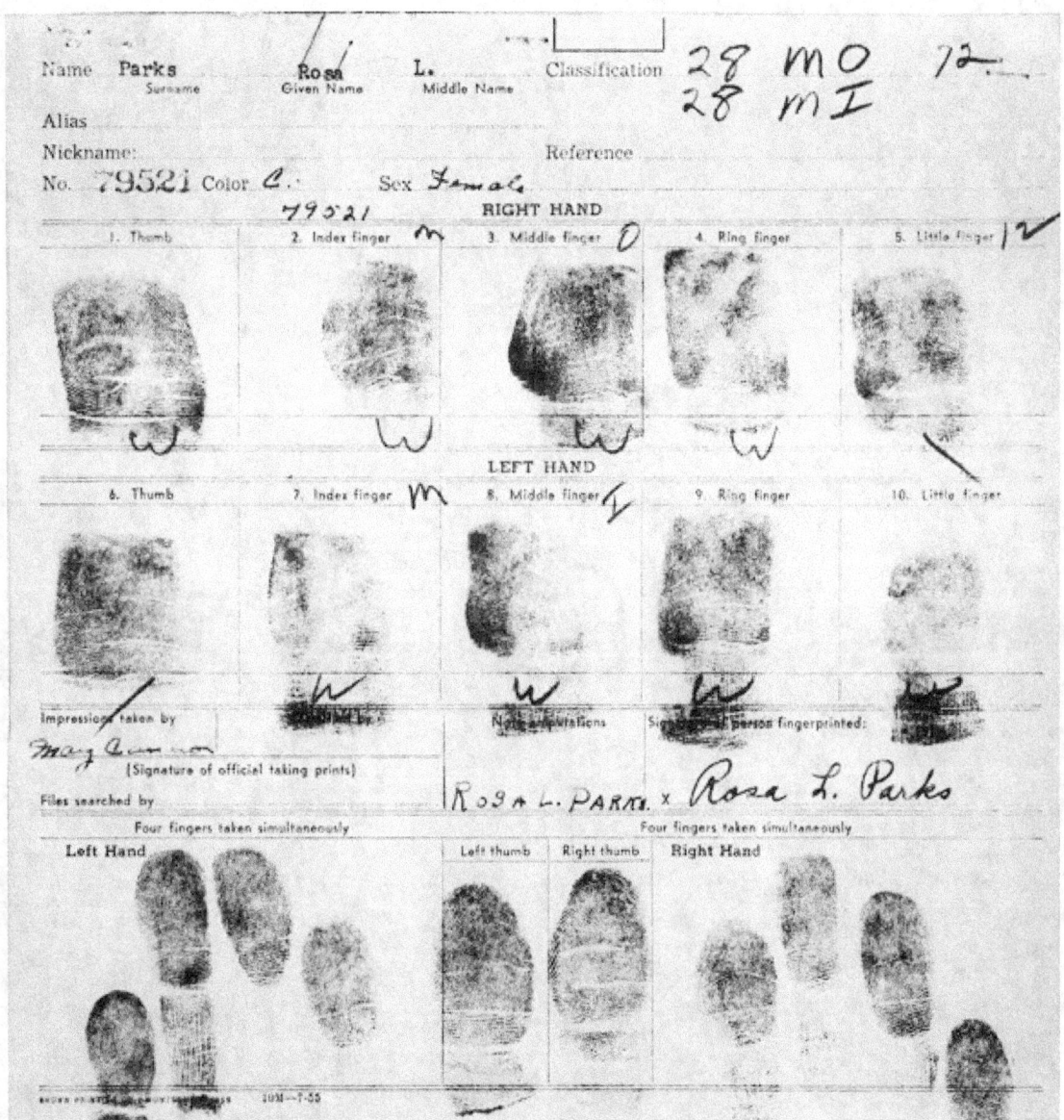

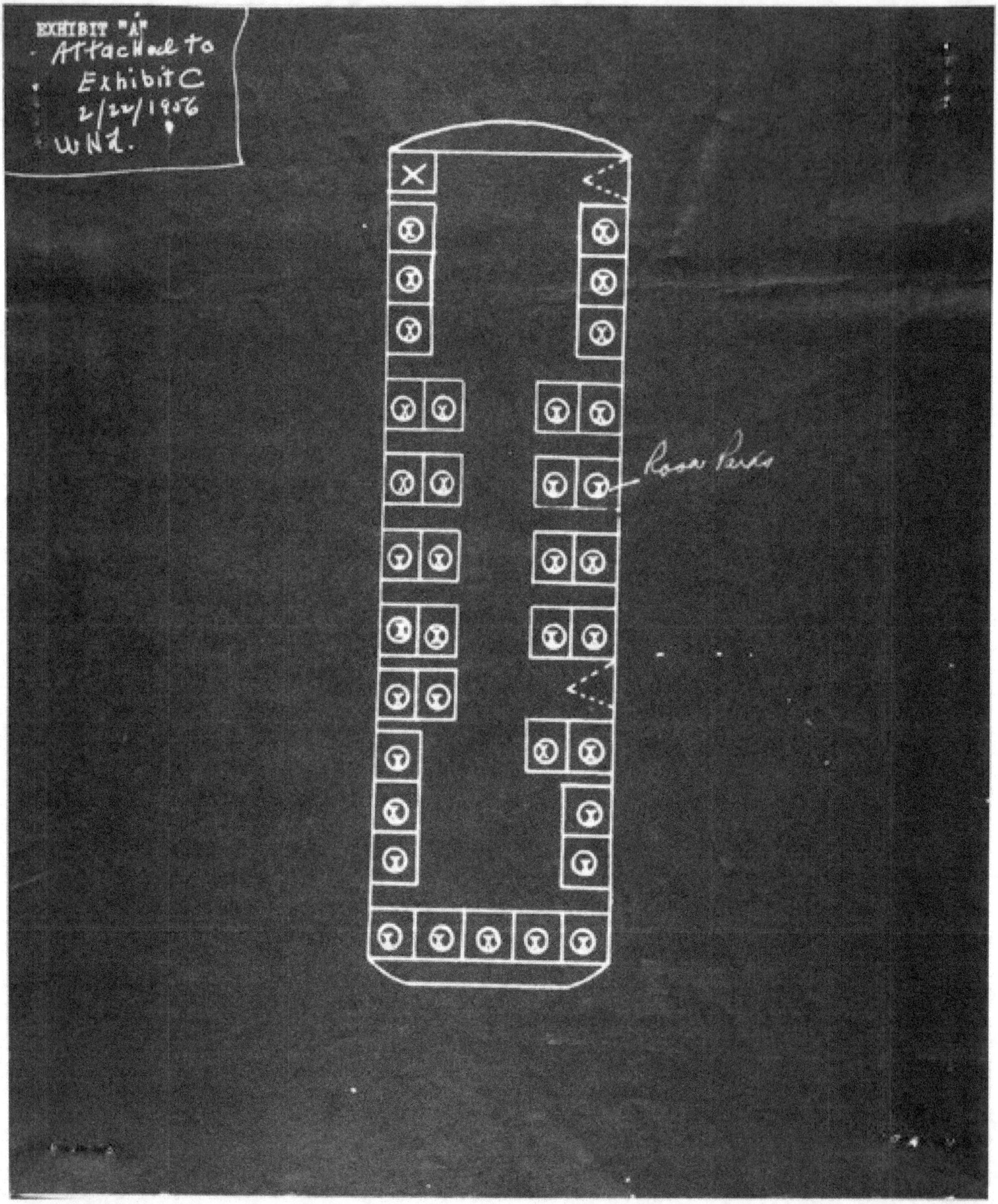

EXHIBIT "A"
Attached to
Exhibit C
2/22/1956
WHd.

Rosa Parks

CIVIL RIGHTS ACT OF 1964

TITLE I - voting

SEC. 101. Section 2004 of the Revised Statutes (42 U.S.C. 1971), as amended by section 131 of the Civil Rights Act of 1957 (71 Stat. 637), and as further amended by section 601 of the Civil Rights Act of 1960 (74 Stat. 90), is further amended as follows:

(a) Insert 1 after (a) in subsection (a) and add at the end of subsection (a) the following new paragraphs:

(2) No person acting under color of law shall

(A) in determining whether any individual is qualified under State law or laws to vote in any Federal election, apply any standard, practice, or procedure different from the standards, practices, or procedures applied under such law or laws to other individuals within the same county, parish, or similar political subdivision who have been found by State officials to be qualified to vote;

(B) deny the right of any individual to vote in any Federal election because of an error or omission on any record or paper relating to any application, registration, or other act requisite to voting, if such error or omission is not material in determining whether such individual is qualified under State law to vote in such election; or

(C) employ any literacy test as a qualification for voting in any Federal election unless (i) such test is administered to each individual and is conducted wholly in writing, and (ii) a certified copy of the test and of the answers given by the individual is furnished to him within twenty-five days of the submission of his request made within the period of time during which records and papers are required to be retained and preserved pursuant to title III of the Civil Rights Act of 1960 (42 U.S.C. 1974--74e; 74 Stat. 88): Provided, however, That the Attorney General may enter into agreements with appropriate State or local authorities that preparation, conduct, and maintenance of such tests in accordance with the provisions of applicable State or local law, including such special provisions as are necessary in the preparation, conduct, and maintenance of such tests for persons who are blind or otherwise physically handicapped, meet the purposes of this subparagraph and constitute compliance therewith.

(3) For purposes of this subsection

(A) The term 'vote' shall have the same meaning as in subsection (e) of this section;

(B) The phrase 'literacy test' includes any test of the ability to read, write, understand, or interpret any matter.

(b) Insert immediately following the period at the end of the first sentence of subsection (c) the following new sentence: If in any such proceeding literacy is a relevant fact there shall be a rebuttable presumption that any person who has not been adjudged an incompetent and who has completed the sixth grade in a public school in, or a private school accredited by, any State or territory, the District of Columbia, or the Commonwealth of Puerto Rico where instruction is carried on predominantly in the English language, possesses sufficient literacy, comprehension, and intelligence to vote in any Federal election.

(c) Add the following subsection (f) and designate the present subsection (f) as subsection (g): (f) When used in subsection (a) or (c) of this section, the words 'Federal election' shall mean any general, special, or primary election held solely or in part for the purpose of electing or selecting any candidate for the office of President, Vice President, presidential elector, Member of the Senate, or Member of the House of Representatives.

(d) Add the following subsection (h):

(h) In any proceeding instituted by the United States in any district court of the United States under this section in which the Attorney General requests a finding of a pattern or practice of discrimination pursuant to subsection (e) of this section the Attorney General, at the time he files the complaint, or any defendant in the proceeding, within twenty days after service upon him of the complaint, may file with the clerk of such court a request that a court of three judges be convened to hear and determine the entire case. A copy of the request for a three-judge court shall be immediately furnished by such clerk to the chief judge of the circuit (or in his absence, the presiding circuit judge of the circuit) in which the case is pending. Upon receipt of the copy of such request it shall be the duty of the chief justice of the circuit or the presiding circuit judge, as the case may be, to designate immediately three judges in such circuit, of whom at least one shall be a circuit judge and another of whom shall be a district judge of the court in which the proceeding was instituted, to hear and determine such case, and it shall be the duty of the judges so designated to assign the case for hearing at the earliest practicable date, to participate in the hearing and determination thereof, and to cause the case to be in every way expedited.

An appeal from the final judgment of such court will lie to the Supreme Court.

In any proceeding brought under subsection (c) of this section to enforce subsection (b) of this section, or in the event neither the Attorney General nor any defendant files a request for a three-judge court in any proceeding authorized by this subsection, it shall be the duty of the chief judge of the district (or in his absence, the acting chief judge) in which the case is pending immediately to designate a judge in such district to hear and determine the case. In the event that no judge in the district is available to hear and determine the case, the chief judge of the district, or the acting chief judge, as the case may be, shall certify this fact to the chief judge of the circuit (or, in his absence, the acting chief judge) who shall then designate a district or circuit judge of the circuit to hear and determine the case.

It shall be the duty of the judge designated pursuant to this section to assign the case for hearing at the earliest practicable date and to cause the case to be in every way expedited.

TITLE II—RELIEF OF PUBLIC DISCRIMINATION

SEC. 201. (a) All persons shall be entitled to the full and equal enjoyment of the goods, services, facilities, and privileges, advantages, and accommodations of any place of public accommodation, as defined in this section, without discrimination or segregation on the ground of race, color, religion, or national origin.

(b) Each of the following establishments which serves the public is a place of public accommodation within the meaning of this title if its operations affect commerce, or if discrimination or segregation by it is supported by State action:

(1) any inn, hotel, motel, or other establishment which provides lodging to transient guests, other than an establishment located within a building which contains not more than five rooms for rent or hire and which is actually occupied by the proprietor of such establishment as his residence;

(2) any restaurant, cafeteria, lunchroom, lunch counter, soda fountain, or other facility principally engaged in selling food for consumption on the premises, including, but not limited to, any such facility located on the premises of any retail establishment; or any gasoline station;

(3) any motion picture house, theater, concert hall, sports arena, stadium or other place of exhibition or entertainment; and

(4) any establishment (A)(i) which is physically located within the premises of any establishment otherwise covered by this subsection, or (ii) within the premises of which is physically located any such covered establishment, and (B) which holds itself out as serving patrons of such covered establishment.

(c) The operations of an establishment affect commerce within the meaning of this title if (1) it is one of the establishments described in paragraph (1) of subsection (b); (2) in the case of an establishment described in paragraph (2) of subsection (b), it serves or offers to serve interstate travelers or a substantial portion of the food which it serves, or gasoline or other products which it sells, has moved in commerce; (3) in the case of an establishment described in paragraph (3) of subsection (b), it customarily presents films, performances, athletic teams, exhibitions, or other sources of entertainment which move in commerce; and (4) in the case of an establishment described in paragraph (4) of subsection (b), it is physically located within the premises of, or there is physically located within its premises, an establishment the operations of which affect commerce within the meaning of this subsection. For purposes of this section, commerce means travel, trade, traffic, commerce, transportation, or communication among the several States, or between the District of Columbia and any State, or between any foreign country or any territory or possession and any State or the District of Columbia, or between points in the same State but through any other State or the District of Columbia or a foreign country.

(d) Discrimination or segregation by an establishment is supported by State action within the meaning of this title if such discrimination or segregation (1) is carried on under color of any law, statute, ordinance, or regulation; or (2) is carried on under color of any custom or usage required or enforced by officials of the State or political subdivision thereof; or (3) is required by action of the State or political subdivision thereof.

(e) The provisions of this title shall not apply to a private club or other establishment not in fact open to the public, except to the extent that the facilities of such establishment are made available to the customers or patrons of an establishment within the scope of subsection (b).

SEC. 202. All persons shall be entitled to be free, at any establishment or place, from discrimination or segregation of any kind on the ground of race, color, religion, or national origin, if such discrimination or segregation is or purports to be required by any law, statute, ordinance, regulation, rule, or order of a State or any agency or political subdivision thereof.

SEC. 203. No person shall (a) withhold, deny, or attempt to withhold or deny, or deprive or attempt to deprive, any person of any right or privilege secured by section 201 or 202, or (b) intimidate, threaten, or coerce, or attempt to intimidate, threaten, or coerce any person with the purpose of interfering with any right or privilege secured by section 201 or 202, or (c) punish or attempt to punish any person for exercising or attempting to exercise any right or privilege secured by section 201 or 202.

SEC. 204. (a) Whenever any person has engaged or there are reasonable grounds to believe that any person is about to engage in any act or practice prohibited by section 203, a civil action for preventive relief, including an application for a permanent or temporary injunction, restraining order, or other order, may be instituted by the person aggrieved and, upon timely application, the court may, in its discretion, permit the Attorney General to intervene in such civil action if he certifies that the case is of general public importance.

Upon application by the complainant and in such circumstances as the court may deem just, the court may appoint an attorney for such complainant and may authorize the commencement of the civil action without the payment of fees, costs, or security.

(b) In any action commenced pursuant to this title, the court, in its discretion, may allow the prevailing party, other than the United States, a reasonable attorney's fee as part of the costs, and the United States shall be liable for costs the same as a private person.

(c) In the case of an alleged act or practice prohibited by this title which occurs in a State, or political subdivision of a State, which has a State or local law prohibiting such act or practice and establishing or authorizing a State or local authority to grant or seek relief from such practice or to institute criminal proceedings with respect thereto upon receiving notice thereof, no civil action may be brought under subsection (a) before the expiration of thirty days after written notice of such alleged act or practice has been given to the appropriate State or local authority by registered mail or in person, provided that the court may stay proceedings in such civil action pending the termination of State or local enforcement proceedings.

(d) In the case of an alleged act or practice prohibited by this title which occurs in a State, or political subdivision of a State, which has no State or local law prohibiting such act or practice, a civil action may be brought under subsection (a): Provided, That the court may refer the matter to the Community Relations Service established by title X of this Act for as long as the court believes there is a reasonable possibility of obtaining voluntary compliance, but for not more than sixty days: Provided further, That upon expiration of such sixty-day period, the court may extend such period for an additional period, not to exceed a cumulative total of one hundred and twenty days, if it believes there then exists a reasonable possibility of securing voluntary compliance.

SEC. 205. The Service is authorized to make a full investigation of any complaint referred to it by the court under section 204(d) and may hold such hearings with respect thereto as may be necessary. The Service shall conduct any hearings with respect to any such complaint in executive session, and shall not release any testimony given therein except by agreement of all parties involved in the complaint with the permission of the court, and the Service shall endeavor to bring about a voluntary settlement between the parties.

SEC. 206. (a) Whenever the Attorney General has reasonable cause to believe that any person or group of persons is engaged in a pattern or practice of resistance to the full enjoyment of any of the rights secured by this title, and that the pattern or practice is of such a nature and is intended to deny the full exercise of the rights herein described, the Attorney General may bring a civil action in the appropriate district court of the United States by filing with it a complaint (1) signed by him (or in his absence the Acting Attorney General), (2) setting forth facts pertaining to such pattern or practice, and (3) requesting such preventive relief, including an application for a permanent or temporary injunction, restraining order or other order against the person or persons responsible for such pattern or practice, as he deems necessary to insure the full enjoyment of the rights herein described.

(b) In any such proceeding the Attorney General may file with the clerk of such court a request that a court of three judges be convened to hear and determine the case. Such request by the Attorney General shall be accompanied by a certificate that, in his opinion, the case is of general public importance. A copy of the certificate and request for a three-judge court shall be immediately furnished by such clerk to the chief judge of the circuit (or in his absence, the presiding circuit judge of the circuit) in which the case is pending. Upon receipt of the copy of such request it shall be the duty of the chief judge of the circuit or the presiding circuit judge, as the case may be, to designate immediately three judges in such circuit, of whom at least one shall be a circuit judge and another of whom shall be a district judge of the court in which the proceeding was instituted, to hear and determine such case, and it shall be the duty of the judges so designated to assign the case for hearing at the earliest practicable date, to participate in the hearing and determination thereof, and to cause the case to be in every way expedited. An appeal from the final judgment of such court will lie to the Supreme Court.

In the event the Attorney General fails to file such a request in any such proceeding, it shall be the duty of the chief judge of the district (or in his absence, the acting chief judge) in which the case is pending immediately to designate a judge in such district to hear and determine the case. In the event that no judge in the district is available to hear and determine the case, the chief judge of the district, or the acting chief judge, as the case may be, shall certify this fact to the chief judge of the circuit (or in his absence, the acting chief judge) who shall then designate a district or circuit judge of the circuit to hear and determine the case.

It shall be the duty of the judge designated pursuant to this section to assign the case for hearing at the earliest practicable date and to cause the case to be in every way expedited.

SEC. 207. (a) The district courts of the United States shall have jurisdiction of proceedings instituted pursuant to this title and shall exercise the same without regard to whether the aggrieved party shall have exhausted any administrative or other remedies that may be provided by law.

(b) The remedies provided in this title shall be the exclusive means of enforcing the rights based on this title, but nothing in this title shall preclude any individual or any State or local agency from asserting any right based on any other Federal or State law not inconsistent with this title, including any statute or ordinance requiring nondiscrimination in public establishments or accommodations, or from pursuing any remedy, civil or criminal, which may be available for the vindication or enforcement of such right.

TITLE III – DESEGREGATION OF PUBLIC FACILITIES

SEC. 301. (a) Whenever the Attorney General receives a complaint in writing signed by an individual to the effect that he is being deprived of or threatened with the loss of his right to the equal protection of the laws, on account of his race, color, religion, or national origin, by being denied equal utilization of any public facility which is owned, operated, or managed by or on behalf of any State or subdivision thereof, other than a public school or public college as defined in section 401 of title IV hereof, and the Attorney General believes the complaint is meritorious and certifies that the signer or signers of such complaint are unable, in his judgment, to initiate and maintain appropriate legal proceedings for relief and that the institution of an action will materially further the orderly progress of desegregation in public facilities, the Attorney General is authorized to institute for or in the name of the United States a civil action in any appropriate district court of the United States against such parties and for such relief as may be appropriate, and such court shall have and shall exercise jurisdiction of proceedings instituted pursuant to this section. The Attorney General may implead as defendants such additional parties as are or become necessary to the grant of effective relief hereunder.

(b) The Attorney General may deem a person or persons unable to initiate and maintain appropriate legal proceedings within the meaning of subsection

(a) of this section when such person or persons are unable, either directly or through other interested persons or organizations, to bear the expense of the litigation or to obtain effective legal representation; or whenever he is satisfied that the institution of such litigation would jeopardize the personal safety, employment, or economic standing of such person or persons, their families, or their property.

SEC. 302. In any action or proceeding under this title the United States shall be liable for costs, including a reasonable attorney's fee, the same as a private person.

SEC. 303. Nothing in this title shall affect adversely the right of any person to sue for or obtain relief in any court against discrimination in any facility covered by this title.

SEC. 304. A complaint as used in this title is a writing or document within the meaning of section 1001, title 18, United States Code.

TITLE IV – DESEGREGATION OF PUBLIC EDUCATION

DEFINITIONS

SEC. 401. As used in this title--

(a) Commissioner means the Commissioner of Education.

(b) Desegregation means the assignment of students to public schools and within such schools without regard to their race, color, religion, or national origin, but desegregation shall not mean the assignment of students to public schools in order to overcome racial imbalance.

(c) Public school means any elementary or secondary educational institution, and public college means any institution of higher education or any technical or vocational school above the secondary school level, provided that such public school or public college is operated by a State, subdivision of a State, or governmental agency within a State, or operated wholly or predominantly from or through the use of governmental funds or property, or funds or property derived from a governmental source.

(d) School board means any agency or agencies which administer a system of one or more public schools and any other agency which is responsible for the assignment of students to or within such system.

SURVEY AND REPORT OF EDUCATIONAL OPPORTUNITIES

SEC. 402. The Commissioner shall conduct a survey and make a report to the President and the Congress, within two years of the enactment of this title, concerning the lack of availability of equal educational opportunities for individuals by reason of race, color, religion, or national origin in public educational institutions at all levels in the United States, its territories and possessions, and the District of Columbia.

TECHNICAL ASSISTANCE

SEC. 403. The Commissioner is authorized, upon the application of any school board, State, municipality, school district, or other governmental unit legally responsible for operating a public school or schools, to render technical assistance to such applicant in the preparation, adoption, and implementation of plans for the desegregation of public schools. Such technical assistance may, among other activities, include making available to such agencies information regarding effective methods of coping with special educational problems occasioned by desegregation, and making available to such agencies personnel of the Office of Education or other persons specially equipped to advise and assist them in coping with such problems.

TRAINING INSTITUTES

SEC. 404. The Commissioner is authorized to arrange, through grants or contracts, with institutions of higher education for the operation of short-term or regular session institutes for special training designed to improve the ability of teachers, supervisors, counselors, and other elementary or secondary school personnel to deal effectively with special educational problems occasioned by desegregation. Individuals who attend such an institute on a full-time basis may be paid stipends for the period of their attendance at such institute in amounts specified by the Commissioner in regulations, including allowances for travel to attend such institute.

GRANTS

SEC. 405. (a) The Commissioner is authorized, upon application of a school board, to make grants to such board to pay, in whole or in part, the cost of--

(1) Giving to teachers and other school personnel inservice training in dealing with problems incident to desegregation, and

(2) Employing specialists to advise in problems incident to desegregation.

(b) In determining whether to make a grant, and in fixing the amount thereof and the terms and conditions on which it will be made, the Commissioner shall take into consideration the amount available for grants under this section and the other applications which are pending before him; the financial condition of the applicant and the other resources available to it; the nature, extent, and gravity of its problems incident to desegregation; and such other factors as he finds relevant.

PAYMENTS

SEC. 406. Payments pursuant to a grant or contract under this title may be made (after necessary adjustments on account of previously made overpayments or underpayments) in advance or by way of reimbursement, and in such installments, as the Commissioner may determine.

SUITS BY THE ATTORNEY GENERAL

SEC. 407. (a) Whenever the Attorney General receives a complaint in writing--

(1) signed by a parent or group of parents to the effect that his or their minor children, as members of a class of persons similarly situated, are being deprived by a school board of the equal protection of the laws, or

(2) signed by an individual, or his parent, to the effect that he has been denied admission to or not permitted to continue in attendance at a public college by reason of race, color, religion, or national origin, and the Attorney General believes the complaint is meritorious and certifies that the signer or signers of such complaint are unable, in his judgment, to initiate and maintain appropriate legal proceedings for relief and that the institution of an action will materially further the orderly achievement of desegregation in public education, the Attorney General is authorized, after giving notice of such complaint to the appropriate school board or college authority and after certifying that he is satisfied that such board or authority has had a reasonable time to adjust the conditions alleged in such complaint, to institute for or in the name of the United States a civil action in any appropriate district court of the United States against such parties and for such relief as may be appropriate, and such court shall have and shall exercise jurisdiction of proceedings instituted pursuant to this section, provided that nothing herein shall empower any official or court of the United States to issue any order seeking to achieve a racial balance in any school by requiring the transportation of pupils or students from one school to another or one school district to another in order to achieve such racial balance, or otherwise enlarge the existing power of the court to insure compliance with constitutional standards. The Attorney General may implead as defendants such additional parties as are or become necessary to the grant of effective relief hereunder.

(b) The Attorney General may deem a person or persons unable to initiate and maintain appropriate legal proceedings within the meaning of subsection

(a) of this section when such person or persons are unable, either directly or through other interested persons or organizations, to bear the expense of the litigation or to obtain effective legal representation; or whenever he is satisfied that the institution of such litigation would jeopardize the personal safety, employment, or economic standing of such person or persons, their families, or their property.

(c) The term parent as used in this section includes any person standing in loco parentis. A complaint as used in this section is a writing or document within the meaning of section 1001, title 18, United States Code.

SEC. 408. In any action or proceeding under this title the United States shall be liable for costs the same as a private person.

SEC. 409. Nothing in this title shall affect adversely the right of any person to sue for or obtain relief in any court against discrimination in public education.

SEC. 410. Nothing in this title shall prohibit classification and assignment for reasons other than race, color, religion, or national origin.

TITLE V – COMMISSION ON CIVIL RIGHTS

SEC. 501. Section 102 of the Civil Rights Act of 1957 (42 U.S.C. 1975a; 71

Stat. 634) is amended to read as follows:

RULES OF PROCEDURE OF THE COMMISSION HEARINGS
SEC. 102. (a) At least thirty days prior to the commencement of any hearing, the Commission shall cause to be published in the Federal Register notice of the date on which such hearing is to commence, the place at which it is to be held and the subject of the hearing. The Chairman, or one designated by him to act as Chairman at a hearing of the Commission, shall announce in an opening statement the subject of the hearing.

(b) A copy of the Commission's rules shall be made available to any witness before the Commission, and a witness compelled to appear before the Commission or required to produce written or other matter shall be served with a copy of the Commission's rules at the time of service of the subpoena.

(c) Any person compelled to appear in person before the Commission shall be accorded the right to be accompanied and advised by counsel, who shall have the right to subject his client to reasonable examination, and to make objections on the record and to argue briefly the basis for such objections. The Commission shall proceed with reasonable dispatch to conclude any hearing in which it is engaged. Due regard shall be had for the convenience and necessity of witnesses.

(d) The Chairman or Acting Chairman may punish breaches of order and decorum by censure and exclusion from the hearings.

(e) If the Commission determines that evidence or testimony at any hearing may tend to defame, degrade, or incriminate any person, it shall receive such evidence or testimony or summary of such evidence or testimony in executive session. The Commission shall afford any person defamed, degraded, or incriminated by such evidence or testimony an opportunity to appear and be heard in executive session, with a reasonable number of additional witnesses requested by him, before deciding to use such evidence or testimony. In the event the Commission determines to release or use such evidence or testimony in such manner as to reveal publicly the identity of the person defamed, degraded, or incriminated, such evidence or testimony, prior to such public release or use, shall be given at a public session, and the Commission shall afford such person an opportunity to appear as a voluntary witness or to file a sworn statement in his behalf and to submit brief and pertinent sworn statements of others. The Commission shall receive and dispose of requests from such person to subpoena additional witnesses.

(f) Except as provided in sections 102 and 105 (f) of this Act, the Chairman shall receive and the Commission shall dispose of requests to subpoena additional witnesses.

(g) No evidence or testimony or summary of evidence or testimony taken in executive session may be released or used in public sessions without the consent of the Commission. Whoever releases or uses in public without the consent of the Commission such evidence or testimony taken in executive session shall be fined not more than $1,000, or imprisoned for not more than one year.

(h) In the discretion of the Commission, witnesses may submit brief and pertinent sworn statements in writing for inclusion in the record. The Commission shall determine the pertinency of testimony and evidence adduced at its hearings.

(i) Every person who submits data or evidence shall be entitled to retain or, on payment of lawfully prescribed costs, procure a copy or transcript thereof, except that a witness in a hearing held in executive session may for good cause be limited to inspection of the official transcript of his testimony. Transcript copies of public sessions may be obtained by the public upon the payment of the cost thereof. An accurate transcript shall be made of the testimony of all witnesses at all hearings, either public or executive sessions, of the Commission or of any subcommittee thereof.

(j) A witness attending any session of the Commission shall receive $6 for each day's attendance and for the time necessarily occupied in going to and returning from the same, and 10 cents per mile for going from and returning to his place of residence. Witnesses who attend at points so far removed from their respective residences as to prohibit return thereto from day to day shall be entitled to an additional allowance of $10 per day for expenses of subsistence including the time necessarily occupied in going to and returning from the place of attendance. Mileage payments shall be tendered to the witness upon service of a subpoena issued on behalf of the Commission or any subcommittee thereof.

(k) The Commission shall not issue any subpoena for the attendance and testimony of witnesses or for the production of written or other matter which would require the presence of the party subpoenaed at a hearing to be held outside of the State wherein the witness is found or resides or is domiciled or transacts business, or has appointed an agent for receipt of service of process except that, in any event, the Commission may issue subpoenas for the attendance and testimony of witnesses and the production of written or other matter at a hearing held within fifty miles of the place where the witness is found or resides or is domiciled or transacts business or has appointed an agent for receipt of service of process.

(l) The Commission shall separately state and currently publish in the Federal Register (1) descriptions of its central and field organization including the established places at which, and methods whereby, the public may secure information or make requests; (2) statements of the general course and method by which its functions are channeled and determined, and (3) rules adopted as authorized by law. No person shall in any manner be subject to or required to resort to rules, organization, or procedure not so published.

SEC. 502. Section 103(a) of the Civil Rights Act of 1957 (42 U.S.C.

1975b(a); 71 Stat. 634) is amended to read as follows:

SEC. 103. (a) Each member of the Commission who is not otherwise in the service of the Government of the United States shall receive the sum of $75 per day for each day spent in the work of the Commission, shall be paid actual travel expenses, and per diem in lieu of subsistence expenses when away from his usual place of residence, in accordance with section 5 of the Administrative Expenses Act of 1946, as amended (5 U.S.C 73b-2; 60 Stat. 808).

SEC. 503. Section 103(b) of the Civil Rights Act of 1957 (42 U.S.C.

1975(b); 71 Stat. 634) is amended to read as follows:

(b) Each member of the Commission who is otherwise in the service of the Government of the United States shall serve without compensation in addition to that received for such other service, but while engaged in the work of the Commission shall be paid actual travel expenses, and per diem in lieu of subsistence expenses when away from his usual place of residence, in accordance with the provisions of the Travel Expenses Act of 1949, as amended

(5 U.S.C. 835--42; 63 Stat. 166).

SEC. 504. (a) Section 104(a) of the Civil Rights Act of 1957 (42 U.S.C. 1975c (a); 71 Stat. 635), as amended, is further amended to read as follows:

DUTIES OF THE COMMISSION
SEC. 104. (a) The Commission shall--

(1) investigate allegations in writing under oath or affirmation that certain citizens of the United States are being deprived of their right to vote and have that vote counted by reason of their color, race, religion, or national origin; which writing, under oath or affirmation, shall set forth the facts upon which such belief or beliefs are based;

(2) study and collect information concerning legal developments constituting a denial of equal protection of the laws under the Constitution because of race, color, religion or national origin or in the administration of justice;

(3) Appraise the laws and policies of the Federal Government with respect to denials of equal protection of the laws under the Constitution because of race, color, religion or national origin or in the administration of justice;

(4) serve as a national clearinghouse for information in respect to denials of equal protection of the laws because of race, color, religion or national origin, including but not limited to the fields of voting, education, housing, employment, the use of public facilities, and transportation, or in the administration of justice;

(5) investigate allegations, made in writing and under oath or affirmation, that citizens of the United States are unlawfully being accorded or denied the right to vote, or to have their votes properly counted, in any election of presidential electors, Members of the United States Senate, or of the House of Representatives, as a result of any patterns or practice of fraud or discrimination in the conduct of such election; and

(6) Nothing in this or any other Act shall be construed as authorizing the Commission, its Advisory Committees, or any person under its supervision or control to inquire into or investigate any membership practices or internal operations of any fraternal organization, any college or university fraternity or sorority, any private club or any religious organization.

(b) The Commission shall submit interim reports to the President and to the Congress at such times as the Commission, the Congress or the President shall deem desirable, and shall submit to the President and to the Congress a final report of its activities, findings, and recommendations not later than January 31, 1968.

SEC. 505. Section 105(a) of the Civil Rights Act of 1957 (42 U.S.C. 1975d (a); 71 Stat. 636) is amended by striking out in the last sentence thereof $50 per diem and inserting in lieu thereof $75 per diem.

SEC. 506. Section 105(f) and section 105(g) of the Civil Rights Act of 1957 (42 U.S.C. 1975d (f) and (g); 71 Stat. 636) are amended to read as follows:

(f) The Commission, or on the authorization of the Commission any subcommittee of two or more members, at least one of whom shall be of each major political party, may, for the purpose of carrying out the provisions of this Act, hold such hearings and act at such times and places as the Commission or such authorized subcommittee may deem advisable. Subpoenas for the attendance and testimony of witnesses or the production of written or other matter may be issued in accordance with the rules of the Commission as contained in section 102 (j) and (k) of this Act, over the signature of the Chairman of the Commission or of such subcommittee, and may be served by any person designated by such Chairman. The holding of hearings by the Commission, or the appointment of a subcommittee to hold hearings pursuant to this subparagraph, must be approved by a majority of the Commission, or by a majority of the members present at a meeting at which at least a quorum of four members is present.

(g) In case of contumacy or refusal to obey a subpoena, any district court of the United States or the United States court of any territory or possession, or the District Court of the United States for the District of Columbia, within the jurisdiction of which the inquiry is carried on or within the jurisdiction of which said person guilty of contumacy or refusal to obey is found or resides or is domiciled or transacts business, or has appointed an agent for receipt of service of process, upon application by the Attorney General of the United States shall have jurisdiction to issue to such person an order requiring such person to appear before the Commission or a subcommittee thereof, there to produce pertinent, relevant and non-privileged evidence if so ordered, or there to give testimony touching the matter under investigation; and any failure to obey such order of the court may be punished by said court as a contempt thereof.

SEC. 507. Section 105 of the Civil Rights Act of 1957 (42 U.S.C. 1975d; 71 Stat. 636), as amended by section 401 of the Civil Rights Act of 1960 (42 U.S.C. 1975d (h); 74 Stat. 89), is further amended by adding a new subsection at the end to read as follows:

(i) The Commission shall have the power to make such rules and regulations as are necessary to carry out the purposes of this Act.

TITLE VI – NONDISCRIMINATION IN FEDERALLY ASSISTED PROGRAMS

SEC. 601. No person in the United States shall, on the ground of race, color, or national origin, be excluded from participation in, be denied the benefits of, or be subjected to discrimination under any program or activity receiving Federal financial assistance.

SEC. 602. Each Federal department and agency which is empowered to extend Federal financial assistance to any program or activity, by way of grant, loan, or contract other than a contract of insurance or guaranty, is authorized and directed to effectuate the provisions of section 601 with respect to such program or activity by issuing rules, regulations, or orders of general applicability which shall be consistent with achievement of the objectives of the statute authorizing the financial assistance in connection with which the action is taken. No such rule, regulation, or order shall become effective unless and until approved by the President. Compliance with any requirement adopted pursuant to this section may be effected (1) by the termination of or refusal to grant or to continue assistance under such program or activity to any recipient as to whom there has been an express finding on the record, after opportunity for hearing, of a failure to comply with such requirement, but such termination or refusal shall be limited to the particular political entity, or part thereof, or other recipient as to whom such a finding has been made and, shall be limited in its effect to the particular program, or part thereof, in which such non-compliance has been so found, or (2) by any other means authorized by law: Provided, however, That no such action shall be taken until the department or agency concerned has advised the appropriate person or persons of the failure to comply with the requirement and has determined that compliance cannot be secured by voluntary means. In the case of any action terminating, or refusing to grant or continue, assistance because of failure to comply with a requirement imposed pursuant to this section, the head of the federal department or agency shall file with the committees of the House and Senate having legislative jurisdiction over the program or activity involved a full written report of the circumstances and the grounds for such action. No such action shall become effective until thirty days have elapsed after the filing of such report.

SEC. 603. Any department or agency action taken pursuant to section 602 shall be subject to such judicial review as may otherwise be provided by law for similar action taken by such department or agency on other grounds. In the case of action, not otherwise subject to judicial review, terminating or refusing to grant or to continue financial assistance upon a finding of failure to comply with any requirement imposed pursuant to section 602, any person aggrieved (including any State or political subdivision thereof and any agency of either) may obtain judicial review of such action in accordance with section 10 of the Administrative Procedure Act, and such action shall not be deemed committed to unreviewable agency discretion within the meaning of that section.

SEC. 604. Nothing contained in this title shall be construed to authorize action under this title by any department or agency with respect to any employment practice of any employer, employment agency, or labor organization except where a primary objective of the Federal financial assistance is to provide employment.

SEC. 605. Nothing in this title shall add to or detract from any existing authority with respect to any program or activity under which Federal financial assistance is extended by way of a contract of insurance or guaranty.

TITLE VII – EQUAL EMPLOYMENT OPPORTUNITY

DEFINITIONS
SEC. 701. For the purposes of this title--

(a) The term person includes one or more individuals, labor unions, partnerships, associations, corporations, legal representatives, mutual companies, joint-stock companies, trusts, unincorporated organizations, trustees, trustees in bankruptcy, or receivers.

(b) The term employer means a person engaged in an industry affecting commerce who has twenty-five or more employees for each working day in each of twenty or more calendar weeks in the current or preceding calendar year, and any agent of such a person, but such term does not include (1) the United States, a corporation wholly owned by the Government of the United States, an Indian tribe, or a State or political subdivision thereof, (2) a bona fide private membership club (other than a labor organization) which is exempt from taxation under section 501(c) of the Internal Revenue Code of 1954: Provided, That during the first year after the effective date prescribed in subsection (a) of section 716, persons having fewer than one hundred employees (and their agents) shall not be considered employers, and, during the second year after such date, persons having fewer than seventy-five employees (and their agents) shall not be considered employers, and, during the third year after such date, persons having fewer than fifty employees (and their agents) shall not be considered employers: Provided further, That it shall be the policy of the United States to insure equal employment opportunities for Federal employees without discrimination because of race, color, religion, sex or national origin and the President shall utilize his existing authority to effectuate this policy.

(c) The term employment agency means any person regularly undertaking with or without compensation to procure employees for an employer or to procure for employees opportunities to work for an employer and includes an agent of such a person; but shall not include an agency of the United States, or an agency of a State or political subdivision of a State, except that such term shall include the United States Employment Service and the system of State and local employment services receiving Federal assistance.

(d) The term labor organization means a labor organization engaged in an industry affecting commerce, and any agent of such an organization, and includes any organization of any kind, any agency, or employee representation committee, group, association, or plan so engaged in which employees participate and which exists for the purpose, in whole or in part, of dealing with employers concerning grievances, labor disputes, wages, rates of pay, hours, or other terms or conditions of employment, and any conference, general committee, joint or system board, or joint council so engaged which is subordinate to a national or international labor organization.

(e) A labor organization shall be deemed to be engaged in an industry affecting commerce if (1) it maintains or operates a hiring hall or hiring office which procures employees for an employer or procures for employees opportunities to work for an employer, or (2) the number of its members (or, where it is a labor organization composed of other labor organizations or their representatives, if the aggregate number of the members of such other labor organization) is (A) one hundred or more during the first year after the effective date prescribed in subsection (a) of section 716, (B) seventy-five or more during the second year after such date or fifty or more during the third year, or (C) twenty-five or more thereafter, and such labor organization--

(1) is the certified representative of employees under the provisions of the National Labor Relations Act, as amended, or the Railway Labor Act, as amended;

(2) although not certified, is a national or international labor organization or a local labor organization recognized or acting as the representative of employees of an employer or employers engaged in an industry affecting commerce; or

(3) has chartered a local labor organization or subsidiary body which is representing or actively seeking to represent employees of employers within the meaning of paragraph (1) or (2); or

(4) has been chartered by a labor organization representing or actively seeking to represent employees within the meaning of paragraph (1) or (2) as the local or subordinate body through which such employees may enjoy membership or become affiliated with such labor organization; or

(5) Is a conference, general committee, joint or system board, or joint council subordinate to a national or international labor organization, which includes a labor organization engaged in an industry affecting commerce within the meaning of any of the preceding paragraphs of this subsection.

(f) The term employee means an individual employed by an employer.

(g) The term commerce means trade, traffic, commerce, transportation, transmission, or communication among the several States; or between a State and any place outside thereof; or within the District of Columbia, or a possession of the United States; or between points in the same State but through a point outside thereof.

(h) The term industry affecting commerce means any activity, business, or industry in commerce or in which a labor dispute would hinder or obstruct commerce or the free flow of commerce and includes any activity or industry affecting commerce within the meaning of the Labor-Management Reporting and Disclosure Act of 1959.

(i) The term State includes a State of the United States, the District of Columbia, Puerto Rico, the Virgin Islands, American Samoa, Guam, Wake Island, The Canal Zone, and Outer Continental Shelf lands defined in the Outer Continental Shelf Lands Act.

EXEMPTION
SEC. 702. This title shall not apply to an employer with respect to the employment of aliens outside any State, or to a religious corporation, association, or society with respect to the employment of individuals of a particular religion to perform work connected with the carrying on by such corporation, association, or society of its religious activities or to an educational institution with respect to the employment of individuals to perform work connected with the educational activities of such institution.

DISCRIMINATION BECAUSE OF RACE, COLOR, RELIGION, SEX, OR NATIONAL ORIGIN
SEC. 703. (a) It shall be an unlawful employment practice for an employer--

(1) to fail or refuse to hire or to discharge any individual, or otherwise to discriminate against any individual with respect to his compensation, terms, conditions, or privileges of employment, because of such individual's race, color, religion, sex, or national origin; or

(2) To limit, segregate, or classify his employees in any way which would deprive or tend to deprive any individual of employment opportunities or otherwise adversely affect his status as an employee, because of such individual's race, color, religion, sex, or national origin.

(b) It shall be an unlawful employment practice for an employment agency to fail or refuse to refer for employment, or otherwise to discriminate against, any individual because of his race, color, religion, sex, or national origin, or to classify or refer for employment any individual on the basis of his race, color, religion, sex, or national origin.

(c) It shall be an unlawful employment practice for a labor organization--

(1) To exclude or to expel from its membership, or otherwise to discriminate against, any individual because of his race, color, religion, sex, or national origin;

(2) to limit, segregate, or classify its membership, or to classify or fail or refuse to refer for employment any individual, in any way which would deprive or tend to deprive any individual of employment opportunities, or would limit such employment opportunities or otherwise adversely affect his status as an employee or as an applicant for employment, because of such individual's race, color, religion, sex, or national origin; or

(3) To cause or attempt to cause an employer to discriminate against an individual in violation of this section.

(d) It shall be an unlawful employment practice for any employer, labor organization, or joint labor-management committee controlling apprenticeship or other training or retraining, including on-the-job training programs to discriminate against any individual because of his race, color, religion, sex, or national origin in admission to, or employment in, any program established to provide apprenticeship or other training.

(e) Notwithstanding any other provision of this title, (1) it shall not be an unlawful employment practice for an employer to hire and employ employees, for an employment agency to classify, or refer for employment any individual, for a labor organization to classify its membership or to classify or refer for employment any individual, or for an employer, labor organization, or joint labor-management committee controlling apprenticeship or other training or retraining programs to admit or employ any individual in any such program, on the basis of his religion, sex, or national origin in those certain instances where religion, sex, or national origin is a bona fide occupational qualification reasonably necessary to the normal operation of that particular business or enterprise, and (2) it shall not be an unlawful employment practice for a school, college, university, or other educational institution or institution of learning to hire and employ employees of a particular religion if such school, college, university, or other educational institution or institution of learning is, in whole or in substantial part, owned, supported, controlled, or managed by a particular religion or by a particular religious corporation, association, or society, or if the curriculum of such school, college, university, or other educational institution or institution of learning is directed toward the propagation of a particular religion.

(f) As used in this title, the phrase unlawful employment practice shall not be deemed to include any action or measure taken by an employer, labor organization, joint labor-management committee, or employment agency with respect to an individual who is a member of the Communist Party of the United States or of any other organization required to register as a Communist-action or Communist-front organization by final order of the Subversive Activities Control Board pursuant to the Subversive Activities Control Act of 1950.

(g) Notwithstanding any other provision of this title, it shall not be an unlawful employment practice for an employer to fail or refuse to hire and employ any individual for any position, for an employer to discharge any individual from any position, or for an employment agency to fail or refuse to refer any individual for employment in any position, or for a labor organization to fail or refuse to refer any individual for employment in any position, if--

(1) the occupancy of such position, or access to the premises in or upon which any part of the duties of such position is performed or is to be performed, is subject to any requirement imposed in the interest of the national security of the United States under any security program in effect pursuant to or administered under any statute of the United States or any Executive order of the President; and

(2) such individual has not fulfilled or has ceased to fulfill that requirement.

(h) Notwithstanding any other provision of this title, it shall not be an unlawful employment practice for an employer to apply different standards of compensation, or different terms, conditions, or privileges of employment pursuant to a bona fide seniority or merit system, or a system which measures earnings by quantity or quality of production or to employees who work in different locations, provided that such differences are not the result of an intention to discriminate because of race, color, religion, sex, or national origin, nor shall it be an unlawful employment practice for an employer to give and to act upon the results of any professionally developed ability test provided that such test, its administration or action upon the results is not designed, intended or used to discriminate because of race, color, religion, sex or national origin. It shall not be an unlawful employment practice under this title for any employer to differentiate upon the basis of sex in determining the amount of the wages or compensation paid or to be paid to employees of such employer if such differentiation is authorized by the provisions of section 6(d) of the Fair Labor Standards Act of 1938, as amended (29 U.S.C. 206(d)).

(i) Nothing contained in this title shall apply to any business or enterprise on or near an Indian reservation with respect to any publicly announced employment practice of such business or enterprise under which a preferential treatment is given to any individual because he is an Indian living on or near a reservation.

(j) Nothing contained in this title shall be interpreted to require any employer, employment agency, labor organization, or joint labor-management committee subject to this title to grant preferential treatment to any individual or to any group because of the race, color, religion, sex, or national origin of such individual or group on account of an imbalance which may exist with respect to the total number or percentage of persons of any race, color, religion, sex, or national origin employed by any employer, referred or classified for employment by any employment agency or labor organization, admitted to membership or classified by any labor organization, or admitted to, or employed in, any apprenticeship or other training program, in comparison with the total number or percentage of persons of such race, color, religion, sex, or national origin in any community, State, section, or other area, or in the available work force in any community, State, section, or other area.

OTHER UNLAWFUL EMPLOYMENT PRACTICES
SEC. 704. (a) It shall be an unlawful employment practice for an employer to discriminate against any of his employees or applicants for employment, for an employment agency to discriminate against any individual, or for a labor organization to discriminate against any member thereof or applicant for membership, because he has opposed, any practice made an unlawful employment practice by this title, or because he has made a charge, testified, assisted, or participated in any manner in an investigation, proceeding, or hearing under this title.

(b) It shall be an unlawful employment practice for an employer, labor organization, or employment agency to print or publish or cause to be printed or published any notice or advertisement relating to employment by such an employer or membership in or any classification or referral for employment by such a labor organization, or relating to any classification or referral for employment by such an employment agency, indicating any preference, limitation, specification, or discrimination, based on race, color, religion, sex, or national origin, except that such a notice or advertisement may indicate a preference, limitation, specification, or discrimination based on religion, sex, or national origin when religion, sex, or national origin is a bona fide occupational qualification for employment.

EQUAL EMPLOYMENT OPPORTUNITY COMMISSION
SEC. 705. (a) There is hereby created a Commission to be known as the Equal Employment Opportunity Commission, which shall be composed of five members, not more than three of whom shall be members of the same political party, who shall be appointed by the President by and with the advice and consent of the Senate. One of the original members shall be appointed for a term of one year, one for a term of two years, one for a term of three years, one for a term of four years, and one for a term of five years, beginning from the date of enactment of this title, but their successors shall be appointed for terms of five years each, except that any individual chosen to fill a vacancy shall be appointed only for the unexpired term of the member whom he shall succeed. The President shall designate one member to serve as Chairman of the Commission, and one member to serve as Vice Chairman. The Chairman shall be responsible on behalf of the Commission for the administrative operations of the Commission, and shall appoint, in accordance with the civil service laws, such officers, agents, attorneys, and employees as it deems necessary to assist it in the performance of its functions and to fix their compensation in accordance with the Classification Act of 1949, as amended. The

Vice Chairman shall act as Chairman in the absence or disability of the Chairman or in the event of a vacancy in that office.

(b) A vacancy in the Commission shall not impair the right of the remaining members to exercise all the powers of the Commission and three members thereof shall constitute a quorum.

(c) The Commission shall have an official seal which shall be judicially noticed.

(d) The Commission shall at the close of each fiscal year report to the Congress and to the President concerning the action it has taken; the names, salaries, and duties of all individuals in its employ and the moneys it has disbursed; and shall make such further reports on the cause of and means of eliminating discrimination and such recommendations for further legislation as may appear desirable.

(e) The Federal Executive Pay Act of 1956, as amended (5 U.S.C. 2201-2209), is further amended--

(1) By adding to section 105 thereof (5 U.S.C. 2204) the following clause:

(32) Chairman, Equal Employment Opportunity Commission; and

(2) By adding to clause (45) of section 106(a) thereof (5 U.S.C. 2205(a)) the following: Equal Employment Opportunity Commission (4).

(f) The principal office of the Commission shall be in or near the District of Columbia, but it may meet or exercise any or all its powers at any other place. The Commission may establish such regional or State offices as it deems necessary to accomplish the purpose of this title.

(g) The Commission shall have power--

(1) To cooperate with and, with their consent, utilize regional, State, local, and other agencies, both public and private, and individuals;

(2) To pay to witnesses whose depositions are taken or who are summoned before the Commission or any of its agents the same witness and mileage fees as are paid to witnesses in the courts of the United States;

(3) To furnish to persons subject to this title such technical assistance as they may request to further their compliance with this title or an order issued thereunder;

(4) Upon the request of (i) any employer, whose employees or some of them, or (ii) any labor organization, whose members or some of them, refuse or threaten to refuse to cooperate in effectuating the provisions of this title, to assist in such effectuation by conciliation or such other remedial action as is provided by this title;

(5) To make such technical studies as are appropriate to effectuate the purposes and policies of this title and to make the results of such studies available to the public;

(6) To refer matters to the Attorney General with recommendations for intervention in a civil action brought by an aggrieved party under section 706, or for the institution of a civil action by the Attorney General under section 707, and to advise, consult, and assist the Attorney General on such matters.

(h) Attorneys appointed under this section may, at the direction of the Commission, appear for and represent the Commission in any case in court.

(i) The Commission shall, in any of its educational or promotional activities, cooperate with other departments and agencies in the performance of such educational and promotional activities.

(j) All officers, agents, attorneys, and employees of the Commission shall be subject to the provisions of section 9 of the Act of August 2, 1939, as amended (the Hatch Act), notwithstanding any exemption contained in such section.

PREVENTION OF UNLAWFUL EMPLOYMENT PRACTICES

SEC. 706. (a) Whenever it is charged in writing under oath by a person claiming to be aggrieved, or a written charge has been filed by a member of the Commission where he has reasonable cause to believe a violation of this title has occurred (and such charge sets forth the facts upon which it is based) that an employer, employment agency, or labor organization has engaged in an unlawful employment practice, the Commission shall furnish such employer, employment agency, or labor organization (hereinafter referred to as the respondent) with a copy of such charge and shall make an investigation of such charge, provided that such charge shall not be made public by the Commission. If the Commission shall determine, after such investigation, that there is reasonable cause to believe that the charge is true, the Commission shall endeavor to eliminate any such alleged unlawful employment practice by informal methods of conference, conciliation, and persuasion. Nothing said or done during and as a part of such endeavors may be made public by the Commission without the written consent of the parties, or used as evidence in a subsequent proceeding. Any officer or employee of the Commission, who shall make public in any manner whatever any information in violation of this subsection shall be deemed guilty of a misdemeanor and upon conviction thereof shall be fined not more than $1,000 or imprisoned not more than one year.

(b) In the case of an alleged unlawful employment practice occurring in a State, or political subdivision of a State, which has a State or local law prohibiting the unlawful employment practice alleged and establishing or authorizing a State or local authority to grant or seek relief from such practice or to institute criminal proceedings with respect thereto upon receiving notice thereof, no charge may be filed under subsection (a) by the person aggrieved before the expiration of sixty days after proceedings have been commenced under the State or local law, unless such proceedings have been earlier terminated, provided that such sixty-day period shall be extended to one hundred and twenty days during the first year after the effective date of such State or local law. If any requirement for the commencement of such proceedings is imposed by a State or local authority other than a requirement of the filing of a written and signed statement of the facts upon which the proceeding is based, the proceeding shall be deemed to have been commenced for the purposes of this subsection at the time such statement is sent by registered mail to the appropriate State or local authority.

(c) In the case of any charge filed by a member of the Commission alleging an unlawful employment practice occurring in a State or political subdivision of a State, which has a State or local law prohibiting the practice alleged and establishing or authorizing a State or local authority to grant or seek relief from such practice or to institute criminal proceedings with respect thereto upon receiving notice thereof, the Commission shall, before taking any action with respect to such charge, notify the appropriate State or local officials and, upon request, afford them a reasonable time, but not less than sixty days (provided that such sixty-day period shall be extended to one hundred and twenty days during the first year after the effective day of such State or local law), unless a shorter period is requested, to act under such State or local law to remedy the practice alleged.

(d) A charge under subsection (a) shall be filed within ninety days after the alleged unlawful employment practice occurred, except that in the case of an unlawful employment practice with respect to which the person aggrieved has followed the procedure set out in subsection (b), such charge shall be filed by the person aggrieved within two hundred and ten days after the alleged unlawful employment practice occurred, or within thirty days after receiving notice that the State or local agency has terminated the proceedings under the State or local, law, whichever is earlier, and a copy of such charge shall be filed by the Commission with the State or local agency.

(e) If within thirty days after a charge is filed with the Commission or within thirty days after expiration of any period of reference under subsection (c) (except that in either case such period may be extended to not more than sixty days upon a determination by the Commission that further efforts to secure voluntary compliance are warranted), the Commission has been unable to obtain voluntary compliance with this title, the Commission shall so notify the person aggrieved and a civil action may, within thirty days thereafter, be brought against the respondent named in the charge (1) by the person claiming to be aggrieved, or (2) if such charge was filed by a member of the Commission, by any person whom the charge alleges was aggrieved by the alleged unlawful employment practice. Upon application by the complainant and in such circumstances as the court may deem just, the court may appoint an attorney for such complainant and may authorize the commencement of the action without the payment of fees, costs, or security. Upon timely application, the court may, in its discretion, permit the Attorney General to intervene in such civil action if he certifies that the case is of general public importance. Upon request, the court may, in its discretion, stay further proceedings for not more than sixty days pending the termination of State or local proceedings described in subsection (b) or the efforts of the Commission to obtain voluntary compliance.

(f) Each United States district court and each United States court of a place subject to the jurisdiction of the United States shall have jurisdiction of actions brought under this title. Such an action may be brought in any judicial district in the State in which the unlawful employment practice is alleged to have been committed, in the judicial district in which the employment records relevant to such practice are maintained and administered, or in the judicial district in which the plaintiff would have worked but for the alleged unlawful employment practice, but if the respondent is not found within any such district, such an action may be brought within the judicial district in which the respondent has his principal office. For purposes of sections 1404 and 1406 of title 28 of the United States Code, the judicial district in which the respondent has his principal office shall in all cases be considered a district in which the action might have been brought.

(g) If the court finds that the respondent has intentionally engaged in or is intentionally engaging in an unlawful employment practice charged in the complaint, the court may enjoin the respondent from engaging in such unlawful employment practice, and order such affirmative action as may be appropriate, which may include reinstatement or hiring of employees, with or without back pay (payable by the employer, employment agency, or labor organization, as the case may be, responsible for the unlawful employment practice). Interim earnings or amounts earnable with reasonable diligence by the person or persons discriminated against shall operate to reduce the back pay otherwise allowable. No order of the court shall require the admission or reinstatement of an individual as a member of a union or the hiring, reinstatement, or promotion of an individual as an employee, or the payment to him of any back pay, if such individual was refused admission, suspended, or expelled or was refused employment or advancement or was suspended or discharged for any reason other than discrimination on account of race, color, religion, sex or national origin or in violation of section 704(a).

(h) The provisions of the Act entitled An Act to amend the Judicial Code and to define and limit the jurisdiction of courts sitting in equity, and for other purposes, approved March 23, 1932 (29 U.S.C. 101-115), shall not apply with respect to civil actions brought under this section.

(i) In any case in which an employer, employment agency, or labor organization fails to comply with an order of a court issued in a civil action brought under subsection (e), the Commission may commence proceedings to compel compliance with such order.

(j) Any civil action brought under subsection (e) and any proceedings brought under subsection (i) shall be subject to appeal as provided in sections 1291 and 1292, title 28, United States Code.

(k) In any action or proceeding under this title the court, in its discretion, may allow the prevailing party, other than the Commission or the United States, a reasonable attorney's fee as part of the costs, and the Commission and the United States shall be liable for costs the same as a private person.

SEC. 707. (a) Whenever the Attorney General has reasonable cause to believe that any person or group of persons is engaged in a pattern or practice of resistance to the full enjoyment of any of the rights secured by this title, and that the pattern or practice is of such a nature and is intended to deny the full exercise of the rights herein described, the Attorney General may bring a civil action in the appropriate district court of the United States by filing with it a complaint (1) signed by him (or in his absence the Acting Attorney General), (2) setting forth facts pertaining to such pattern or practice, and (3) requesting such relief, including an application for a permanent or temporary injunction, restraining order or other order against the person or persons responsible for such pattern or practice, as he deems necessary to insure the full enjoyment of the rights herein described.

(b) The district courts of the United States shall have and shall exercise jurisdiction of proceedings instituted pursuant to this section, and in any such proceeding the Attorney General may file with the clerk of such court a request that a court of three judges be convened to hear and determine the case. Such request by the Attorney General shall be accompanied by a certificate that, in his opinion, the case is of general public importance. A copy of the certificate and request for a three-judge court shall be immediately furnished by such clerk to the chief judge of the circuit (or in his absence, the presiding circuit judge of the circuit) in which the case is pending. Upon receipt of such request it shall be the duty of the chief judge of the circuit or the presiding circuit judge, as the case may be, to designate immediately three judges in such circuit, of whom at least one shall be a circuit judge and another of whom shall be a district judge of the court in which the proceeding was instituted, to hear and determine such case, and it shall be the duty of the judges so designated to assign the case for hearing at the earliest practicable date, to participate in the hearing and determination thereof, and to cause the case to be in every way expedited. An appeal from the final judgment of such court will lie to the Supreme Court.

In the event the Attorney General fails to file such a request in any such proceeding, it shall be the duty of the chief judge of the district (or in his absence, the acting chief judge) in which the case is pending immediately to designate a judge in such district to hear and determine the case. In the event that no judge in the district is available to hear and determine the case, the chief judge of the district, or the acting chief judge, as the case may be, shall certify this fact to the chief judge of the circuit (or in his absence, the acting chief judge) who shall then designate a district or circuit judge of the circuit to hear and determine the case.

It shall be the duty of the judge designated pursuant to this section to assign the case for hearing at the earliest practicable date and to cause the case to be in every way expedited.

EFFECT ON STATE LAWS
SEC. 708. Nothing in this title shall be deemed to exempt or relieve any person from any liability, duty, penalty, or punishment provided by any present or future law of any State or political subdivision of a State, other than any such law which purports to require or permit the doing of any act which would be an unlawful employment practice under this title.

INVESTIGATIONS, INSPECTIONS, RECORDS, STATE AGENCIES
SEC. 709. (a) In connection with any investigation of a charge filed under section 706, the Commission or its

designated representative shall at all reasonable times have access to, for the purposes of examination, and the right to copy any evidence of any person being investigated or proceeded against that relates to unlawful employment practices covered by this title and is relevant to the charge under investigation.

(b) The Commission may cooperate with State and local agencies charged with the administration of State fair employment practices laws and, with the consent of such agencies, may for the purpose of carrying out its functions and duties under this title and within the limitation of funds appropriated specifically for such purpose, utilize the services of such agencies and their employees and, notwithstanding any other provision of law, may reimburse such agencies and their employees for services rendered to assist the Commission in carrying out this title. In furtherance of such cooperative efforts, the Commission may enter into written agreements with such State or local agencies and such agreements may include provisions under which the Commission shall refrain from processing a charge in any cases or class of cases specified in such agreements and under which no person may bring a civil action under section 706 in any cases or class of cases so specified, or under which the Commission shall relieve any person or class of persons in such State or locality from requirements imposed under this section. The Commission shall rescind any such agreement whenever it determines that the agreement no longer serves the interest of effective enforcement of this title.

(c) Except as provided in subsection (d), every employer, employment agency, and labor organization subject to this title shall (1) make and keep such records relevant to the determinations of whether unlawful employment practices have been or are being committed, (2) preserve such records for such periods, and (3) make such reports therefrom, as the Commission shall prescribe by regulation or order, after public hearing, as reasonable, necessary, or appropriate for the enforcement of this title or the regulations or orders thereunder. The Commission shall, by regulation, require each employer, labor organization, and joint labor-management committee subject to this title which controls an apprenticeship or other training program to maintain such records as are reasonably necessary to carry out the purpose of this title, including, but not limited to, a list of applicants who wish to participate in such program, including the chronological order in which such applications were received, and shall furnish to the Commission, upon request, a detailed description of the manner in which persons are selected to participate in the apprenticeship or other training program. Any employer, employment agency, labor organization, or joint labor-management committee which believes that the application to it of any regulation or order issued under this section would result in undue hardship may (1) apply to the Commission for an exemption from the application of such regulation or order, or (2) bring a civil action in the United States district court for the district where such records are kept. If the Commission or the court, as the case may be, finds that the application of the regulation or order to the employer, employment agency, or labor organization in question would impose an undue hardship, the Commission or the court, as the case may be, may grant appropriate relief.

(d) The provisions of subsection (c) shall not apply to any employer, employment agency, labor organization, or joint labor-management committee with respect to matters occurring in any State or political subdivision thereof which has a fair employment practice law during any period in which such employer, employment agency, labor organization, or joint labor-management committee is subject to such law, except that the Commission may require such notations on records which such employer, employment agency, labor organization, or joint labor-management committee keeps or is required to keep as are necessary because of differences in coverage or methods of enforcement between the State or local law and the provisions of this title. Where an employer is required by Executive Order 10925, issued March 6, 1961, or by any other Executive order prescribing fair employment practices for Government contractors and subcontractors, or by rules or regulations issued thereunder, to file reports relating to his employment practices with any Federal agency or committee, and he is substantially in compliance with such requirements, the Commission shall not require him to file additional reports pursuant to subsection (c) of this section.

(e) It shall be unlawful for any officer or employee of the Commission to make public in any manner whatever any information obtained by the Commission pursuant to its authority under this section prior to the institution of any proceeding under this title involving such information. Any officer or employee of the Commission who shall make public in any manner whatever any information in violation of this subsection shall be guilty of a misdemeanor and upon conviction thereof, shall be fined not more than $1,000, or imprisoned not more than one year.

INVESTIGATORY POWERS

SEC. 710. (a) For the purposes of any investigation of a charge filed under the authority contained in section 706, the Commission shall have authority to examine witnesses under oath and to require the production of documentary evidence relevant or material to the charge under investigation.

(b) If the respondent named in a charge filed under section 706 fails or refuses to comply with a demand of the Commission for permission to examine or to copy evidence in conformity with the provisions of section 709(a), or if any person required to comply with the provisions of section 709 (c) or (d) fails or refuses to do so, or if any person fails or refuses to comply with a demand by the Commission to give testimony under oath, the United States district court for the district in which such person is found, resides, or transacts business, shall, upon application of the Commission, have jurisdiction to issue to such person an order requiring him to comply with the provisions of section 709 (c) or (d) or to comply with the demand of the Commission, but the attendance of a witness may not be required outside the State where he is found, resides, or transacts business and the production of evidence may not be required outside the State where such evidence is kept.

(c) Within twenty days after the service upon any person charged under section 706 of a demand by the Commission for the production of documentary evidence or for permission to examine or to copy evidence in conformity with the provisions of section 709(a), such person may file in the district court of the United States for the judicial district in which he resides, is found, or transacts business, and serve upon the Commission a petition for an order of such court modifying or setting aside such demand. The time allowed for compliance with the demand in whole or in part as deemed proper and ordered by the court shall not run during the pendency of such petition in the court. Such petition shall specify each ground upon which the petitioner relies in seeking such relief, and may be based upon any failure of such demand to comply with the provisions of this title or with the limitations generally applicable to compulsory process or upon any constitutional or other legal right or privilege of such person. No objection which is not raised by such a petition may be urged in the defense to a proceeding initiated by the Commission under subsection (b) for enforcement of such a demand unless such proceeding is commenced by the Commission prior to the expiration of the twenty-day period, or unless the court determines that the defendant could not reasonably have been aware of the availability of such ground of objection.

(d) In any proceeding brought by the Commission under subsection (b), except as provided in subsection (c) of this section, the defendant may petition the court for an order modifying or setting aside the demand of the Commission.

SEC. 711. (a) Every employer, employment agency, and labor organization, as the case may be, shall post and keep posted in conspicuous places upon its premises where notices to employees, applicants for employment, and members are customarily posted a notice to be prepared or approved by the Commission setting forth excerpts from or, summaries of, the pertinent provisions of this title and information pertinent to the filing of a complaint.

(b) A willful violation of this section shall be punishable by a fine of not more than $100 for each separate offense.

VETERANS' PREFERENCE
SEC. 712. Nothing contained in this title shall be construed to repeal or modify any Federal, State, territorial, or local law creating special rights or preference for veterans.

RULES AND REGULATIONS
SEC. 713. (a) The Commission shall have authority from time to time to issue, amend, or rescind suitable procedural regulations to carry out the provisions of this title. Regulations issued under this section shall be in conformity with the standards and limitations of the Administrative Procedure Act.

(b) In any action or proceeding based on any alleged unlawful employment practice, no person shall be subject to any liability or punishment for or on account of (1) the commission by such person of an unlawful employment practice if he pleads and proves that the act or omission complained of was in good faith, in conformity with, and in reliance on any written interpretation or opinion of the Commission, or (2) the failure of such person to publish and file any information required by any provision of this title if he pleads and proves that he failed to publish and file such information in good faith, in conformity with the instructions of the Commission issued under this title regarding the filing of such information. Such a defense, if established, shall be a bar to the action or proceeding, notwithstanding that (A) after such act or omission, such interpretation or opinion is modified or rescinded or is determined by judicial authority to be invalid or of no legal effect, or (B) after publishing or filing the description and annual reports, such publication or filing is determined by judicial authority not to be in conformity with the requirements of this title.

FORCIBLY RESISTING THE COMMISSION OR ITS REPRESENTATIVES
SEC. 714. The provisions of section 111, title 18, United States Code, shall apply to officers, agents, and employees of the Commission in the performance of their official duties.

SPECIAL STUDY BY SECRETARY OF LABOR
SEC. 715. The Secretary of Labor shall make a full and complete study of the factors which might tend to result in discrimination in employment because of age and of the consequences of such discrimination on the economy and individuals affected. The Secretary of Labor shall make a report to the Congress not later than June 30, 1965, containing the results of such study and shall include in such report such recommendations for legislation to prevent arbitrary discrimination in employment because of age as he determines advisable.

EFFECTIVE DATE
SEC. 716. (a) This title shall become effective one year after the date of its enactment.

(b) Notwithstanding subsection (a), sections of this title other than sections 703, 704, 706, and 707 shall become effective immediately.

(c) The President shall, as soon as feasible after the enactment of this title, convene one or more conferences for the purpose of enabling the leaders of groups whose members will be affected by this title to become familiar with the rights afforded and obligations imposed by its provisions, and for the purpose of making plans which will result in the fair and effective administration of this title when all of its provisions become effective. The President shall invite the participation in such conference or conferences of (1) the members of the President's Committee on Equal Employment Opportunity, (2) the members of the Commission on Civil Rights, (3) representatives of State and local agencies engaged in furthering equal employment opportunity, (4) representatives of private agencies engaged in furthering equal employment opportunity, and (5) representatives of employers, labor organizations, and employment agencies who will be subject to this title.

TITLE VIII – REGISTRATION AND VOTING STATISTICS

SEC. 801. The Secretary of Commerce shall promptly conduct a survey to compile registration and voting statistics in such geographic areas as may be recommended by the Commission on Civil Rights. Such a survey and compilation shall, to the extent recommended by the Commission on Civil Rights, only include a count of persons of voting age by race, color, and national origin, and determination of the extent to which such persons are registered to vote, and have voted in any statewide primary or general election in which the Members of the United States House of Representatives are nominated or elected, since January 1, 1960. Such information shall also be collected and compiled in connection with the Nineteenth Decennial Census, and at such other times as the Congress may prescribe. The provisions of section 9 and chapter 7 of title 13, United States Code, shall apply to any survey, collection, or compilation of registration and voting statistics carried out under this title: Provided, however, That no person shall be compelled to disclose his race, color, national origin, or questioned about his political party affiliation, how he voted, or the reasons therefore, nor shall any penalty be imposed for his failure or refusal to make such disclosure. Every person interrogated orally, by written survey or questionnaire or by any other means with respect to such information shall be fully advised with respect to his right to fail or refuse to furnish such information.

TITLE IX – INTERVENTION AND PROCEDURE AFTER REMOVAL IN CIVIL RIGHTS CASES

SEC. 901. Title 28 of the United States Code, section 1447(d), is amended to read as follows:

An order remanding a case to the State court from which it was removed is not reviewable on appeal or otherwise, except that an order remanding a case to the State court from which it was removed pursuant to section 1443 of this title shall be reviewable by appeal or otherwise.

SEC. 902. Whenever an action has been commenced in any court of the United States seeking relief from the denial of equal protection of the laws under the fourteenth amendment to the Constitution on account of race, color, religion, or national origin, the Attorney General for or in the name of the United States may intervene in such action upon timely application if the Attorney General certifies that the case is of general public importance. In such action the United States shall be entitled to the same relief as if it had instituted the action.

TITLE X – ESTABLISHMENT OF COMMUNITY RELATIONS SERVICE

SEC. 1001. (a) There is hereby established in and as a part of the Department of Commerce a Community Relations Service (hereinafter referred to as the Service), which shall be headed by a Director who shall be appointed by the President with the advice and consent of the Senate for a term of four years. The Director is authorized to appoint, subject to the civil service laws and regulations, such other personnel as may be necessary to enable the Service to carry out its functions and duties, and to fix their compensation in accordance with the Classification Act of 1949, as amended. The Director is further authorized to procure services as authorized by section 15 of the Act of August 2, 1946 (60 Stat. 810; 5 U.S.C. 55(a)), but at rates for individuals not in excess of $75 per diem.

(b) Section 106(a) of the Federal Executive Pay Act of 1956, as amended (5 U.S.C. 2205(a)), is further amended by adding the following clause thereto:

(52) Director, Community Relations Service.

SEC. 1002. It shall be the function of the Service to provide assistance to communities and persons therein in resolving disputes, disagreements, or difficulties relating to discriminatory practices based on race, color, or national origin which impair the rights of persons in such communities under the Constitution or laws of the United States or which affect or may affect interstate commerce. The Service may offer its services in cases of such disputes, disagreements, or difficulties whenever, in its judgment, peaceful relations among the citizens of the community involved are threatened thereby, and it may offer its services either upon its own motion or upon the request of an appropriate State or local official or other interested person.

SEC. 1003. (a) The Service shall, whenever possible, in performing its functions, seek and utilize the cooperation of appropriate State or local, public, or private agencies.

(b) The activities of all officers and employees of the Service in providing conciliation assistance shall be conducted in confidence and without publicity, and the Service shall hold confidential any information acquired in the regular performance of its duties upon the understanding that it would be so held. No officer or employee of the Service shall engage in the performance of investigative or prosecuting functions of any department or agency in any litigation arising out of a dispute in which he acted on behalf of the Service. Any officer or other employee of the Service, who shall make public in any manner whatever any information in violation of this subsection, shall be deemed guilty of a misdemeanor and, upon conviction thereof, shall be fined not more than $1,000 or imprisoned not more than one year.

SEC. 1004. Subject to the provisions of sections 205 and 1003(b), the Director shall, on or before January 31 of each year, submit to the Congress a report of the activities of the Service during the preceding fiscal year.

TITLE XI – MISCELLANEOUS

SEC. 1101. In any proceeding for criminal contempt arising under title II, III, IV, V, VI, or VII of this Act, the accused, upon demand therefor, shall be entitled to a trial by jury, which shall conform as near as may be to the practice in criminal cases. Upon conviction, the accused shall not be fined more than $1,000 or imprisoned for more than six months.

This section shall not apply to contempts committed in the presence of the court, or so near thereto as to obstruct the administration of justice, nor to the misbehavior, misconduct, or disobedience of any officer of the court in respect to writs, orders, or process of the court. No person shall be convicted of criminal contempt hereunder unless the act or omission constituting such contempt shall have been intentional, as required in other cases of criminal contempt.

Nor shall anything herein be construed to deprive courts of their power, by civil contempt proceedings, without a jury, to secure compliance with or to prevent obstruction of, as distinguished from punishment for violations of, any lawful writ, process, order, rule, decree, or command of the court in accordance with the prevailing usages of law and equity, including the power of detention.

SEC. 1102. No person should be put twice in jeopardy under the laws of the United States for the same act or omission. For this reason, an acquittal or conviction in a prosecution for a specific crime under the laws of the United States shall bar a proceeding for criminal contempt, which is based upon the same act or omission and which arises under the provisions of this Act; and an acquittal or conviction in a proceeding for criminal contempt, which arises under the provisions of this Act, shall bar a prosecution for a specific crime under the laws of the United States based upon the same act or omission.

SEC. 1103. Nothing in this Act shall be construed to deny, impair, or otherwise affect any right or authority of the Attorney General or of the United States or any agency or officer thereof under existing law to institute or intervene in any action or proceeding.

SEC. 1104. Nothing contained in any title of this Act shall be construed as indicating an intent on the part of Congress to occupy the field in which any such title operates to the exclusion of State laws on the same subject matter, nor shall any provision of this Act be construed as invalidating any provision of State law unless such provision is inconsistent with any of the purposes of this Act, or any provision thereof.

SEC. 1105. There are hereby authorized to be appropriated such sums as are necessary to carry out the provisions of this Act.

SEC. 1106. If any provision of this Act or the application thereof to any person or circumstances is held invalid, the remainder of the Act and the application of the provision to other persons not similarly situated or to other circumstances shall not be affected thereby.

Henry Highland Garnet

An Address to the Slaves of the United States of America

The National Negro Convention of 1843

Brethren and Fellow Citizens:—Your brethren of the North, East, and West have been accustomed to meet together in National Conventions, to sympathize with each other, and to weep over your unhappy condition. In these meetings we have addressed all classes of the free, but we have never, until this time, sent a word of consolation and advice to you. We have been contented in sitting still and mourning over your sorrows, earnestly hoping that before this day your sacred liberty would have been restored. But, we have hoped in vain. Years have rolled on, and tens of thousands have been borne on streams of blood and tears, to the shores of eternity. While you have been oppressed, we have also been partakers with you; nor can we be free while you are enslaved. We, therefore, write to you as being bound with you. Many of you are bound to us, not only by the ties of a common humanity, but we are connected by the more tender relations of parents, wives, husbands, children, brothers, and sisters, and friends. As such we most affectionately address you.

Slavery has fixed a deep gulf between you and us, and while it shuts out from you the relief and consolation which your friends would willingly render, it affects and persecutes you with a fierceness which we might not expect to see in the fiends of hell. But still the Almighty Father of mercies has left to us a glimmering ray of hope, which shines out like a lone star in a cloudy sky. Mankind are becoming wiser, and better—the oppressor's power is fading, and you, every day, are becoming better informed, and more numerous. Your grievances, brethren, are many. We shall not attempt, in this short address, to present to the world all the dark catalogue of this nation's sins, which have been committed upon an innocent people. Nor is it indeed necessary, for you feel them from day to day, and all the civilized world look upon them with amazement.

Two hundred and twenty seven years ago, the first of our injured race were brought to the shores of America. They came not with glad spirits to select their homes in the New World. They came not with their own consent, to find an unmolested enjoyment of the blessings of this fruitful soil. The first dealings they had with men calling themselves Christians, exhibited to them the worst features of corrupt and sordid hearts; and convinced them that no cruelty is too great, no villainy and no robbery too abhorrent for even enlightened men to perform, when influenced by avarice and lust. Neither did they come flying upon the wings of Liberty, to a land of freedom. But they came with broken hearts, from their beloved native land, and were doomed to unrequited toil and deep degradation. Nor did the evil of their bondage end at their emancipation by death. Succeeding generations inherited their chains, and millions have come from eternity into time, and have returned again to the world of spirits, cursed and ruined by American slavery.

The propagators of the system, or their immediate ancestors, very soon discovered its growing evil, and its tremendous wickedness, and secret promises were made to destroy it. The gross inconsistency of a people holding slaves, who had themselves "ferried o'er the wave" for freedom's sake, was too apparent to be entirely overlooked. The voice of Freedom cried, "Emancipate yourselves." Humanity supplicated with tears for the deliverance of the children of Africa. Wisdom urged her solemn plea. The bleeding captive plead his innocence, and pointed to Christianity who stood weeping at the cross. Jehovah frowned upon the nefarious institution, and thunderbolts, red with vengeance, struggled to leap forth to blast the guilty wretches who maintained it. But all was in vain. Slavery had stretched its dark wings of death over the land, the Church stood silently by the priests prophesied falsely, and the people loved to have it so. Its throne is established, and now it reigns triumphant.

Nearly three millions of your fellow citizens are prohibited by law and public opinion, (which in this country is stronger than law,) from reading the Book of Life. Your intellect has been destroyed as much as possible, and every ray of light they have attempted to shut out from your minds. The oppressors themselves have become involved in the ruin. They have become weak, sensual, and rapacious—they have cursed you—they have cursed themselves—they have cursed the earth which they have trod.

The colonists threw the blame upon England. They said that the mother country entailed the evil upon them, and that they would rid themselves of it if they could. The world thought they were sincere, and the philanthropic pitied them. But time soon tested their sincerity.

In a few years the colonists grew strong, and severed themselves from the British Government. Their independence was declared, and they took their station among the sovereign powers of the earth. The declaration was a glorious document. Sages admired it, and the patriotic of every nation reverenced the God like sentiments which it contained. When the power of Government returned to their hands, did they emancipate the slaves? No; they rather added new links to our chains. Were they ignorant of the principles of Liberty? Certainly they were not. The sentiments of their revolutionary orators fell in burning eloquence upon their hearts, and with one voice they cried, Liberty or Death. Oh what a sentence was that! It ran from soul to soul like electric fire, and nerved the arm of thousands to fight in the holy cause of Freedom. Among the diversity of opinions that are entertained in regard to physical resistance, there are but a few found to gainsay that stern declaration. We are among those who do not. Slavery! How much misery is comprehended in that single word. What mind is there that does not shrink from its direful effects? Unless the image of God be obliterated from the soul, all men cherish the love of Liberty. The nice discerning political economist does not regard the sacred right more than the untutored African who roams in the wilds of Congo. Nor has the one more right to the full enjoyment of his freedom than the other. In every man's mind the good seeds of liberty are planted, and he who brings his fellow down so low, as to make him contented with a condition of slavery, commits the highest crime against God and man. Brethren, your oppressors aim to do this. They endeavor to make you as much like brutes as possible. When they have blinded the eyes of your mind when they have embittered the sweet waters of life then, and not till then, has American slavery done its perfect work.

To such degredation it is sinful in the extreme for you to make voluntary submission! The divine commandments you are in duty bound to reverence and obey. If you do not obey them, you will surely meet with the displeasure of the Almighty. He requires you to love him supremely, and your neighbor as yourself—to keep the Sabbath day holy—to search the Scriptures—and bring up your children with respect for his laws, and to worship no other God but him. But slavery sets all these at nought, and hurls defiance in the face of Jehovah. The forlorn condition in which you are placed, does not destroy your moral obligation to God. You are not certain of heaven, because you suffer yourselves to remain in a state of slavery, where you cannot obey the commandments of the Sovereign of the universe. If the ignorance of slavery is a passport to heaven, then it is a blessing, and no curse, and you should rather desire its perpetuity than its abolition. God will not receive slavery, nor ignorance, nor any other state of mind, for love and obedience to him. Your condition does not absolve you from your moral obligation. The diabolical injustice by which your liberties are cloven down, NEITHER GOD, NOR ANGELS, OR JUST MEN, COMMAND YOU TO SUFFER FOR A SINGLE MOMENT. THEREFORE IT IS YOUR SOLEMN AND IMPERATIVE DUTY TO USE EVERY MEANS, BOTH MORAL, INTELLECTUAL, AND PHYSICAL THAT PROMISES SUCCESS. If a band of heathen men should attempt to enslave a race of Christians, and to place their children under the influence of some false religion, surely Heaven would frown upon the men who would not resist such aggression, even to death. If, on the other hand, a band of Christians should attempt to enslave h race of heathen men, and to entail slavery upon them, and to keep them in heathenism in the midst of Christianity, the God of heaven would smile upon every effort which the injured might make to disenthrall themselves.

Brethren, it is as wrong for your lordly oppressors to keep you in slavery, as it was for the man thief to steal our ancestors from the coast of Africa. You should therefore now use the same manner of resistance, as would have been just in our ancestors when the bloody foot prints of the first remorseless soul thief was placed upon the shores of our fatherland. The humblest peasant is as free in the sight of God as the proudest monarch that ever swayed a sceptre. Liberty is a spirit sent out from God, and like its great Author, is no respecter of persons.

Brethren, the time has come when you must act for yourselves. It is an old and true saying that, "if hereditary bondmen would be free, they must themselves strike the blow." You can plead your own cause, and do the work of emancipation better than any others. The nations of the world are moving in the great cause of universal freedom, and some of them at least will, ere long, do you justice. The combined powers of Europe have placed their broad seal of disapprobation upon the African slave trade. But in the slaveholding parts of the United States, the trade is as brisk as ever. They buy and sell you as though you were brute beasts. The North has done much—her opinion of slavery in the abstract is known. But in regard to the South, we adopt the opinion of the New York Evangelist—We have advanced so far, that the cause apparently waits for a more effectual door to be thrown open than has been yet. We are about to point out that more effectual door. Look around you, and behold the bosoms of your loving wives heaving with untold agonies! Hear the cries of your poor children!

Remember the stripes your fathers bore. Think of the torture and disgrace of your noble mothers. Think of your wretched sisters, loving virtue and purity, as they are driven into concubinage and are exposed to the unbridled lusts of incarnate devils. Think of the undying glory that hangs around the ancient name of Africa—and forget not that you are native born American citizens, and as such, you are justly entitled to all the rights that are granted to the freest. Think how many tears you have poured out upon the soil which you have cultivated with unrequited toil and enriched with your blood; and then go to your lordly enslavers and tell them plainly, that you are determined to be free. Appeal to their sense of justice, and tell them that they have no more right to oppress you, than you have to enslave them. Entreat them to remove the grievous burdens which they have imposed upon you, and to remunerate you for your labor. Promise them renewed diligence in the cultivation of the soil, if they will render to you an equivalent for your services. Point them to the increase of happiness and prosperity in the British West Indies since the Act of Emancipation. Tell them in language which they cannot misunderstand, of the exceeding sinfulness of slavery, and of a future judgment, and of the righteous retributions of an indignant God. Inform them that all you desire is freedom! and that nothing else will suffice. Do this, and for ever after cease to toil for the heartless tyrants, who give you no other reward but stripes and abuse. If they then commence the work of death, they, and not you, will be responsible for the consequences. You had better all die immediately, than live slaves and entail your wretchedness upon your posterity. If you would be free in this generation, here is your only hope. However much you and all of us may desire it, there is not much hope of redemption without the shedding of blood. If you must bleed, let it all come at once—rather die freemen, than live to be slaves. It is impossible like the children of Israel, to make a grand exodus from the land of bondage. The Pharaohs are on both sides of the blood red waters! You cannot move en masse, to the dominions of the British Queen—nor can you pass through Florida and overrun Texas, and at last find peace in Mexico. The propagators of American slavery are spending their blood and treasure, that they may plant the black flag in the heart of Mexico and riot in the halls of the Montezumas. In the language of the Rev. Robert Hall, when addressing the volunteers of Bristol, who were rushing forth to repel the invasion of Napoleon, who threatened to lay waste the fair homes of England, "Religion is too much interested in your behalf, not to shed over you her most gracious influences."

You will not be compelled to spend much time in order to become inured to hardships. From the first moment that you breathed the air of heaven, you have been accustomed to nothing else but hardships. The heroes of the American Revolution were never put upon harder fare than a peck of corn and a few herrings per week. You have not become enervated by the luxuries of life. Your sternest energies have been beaten out upon the anvil of severe trial. Slavery has done this, to make you subservient, to its own purposes; but it has done more than this, it has prepared you for any emergency. If you receive good treatment, it is what you could hardly expect; if you meet with pain, sorrow, and even death, these are the common lot of slaves.

Fellow men! Patient sufferers! behold your dearest rights crushed to the earth! See your sons murdered, and your wives, mothers and sisters doomed to prostitution. In the name of the merciful God, and by all that life is worth, let it no longer be a debatable question whether it is better to choose Liberty or death.

In 1822, Denmark Veazie, of South Carolina, formed a plan for the liberation of his fellow men. In the whole history of human efforts to overthrow slavery, a more complicated and tremendous plan was never formed. He was betrayed by the treachery of his own people, and died a martyr to freedom. Many a brave hero fell, but history, faithful to her high trust, will transcribe his name on the same monument with Moses, Hampden, Tell, Bruce and Wallace, Toussaint L'Ouverture, Lafayette and Washington. That tremendous movement shook the whole empire of slavery. The guilty soul thieves were overwhelmed with fear. It is a matter of fact, that at that time, and in consequence of the threatened revolution, the slave States talked strongly of emancipation. But they blew but one blast of the trumpet of freedom and then laid it aside. As these men became quiet, the slaveholders ceased to talk about emancipation; and now behold your condition today! Angels sigh over it, and humanity has long since exhausted her tears in weeping on your account!

The patriotic Nathaniel Turner followed Denmark Veazie. He was goaded to desperation by wrong and injustice. By despotism, his name has been recorded on the list of infamy, and future generations will remember him among the noble and brave.

Next arose the immortal Joseph Cinque, the hero of the Amistad. He was a native African, and by the help of God he emancipated a whole ship load of his fellow men on the high seas. And he now sings of liberty on the sunny hills of Africa and beneath his native palm trees, where he hears the lion roar and feels himself as free as that king of the forest.

Next arose Madison Washington that bright star of freedom, and took his station in the constellation of true heroism. He was a slave on board the brig Creole, of Richmond, bound to New Orleans, that great slave mart, with a hundred and four others. Nineteen struck for liberty or death. But one life was taken, and the whole were emancipated, and the vessel was carried into Nassau, New Providence.

Noble men! Those who have fallen in freedom's conflict, their memories will be cherished by the true hearted and the God fearing in all future generations; those who are living, their names are surrounded by a halo of glory.

Brethren, arise, arise! Strike for your lives and liberties. Now is the day and the hour. Let every slave throughout the land do this, and the days of slavery are numbered. You cannot be more oppressed than you have been—you cannot suffer greater cruelties than you have already. Rather die free men than live to be slaves. Remember that you are four millions!

It is in your power so to torment the God cursed slaveholders that they will be glad to let you go free. If the scale was turned, and black men were the masters and white men the slaves, every destructive agent and element would be employed to lay the oppressor low. Danger and death would hang over their heads day and night. Yes, the tyrants would meet with plagues more terrible than those of Pharaoh. But you are a patient people. You act as though, you were made for the special use of these devils. You act as though your daughters were born to pamper the lusts of your masters and overseers. And worse than all, you tamely submit while your lords tear your wives from your embraces and defile them before your eyes. In the name of God, we ask, are you men? Where is the blood of your fathers? Has it all run out of your veins? Awake, awake; millions of voices are calling you! Your dead fathers speak to you from their graves. Heaven, as with a voice of thunder, calls on you to arise from the dust.

Let your motto be resistance! resistance! resistance! No oppressed people have ever secured their liberty without resistance. What kind of resistance you had better make, you must decide by the circumstances that surround you, and according to the suggestion of expediency. Brethren, adieu! Trust in the living God. Labor for the peace of the human race, and remember that you are four millions!

Sojourner Truth

Ain't I a Woman?

May 28, 1851

Well, children, where there is so much racket there must be something out of kilter. I think that 'twixt the negroes of the South and the women of the North, all talking about rights, the white men will be in a fix pretty soon. But what's all this here talking about? That man over there says that women need to be helped into carriages and lifted over ditches, and to have the best place everywhere. Nobody ever helps me into carriages, or over mud-puddles, or gives me any best place! And ain't I a woman?

Look at me! Look at my arm! I could have ploughed and planted, and gathered into barns, and no man could head me! And ain't I a woman?

I could work as much and eat as much as a man- when I could get it- and bear the lash as well! And ain't I a woman?

I have borne thirteen children, and seen them most all sold off to slavery, and when I cried out with my mother's grief, none but Jesus heard me! And ain't I a woman?

Then they talk about this thing in the head; what's this they call it? [Intellect, somebody whispers] That's it, honey. What's that got to do with women's rights or negro's rights? If my cup won't hold but a pint, and yours holds a quart, wouldn't you be mean not to let me have my little half measure-full? Then that little man in black there, he says women can't have as much rights as men, 'cause Christ wasn't a woman! Where did your Christ come from? Where did your Christ come from? From God and a woman! Man had nothing to do with Him. If the first woman God ever made was strong enough to turn the world upside down all alone, these women together ought to be able to turn it back, and get it right side up again!

And now they is asking to do it, the men better let them. Obliged to you for hearing me, and now old Sojourner ain't got nothing more to say.

Frederick Douglass

What to the Slave is the Fourth of July?

July 5, 1852

Mr. President, Friends and Fellow Citizens:

He who could address this audience without a quailing sensation, has stronger nerves than I have. I do not remember ever to have appeared as a speaker before any assembly more shrinkingly, nor with greater distrust of my ability, than I do this day. A feeling has crept over me, quite unfavorable to the exercise of my limited powers of speech. The task before me is one which requires much previous thought and study for its proper performance. I know that apologies of this sort are generally considered flat and unmeaning. I trust, however, that mine will not be so considered. Should I seem at ease, my appearance would much misrepresent me. The little experience I have had in addressing public meetings, in country schoolhouses, avails me nothing on the present occasion.

The papers and placards say, that I am to deliver a 4th [of] July oration. This certainly sounds large, and out of the common way, for it is true that I have often had the privilege to speak in this beautiful Hall, and to address many who now honor me with their presence. But neither their familiar faces, nor the perfect gage I think I have of Corinthian Hall, seems to free me from embarrassment.

The fact is, ladies and gentlemen, the distance between this platform and the slave plantation, from which I escaped, is considerable — and the difficulties to be overcome in getting from the latter to the former, are by no means slight. That I am here to-day is, to me, a matter of astonishment as well as of gratitude. You will not, therefore, be surprised, if in what I have to say I evince no elaborate preparation, nor grace my speech with any high sounding exordium. With little experience and with less learning, I have been able to throw my thoughts hastily and imperfectly together; and trusting to your patient and generous indulgence, I will proceed to lay them before you.

This, for the purpose of this celebration, is the 4th of July. It is the birthday of your National Independence, and of your political freedom. This, to you, is what the Passover was to the emancipated people of God. It carries your minds back to the day, and to the act of your great deliverance; and to the signs, and to the wonders, associated with that act, and that day. This celebration also marks the beginning of another year of your national life; and reminds you that the Republic of America is now 76 years old. I am glad, fellow-citizens, that your nation is so young. Seventy-six years, though a good old age for a man, is but a mere speck in the life of a nation. Three score years and ten is the allotted time for individual men; but nations number their years by thousands. According to this fact, you are, even now, only in the beginning of your national career, still lingering in the period of childhood. I repeat, I am glad this is so. There is hope in the thought, and hope is much needed, under the dark clouds which lower above the horizon. The eye of the reformer is met with angry flashes, portending disastrous times; but his heart may well beat lighter at the thought that America is young, and that she is still in the impressible stage of her existence. May he not hope that high lessons of wisdom, of justice and of truth, will yet give direction to her destiny? Were the nation older, the patriot's heart might be sadder, and the reformer's brow heavier. Its future might be shrouded in gloom, and the hope of its prophets go out in sorrow.

There is consolation in the thought that America is young. Great streams are not easily turned from channels, worn deep in the course of ages. They may sometimes rise in quiet and stately majesty, and inundate the land, refreshing and fertilizing the earth with their mysterious properties. They may also rise in wrath and fury, and bear away, on their angry waves, the accumulated wealth of years of toil and hardship. They, however, gradually flow back to the same old channel, and flow on as serenely as ever. But, while the river may not be turned aside, it may dry up, and leave nothing behind but the withered branch, and the unsightly rock, to howl in the abyss-sweeping wind, the sad tale of departed glory. As with rivers so with nations.

Fellow-citizens, I shall not presume to dwell at length on the associations that cluster about this day. The simple story of it is that, 76 years ago, the people of this country were British subjects. The style and title of your "sovereign people" (in which you now glory) was not then born. You were under the British Crown. Your fathers esteemed the English Government as the home government; and England as the fatherland. This home government, you know, although a considerable distance from your home, did, in the exercise of its parental prerogatives, impose upon its colonial children, such restraints, burdens and limitations, as, in its mature judgment, it deemed wise, right and proper.

But, your fathers, who had not adopted the fashionable idea of this day, of the infallibility of government, and the absolute character of its acts, presumed to differ from the home government in respect to the wisdom and the justice of some of those burdens and restraints. They went so far in their excitement as to pronounce the measures of government unjust, unreasonable, and oppressive, and altogether such as ought not to be quietly submitted to. I scarcely need say, fellow-citizens, that my opinion of those measures fully accords with that of your fathers. Such a declaration of agreement on my part would not be worth much to anybody. It would, certainly, prove nothing, as to what part I might have taken, had I lived during the great controversy of 1776. To say now that America was right, and England wrong, is exceedingly easy. Everybody can say it; the dastard, not less than the noble brave, can flippantly discant on the tyranny of England towards the American Colonies. It is fashionable to do so; but there was a time when to pronounce against England, and in favor of the cause of the colonies, tried men's souls. They who did so were accounted in their day, plotters of mischief, agitators and rebels, dangerous men. To side with the right, against the wrong, with the weak against the strong, and with the oppressed against the oppressor! here lies the merit, and the one which, of all others, seems unfashionable in our day. The cause of liberty may be stabbed by the men who glory in the deeds of your fathers. But, to proceed.

Feeling themselves harshly and unjustly treated by the home government, your fathers, like men of honesty, and men of spirit, earnestly sought redress. They petitioned and remonstrated; they did so in a decorous, respectful, and loyal manner. Their conduct was wholly unexceptionable. This, however, did not answer the purpose. They saw themselves treated with sovereign indifference, coldness and scorn. Yet they persevered. They were not the men to look back.

As the sheet anchor takes a firmer hold, when the ship is tossed by the storm, so did the cause of your fathers grow stronger, as it breasted the chilling blasts of kingly displeasure. The greatest and best of British statesmen admitted its justice, and the loftiest eloquence of the British Senate came to its support. But, with that blindness which seems to be the unvarying characteristic of tyrants, since Pharaoh and his hosts were drowned in the Red Sea, the British Government persisted in the exactions complained of. The madness of this course, we believe, is admitted now, even by England; but we fear the lesson is wholly lost on our present ruler.

Oppression makes a wise man mad. Your fathers were wise men, and if they did not go mad, they became restive under this treatment. They felt themselves the victims of grievous wrongs, wholly incurable in their colonial capacity. With brave men there is always a remedy for oppression. Just here, the idea of a total separation of the colonies from the crown was born! It was a startling idea, much more so, than we, at this distance of time, regard it. The timid and the prudent (as has been intimated) of that day, were, of course, shocked and alarmed by it.

Such people lived then, had lived before, and will, probably, ever have a place on this planet; and their course, in respect to any great change, (no matter how great the good to be attained, or the wrong to be redressed by it), may be calculated with as much precision as can be the course of the stars. They hate all changes, but silver, gold and copper change! Of this sort of change they are always strongly in favor.

These people were called Tories in the days of your fathers; and the appellation, probably, conveyed the same idea that is meant by a more modern, though a somewhat less euphonious term, which we often find in our papers, applied to some of our old politicians. Their opposition to the then dangerous thought was earnest and powerful; but, amid all their terror and affrighted vociferations against it, the alarming and revolutionary idea moved on, and the country with it.

On the 2d of July, 1776, the old Continental Congress, to the dismay of the lovers of ease, and the worshipers of property, clothed that dreadful idea with all the authority of national sanction. They did so in the form of a resolution; and as we seldom hit upon resolutions, drawn up in our day whose transparency is at all equal to this, it may refresh your minds and help my story if I read it. "Resolved, That these united colonies are, and of right, ought to be free and Independent States; that they are absolved from all allegiance to the British Crown; and that all political connection between them and the State of Great Britain is, and ought to be, dissolved."

Citizens, your fathers made good that resolution. They succeeded; and to-day you reap the fruits of their success. The freedom gained is yours; and you, therefore, may properly celebrate this anniversary. The 4th of July is the first great fact in your nation's history — the very ring-bolt in the chain of your yet undeveloped destiny.

Pride and patriotism, not less than gratitude, prompt you to celebrate and to hold it in perpetual remembrance. I have said that the Declaration of Independence is the ring-bolt to the chain of your nation's destiny; so, indeed, I regard it. The principles contained in that instrument are saving principles. Stand by those principles, be true to them on all occasions, in all places, against all foes, and at whatever cost.

From the round top of your ship of state, dark and threatening clouds may be seen. Heavy billows, like mountains in the distance, disclose to the leeward huge forms of flinty rocks! That bolt drawn, that chain broken, and all is lost. Cling to this day — cling to it, and to its principles, with the grasp of a storm-tossed mariner to a spar at midnight.

The coming into being of a nation, in any circumstances, is an interesting event. But, besides general considerations, there were peculiar circumstances which make the advent of this republic an event of special attractiveness. The whole scene, as I look back to it, was simple, dignified and sublime.

The population of the country, at the time, stood at the insignificant number of three millions. The country was poor in the munitions of war. The population was weak and scattered, and the country a wilderness unsubdued. There were then no means of concert and combination, such as exist now. Neither steam nor lightning had then been reduced to order and discipline. From the Potomac to the Delaware was a journey of many days. Under these, and innumerable other disadvantages, your fathers declared for liberty and independence and triumphed.

Fellow citizens, I am not wanting in respect for the fathers of this republic. The signers of the Declaration of Independence were brave men. They were great men too — great enough to give fame to a great age. It does not often happen to a nation to raise, at one time, such a number of truly great men. The point from which I am compelled to view them is not, certainly, the most favorable; and yet I cannot contemplate their great deeds with less than admiration. They were statesmen, patriots and heroes, and for the good they did, and the principles they contended for, I will unite with you to honor their memory.

They loved their country better than their own private interests; and, though this is not the highest form of human excellence, all will concede that it is a rare virtue, and that when it is exhibited, it ought to command respect. He who will, intelligently, lay down his life for his country, is a man whom it is not in human nature to despise. Your fathers staked their lives, their fortunes, and their sacred honor, on the cause of their country. In their admiration of liberty, they lost sight of all other interests.

They were peace men, but they preferred revolution to peaceful submission to bondage. They were quiet men, but they did not shrink from agitating against oppression. They showed forbearance, but that they knew its limits. They believed in order, but not in the order of tyranny.

With them, nothing was "settled" that was not right. With them, justice, liberty and humanity were "final;" not slavery and oppression. You may well cherish the memory of such men. They were great in their day and generation. Their solid manhood stands out the more as we contrast it with these degenerate times.

How circumspect, exact and proportionate were all their movements! How unlike the politicians of an hour! Their statesmanship looked beyond the passing moment, and stretched away in strength into the distant future. They seized upon eternal principles, and set a glorious example in their defense. Mark them!

Fully appreciating the hardship to be encountered, firmly believing in the right of their cause, honorably inviting the scrutiny of an on-looking world, reverently appealing to heaven to attest their sincerity, soundly comprehending the solemn responsibility they were about to assume, wisely measuring the terrible odds against them, your fathers, the fathers of this republic, did, most deliberately, under the inspiration of a glorious patriotism, and with a sublime faith in the great principles of justice and freedom, lay deep the corner-stone of the national superstructure, which has risen and still rises in grandeur around you.

Of this fundamental work, this day is the anniversary. Our eyes are met with demonstrations of joyous enthusiasm. Banners and pennants wave exultingly on the breeze. The din of business, too, is hushed. Even Mammon seems to have quitted his grasp on this day. The ear-piercing fife and the stirring drum unite their accents with the ascending peal of a thousand church bells. Prayers are made, hymns are sung, and sermons are preached in honor of this day; while the quick martial tramp of a great and multitudinous nation, echoed back by all the hills, valleys and mountains of a vast continent, bespeak the occasion one of thrilling and universal interest — a nation's jubilee.

Friends and citizens, I need not enter further into the causes which led to this anniversary. Many of you understand them better than I do. You could instruct me in regard to them. That is a branch of knowledge in which you feel, perhaps, a much deeper interest than your speaker. The causes which led to the separation of the colonies from the British crown have never lacked for a tongue. They have all been taught in your common schools, narrated at your firesides, unfolded from your pulpits, and thundered from your legislative halls, and are as familiar to you as household words. They form the staple of your national poetry and eloquence.

I remember, also, that, as a people, Americans are remarkably familiar with all facts which make in their own favor. This is esteemed by some as a national trait — perhaps a national weakness. It is a fact, that whatever makes for the wealth or for the reputation of Americans, and can be had cheap! will be found by Americans. I shall not be charged with slandering Americans, if I say I think the American side of any question may be safely left in American hands.

I leave, therefore, the great deeds of your fathers to other gentlemen whose claim to have been regularly descended will be less likely to be disputed than mine! My business, if I have any here to-day, is with the present. The accepted time with God and his cause is the ever-living now.

Trust no future, however pleasant,
Let the dead past bury its dead;
Act, act in the living present,
Heart within, and God overhead.

We have to do with the past only as we can make it useful to the present and to the future. To all inspiring motives, to noble deeds which can be gained from the past, we are welcome. But now is the time, the important time. Your fathers have lived, died, and have done their work, and have done much of it well. You live and must die, and you must do your work. You have no right to enjoy a child's share in the labor of your fathers, unless your children are to be blest by your labors. You have no right to wear out and waste the hard-earned fame of your fathers to cover your indolence. Sydney Smith tells us that men seldom eulogize the wisdom and virtues of their fathers, but to excuse some folly or wickedness of their own. This truth is not a doubtful one. There are illustrations of it near and remote, ancient and modern. It was fashionable, hundreds of years ago, for the children of Jacob to boast, we have "Abraham to our father," when they had long lost Abraham's faith and spirit. That people contented themselves under the shadow of Abraham's great name, while they repudiated the deeds which made his name great. Need I remind you that a similar thing is being done all over this country to-day? Need I tell you that the Jews are not the only people who built the tombs of the prophets, and garnished the sepulchres of the righteous? Washington could not die till he had broken the chains of his slaves. Yet his monument is built up by the price of human blood, and the traders in the bodies and souls of men shout; "We have Washington to *our father*." Alas! that it should be so; yet so it is.

The evil that men do, lives after them, The good is oft-interred with their bones.

Fellow citizens, pardon me, allow me to ask, why am I called upon to speak here to-day? What have I, or those I represent, to do with your national independence? Are the great principles of political freedom and of natural justice, embodied in that Declaration of Independence, extended to us? And am I, therefore, called upon to bring our humble offering to the national altar, and to confess the benefits and express devout gratitude for the blessings resulting from your independence to us?

Would to God, both for your sakes and ours, that an affirmative answer could be truthfully returned to these questions! Then would my task be light, and my burden easy and delightful. For who is there so cold, that a nation's sympathy could not warm him? Who so obdurate and dead to the claims of gratitude, that would not thankfully acknowledge such priceless benefits? Who so stolid and selfish, that would not give his voice to swell the hallelujahs of a nation's jubilee, when the chains of servitude had been torn from his limbs? I am not that man. In a case like that, the dumb might eloquently speak, and the "lame man leap as an hart."

But, such is not the state of the case. I say it with a sad sense of the disparity between us. I am not included within the pale of this glorious anniversary! Your high independence only reveals the immeasurable distance between us. The blessings in which you, this day, rejoice, are not enjoyed in common. The rich inheritance of justice, liberty, prosperity and independence, bequeathed by your fathers, is shared by you, not by me. The sunlight that brought life and healing to you, has brought stripes and death to me. This Fourth (of) July is *yours*, not *mine*. *You* may rejoice, *I* must mourn. To drag a man in fetters into the grand illuminated temple of liberty, and call upon him to join you in joyous anthems, were inhuman mockery and sacrilegious irony. Do you mean, citizens, to mock me, by asking me to speak today? If so, there is a parallel to your conduct. And let me warn you that it is dangerous to copy the example of a nation whose crimes, lowering up to heaven, were thrown down by the breath of the Almighty, burying that nation in irrecoverable ruin! I can to-day take up the plaintive lament of a peeled and woe-smitten people!

"By the rivers of Babylon, there we sat down. Yea! We wept when we remembered Zion. We hanged our harps upon the willows in the midst thereof. For there, they that carried us away captive, required of us a song; and they who wasted us required of us mirth, saying, sing us one of the songs of Zion. How can we sing the Lord's song in a strange land? If I forget thee, O Jerusalem, let my right hand forget her cunning. If I do not remember thee, let my tongue cleave to the roof of my mouth."

Fellow-citizens; above your national, tumultuous joy, I hear the mournful wail of millions! whose chains, heavy and grievous yesterday, are, to-day, rendered more intolerable by the jubilee shouts that reach them. If I do forget, if I do not faithfully remember those bleeding children of sorrow this day, "may my right hand forget her cunning, and may my tongue cleave to the roof of my mouth!" To forget them, to pass lightly over their wrongs, and to chime in with the popular theme, would be treason most scandalous and shocking, and would make me a reproach before God and the world. My subject, then fellow-citizens, is AMERICAN SLAVERY. I shall see, this day, and its popular characteristics, from the slave's point of view. Standing, there, identified with the American bondman, making his wrongs mine, I do not hesitate to declare, with all my soul, that the character and conduct of this nation never looked blacker to me than on this 4th of July! Whether we turn to the declarations of the past, or to the professions of the present, the conduct of the nation seems equally hideous and revolting. America is false to the past, false to the present, and solemnly binds herself to be false to the future. Standing with God and the crushed and bleeding slave on this occasion, I will, in the name of humanity which is outraged, in the name of liberty which is fettered, in the name of the constitution and the Bible, which are disregarded and trampled upon, dare to call in question and to denounce, with all the emphasis I can command, everything that serves to perpetuate slavery — the great sin and shame of America! "I will not equivocate; I will not excuse;" I will use the severest language I can command; and yet not one word shall escape me that any man, whose judgment is not blinded by prejudice, or who is not at heart a slaveholder, shall not confess to be right and just.

But I fancy I hear some one of my audience say, it is just in this circumstance that you and your brother abolitionists fail to make a favorable impression on the public mind. Would you argue more, and denounce less, would you persuade more, and rebuke less, your cause would be much more likely to succeed. But, I submit, where all is plain there is nothing to be argued. What point in the anti-slavery creed would you have me argue? On what branch of the subject do the people of this country need light? Must I undertake to prove that the slave is a man? That point is conceded already. Nobody doubts it. The slaveholders themselves acknowledge it in the enactment of laws for their government. They acknowledge it when they punish disobedience on the part of the slave. There are seventy-two crimes in the State of Virginia, which, if committed by a black man, (no matter how ignorant he be), subject him to the punishment of death; while only two of the same crimes will subject a white man to the like punishment. What is this but the acknowledgement that the slave is a moral, intellectual and responsible being? The manhood of the slave is conceded. It is admitted in the fact that Southern statute books are covered with enactments forbidding, under severe fines and penalties, the teaching of the slave to read or to write. When you can point to any such laws, in reference to the beasts of the field, then I may consent to argue the manhood of the slave. When the dogs in your streets, when the fowls of the air, when the cattle on your hills, when the fish of the sea, and the reptiles that crawl, shall be unable to distinguish the slave from a brute,*then* will I argue with you that the slave is a man!

For the present, it is enough to affirm the equal manhood of the Negro race. Is it not astonishing that, while we are ploughing, planting and reaping, using all kinds of mechanical tools, erecting houses, constructing bridges, building ships, working in metals of brass, iron, copper, silver and gold; that, while we are reading, writing and cyphering, acting as clerks, merchants and secretaries, having among us lawyers, doctors, ministers, poets, authors, editors, orators and teachers; that, while we are engaged in all manner of enterprises common to other men, digging gold in California, capturing the whale in the Pacific, feeding sheep and cattle on the hill-side, living, moving, acting, thinking, planning, living in families as husbands, wives and children, and, above all, confessing and worshipping the Christian's God, and looking hopefully for life and immortality beyond the grave, we are called upon to prove that we are men!

Would you have me argue that man is entitled to liberty? that he is the rightful owner of his own body? You have already declared it. Must I argue the wrongfulness of slavery? Is that a question for Republicans? Is it to be settled by the rules of logic and argumentation, as a matter beset with great difficulty, involving a doubtful application of the principle of justice, hard to be understood? How should I look to-day, in the presence of Americans, dividing, and subdividing a discourse, to show that men have a natural right to freedom? speaking of it relatively, and positively, negatively, and affirmatively. To do so, would be to make myself ridiculous, and to offer an insult to your understanding. — There is not a man beneath the canopy of heaven, that does not know that slavery is wrong *for him*.

What, am I to argue that it is wrong to make men brutes, to rob them of their liberty, to work them without wages, to keep them ignorant of their relations to their fellow men, to beat them with sticks, to flay their flesh with the lash, to load their limbs with irons, to hunt them with dogs, to sell them at auction, to sunder their families, to knock out their teeth, to burn their flesh, to starve them into obedience and submission to their masters? Must I argue that a system thus marked with blood, and stained with pollution, is *wrong*? No! I will not. I have better employments for my time and strength than such arguments would imply.

What, then, remains to be argued? Is it that slavery is not divine; that God did not establish it; that our doctors of divinity are mistaken? There is blasphemy in the thought. That which is inhuman, cannot be divine! Who can reason on such a proposition? They that can, may; I cannot. The time for such argument is passed.

At a time like this, scorching irony, not convincing argument, is needed. O! had I the ability, and could I reach the nation's ear, I would, to-day, pour out a fiery stream of biting ridicule, blasting reproach, withering sarcasm, and stern rebuke. For it is not light that is needed, but fire; it is not the gentle shower, but thunder. We need the storm, the whirlwind, and the earthquake. The feeling of the nation must be quickened; the conscience of the nation must be roused; the propriety of the nation must be startled; the hypocrisy of the nation must be exposed; and its crimes against God and man must be proclaimed and denounced.

What, to the American slave, is your 4th of July? I answer: a day that reveals to him, more than all other days in the year, the gross injustice and cruelty to which he is the constant victim. To him, your celebration is a sham; your boasted liberty, an unholy license; your national greatness, swelling vanity; your sounds of rejoicing are empty and heartless; your denunciations of tyrants, brass fronted impudence; your shouts of liberty and equality, hollow mockery; your prayers and hymns, your sermons and thanksgivings, with all your religious parade, and solemnity, are, to him, mere bombast, fraud, deception, impiety, and hypocrisy — a thin veil to cover up crimes which would disgrace a nation of savages. There is not a nation on the earth guilty of practices, more shocking and bloody, than are the people of these United States, at this very hour.

Go where you may, search where you will, roam through all the monarchies and despotisms of the old world, travel through South America, search out every abuse, and when you have found the last, lay your facts by the side of the everyday practices of this nation, and you will say with me, that, for revolting barbarity and shameless hypocrisy, America reigns without a rival.

Take the American slave-trade, which, we are told by the papers, is especially prosperous just now. Ex-Senator Benton tells us that the price of men was never higher than now. He mentions the fact to show that slavery is in no danger. This trade is one of the peculiarities of American institutions. It is carried on in all the large towns and cities in one-half of this confederacy; and millions are pocketed every year, by dealers in this horrid traffic. In several states, this trade is a chief source of wealth. It is called (in contradistinction to the foreign slave-trade) *"the internal slave trade."* It is, probably, called so, too, in order to divert from it the horror with which the foreign slave-trade is contemplated. That trade has long since been denounced by this government, as piracy. It has been denounced with burning words, from the high places of the nation, as an execrable traffic. To arrest it, to put an end to it, this nation keeps a squadron, at immense cost, on the coast of Africa. Everywhere, in this country, it is safe to speak of this foreign slave-trade, as a most inhuman traffic, opposed alike to the laws of God and of man. The duty to extirpate and destroy it, is admitted even by our DOCTORS OF DIVINITY. In order to put an end to it, some of these last have consented that their colored brethren (nominally free) should leave this country, and establish themselves on the western coast of Africa! It is, however, a notable fact that, while so much execration is poured out by Americans upon those engaged in the foreign slave-trade, the men engaged in the slave-trade between the states pass without condemnation, and their business is deemed honorable.

Behold the practical operation of this internal slave-trade, the American slave-trade, sustained by American politics and America religion. Here you will see men and women reared like swine for the market. You know what is a swine-drover? I will show you a man-drover. They inhabit all our Southern States. They perambulate the country, and crowd the highways of the nation, with droves of human stock. You will see one of these human flesh-jobbers, armed with pistol, whip and bowie-knife, driving a company of a hundred men, women, and children, from the Potomac to the slave market at New Orleans. These wretched people are to be sold singly, or in lots, to suit purchasers. They are food for the cotton-field, and the deadly sugar-mill. Mark the sad procession, as it moves wearily along, and the inhuman wretch who drives them. Hear his savage yells and his blood-chilling oaths, as he hurries on his affrighted captives! There, see the old man, with locks thinned and gray. Cast one glance, if you please, upon that young mother, whose shoulders are bare to the scorching sun, her briny tears falling on the brow of the babe in her arms. See, too, that girl of thirteen, weeping, *yes*! Weeping, as she thinks of the mother from whom she has been torn! The drove moves tardily. Heat and sorrow have nearly consumed their strength; suddenly you hear a quick snap, like the discharge of a rifle; the fetters clank, and the chain rattles simultaneously; your ears are saluted with a scream, that seems to have torn its way to the center of your soul! The crack you heard, was the sound of the slave-whip; the scream you heard, was from the woman you saw with the babe. Her speed had faltered under the weight of her child and her chains! that gash on her shoulder tells her to move on. Follow the drove to New Orleans. Attend the auction; see men examined like horses; see the forms of women rudely and brutally exposed to the shocking gaze of American slave-buyers. See this drove sold and separated forever; and never forget the deep, sad sobs that arose from that scattered multitude. Tell me citizens, WHERE, under the sun, you can witness a spectacle more fiendish and shocking. Yet this is but a glance at the American slave-trade, as it exists, at this moment, in the ruling part of the United States.

I was born amid such sights and scenes. To me the American slave-trade is a terrible reality. When a child, my soul was often pierced with a sense of its horrors. I lived on Philpot Street, Fell's Point, Baltimore, and have watched from the wharves, the slave ships in the Basin, anchored from the shore, with their cargoes of human flesh, waiting for favorable winds to waft them down the Chesapeake. There was, at that time, a grand slave mart kept at the head of Pratt Street, by Austin Woldfolk. His agents were sent into every town and county in Maryland, announcing their arrival, through the papers, and on flaming "*hand-bills*," headed CASH FOR NEGROES. These men were generally well dressed men, and very captivating in their manners. Ever ready to drink, to treat, and to gamble. The fate of many a slave has depended upon the turn of a single card; and many a child has been snatched from the arms of its mother by bargains arranged in a state of brutal drunkenness.

The flesh-mongers gather up their victims by dozens, and drive them, chained, to the general depot at Baltimore. When a sufficient number have been collected here, a ship is chartered, for the purpose of conveying the forlorn crew to Mobile, or to New Orleans. From the slave prison to the ship, they are usually driven in the darkness of night; for since the antislavery agitation, a certain caution is observed.

In the deep still darkness of midnight, I have been often aroused by the dead heavy footsteps, and the piteous cries of the chained gangs that passed our door. The anguish of my boyish heart was intense; and I was often consoled, when speaking to my mistress in the morning, to hear her say that the custom was very wicked; that she hated to hear the rattle of the chains, and the heart-rending cries. I was glad to find one who sympathized with me in my horror.

Fellow citizens, this murderous traffic is, today, in active operation in this boasted republic. In the solitude of my spirit, I see clouds of dust raised on the highways of the South; I see the bleeding footsteps; I hear the doleful wail of fettered humanity, on the way to the slave-markets, where the victims are to be sold like *horses*, *sheep*, and *swine*, knocked off to the highest bidder. There I see the tenderest ties ruthlessly broken, to gratify the lust, caprice and rapacity of the buyers and sellers of men. My soul sickens at the sight.

Is this the land your Fathers loved,
The freedom which they toiled to win?
Is this the earth whereon they moved?
Are these the graves they slumber in?

But a still more inhuman, disgraceful, and scandalous state of things remains to be presented. By an act of the American Congress, not yet two years old, slavery has been nationalized in its most horrible and revolting form. By that act, Mason and Dixon's line has been obliterated; New York has become as Virginia; and the power to hold, hunt, and sell men, women, and children as slaves remains no longer a mere state institution, but is now an institution of the whole United States. The power is co-extensive with the Star-Spangled Banner and American Christianity. Where these go, may also go the merciless slave-hunter. Where these are, man is not sacred. He is a bird for the sportsman's gun. By that most foul and fiendish of all human decrees, the liberty and person of every man are put in peril. Your broad republican domain is hunting ground for *men*. Not for thieves and robbers, enemies of society, merely, but for men guilty of no crime. Your lawmakers have commanded all good citizens to engage in this hellish sport. Your President, your Secretary of State, our lords, nobles, and ecclesiastics, enforce, as a duty you owe to your free and glorious country, and to your God, that you do this accursed thing.

Not fewer than forty Americans have, within the past two years, been hunted down and, without a moment's warning, hurried away in chains, and consigned to slavery and excruciating torture. Some of these have had wives and children, dependent on them for bread; but of this, no account was made. The right of the hunter to his prey stands superior to the right of marriage, and to *all* rights in this republic, the rights of God included! For black men there are neither law, justice, humanity, not religion. The Fugitive Slave *Law* makes mercy to them a crime; and bribes the judge who tries them. An American judge gets ten dollars for every victim he consigns to slavery, and five, when he fails to do so. The oath of any two villains is sufficient, under this hell-black enactment, to send the most pious and exemplary black man into the remorseless jaws of slavery! His own testimony is nothing. He can bring no witnesses for himself. The minister of American justice is bound by the law to hear but *one* side; and *that* side, is the side of the oppressor. Let this damning fact be perpetually told. Let it be thundered around the world, that, in tyrant-killing, king-hating, people-loving, democratic, Christian America, the seats of justice are filled with judges, who hold their offices under an open and palpable *bribe*, and are bound, in deciding in the case of a man's liberty, hear only his accusers!

In glaring violation of justice, in shameless disregard of the forms of administering law, in cunning arrangement to entrap the defenseless, and in diabolical intent, this Fugitive Slave Law stands alone in the annals of tyrannical legislation. I doubt if there be another nation on the globe, having the brass and the baseness to put such a law on the statute-book. If any man in this assembly thinks differently from me in this matter, and feels able to disprove my statements, I will gladly confront him at any suitable time and place he may select.

I take this law to be one of the grossest infringements of Christian Liberty, and, if the churches and ministers of our country were not stupidly blind, or most wickedly indifferent, they, too, would so regard it.

At the very moment that they are thanking God for the enjoyment of civil and religious liberty, and for the right to worship God according to the dictates of their own consciences, they are utterly silent in respect to a law which robs religion of its chief significance, and makes it utterly worthless to a world lying in wickedness. Did this law concern the "mint, anise, and cumin", abridge the right to sing psalms, to partake of the sacrament, or to engage in any of the ceremonies of religion, it would be smitten by the thunder of a thousand pulpits. A general shout would go up from the church, demanding *repeal, repeal, instant repeal*! And it would go hard with that politician who presumed to solicit the votes of the people without inscribing this motto on his banner. Further, if this demand were not complied with, another Scotland would be added to the history of religious liberty, and the stern old Covenanters would be thrown into the shade. A John Knox would be seen at every church door, and heard from every pulpit, and Fillmore would have no more quarter than was shown by Knox, to the beautiful, but treacherous queen Mary of Scotland. The fact that the church of our country, (with fractional exceptions), does not esteem "the Fugitive Slave Law" as a declaration of war against religious liberty, implies that that church regards religion simply as a form of worship, an empty ceremony, and *not* a vital principle, requiring active benevolence, justice, love and good will towards man. It esteems sacrifice above mercy; psalm-singing above right doing; solemn meetings above practical righteousness. A worship that can be conducted by persons who refuse to give shelter to the houseless, to give bread to the hungry, clothing to the naked, and who enjoin obedience to a law forbidding these acts of mercy, is a curse, not a blessing to mankind. The Bible addresses all such persons as "scribes, Pharisees, hypocrites, who pay tithe of *mint, anise*, and *cumin*, and have omitted the weightier matters of the law, judgment, mercy and faith."

But the church of this country is not only indifferent to the wrongs of the slave, it actually takes sides with the oppressors. It has made itself the bulwark of American slavery, and the shield of American slave-hunters. Many of its most eloquent Divines. who stand as the very lights of the church, have shamelessly given the sanction of religion and the Bible to the whole slave system. They have taught that man may, properly, be a slave; that the relation of master and slave is ordained of God; that to send back an escaped bondman to his master is clearly the duty of all the followers of the Lord Jesus Christ; and this horrible blasphemy is palmed off upon the world for Christianity.

For my part, I would say, welcome infidelity! Welcome atheism! Welcome anything! In preference to the gospel, *as preached by those Divines*! They convert the very name of religion into an engine of tyranny, and barbarous cruelty, and serve to confirm more infidels, in this age, than all the infidel writings of Thomas Paine, Voltaire, and Bolingbroke, put together, have done! These ministers make religion a cold and flinty-hearted thing, having neither principles of right action, nor bowels of compassion. They strip the love of God of its beauty, and leave the throng of religion a huge, horrible, repulsive form. It is a religion for oppressors, tyrants, man-stealers, and *thugs*. It is not that "*pure and undefiled religion*" which is from above, and which is "*first pure, then peaceable, easy to be entreated,* full of mercy and good fruits, *without partiality, and without hypocrisy.*" But a religion which favors the rich against the poor; which exalts the proud above the humble; which divides mankind into two classes, tyrants and slaves; which says to the man in chains, *stay there*; and to the oppressor, *oppress on*; it is a religion which may be professed and enjoyed by all the robbers and enslavers of mankind; it makes God a respecter of persons, denies his fatherhood of the race, and tramples in the dust the great truth of the brotherhood of man.

All this we affirm to be true of the popular church, and the popular worship of our land and nation — a religion, a church, and a worship which, on the authority of inspired wisdom, we pronounce to be an abomination in the sight of God. In the language of Isaiah, the American church might be well addressed, "Bring no more vain ablations; incense is an abomination unto me: the new moons and Sabbaths, the calling of assemblies, I cannot away with; it is iniquity even the solemn meeting. Your new moons and your appointed feasts my soul hateth. They are a trouble to me; I am weary to bear them; and when ye spread forth your hands I will hide mine eyes from you. Yea! when ye make many prayers, I will not hear. Your hands are full of blood! Cease to do evil, learn to do well, seek judgment, relieve the oppressed, judge for the fatherless, plead for the widow."

The American church is guilty, when viewed in connection with what it is doing to uphold slavery; but it is superlatively guilty when viewed in connection with its ability to abolish slavery. The sin of which it is guilty is one of omission as well as of commission. Albert Barnes but uttered what the common sense of every man at all observant of the actual state of the case will receive as truth, when he declared that "There is no power out of the church that could sustain slavery an hour, if it were not sustained in it."

Let the religious press, the pulpit, the Sunday school, the conference meeting, the great ecclesiastical, missionary, Bible and tract associations of the land array their immense powers against slavery and slave-holding; and the whole system of crime and blood would be scattered to the winds; and that they do not do this involves them in the most awful responsibility of which the mind can conceive.

In prosecuting the anti-slavery enterprise, we have been asked to spare the church, to spare the ministry; but *how*, we ask, could such a thing be done? We are met on the threshold of our efforts for the redemption of the slave, by the church and ministry of the country, in battle arrayed against us; and we are compelled to fight or flee. From *what* quarter, I beg to know, has proceeded a fire so deadly upon our ranks, during the last two years, as from the Northern pulpit? As the champions of oppressors, the chosen men of American theology have appeared — men, honored for their so-called piety, and their real learning. The Lords of Buffalo, the Springs of New York, the

Lathrops of Auburn, the Coxes and Spencers of Brooklyn, the Gannets and Sharps of Boston, the Deweys of Washington, and other great religious lights of the land have, in utter denial of the authority of *Him* by whom they professed to be called to the ministry, deliberately taught us, against the example or the Hebrews and against the remonstrance of the Apostles, they teach *that we ought to obey man's law before the law of God.*

    My spirit wearies of such blasphemy; and how such men can be supported, as the "standing types and representatives of Jesus Christ," is a mystery which I leave others to penetrate. In speaking of the American church, however, let it be distinctly understood that I mean the great mass of the religious organizations of our land. There are exceptions, and I thank God that there are. Noble men may be found, scattered all over these Northern States, of whom Henry Ward Beecher of Brooklyn, Samuel J. May of Syracuse, and my esteemed friend (Rev. R. R. Raymond) on the platform, are shining examples; and let me say further, that upon these men lies the duty to inspire our ranks with high religious faith and zeal, and to cheer us on in the great mission of the slave's redemption from his chains.

    One is struck with the difference between the attitude of the American church towards the anti-slavery movement, and that occupied by the churches in England towards a similar movement in that country. There, the church, true to its mission of ameliorating, elevating, and improving the condition of mankind, came forward promptly, bound up the wounds of the West Indian slave, and restored him to his liberty. There, the question of emancipation was a high religious question. It was demanded, in the name of humanity, and according to the law of the living God. The Sharps, the Clarksons, the Wilberforces, the Buxtons, and Burchells and the Knibbs, were alike famous for their piety, and for their philanthropy. The anti-slavery movement *there* was not an anti-church movement, for the reason that the church took its full share in prosecuting that movement: and the anti-slavery movement in this country will cease to be an anti-church movement, when the church of this country shall assume a favorable, instead of a hostile position towards that movement. Americans! your republican politics, not less than your republican religion, are flagrantly inconsistent. You boast of your love of liberty, your superior civilization, and your pure Christianity, while the whole political power of the nation (as embodied in the two great political parties), is solemnly pledged to support and perpetuate the enslavement of three millions of your countrymen. You hurl your anathemas at the crowned headed tyrants of Russia and Austria, and pride yourselves on your Democratic institutions, while you yourselves consent to be the mere *tools* and *body-guards* of the tyrants of

Virginia and Carolina. You invite to your shores fugitives of oppression from abroad, honor them with banquets, greet them with ovations, cheer them, toast them, salute them, protect them, and pour out your money to them like water; but the fugitives from your own land you advertise, hunt, arrest, shoot and kill. You glory in your refinement and your universal education yet you maintain a system as barbarous and dreadful as ever stained the character of a nation — a system begun in avarice, supported in pride, and perpetuated in cruelty. You shed tears over fallen Hungary, and make the sad story of her wrongs the theme of your poets, statesmen and orators, till your gallant sons are ready to fly to arms to vindicate her cause against her oppressors; but, in regard to the ten thousand wrongs of the American slave, you would enforce the strictest silence, and would hail him as an enemy of the nation who dares to make those wrongs the subject of public discourse! You are all on fire at the mention of liberty for France or for Ireland; but are as cold as an iceberg at the thought of liberty for the enslaved of America. You discourse eloquently on the dignity of labor; yet, you sustain a system which, in its very essence, casts a stigma upon labor. You can bare your bosom to the storm of British artillery to throw off a three-penny tax on tea, and yet wring the last hard-earned farthing from the grasp of the black laborers of your country. You profess to believe "that, of one blood, God made all nations of men to dwell on the face of all the earth," and hath commanded all men, everywhere to love one another; yet you notoriously hate, (and glory in your hatred), all men whose skins are not colored like your own.

You declare, before the world, and are understood by the world to declare, that you "*hold these truths to be self-evident, that all men are created equal; and are endowed by their Creator with certain inalienable rights; and that, among these are, life, liberty, and the pursuit of happiness*;" and yet, you hold securely, in a bondage which, according to your own Thomas Jefferson, "*is worse than ages of that which your fathers rose in rebellion to oppose*," a *seventh part* of the inhabitants of your country.

Fellow citizens! I will not enlarge further on your national inconsistencies. The existence of slavery in this country brands your republicanism as a sham, your humanity as a base pretence, and your Christianity as a lie. It destroys your moral power abroad; it corrupts your politicians at home. It saps the foundation of religion; it makes your name a hissing, and a bye-word to a mocking earth. It is the antagonistic force in your government, the only thing that seriously disturbs and endangers your *Union*. It fetters your progress; it is the enemy of improvement, the deadly foe of education; it fosters pride; it breeds insolence; it promotes vice; it shelters crime; it is a curse to the earth that supports it; and yet, you cling to it, as if it were the sheet anchor of all your hopes. Oh! Be warned! Be warned! a horrible reptile is coiled up in your nation's bosom; the venomous creature is nursing at the tender breast of your youthful republic; *for the love of God*, tear away, and fling from you the hideous monster, and *let the weight of twenty millions crush and destroy it forever*!

But it is answered in reply to all this, that precisely what I have now denounced is, in fact, guaranteed and sanctioned by the Constitution of the United States; that the right to hold and to hunt slaves is a part of that Constitution framed by the illustrious Fathers of this Republic.

Then, I dare to affirm, notwithstanding all I have said before, your fathers stooped, basely stooped:

To palter with us in a double sense:
And keep the word of promise to the ear,
But break it to the heart.

And instead of being the honest men I have before declared them to be, they were the veriest imposters that ever practiced on mankind. This is the inevitable conclusion, and from it there is no escape. But I differ from those who charge this baseness on the framers of the Constitution of the United States. It is a slander upon their memory, at least, so I believe. There is not time now to argue the constitutional question at length — nor have I the ability to discuss it as it ought to be discussed. The subject has been handled with masterly power by Lysander Spooner, Esq., by William Goodell, by Samuel E. Sewall, Esq., and last, though not least, by Gerritt Smith, Esq. These gentlemen have, as I think, fully and clearly vindicated the Constitution from any design to support slavery for an hour.

Fellow citizens! There is no matter in respect to which, the people of the North have allowed themselves to be so ruinously imposed upon, as that of the pro-slavery character of the Constitution. In that instrument I hold there is neither warrant, license, nor sanction of the hateful thing; but, interpreted as it ought to be interpreted, the Constitution is a GLORIOUS LIBERTY DOCUMENT. Read its preamble, consider its purposes. Is slavery among them? Is it at the gateway? Or is it in the temple? It is neither. While I do not intend to argue this question on the present occasion, let me ask, if it be not somewhat singular that, if the Constitution were intended to be, by its framers and adopters, a slave-holding instrument, why neither slavery, slaveholding, nor slave can anywhere be found in it. What would be thought of an instrument, drawn up, legally drawn up, for the purpose of entitling the city of Rochester to a track of land, in which no mention of land was made? Now, there are certain rules of interpretation, for the proper understanding of all legal instruments. These rules are well established. They are plain, common-sense rules, such as you and I, and all of us, can understand and apply, without having passed years in the study of law. I scout the idea that the question of the constitutionality or unconstitutionality of slavery is not a question for the people. I hold that every American citizen has a right to form an opinion of the constitution, and to propagate that opinion, and to use all honorable means to make his opinion the prevailing one. Without this right, the liberty of an American citizen would be as insecure as that of a Frenchman. Ex-Vice-President Dallas tells us that the Constitution is an object to which no American mind can be too attentive, and no American heart too devoted. He further says, the Constitution, in its words, is plain and intelligible, and is meant for the home-bred, unsophisticated understandings of our fellow-citizens. Senator Berrien tell us that the Constitution is the fundamental law, that which controls all others. The charter of our liberties, which every citizen has a personal interest in understanding thoroughly. The testimony of Senator Breese, Lewis Cass, and many others that might be named, who are everywhere esteemed as sound lawyers, so regard the constitution. I take it, therefore, that it is not presumption in a private citizen to form an opinion of that instrument.

Now, take the Constitution according to its plain reading, and I defy the presentation of a single pro-slavery clause in it. On the other hand it will be found to contain principles and purposes, entirely hostile to the existence of slavery.

I have detained my audience entirely too long already. At some future period I will gladly avail myself of an opportunity to give this subject a full and fair discussion.

Allow me to say, in conclusion, notwithstanding the dark picture I have this day presented of the state of the nation, I do not despair of this country. There are forces in operation, which must inevitably work the downfall of slavery. "The arm of the Lord is not shortened," and the doom of slavery is certain. I, therefore, leave off where I began, with hope. While drawing encouragement from the Declaration of Independence, the great principles it contains, and the genius of American Institutions, my spirit is also cheered by the obvious tendencies of the age. Nations do not now stand in the same relation to each other that they did ages ago. No nation can now shut itself up from the surrounding world, and trot round in the same old path of its fathers without interference. The time was when such could be done. Long established customs of hurtful character could formerly fence themselves in, and do their evil work with social impunity. Knowledge was then confined and enjoyed by the privileged few, and the multitude walked on in mental darkness. But a change has now come over the affairs of mankind. Walled cities and empires have become unfashionable. The arm of commerce has borne away the gates of the strong city. Intelligence is penetrating the darkest corners of the globe. It makes its pathway over and under the sea, as well as on the earth. Wind, steam, and lightning are its chartered agents. Oceans no longer divide, but link nations together. From Boston to London is now a holiday excursion. Space is comparatively annihilated. Thoughts expressed on one side of the Atlantic, are distinctly heard on the other. The far off and almost fabulous Pacific rolls in grandeur at our feet. The Celestial Empire, the mystery of ages, is being solved. The fiat of the Almighty, "Let there be Light," has not yet spent its force. No abuse, no outrage whether in taste, sport or avarice, can now hide itself from the all-pervading light. The iron shoe, and crippled foot of China must be seen, in contrast with nature. Africa must rise and put on her yet unwoven garment. "Ethiopia shall stretch out her hand unto God." In the fervent aspirations of William Lloyd Garrison, I say, and let every heart join in saying it:

God speed the year of jubilee
The wide world o'er
When from their galling chains set free,
Th' oppress'd shall vilely bend the knee,

And wear the yoke of tyranny
Like brutes no more.
That year will come, and freedom's reign,
To man his plundered fights again
Restore.

God speed the day when human blood
Shall cease to flow!
In every clime be understood,
The claims of human brotherhood,
And each return for evil, good,
Not blow for blow;
That day will come all feuds to end.
And change into a faithful friend
Each foe.

God speed the hour, the glorious hour,
When none on earth

Shall exercise a lordly power,
Nor in a tyrant's presence cower;
But all to manhood's stature tower,
By equal birth!
That hour will come, to each, to all,
And from his prison-house, the thrall
Go forth.

Until that year, day, hour, arrive,
With head, and heart, and hand I'll strive,
To break the rod, and rend the gyve,
The spoiler of his prey deprive —
So witness Heaven!
And never from my chosen post,
Whate'er the peril or the cost,
Be driven.

Malcom X

The Ballot or the Bullet

April 3, 1964

Mr. Moderator, Brother Lomax, brothers and sisters, friends and enemies: I just can't believe everyone in here is a friend, and I don't want to leave anybody out. The question tonight, as I understand it, is "The Negro Revolt, and Where Do We Go From Here?" or What Next?" In my little humble way of understanding it, it points toward either the ballot or the bullet.

Before we try and explain what is meant by the ballot or the bullet, I would like to clarify something concerning myself. I'm still a Muslim; my religion is still Islam. That's my personal belief. Just as Adam Clayton Powell is a Christian minister who heads the Abyssinian Baptist Church in New York, but at the same time takes part in the political struggles to try and bring about rights to the black people in this country; and Dr. Martin Luther King is a Christian minister down in Atlanta, Georgia, who heads another organization fighting for the civil rights of black people in this country; and Reverend Galamison, I guess you've heard of him, is another Christian minister in New York who has been deeply involved in the school boycotts to eliminate segregated education; well, I myself am a minister, not a Christian minister, but a Muslim minister; and I believe in action on all fronts by whatever means necessary.

Although I'm still a Muslim, I'm not here tonight to discuss my religion. I'm not here to try and change your religion. I'm not here to argue or discuss anything that we differ about, because it's time for us to submerge our differences and realize that it is best for us to first see that we have the same problem, a common problem, a problem that will make you catch hell whether you're a Baptist, or a Methodist, or a Muslim, or a nationalist. Whether you're educated or illiterate, whether you live on the boulevard or in the alley, you're going to catch hell just like I am. We're all in the same boat and we all are going to catch the same hell from the same man. He just happens to be a white man. All of us have suffered here, in this country, political oppression at the hands of the white man, economic exploitation at the hands of the white man, and social degradation at the hands of the white man.

Now in speaking like this, it doesn't mean that we're anti-white, but it does mean we're anti-exploitation, we're anti-degradation, we're anti-oppression. And if the white man doesn't want us to be anti-him, let him stop oppressing and exploiting and degrading us. Whether we are Christians or Muslims or nationalists or agnostics or atheists, we must first learn to forget our differences. If we have differences, let us differ in the closet; when we come out in front, let us not have anything to argue about until we get finished arguing with the man. If the late President Kennedy could get together with Khrushchev and exchange some wheat, we certainly have more in common with each other than Kennedy and Khrushchev had with each other.

If we don't do something real soon, I think you'll have to agree that we're going to be forced either to use the ballot or the bullet. It's one or the other in 1964. It isn't that time is running out -- time has run out!

1964 threatens to be the most explosive year America has ever witnessed. The most explosive year. Why? It's also a political year. It's the year when all of the white politicians will be back in the so-called Negro community jiving you and me for some votes. The year when all of the white political crooks will be right back in your and my community with their false promises, building up our hopes for a letdown, with their trickery and their treachery, with their false promises which they don't intend to keep. As they nourish these dissatisfactions, it can only lead to one thing, an explosion; and now we have the type of black man on the scene in America today -- I'm sorry, Brother Lomax -- who just doesn't intend to turn the other cheek any longer.

Don't let anybody tell you anything about the odds are against you. If they draft you, they send you to Korea and make you face 800 million Chinese. If you can be brave over there, you can be brave right here. These odds aren't as great as those odds. And if you fight here, you will at least know what you're fighting for.

I'm not a politician, not even a student of politics; in fact, I'm not a student of much of anything. I'm not a Democrat. I'm not a Republican, and I don't even consider myself an American. If you and I were Americans, there'd be no problem. Those Honkies that just got off the boat, they're already Americans; Polacks are already Americans; the Italian refugees are already Americans. Everything that came out of Europe, every blue-eyed thing, is already an American. And as long as you and I have been over here, we aren't Americans yet.

Well, I am one who doesn't believe in deluding myself. I'm not going to sit at your table and watch you eat, with nothing on my plate, and call myself a diner. Sitting at the table doesn't make you a diner, unless you eat some of what's on that plate. Being here in America doesn't make you an American. Being born here in America doesn't make you an American. Why, if birth made you American, you wouldn't need any legislation; you wouldn't need any amendments to the Constitution; you wouldn't be faced with civil-rights filibustering in Washington, D.C., right now. They don't have to pass civil-rights legislation to make a Polack an American.

No, I'm not an American. I'm one of the 22 million black people who are the victims of Americanism. One of the 22 million black people who are the victims of democracy, nothing but disguised hypocrisy. So, I'm not standing here speaking to you as an American, or a patriot, or a flag-saluter, or a flag-waver; no, not I. I'm speaking as a victim of this American system. And I see America through the eyes of the victim. I don't see any American dream; I see an American nightmare.

These 22 million victims are waking up. Their eyes are coming open. They're beginning to see what they used to only look at. They're becoming politically mature. They are realizing that there are new political trends from coast to coast. As they see these new political trends, it's possible for them to see that every time there's an election the races are so close that they have to have a recount. They had to recount in Massachusetts to see who was going to be governor, it was so close. It was the same way in Rhode Island, in Minnesota, and in many other parts of the country. And the same with Kennedy and Nixon when they ran for president. It was so close they had to count all over again. Well, what does this mean? It means that when white people are evenly divided, and black people have a bloc of votes of their own, it is left up to them to determine who's going to sit in the White House and who's going to be in the dog house.

It was the black man's vote that put the present administration in Washington, D.C. Your vote, your dumb vote, your ignorant vote, your wasted vote put in an administration in Washington, D.C., that has seen fit to pass every kind of legislation imaginable, saving you until last, then filibustering on top of that. And your and my leaders have the audacity to run around clapping their hands and talk about how much progress we're making. And what a good president we have. If he wasn't good in Texas, he sure can't be good in Washington, D.C. Because Texas is a lynch state. It is in the same breath as Mississippi, no different; only they lynch you in Texas with a Texas accent and lynch you in Mississippi with a Mississippi accent. And these Negro leaders have the audacity to go and have some coffee in the White House with a Texan, a Southern cracker -- that's all he is -- and then come out and tell you and me that he's going to be better for us because, since he's from the South, he knows how to deal with the

Southerners. What kind of logic is that? Let Eastland be president, he's from the South too. He should be better able to deal with them than Johnson.

In this present administration they have in the House of Representatives 257 Democrats to only 177 Republicans. They control two-thirds of the House vote. Why can't they pass something that will help you and me? In the Senate, there are 67 senators who are of the Democratic Party. Only 33 of them are Republicans. Why, the Democrats have got the government sewed up, and you're the one who sewed it up for them. And what have they given you for it? Four years in office, and just now getting around to some civil-rights legislation. Just now, after everything else is gone, out of the way, they're going to sit down now and play with you all summer long -- the same old giant con game that they call filibuster. All those are in cahoots together. Don't you ever think they're not in cahoots together, for the man that is heading the civil-rights filibuster is a man from Georgia named Richard Russell. When Johnson became president, the first man he asked for when he got back to Washington, D.C., was "Dicky" -- that's how tight they are. That's his boy, that's his pal, that's his buddy. But they're playing that old con game. One of them makes believe he's for you, and he's got it fixed where the other one is so tight against you, he never has to keep his promise.

So it's time in 1964 to wake up. And when you see them coming up with that kind of conspiracy, let them know your eyes are open. And let them know you -- something else that's wide open too. It's got to be the ballot or the bullet. The ballot or the bullet. If you're afraid to use an expression like that, you should get on out of the country; you should get back in the cotton patch; you should get back in the alley. They get all the Negro vote, and after they get it, the Negro gets nothing in return. All they did when they got to Washington was give a few big Negroes big jobs. Those big Negroes didn't need big jobs, they already had jobs. That's camouflage, that's trickery, that's treachery, window-dressing. I'm not trying to knock out the Democrats for the Republicans. We'll get to them in a minute. But it is true; you put the Democrats first and the Democrats put you last.

Look at it the way it is. What alibis do they use, since they control Congress and the Senate? What alibi do they use when you and I ask, "Well, when are you going to keep your promise?" They blame the Dixiecrats. What is a Dixiecrat? A Democrat. A Dixiecrat is nothing but a Democrat in disguise. The titular head of the Democrats is also the head of the Dixiecrats, because the Dixiecrats are a part of the Democratic Party. The Democrats have never kicked the Dixiecrats out of the party. The Dixiecrats bolted themselves once, but the Democrats didn't put them out. Imagine, these lowdown Southern segregationists put the Northern Democrats down. But the Northern Democrats have never put the Dixiecrats down. No, look at that thing the way it is. They have got a con game going on, a political con game, and you and I are in the middle. It's time for you and me to wake up and start looking at it like it is, and trying to understand it like it is; and then we can deal with it like it is.

The Dixiecrats in Washington, D.C., control the key committees that run the government. The only reason the Dixiecrats control these committees is because they have seniority. The only reason they have seniority is because they come from states where Negroes can't vote. This is not even a government that's based on democracy. It. is not a government that is made up of representatives of the people. Half of the people in the South can't even vote. Eastland is not even supposed to be in Washington. Half of the senators and congressmen who occupy these key positions in Washington, D.C., are there illegally, are there unconstitutionally.

I was in Washington, D.C., a week ago Thursday, when they were debating whether or not they should let the bill come onto the floor. And in the back of the room where the Senate meets, there's a huge map of the United States, and on that map it shows the location of Negroes throughout the country. And it shows that the Southern section of the country, the states that are most heavily concentrated with Negroes, are the ones that have senators and congressmen standing up filibustering and doing all other kinds of trickery to keep the Negro from being able to vote. This is pitiful. But it's not pitiful for us any longer; it's actually pitiful for the white man, because soon now, as the Negro awakens a little more and sees the vise that he's in, sees the bag that he's in, sees the real game that he's in, then the Negro's going to develop a new tactic.

These senators and congressmen actually violate the constitutional amendments that guarantee the people of that particular state or county the right to vote. And the Constitution itself has within it the machinery to expel any representative from a state where the voting rights of the people are violated. You don't even need new legislation. Any person in Congress right now, who is there from a state or a district where the voting rights of the people are violated, that particular person should be expelled from Congress. And when you expel him, you've removed one of the obstacles in the path of any real meaningful legislation in this country. In fact, when you expel them, you don't need new legislation, because they will be replaced by black representatives from counties and districts where the black man is in the majority, not in the minority.

If the black man in these Southern states had his full voting rights, the key Dixiecrats in Washington, D. C., which means the key Democrats in Washington, D.C., would lose their seats. The Democratic Party itself would lose its power. It would cease to be powerful as a party. When you see the amount of power that would be lost by the Democratic Party if it were to lose the Dixiecrat wing, or branch, or element, you can see where it's against the interests of the Democrats to give voting rights to Negroes in states where the Democrats have been in complete power and authority ever since the Civil War. You just can't belong to that Party without analyzing it.

I say again, I'm not anti-Democrat, I'm not anti-Republican, I'm not anti anything. I'm just questioning their sincerity, and some of the strategy that they've been using on our people by promising them promises that they don't intend to keep. When you keep the Democrats in power, you're keeping the Dixiecrats in power. I doubt that my good Brother Lomax will deny that. A vote for a Democrat is a vote for a Dixiecrat. That's why, in 1964, it's time now for you and me to become more politically mature and realize what the ballot is for; what we're supposed to get when we cast a ballot; and that if we don't cast a ballot, it's going to end up in a situation where we're going to have to cast a bullet. It's either a ballot or a bullet.

In the North, they do it a different way. They have a system that's known as gerrymandering, whatever that means. It means when Negroes become too heavily concentrated in a certain area, and begin to gain too much political power, the white man comes along and changes the district lines. You may say, "Why do you keep saying white man?" Because it's the white man who does it. I haven't ever seen any Negro changing any lines. They don't let him get near the line. It's the white man who does this. And usually, it's the white man who grins at you the most, and pats you on the back, and is supposed to be your friend. He may be friendly, but he's not your friend.

So, what I'm trying to impress upon you, in essence, is this: You and I in America are faced not with a segregationist conspiracy, we're faced with a government conspiracy. Everyone who's filibustering is a senator -- that's the government. Everyone who's finagling in Washington, D.C., is a congressman -- that's the government. You don't have anybody putting blocks in your path but people who are a part of the government. The same government that you go abroad to fight for and die for is the government that is in a conspiracy to deprive you of your voting rights, deprive you of your economic opportunities, deprive you of decent housing, deprive you of decent education. You don't need to go to the employer alone, it is the government itself, the government of America that is responsible for the oppression and exploitation and degradation of black people in this country. And you should drop it in their lap. This government has failed the Negro. This so-called democracy has failed the Negro. And all these white liberals have definitely failed the Negro.

So, where do we go from here? First, we need some friends. We need some new allies. The entire civil-rights struggle needs a new interpretation, a broader interpretation. We need to look at this civil-rights thing from another angle -- from the inside as well as from the outside. To those of us whose philosophy is black nationalism, the only way you can get involved in the civil rights struggle is give it a new interpretation. That old interpretation excluded us. It kept us out. So, we're giving a new interpretation to the civil-rights struggle, an interpretation that will enable us to come into it, take part in it. And these handkerchief-heads who have been dillydallying and pussy footing and compromising -- we don't intend to let them pussyfoot and dillydally and compromise any longer.

How can you thank a man for giving you what's already yours? How then can you thank him for giving you only part of what's already yours? You haven't even made progress, if what's being given to you, you should have had already. That's not progress. And I love my Brother Lomax, the way he pointed out we're right back where we were in 1954. We're not even as far up as we were in 1954. We're behind where we were in 1954. There's more segregation now than there was in 1954. There's more racial animosity, more racial hatred, more racial violence today in 1964, than there was in 1954. Where is the progress?

And now you're facing a situation where the young Negro's coming up. They don't want to hear that "turn the-other-cheek" stuff, no. In Jacksonville, those were teenagers, they were throwing Molotov cocktails. Negroes have never done that before. But it shows you there's a new deal coming in. There's new thinking coming in. There's new strategy coming in. It'll be Molotov cocktails this month, hand grenades next month, and something else next month. It'll be ballots, or it'll be bullets. It'll be liberty, or it will be death. The only difference about this kind of death -- it'll be reciprocal. You know what is meant by "reciprocal"? That's one of Brother Lomax's words. I stole it from him. I don't usually deal with those big words because I don't usually deal with big people. I deal with small people. I find you can get a whole lot of small people and whip hell out of a whole lot of big people. They haven't got anything to lose, and they've got every thing to gain. And they'll let you know in a minute: "It takes two to tango; when I go, you go."

The black nationalists, those whose philosophy is black nationalism, in bringing about this new interpretation of the entire meaning of civil rights, look upon it as meaning, as Brother Lomax has pointed out, equality of opportunity. Well, we're justified in seeking civil rights, if it means equality of opportunity, because all we're doing there is trying to collect for our investment. Our mothers and fathers invested sweat and blood. Three hundred and ten years we worked in this country without a dime in return -- I mean without a dime in return. You let the white man walk around here talking about how rich this country is, but you never stop to think how it got rich so quick. It got rich because you made it rich.

You take the people who are in this audience right now. They're poor. We're all poor as individuals. Our weekly salary individually amounts to hardly anything. But if you take the salary of everyone in here collectively, it'll fill up a whole lot of baskets. It's a lot of wealth. If you can collect the wages of just these people right here for a year, you'll be rich -- richer than rich. When you look at it like that, think how rich Uncle Sam had to become, not with this handful, but millions of black people. Your and my mother and father, who didn't work an eight-hour shift, but worked from "can't see" in the morning until "can't see" at night, and worked for nothing, making the white man rich, making Uncle Sam rich. This is our investment. This is our contribution, our blood.

Not only did we give of our free labor, we gave of our blood. Every time he had a call to arms, we were the first ones in uniform. We died on every battlefield the white man had. We have made a greater sacrifice than anybody who's standing up in America today. We have made a greater contribution and have collected less. Civil rights, for those of us whose philosophy is black nationalism, means: "Give it to us now. Don't wait for next year. Give it to us yesterday, and that's not fast enough."

I might stop right here to point out one thing. Whenever you're going after something that belongs to you, anyone who's depriving you of the right to have it is a criminal. Understand that. Whenever you are going after something that is yours, you are within your legal rights to lay claim to it. And anyone who puts forth any effort to deprive you of that which is yours, is breaking the law, is a criminal. And this was pointed out by the Supreme Court decision. It outlawed segregation.

Which means segregation is against the law. Which means a segregationist is breaking the law. A segregationist is a criminal. You can't label him as anything other than that. And when you demonstrate against segregation, the law is on your side. The Supreme Court is on your side.

Now, who is it that opposes you in carrying out the law? The police department itself. With police dogs and clubs. Whenever you demonstrate against segregation, whether it is segregated education, segregated housing, or anything else, the law is on your side, and anyone who stands in the way is not the law any longer. They are breaking the law; they are not representatives of the law. Any time you demonstrate against segregation and a man has the audacity to put a police dog on you, kill that dog, kill him, I'm telling you, kill that dog. I say it, if they put me in jail tomorrow, kill that dog. Then you'll put a stop to it. Now, if these white people in here don't want to see that kind of action, get down and tell the mayor to tell the police department to pull the dogs in. That's all you have to do. If you don't do it, someone else will.

If you don't take this kind of stand, your little children will grow up and look at you and think "shame." If you don't take an uncompromising stand, I don't mean go out and get violent; but at the same time you should never be nonviolent unless you run into some nonviolence. I'm nonviolent with those who are nonviolent with me. But when you drop that violence on me, then you've made me go insane, and I'm not responsible for what I do. And that's the way every Negro should get. Any time you know you're within the law, within your legal rights, within your moral rights, in accord with justice, then die for what you believe in. But don't die alone. Let your dying be reciprocal. This is what is meant by equality. What's good for the goose is good for the gander.

When we begin to get in this area, we need new friends, we need new allies. We need to expand the civil-rights struggle to a higher level -- to the level of human rights. Whenever you are in a civil-rights struggle, whether you know it or not, you are confining yourself to the jurisdiction of Uncle Sam. No one from the outside world can speak out in your behalf as long as your struggle is a civil-rights struggle. Civil rights comes within the domestic affairs of this country. All of our African brothers and our Asian brothers and our Latin-American brothers cannot open their mouths and interfere in the domestic affairs of the United States. And as long as it's civil rights, this comes under the jurisdiction of Uncle Sam.

But the United Nations has what's known as the charter of human rights; it has a committee that deals in human rights. You may wonder why all of the atrocities that have been committed in Africa and in Hungary and in Asia, and in Latin America are brought before the UN, and the Negro problem is never brought before the UN. This is part of the conspiracy. This old, tricky blue eyed liberal who is supposed to be your and my friend, supposed to be in our corner, supposed to be subsidizing our struggle, and supposed to be acting in the capacity of an adviser, never tells you anything about human rights. They keep you wrapped up in civil rights. And you spend so much time barking up the civil-rights tree, you don't even know there's a human-rights tree on the same floor.

When you expand the civil-rights struggle to the level of human rights, you can then take the case of the black man in this country before the nations in the UN. You can take it before the General Assembly. You can take Uncle Sam before a world court. But the only level you can do it on is the level of human rights. Civil rights keeps you under his restrictions, under his jurisdiction. Civil rights keeps you in his pocket. Civil rights means you're asking Uncle Sam to treat you right. Human rights are something you were born with. Human rights are your God-given rights. Human rights are the rights that are recognized by all nations of this earth. And any time any one violates your human rights, you can take them to the world court.

Uncle Sam's hands are dripping with blood, dripping with the blood of the black man in this country. He's the earth's number-one hypocrite. He has the audacity -- yes, he has -- imagine him posing as the leader of the free world. The free world! And you over here singing "We Shall Overcome." Expand the civil-rights struggle to the level of human rights. Take it into the United Nations, where our African brothers can throw their weight on our side, where our Asian brothers can throw their weight on our side, where our Latin-American brothers can throw their weight on our side, and where 800 million Chinamen are sitting there waiting to throw their weight on our side.

Let the world know how bloody his hands are. Let the world know the hypocrisy that's practiced over here. Let it be the ballot or the bullet. Let him know that it must be the ballot or the bullet.

When you take your case to Washington, D.C., you're taking it to the criminal who's responsible; it's like running from the wolf to the fox. They're all in cahoots together. They all work political chicanery and make you look like a chump before the eyes of the world. Here you are walking around in America, getting ready to be drafted and sent abroad, like a tin soldier, and when you get over there, people ask you what are you fighting for, and you have to stick your tongue in your cheek. No, take Uncle Sam to court, take him before the world.

By ballot I only mean freedom. Don't you know -- I disagree with Lomax on this issue -- that the ballot is more important than the dollar? Can I prove it? Yes. Look in the UN. There are poor nations in the UN; yet those poor nations can get together with their voting power and keep the rich nations from making a move. They have one nation -- one vote, everyone has an equal vote. And when those brothers from Asia, and Africa and the darker parts of this earth get together, their voting power is sufficient to hold Sam in check. Or Russia in check. Or some other section of the earth in check. So, the ballot is most important.

Right now, in this country, if you and I, 22 million African-Americans -- that's what we are -- Africans who are in America. You're nothing but Africans. Nothing but Africans. In fact, you'd get farther calling yourself African instead of Negro. Africans don't catch hell. You're the only one catching hell. They don't have to pass civil-rights bills for Africans. An African can go anywhere he wants right now. All you've got to do is tie your head up. That's right, go anywhere you want. Just stop being a Negro. Change your name to Hoogagagooba. That'll show you how silly the white man is. You're dealing with a silly man. A friend of mine who's very dark put a turban on his head and went into a restaurant in Atlanta before they called themselves desegregated. He went into a white restaurant, he sat down, they served him, and he said, "What would happen if a Negro came in here? And there he's sitting, black as night, but because he had his head wrapped up the waitress looked back at him and says, "Why, there wouldn't no nigger dare come in here."

So, you're dealing with a man whose bias and prejudice are making him lose his mind, his intelligence, every day. He's frightened. He looks around and sees what's taking place on this earth, and he sees that the pendulum of time is swinging in your direction. The dark people are waking up. They're losing their fear of the white man. No place where he's fighting right now is he winning. Everywhere he's fighting, he's fighting someone your and my complexion. And they're beating him. He can't win any more. He's won his last battle. He failed to win the Korean War. He couldn't win it. He had to sign a truce. That's a loss.

Any time Uncle Sam, with all his machinery for warfare, is held to a draw by some rice eaters, he's lost the battle. He had to sign a truce. America's not supposed to sign a truce. She's supposed to be bad. But she's not bad any more. She's bad as long as she can use her hydrogen bomb, but she can't use hers for fear Russia might use hers. Russia can't use hers, for fear that Sam might use his. So, both of them are weapon-less. They can't use the weapon because each's weapon nullifies the other's. So the only place where action can take place is on the ground. And the white man can't win another war fighting on the ground. Those days are over The black man knows it, the brown man knows it, the red man knows it, and the yellow man knows it. So they engage him in guerrilla warfare. That's not his style. You've got to have heart to be a guerrilla warrior, and he hasn't got any heart. I'm telling you now.

I just want to give you a little briefing on guerrilla warfare because, before you know it, before you know it. It takes heart to be a guerrilla warrior because you're on your own. In conventional warfare you have tanks and a whole lot of other people with you to back you up -- planes over your head and all that kind of stuff. But a guerrilla is on his own. All you have is a rifle, some sneakers and a bowl of rice, and that's all you need -- and a lot of heart. The Japanese on some of those islands in the Pacific, when the American soldiers landed, one Japanese sometimes could hold the whole army off. He'd just wait until the sun went down, and when the sun went down they were all equal. He would take his little blade and slip from bush to bush, and from American to American. The white soldiers couldn't cope with that. Whenever you see a white soldier that fought in the Pacific, he has the shakes, he has a nervous condition, because they scared him to death.

The same thing happened to the French up in French Indochina. People who just a few years previously were rice farmers got together and ran the heavily-mechanized French army out of Indochina. You don't need it -- modern warfare today won't work. This is the day of the guerrilla. They did the same thing in Algeria. Algerians, who were nothing but Bedouins, took a rine and sneaked off to the hills, and de Gaulle and all of his highfalutin' war machinery couldn't defeat those guerrillas. Nowhere on this earth does the white man win in a guerrilla warfare. It's not his speed. Just as guerrilla warfare is prevailing in Asia and in parts of Africa and in parts of Latin America, you've got to be mighty naive, or you've got to play the black man cheap, if you don't think some day he's going to wake up and find that it's got to be the ballot or the bullet.

I would like to say, in closing, a few things concerning the Muslim Mosque, Inc., which we established recently in New York City. It's true we're Muslims and our religion is Islam, but we don't mix our religion with our politics and our economics and our social and civil activities -- not any more we keep our religion in our mosque. After our religious services are over, then as Muslims we become involved in political action, economic action and social and civic action. We become involved with anybody, anywhere, any time and in any manner that's designed to eliminate the evils, the political, economic and social evils that are afflicting the people of our community.

The political philosophy of black nationalism means that the black man should control the politics and the politicians in his own community; no more. The black man in the black community has to be re-educated into the science of politics so he will know what politics is supposed to bring him in return. Don't be throwing out any ballots. A ballot is like a bullet. You don't throw your ballots until you see a target, and if that target is not within your reach, keep your ballot in your pocket.

The political philosophy of black nationalism is being taught in the Christian church. It's being taught in the NAACP. It's being taught in CORE meetings. It's being taught in SNCC Student Nonviolent Coordinating Committee meetings. It's being taught in Muslim meetings. It's being taught where nothing but atheists and agnostics come together. It's being taught everywhere. Black people are fed up with the dillydallying, pussyfooting, compromising approach that we've been using toward getting our freedom. We want freedom now, but we're not going to get it saying "We Shall Overcome." We've got to fight until we overcome.

The economic philosophy of black nationalism is pure and simple. It only means that we should control the economy of our community. Why should white people be running all the stores in our community? Why should white people be running the banks of our community? Why should the economy of our community be in the hands of the white man? Why? If a black man can't move his store into a white community, you tell me why a white man should move his store into a black community. The philosophy of black nationalism involves a re-education program in the black community in regards to economics. Our people have to be made to see that any time you take your dollar out of your community and spend it in a community where you don't live, the community where you live will get poorer and poorer, and the community where you spend your money will get richer and richer.

Then you wonder why where you live is always a ghetto or a slum area. And where you and I are concerned, not only do we lose it when we spend it out of the community, but the white man has got all our stores in the community tied up; so that though we spend it in the community, at sundown the man who runs the store takes it over across town somewhere. He's got us in a vise. So the economic philosophy of black nationalism means in every church, in every civic organization, in every fraternal order, it's time now for our people to be come conscious of the importance of controlling the economy of our community. If we own the stores, if we operate the businesses, if we try and establish some industry in our own community, then we're developing to the position where we are creating employment for our own kind. Once you gain control of the economy of your own community, then you don't have to picket and boycott and beg some cracker downtown for a job in his business.

The social philosophy of black nationalism only means that we have to get together and remove the evils, the vices, alcoholism, drug addiction, and other evils that are destroying the moral fiber of our community. We ourselves have to lift the level of our community, the standard of our community to a higher level, make our own society beautiful so that we will be satisfied in our own social circles and won't be running around here trying to knock our way into a social circle where we're not wanted. So I say, in spreading a gospel such as black nationalism, it is not designed to make the black man re-evaluate the white man -- you know him already -- but to make the black man re-evaluate himself. Don't change the white man's mind -- you can't change his mind, and that whole thing about appealing to the moral conscience of America -- America's conscience is bankrupt. She lost all conscience a long time ago. Uncle Sam has no conscience.

They don't know what morals are. They don't try and eliminate an evil because it's evil, or because it's illegal, or because it's immoral; they eliminate it only when it threatens their existence. So you're wasting your time appealing to the moral conscience of a bankrupt man like Uncle Sam. If he had a conscience, he'd straighten this thing out with no more pressure being put upon him. So it is not necessary to change the white man's mind. We have to change our own mind. You can't change his mind about us. We've got to change our own minds about each other. We have to see each other with new eyes. We have to see each other as brothers and sisters. We have to come together with warmth so we can develop unity and harmony that's necessary to get this problem solved ourselves. How can we do this? How can we avoid jealousy? How can we avoid the suspicion and the divisions that exist in the community? I'll tell you how.

I have watched how Billy Graham comes into a city, spreading what he calls the gospel of Christ, which is only white nationalism. That's what he is. Billy Graham is a white nationalist; I'm a black nationalist. But since it's the natural tendency for leaders to be jealous and look upon a powerful figure like Graham with suspicion and envy, how is it possible for him to come into a city and get all the cooperation of the church leaders? Don't think because they're church leaders that they don't have weaknesses that make them envious and jealous -- no, everybody's got it. It's not an accident that when they want to choose a cardinal, as Pope I over there in Rome, they get in a closet so you can't hear them cussing and fighting and carrying on.

Billy Graham comes in preaching the gospel of Christ. He evangelizes the gospel. He stirs everybody up, but he never tries to start a church. If he came in trying to start a church, all the churches would be against him. So, he just comes in talking about Christ and tells everybody who gets Christ to go to any church where Christ is; and in this way the church cooperates with him. So we're going to take a page from his book.

Our gospel is black nationalism. We're not trying to threaten the existence of any organization, but we're spreading the gospel of black nationalism. Anywhere there's a church that is also preaching and practicing the gospel of black nationalism, join that church. If the NAACP is preaching and practicing the gospel of black nationalism, join the NAACP. If CORE is spreading and practicing the gospel of black nationalism, join CORE. Join any organization that has a gospel that's for the uplift of the black man. And when you get into it and see them pussyfooting or compromising, pull out of it because that's not black nationalism. We'll find another one. And in this manner, the organizations will increase in number and in quantity and in quality, and by August, it is then our intention to have a black nationalist convention which will consist of delegates from all over the country who are interested in the political, economic and social philosophy of black nationalism. After these delegates convene, we will hold a seminar; we will hold discussions; we will listen to everyone. We want to hear new ideas and new solutions and new answers. And at that time, if we see fit then to form a black nationalist party, we'll form a black nationalist party. If it's necessary to form a black nationalist army, we'll form a black nationalist army. It'll be the ballot or the bullet. It'll be liberty or it'll be death.

It's time for you and me to stop sitting in this country, letting some cracker senators, Northern crackers and Southern crackers, sit there in Washington, D.C., and come to a conclusion in their mind that you and I are supposed to have civil rights. There's no white man going to tell me anything about my rights. Brothers and sisters, always remember, if it doesn't take senators and congressmen and presidential proclamations to give freedom to the white man, it is not necessary for legislation or proclamation or Supreme Court decisions to give freedom to the black man. You let that white man know, if this is a country of freedom, let it be a country of freedom; and if it's not a country of freedom, change it.

We will work with anybody, anywhere, at any time, who is genuinely interested in tackling the problem head-on, nonviolently as long as the enemy is nonviolent, but violent when the enemy gets violent. We'll work with you on the voter-registration drive, we'll work with you on rent strikes, we'll work with you on school boycotts; I don't believe in any kind of integration; I'm not even worried about it, because I know you're not going to get it anyway; you're not going to get it because you're afraid to die; you've got to be ready to die if you try and force yourself on the white man, because he'll get just as violent as those crackers in Mississippi, right here in Cleveland. But we will still work with you on the school boycotts because we're against a segregated school system. A segregated school system produces children who, when they graduate, graduate with crippled minds. But this does not mean that a school is segregated because it's all black. A segregated school means a school that is controlled by people who have no real interest in it whatsoever.

Let me explain what I mean. A segregated district or community is a community in which people live, but outsiders control the politics and the economy of that community. They never refer to the white section as a segregated community. It's the all-Negro section that's a segregated community. Why? The white man controls his own school, his own bank, his own economy, his own politics, his own everything, his own community; but he also controls yours. When you're under someone else's control, you're segregated. They'll always give you the lowest or the worst that there is to offer, but it doesn't mean you're segregated just because you have your own. You've got to control your own. Just like the white man has control of his, you need to control yours.

You know the best way to get rid of segregation? The white man is more afraid of separation than he is of integration. Segregation means that he puts you away from him, but not far enough for you to be out of his jurisdiction; separation means you're gone. And the white man will integrate faster than he'll let you separate. So we will work with you against the segregated school system because it's criminal, because it is absolutely destructive, in every way imaginable, to the minds of the children who have to be exposed to that type of crippling education.

Last but not least, I must say this concerning the great controversy over rifles and shotguns. The only thing that I've ever said is that in areas where the government has proven itself either unwilling or unable to defend the lives and the property of Negroes, it's time for Negroes to defend themselves. Article number two of the constitutional amendments provides you and me the right to own a rifle or a shotgun. It is constitutionally legal to own a shotgun or a rifle. This doesn't mean you're going to get a rifle and form battalions and go out looking for white folks, although you'd be within your rights -- I mean, you'd be justified; but that would be illegal and we don't do anything illegal. If the white man doesn't want the black man buying rifles and shotguns, then let the government do its job.

That's all. And don't let the white man come to you and ask you what you think about what Malcolm says -- why, you old Uncle Tom. He would never ask you if he thought you were going to say,

"Amen!" No, he is making a Tom out of you." So, this doesn't mean forming rifle clubs and going out looking for people, but it is time, in 1964, if you are a man, to let that man know. If he's not going to do his job in running the government and providing you and me with the protection that our taxes are supposed to be for, since he spends all those billions for his defense budget, he certainly can't begrudge you and me spending $12 or $15 for a single-shot, or double-action. I hope you understand. Don't go out shooting people, but any time -- brothers and sisters, and especially the men in this audience; some of you wearing Congressional Medals of Honor, with shoulders this wide, chests this big, muscles that big -- any time you and I sit around and read where they bomb a church and murder in cold blood, not some grownups, but four little girls while they were praying to the same God the white man taught them to pray to, and you and I see the government go down and can't find who did it.

Why, this man, he can find Eichmann hiding down in Argentina somewhere. Let two or three American soldiers, who are minding somebody else's business way over in South Vietnam, get killed, and he'll send battleships, sticking his nose in their business. He wanted to send troops down to Cuba and make them have what he calls free elections -- this old cracker who doesn't have free elections in his own country.

No, if you never see me another time in your life, if I die in the morning, I'll die saying one thing: the ballot or the bullet, the ballot or the bullet.

If a Negro in 1964 has to sit around and wait for some cracker senator to filibuster when it comes to the rights of black people, why, you and I should hang our heads in shame. You talk about a march on Washington in 1963, you haven't seen anything. There's some more going down in '64.

And this time they're not going like they went last year. They're not going singing "We Shall Overcome." They're not going with white friends. They're not going with placards already painted for them. They're not going with round-trip tickets. They're going with one way tickets. And if they don't want that non-nonviolent army going down there, tell them to bring the filibuster to a halt.

The black nationalists aren't going to wait. Lyndon B. Johnson is the head of the Democratic Party. If he's for civil rights, let him go into the Senate next week and declare himself. Let him go in there right now and declare himself. Let him go in there and denounce the Southern branch of his party. Let him go in there right now and take a moral stand -- right now, not later. Tell him, don't wait until election time. If he waits too long, brothers and sisters, he will be responsible for letting a condition develop in this country which will create a climate that will bring seeds up out of the ground with vegetation on the end of them looking like something these people never dreamed of. In 1964, it's the ballot or the bullet.

Thank you.

Barack Obama

Knox College Commencement Address

June 4, 2005

Good morning President Taylor, Board of Trustees, faculty, parents, family, friends, the community of Galesburg, the class of 1955 -- which I understand was out partying last night, and yet still showed up here on time -- and most of all, the Class of 2005. Congratulations on your graduation, and thank you -- thank you for the honor of allowing me to be a part of it. Thank you also, Mr. President, for this honorary degree. It was only a couple of years ago that I stopped paying my student loans in law school. Had I known it was this easy, I would have ran [sic] for the United States Senate earlier.

You know, it has been about six months now since you sent me to Washington as your United States Senator. I recognize that not all of you voted for me, so for those of you muttering under your breath "I didn't send you anywhere," that's ok too. Maybe we'll hold. What do you call it? A little Pumphandle after the ceremony. Change your mind for the next time.

It has been a fascinating journey thus far. Each time I walk onto the Senate floor, I'm reminded of the history, for good and for ill that has been made there. But there have been a few surreal moments. For example, I remember the day before I was sworn in, myself and my staff, we decided to hold a press conference in our office. Now, keep in mind that I am ranked 99th in seniority. I was proud that I wasn't ranked dead last until I found out that it's just because Illinois is bigger than Colorado. So I'm 99th in seniority, and all the reporters are crammed into the tiny transition office that I have, which is right next to the janitor's closet in the basement of the Dirksen Office Building. It's my first day in the building, I have not taken a single vote, I have not introduced one bill, had not even sat down in my desk, and this very earnest reporter raises his hand and says:

"Senator Obama, what is your place in history?"

I did what you just did, which is laugh out loud. I said, "place in history?" I thought he was kidding. At that point, I wasn't even sure the other Senators would save a place for me at the cool kids' table. But as I was thinking about the words to share with this class, about what's next, about what's possible, and what opportunities lay ahead, I actually think it's not a bad question for you, the class of 2005, to ask yourselves: What will be your place in history?

In other eras, across distant lands, this question could be answered with relative ease and certainty. As a servant in Rome, you knew you'd spend your life forced to build somebody else's Empire. As a peasant in 11th Century China, you knew that no matter how hard you worked, the local warlord might come and take everything you had -- and you also knew that famine might come knocking at the door. As a subject of King George, you knew that your freedom of worship and your freedom to speak and to build your own life would be ultimately limited by the throne. And then America happened.

A place where destiny was not a destination, but a journey to be shared and shaped and remade by people who had the gall, the temerity to believe that, against all odds, they could form "a more perfect union" on this new frontier.

And as people around the world began to hear the tale of the lowly colonists who overthrew an empire for the sake of an idea, they started to come. Across oceans and the ages, they settled in Boston and Charleston, Chicago and St. Louis, Kalamazoo and Galesburg, to try and build their own American Dream. This collective dream moved forward imperfectly -- it was scarred by our treatment of native peoples, betrayed by slavery, clouded by the subjugation of women, shaken by war and depression. And yet, brick by brick, rail by rail, calloused hand by calloused hand, people kept dreaming, and building, and working, and marching, and petitioning their government, until they made America a land where the question of our place in history is not answered for us. It's answered by us.

Have we failed at times? Absolutely. Will you occasionally fail when you embark on your own American journey? You surely will. But the test is not perfection.
The true test of the American ideal is whether we're able to recognize our failings and then rise together to meet the challenges of our time. Whether we allow ourselves to be shaped by events and history, or whether we act to shape them. Whether chance of birth or circumstance decides life's big winners and losers, or whether we build a community where, at the very least, everyone has a chance to work hard, get ahead, and reach their dreams. We have faced this choice before.

At the end of the Civil War, when farmers and their families began moving into the cities to work in the big factories that were sprouting up all across America, we had to decide: Do we do nothing and allow captains of industry and robber barons to run roughshod over the economy and workers by competing to see who can pay the lowest wages at the worst working conditions? Or do we try to make the system work by setting up basic rules for the market, instituting the first public schools, busting up monopolies, letting workers organize into unions? We chose to act, and we rose together.

When the irrational exuberance of the Roaring Twenties came crashing down with the stock market, we had to decide: do we follow the call of leaders who would do nothing, or the call of a leader who, perhaps because of his physical paralysis, refused to accept political paralysis?

We chose to act -- regulating the market, putting people back to work, expanding bargaining rights to include health care and a secure retirement -- and together we rose.

When World War II required the most massive home front mobilization in history and we needed every single American to lend a hand, we had to decide: Do we listen to skeptics who told us it wasn't possible to produce that many tanks and planes? Or, did we build Roosevelt's Arsenal for Democracy and grow our economy even further by providing our returning heroes with a chance to go to college and own their own home? Again, we chose to act, and again, we rose together.

Today, at the beginning of this young century, we have to decide again. But this time, it is your turn to choose.

Here in Galesburg, you know what this new challenge is. You've seen it. All of you, your first year in college saw what happened at 9/11. It's already been noted, the degree to which your lives will be intertwined with the war on terrorism that currently is taking place. But what you've also seen, perhaps not as spectacularly, is the fact that when you drive by the old Maytag plant around lunchtime, no one walks out anymore. I saw it during the campaign when I met union guys who worked at the plant for 20, 30 years and now wonder what they're gonna do at the age of 55 without a pension or health care; when I met the man whose son needed a new liver but because he'd been laid off, didn't know if he could afford to provide his child the care that he needed.

It's as if someone changed the rules in the middle of the game and no wonder -- no one bothered to tell these folks. And, in reality, the rules have changed.

It started with technology and automation that rendered entire occupations obsolete. When was the last time anybody here stood in line for the bank teller instead of going to the ATM, or talked to a switchboard operator? Then it continued when companies like Maytag were able to pick up and move their factories to some under developed country where workers were a lot cheaper than they are in the United States.

As Tom Friedman points out in his new book, The World Is Flat, over the last decade or so, these forces, technology and globalization, have combined like never before. So that while most of us have been paying attention to how much easier technology has made our own lives, sending e-mails back and forth on our blackberries, surfing the Web on our cell phones, instant messaging with friends across the world, a quiet revolution has been breaking down barriers and connecting the world's economies. Now business not only has the ability to move jobs wherever there's a factory, but wherever there's an internet connection.

Countries like India and China realized this. They understand that they no longer need to be just a source of cheap labor or cheap exports. They can compete with us on a global scale. The one resource they needed were skilled, educated workers. So they started schooling their kids earlier, longer, with a greater emphasis on math and science and technology, until their most talented students realized they don't have to come to America to have a decent life -- they can stay right where they are.

The result? China is graduating four times the number of engineers that the United States is graduating. Not only are those Maytag employees competing with Chinese and Indian and Indonesian and Mexican workers, you are too. Today, accounting firms are e-mailing your tax returns to workers in India who will figure them out and send them back to you as fast as any worker in Illinois or Indiana could.

When you lose your luggage in Boston at an airport, tracking it down may involve a call to an agent in Bangalore, who will find it by making a phone call to Baltimore. Even the Associated Press has outsourced some of their jobs to writers all over the world who can send in a story at a click of a mouse.

As Prime Minister Tony Blair has said, in this new economy, "Talent is the 21st century wealth." If you've got the skills, you've got the education, and you have the opportunity to upgrade and improve both, you'll be able to compete and win anywhere. If not, the fall will be further and harder than it ever was before.

So what do we do about this? How does America find its way in this new, global economy? What will our place in history be?

Like so much of the American story, once again, we face a choice. Once again, there are those who believe that there isn't much we can do about this as a nation. That the best idea is to give everyone one big refund on their government -- divvy it up by individual portions, in the form of tax breaks, hand it out, and encourage everyone to use their share to go buy their own health care, their own retirement plan, their own child care, their own education, and so on.

In Washington, they call this the Ownership Society. But in our past there has been another term for it -- Social Darwinism -- every man or woman for him or herself. It's a tempting idea, because it doesn't require much thought or ingenuity. It allows us to say that those whose health care or tuition may rise faster than they can afford -- tough luck. It allows us to say to the Maytag workers who have lost their job -- life isn't fair. It lets us say to the child who was born into poverty -- pull yourself up by your bootstraps. And it is especially tempting because each of us believes we will always be the winner in life's lottery, that we're the one who will be the next Donald Trump, or at least we won't be the chump who Donald Trump says: "You're fired!"

But there is a problem. It won't work. It ignores our history. It ignores the fact that it's been government research and investment that made the railways possible and the internet possible. It's been the creation of a massive middle class, through decent wages and benefits and public schools that allowed us all to prosper. Our economic dependence depended on individual initiative. It depended on a belief in the free market; but it has also depended on our sense of mutual regard for each other, the idea that everybody has a stake in the country, that we're all in it together and everybody's got a shot at opportunity. That's what's produced our unrivaled political stability.

And so if we do nothing in the face of globalization, more people will continue to lose their health care. Fewer kids will be able to afford the diploma you're about to receive.

More companies like United Airlines won't be able to provide pensions for their employees. And those Maytag workers will be joined in the unemployment line by any worker whose skills can be bought and sold on the global market.

So today I'm here to tell you what most of you already know. This is not us -- the option that I just mentioned. Doing nothing. It's not how our story ends -- not in this country. America is a land of big dreamers and big hopes.

It is this hope that has sustained us through revolution and civil war, depression and world war, a struggle for civil and social rights and the brink of nuclear crisis. And it is because our dreamers dreamed that we have emerged from each challenge more united, more prosperous, and more admired than before.

So let's dream. Instead of doing nothing or simply defending 20th century solutions, let's imagine together what we could do to give every American a fighting chance in the 21st century.

What if we prepared every child in America with the education and skills they need to compete in the new economy? If we made sure that college was affordable for everyone who wanted to go? If we walked up to those Maytag workers and we said "Your old job is not coming back, but a new job will be there because we're going to seriously retrain you and there's life-long education that's waiting for you -- the sorts of opportunities that Knox has created with the Strong Futures scholarship program.

What if no matter where you worked or how many times you switched jobs, you had health care and a pension that stayed with you always, so you all had the flexibility to move to a better job or start a new business? What if instead of cutting budgets for research and development and science, we fueled the genius and the innovation that will lead to the new jobs and new industries of the future?

Right now, all across America, there are amazing discoveries being made. If we supported these discoveries on a national level, if we committed ourselves to investing in these possibilities, just imagine what it could do for a town like Galesburg. Ten or twenty years down the road, that old Maytag plant could re-open its doors as an Ethanol refinery that turned corn into fuel. Down the street, a biotechnology research lab could open up on the cusp of discovering a cure for cancer. And across the way, a new auto company could be busy churning out electric cars. The new jobs created would be filled by American workers trained with new skills and a world-class education.

All of that is possible but none of it will come easy. Every one of us is going to have to work more, read more, train more, think more. We will have to slough off some bad habits -- like driving gas guzzlers that weaken our economy and feed our enemies abroad. Our children will have to turn off the TV set once in a while and put away the video games and start hitting the books. We'll have to reform institutions, like our public schools, that were designed for an earlier time. Republicans will have to recognize our collective responsibilities, even as Democrats recognize that we have to do more than just defend old programs.

It won't be easy, but it can be done. It can be our future. We have the talent and the resources and brainpower. But now we need the political will. We need a national commitment. And we need each of you.

Now, no one can force you to meet these challenges. If you want, it will be pretty easy for you to leave here today and not give another thought to towns like Galesburg and the challenges they face. There is no community service requirement in the real world; no one is forcing you to care. You can take your diploma, walk off this stage, and go chasing after the big house, and the nice suits, and all the other things that our money culture says that you should want, that you should aspire to, that you can buy.

But I hope you don't walk away from the challenge. Focusing your life solely on making a buck shows a certain poverty of ambition. It asks too little of yourself. You need to take up the challenges that we face as a nation and make them your own. Not because you have a debt to those who helped you get here, although you do have that debt. Not because you have an obligation to those who are less fortunate than you, although I do think you do have that obligation. It's primarily because you have an obligation to yourself. Because individual salvation has always depended on collective salvation. Because it's only when you hitch your wagon to something larger than yourself that you realize your true potential.

And I know that all of you are wondering how you'll do this, the challenges seem so big. They seem so difficult for one person to make a difference.

But we know it can be done. Because where you're sitting, in this very place, in this town, it's happened before.

Nearly two centuries ago, before civil rights, before voting rights, before Abraham Lincoln, before the Civil War, before all of that, America was stained by the sin of slavery. In the sweltering heat of southern plantations, men and women who looked like me could not escape the life of pain and servitude in which they were sold. And yet, year after year, as this moral cancer ate away at the American ideals of liberty and equality, the nation was silent. But its people didn't stay silent for long.

One by one, abolitionists emerged to tell their fellow Americans that this would not be our place in history -- that this was not the America that had captured the imagination of the world.

This resistance that they met was fierce, and some paid with their lives. But they would not be deterred, and they soon spread out across the country to fight for their cause. One man from New York went west, all the way to the prairies of Illinois to start a colony. And here in Galesburg, freedom found a home.

Here in Galesburg, the main depot for the Underground Railroad in Illinois, escaped slaves could roam freely on the streets and take shelter in people's homes. And when their masters or the police would come for them, the people of this town would help them escape north, some literally carrying them in their arms to freedom.

Think about the risks that involved. If they were caught abetting a fugitive, you could've been jailed or lynched. It would have been simple for these townspeople to turn the other way; to go live their lives in a private peace. And yet, they didn't do that. Why?

Because they knew that we were all Americans; that we were all brothers and sisters; the same reason that a century later, young men and women your age would take Freedom Rides down south, to work for the Civil Rights movement. The same reason that black women would walk instead of ride a bus after a long day of doing somebody else's laundry and cleaning somebody else's kitchen. Because they were marching for freedom.

Today, on this day of possibility, we stand in the shadow of a lanky, raw-boned man with little formal education who once took the stage at Old Main and told the nation that if anyone did not believe the American principles of freedom and equality, that those principles were timeless and all-inclusive, they should go rip that page out of the Declaration of Independence.

My hope for all of you is that as you leave here today, you decide to keep these principles alive in your own life and in the life of this country. You will be tested. You won't always succeed. But know that you have it within your power to try. That generations who have come before you faced these same fears and uncertainties in their own time. And that through our collective labor, and through God's providence, and our willingness to shoulder each other's burdens, America will continue on its precious journey towards that distant horizon, and a better day.

Thank you so much class of 2005, and congratulations on your graduation. Thank you.

www.ingramcontent.com/pod-product-compliance
Lightning Source LLC
Chambersburg PA
CBHW080918180426
43192CB00040B/2446